ALSO BY MICHAEL BESCHLOSS

*The Conquerors: Roosevelt, Truman and the
Destruction of Hitler's Germany* (2002)

Reaching for Glory: Lyndon Johnson's Secret Tapes, 1964–1965 (2001)

Taking Charge: The Johnson White House Tapes, 1963–1964 (1997)

At the Highest Levels: The Inside Story of the End of the Cold War
(with Strobe Talbott, 1993)

The Crisis Years: Kennedy and Khrushchev, 1960–1963 (1991)

Mayday: Eisenhower, Khrushchev and the U-2 Affair (1986)

Kennedy and Roosevelt: The Uneasy Alliance (1980)

PRESIDENTIAL COURAGE

Brave Leaders and How They Changed America 1789–1989

MICHAEL BESCHLOSS

SIMON & SCHUSTER

New York ★ London ★ Toronto ★ Sydney

SIMON & SCHUSTER
1230 Avenue of the Americas
New York, NY 10020

First Simon & Schuster hardcover edition May 2007

SIMON & SCHUSTER and colophon are registered
trademarks of Simon & Schuster, Inc.

For information about special discounts for bulk purchases,
please contact Simon & Schuster Special Sales at
1-800-456-6798 or business@simonandschuster.com

Designed by Dana Sloan

Manufactured in the United States of America

1   3   5   7   9   10   8   6   4   2

Library of Congress Cataloging-in-Publication Data

Beschloss, Michael R.
Presidential courage : brave leaders and how they changed America,
1789–1989 / Michael Beschloss.
p.   cm.
Includes bibliographical references and index.
1. Presidents—United States—Biography—Anecdotes.
2. Courage—United States—Case studies.   3. United States—
Politics and government—Decision making—Case studies.
4. United States—Foreign relations—Decision making—
Case studies.   I. Title.
E176.1.B47   2007
973.09'9—dc22   2007001111
ISBN-13: 978-0-684-85705-3
ISBN-10:   0-684-85705-7

Illustration credits will be found on page 431.

For Afsaneh Mashayekhi Beschloss

PREFACE

This book shows how American Presidents have, at crucial moments, made courageous decisions for the national interest although they knew they might be jeopardizing their careers.

It suggests that throughout our history, at times of crisis and urgent national need, it has been important for Presidents to summon the courage to dismiss what is merely popular—and the wisdom to do that for causes that later Americans will come to admire.

Starting with George Washington, who established this expectation, the book suggests that without such displays of Presidential courage, America would be a lesser country—or it might not exist at all.

The Presidents in this book are not saints, but anxious, self-protective politicians. Each of them tried to escape having to walk through fire. But that is why their tales are so especially gripping. While agonizing over what was right—like most of us, but on a vast, historical stage—they took strength from family, friends, private convictions and, sometimes, religious faith.

This volume is not intended to include all of our greatest Presidents, or all of our bravest. Instead it seeks to show how, in the unending stream of our history, brave leaders took risks of different kinds and magnitude on major, abiding issues—war and peace, human rights, the proper balance of power between the federal government and American business and finance.

The political culture of our time—the instant communications, polls and oceans of money—may inhibit future American leaders from performing such well-considered acts of bravery. Recalling how some of our Presidents past struggled to make vital decisions that ultimately proved to be both wise and courageous should inspire us always to expect more.

CONTENTS

Contents

Contents

PRESIDENTIAL
COURAGE

CHAPTER ONE

A SPEEDY DEATH TO GENERAL WASHINGTON!

In August 1795, at Mount Vernon, drenched by what he called a "violent Rain," George Washington nervously paced down a garden path, elegantly covered by crushed oyster shells.

He was desperate to return to the national capital of Philadelphia, but the biblical torrents had washed out roads and bridges. Adding to his frustration, his mail had been cut off.

Back inside, as the rains pelted his red shingle roof, spinning the dove-of-peace weathervane, the President bent over his candlelit desk, dipped a quill in black ink and tensely scratched out letter after letter. He was feeling "serious anxiety" in a time of "trouble and perplexities."

For twenty years, since the start of the Revolution, he had taken as his due the bands playing "The Hero Comes!" and the lightstruck Americans cheering "the man who unites all hearts." His anointment as President by the Electoral College in 1788 and 1792 had been unanimous.

But now the national adoration for Washington was fading. Americans had learned that a secret treaty negotiated by his envoy John Jay made demands that many found humiliating. One member of Congress said the fury against "that damned treaty" was moving "like an electric velocity to every state in the Union."

As the public tempest had swelled, some wanted Washington impeached. Cartoons showed the President being marched to a guillotine.

Even in the President's beloved Virginia, Revolutionary veterans raised glasses and cried, "A speedy Death to General Washington!"

With the national surge of anger toward Washington, some Americans complained that he was living as luxuriously as George III, the monarch they had fought a revolution to escape. Using old forgeries, several columnists insisted that Washington had been secretly bribed during the war by British agents.

Still others charged that the President stole military credit from soldiers who had bled and died: "With what justice do you monopolize the glories of the American Revolution?"

Reeling from the blows, the sixty-three-year-old Washington wrote that the "infamous scribblers" were calling him "a common pickpocket" in "such exaggerated and indecent terms as could scarcely be applied to a Nero."

One still-friendly gazette moaned, "Washington has been classed with tyrants, and calumniated as the enemy of his country. Weep for the national character of America, for, in ingratitude to her Washington, it is sullied and debased throughout the globe!"

President Washington had brought the national furor upon himself by trying to avert a new war with Great Britain that threatened to strangle his infant nation in its cradle.

In the spring of 1794, the British were arming Indians and spurring them to attack Americans trying to settle the new frontier lands that would one day include Ohio and Michigan. London was reneging on its pledge, made in the peace treaty ending the Revolutionary War, to vacate royal forts in the trans-Appalachian West—Oswego, Niagara, Detroit, Michilimackinac.

Since Britain was at war with France, British captains seized U.S. ships trading with the French West Indies. Renouncing the agreed-upon border between the U.S. and Canada, Britain's governor in Quebec predicted a new Anglo-American war "within a year."

Former Secretary of State Thomas Jefferson, who hated England and adored France, demanded retaliation against the British. But Secretary of the Treasury Alexander Hamilton warned the President not to plunge into a war that America could not win.

*   *   *

The religious Martha Washington could not abide Hamilton's Byzantine intrigues or his infidelities to his wife, Elizabeth. When Martha adopted a tomcat, she named it "Hamilton."

But for the President, who knew his own shortcomings, Hamilton was an endless fount of provocative ideas, tactics and language.

During his first term, Washington had told Hamilton and Jefferson that their gladiatorial clashes over foreign policy, economics and personalities were "tearing our vitals" and had to stop.

Instead, Jefferson quit in 1793 and organized an opposition. The new political chasm between Federalists and Jefferson's Republicans killed Washington's old dream of eternal national unity with no need for political parties.

Retaining the President's ear, Hamilton urged him to send an "envoy extraordinary" to London. A new Anglo-American treaty could secure U.S. trade on the Atlantic and the Great Lakes, giving their country time to build its economy and defenses and settle its frontier. Then if America one day had to fight off Britain, it would be far better prepared.

Washington agreed, but he knew Hamilton must not be the envoy. That would inflame the Jeffersonians. Instead, at Hamilton's suggestion, he chose the aristocratic Chief Justice, John Jay of New York.

Privately Jay warned his wife that America might well have to battle England. But in May 1794, before sailing from lower Manhattan to London, he promised a cheering crowd he would do "everything" to "secure the blessings of peace."

Soon after Jay's departure, the British reclaimed and fortified one of their old posts on American territory near Detroit.

Having jeopardized his prestige to talk with Britain, Washington was furious. He wrote Jay it was "the most open and daring act of the British agents in America." Every "well informed" American knew that the British were instigating "all the difficulties that we encounter with the Indians . . . the murders of helpless women and innocent children."

He noted that some wished him to turn the other cheek: "I answer NO! . . . It will be impossible to keep this country in a state of amity with G. Britain long if the Posts are not surrendered."

Jay got the British to forgo such aggravations while they bargained.

[3]

He assured Washington that Britain felt it was having a "family quarrel" with America, "and that it is Time it should be made up."

Jay reported that, excepting the King, the British respected no one more than George Washington. With such "perfect and universal Confidence" in Washington's "personal character," they had taken Jay's presence in London "as a strong Proof of your Desire to preserve Peace."

By the start of 1795, Washington heard rumors that Jay had managed to broker a treaty, but the expected dispatch case never arrived.

As it turned out, after making a deal in November, Jay had sent the President two copies of the treaty documents by a British ship that was seized by the French on the Atlantic. British sailors had thrown the papers overboard to keep them from French hands.

That spring, another ship brought duplicates to Norfolk, Virginia. By stagecoach and horseback, a mud-caked, frostbitten messenger rushed them to Philadelphia, where Washington received them at the President's House at 190 High Street.

In 1790, when Washington and his government moved from New York City to the temporary capital of Philadelphia, there was no official mansion for the President.

Thus the great man paid three thousand dollars a year to rent the four-story red-brick house owned by Robert Morris, financier of the Revolution and Senator from Pennsylvania.* Morris graciously moved next door to accommodate his old friend.

Washington found it "the best *Single house* in the City" but still "inadequate" for him. For instance, there were "good stables, but for twelve horses only."

During renovations, which Washington financed, a house painter allegedly attacked one of the President's housemaids, who shrieked. Face daubed with shaving cream, the half-dressed Washington was said to have kicked the painter down the stairs, crying, "I will have no woman insulted in my house!"

---

* Washington's rent would be about sixty thousand dollars today. When Philadelphia ceased to be the national capital in 1800, the ex-Presidential mansion was broken up into shops and a hotel. In 1832, it was demolished. By the early twentieth century, the land where Washington's home once stood was the site of a public restroom.

George Washington's rented Philadelphia residence—"the best *Single house* in the City"

The President's servants included eight black slaves selected from the almost three hundred who lived at Mount Vernon. Knowing that Pennsylvania law freed any slave residing there for six months or more, Washington and Martha made sure that each of their slaves was quietly sent home to Virginia every five months or so.

"I wish to have it accomplished under pretext that I may deceive both them and the Public," the General wrote a trusted aide, insisting that the ruse "be known to none but yourself and Mrs. Washington."

Upstairs at his mansion, Washington frowned at Jay's "Treaty of Amity, Commerce and Navigation." He knew that if he approved it, Americans would excoriate him for truckling to their old oppressor across the sea.

Most inflammatory was Article Twelve: America could trade with the West Indies, but not with large vessels. Nor could the U.S. export any products natural to those islands.

Jay's deal would also cosset the lucrative British fur trade in the American Northwest. The U.S. would pledge never to seize British assets in

America, surrendering an important potential weapon for America's defense.

The treaty would also allow the British to keep on halting U.S. exports to France—and to escape paying reparations for American slaves they had carried off during the Revolutionary War.*

To keep public indignation from building against the treaty before he sent it to the Senate, Washington ordered Secretary of State Edmund Randolph to keep its contents "rigidly" secret "from every person on earth"—even the rest of his Cabinet.

Unlike his successors, Washington took literally the Constitution's demand that a President ask the Senate's "advice and consent" on treaties. He would not finally decide whether to approve Jay's Treaty until the Senate voted.

Vice President John Adams feared the pact would be political trouble. "A Battle Royal I expect at its Ratification, and snarling enough afterwards," he wrote his wife, Abigail. "I am very much afraid of this Treaty! . . . Be very carefull, my dearest Friend, of what you say. . . . The Times are perilous."

On Monday morning, June 8, 1795, two dozen U.S. Senators in powdered wigs and ruffled shirts sat down in Philadelphia's Congress Hall for a special closed-door session on Jay's Treaty.

Washington had insisted that the men in the emerald green Senate chamber discuss the treaty in absolute secrecy.

The *Aurora*, published in Philadelphia by Benjamin Franklin Bache, the Francophile, anti-Washington grandson of the famous Founder, howled that *"the secrecy* of the Senate" was an insult to "THE SOVEREIGNTY of the people."

With no desire to pay for Bache's "daily outrages" against decency, the President had long ago canceled his *Aurora* subscription.

During two weeks of debate, Republican Aaron Burr of New York tried to pit Southern Senators against Jay's Treaty by demanding that Britain pay up for the "Negroes and other property" it had stolen—mainly from the American South.

---

* Other issues like U.S. payment of old British debts, the Canadian border and British compensation for seizing U.S. vessels and property were to be decided by commissions.

But Southerners were far more aggrieved by Article Twelve's threat to their exports. Alexander Hamilton, by now a private citizen in New York City, advised Washington to scrap the article in order to save the treaty in the Senate.

The President did so, and by a bare two-thirds vote along party lines, the Senate sent Jay's Treaty to the President's House for Washington to sign.

To Washington's exasperation, the treaty's contents were no longer secret. A Virginia Republican Senator who reviled it passed a copy to the French minister in Philadelphia, who gave it to Ben Bache.

Flamboyantly, the *Aurora* ripped the veil off what it called Jay's "illegitimately begotten" treaty, that "imp of darkness" approved by a "secret lodge" of Senators.

Bache published the entire text in a pamphlet, which he sold up and down the Eastern Seaboard for twenty-five cents. His wife, Peggy, had no opinion about Jay's Treaty. She simply hoped the proceeds would buy her family a new house.

Fulminating that Jay's Treaty had "made its public entry into the Gazettes," Washington knew that Bache's attacks were just the start of a national onslaught.

At midnight of Independence Day 1795, a Philadelphia throng burned a copy of the treaty and an effigy of John Jay.

Crowds in other cities followed suit. Jay mordantly joked that soon he could walk through all of the fifteen United States by night, illuminated only by the glow of all of his effigies burning.

Bitter doggerel described the President's envoy crawling on his belly to King George:

> May it please your Highness, I, John Jay
> Have traveled all this mighty way. . . .
> To show all others I surpass
> In love, by kissing of your ___.

Girding himself for battle from his home seat of Monticello, Thomas Jefferson found Jay's Treaty an "execrable . . . infamous act" by the "Anglomen of this country." He warned, "Acquiescence under insult is not the way to escape war."

Burning of John Jay's effigy

*   *   *

With steam rising from Philadelphia's gravel streets, Washington pondered whether to sign the treaty.

From New York, Hamilton wrote the President that his decision should be "simple and plain." Except for Article Twelve, Jay's pact was "in no way inconsistent with national honor" and would avert a ruinous war.

Then in early July, a new British insult—a "Provision Order" that U.S. grain ships sailing toward France be stopped, their cargo confiscated.

Edmund Randolph advised the President not to sign the treaty until Britain canceled the Provision Order. Washington asked him to so inform the British minister, George Hammond.

Hammond asked Randolph whether Britain could suspend the order long enough to relieve the President's political problems in signing the treaty, then reinstate it. Randolph gave him no answer.

When the Secretary of State reported the conversation, Washington sharply told him that he should have told Hammond that the President would "never" sign the treaty unless the Provision Order was permanently revoked.

The protest was spreading. When Hamilton defended Jay's Treaty in front of New York's City Hall, people threw rocks, leaving his face bloody. Someone joked that the crowd had "tried to knock out Hamilton's brains to reduce him to equality with themselves."

In Boston Harbor, mobs set a British ship aflame. In Philadelphia, they cried, "Kick this damned treaty to hell!"

Spearing a copy of Jay's pact with a sharp pole, the revelers marched it to Minister Hammond's house, burned it on his doorstep and broke his windows, with Hammond and his family cowering inside.

Thomas Jefferson had not seen the American "public pulse beat so full" on "any subject since the Declaration of Independence."

The new Treasury Secretary, Oliver Wolcott, feared the demonstrations might signal the British that Americans sought war. He wrote his mentor Hamilton, "The country rising into flame, their Minister's house insulted by a Mob—their flag dragged through the Streets . . . & burnt. . . . Can they believe that we desire peace?"

Washington found it "extremely embarrassing" for the British to "see the people of this country divided," with such "violent opposition" to "their own government."

He told John Adams he suspected the demonstrations had been inspired by some sinister "pre-concerted plan" to ignite an "explosion in all parts" of the fifteen states.

As the man who had sent Jay to London, the President knew that he could be immolated by the firestorm.

One Federalist gazette mourned that "to follow Washington is now to be a Tory, and to deserve tar and feathers."

━━━━◆◆◆━━━━

CHAPTER TWO

KICK THIS TREATY TO HELL!

By mid-July 1795, Washington yearned to escape the "suffocating" Philadelphia summer and sleep under the roof of his "Home House" at Mount Vernon.

There, after "relaxation" and "well-informed investigation," he would decide "without passion" what to do about Jay's Treaty. He would not return to Philadelphia until the autumn chill vanquished the season's yellow fever epidemic.

He wrote his Mount Vernon overseer, "Have Veal, Mutton and Lambs in good order . . . for we already know that many intend to visit us."

After receiving two Indian chiefs, Washington climbed into a two-horse phaeton, followed by Martha and her grandchildren in a four-horse coach.

He found the bumpy six-day journey home "hot and disagreeable." One of his horses buckled under the heat and died.

Stopping in Baltimore, Washington was handed a petition from Boston Selectmen against Jay's Treaty—"no doubt" intended, he wrote, to make him "embarrassed."

Reaching Mount Vernon, the President told his diary, "Small Westerly breeze—quite clear."

In the mornings, he rose early for horseback rides across the ancestral domain he had so exquisitely transformed. The cultivated beauty and timeless certitudes of his plantation always steeled and grounded him for the unpredictable battles of the outside world.

He wrote that "nothing pleases me better" than to see his farmlands "trim, handsome and thriving"—and "nothing hurts me more than to find them otherwise."*

During his rides, Washington wore a broad-brimmed straw hat, his white hair in a single braid flopping behind his shoulders as he surveyed his architecture, crops and gardens, pungent with warm, newly laid fertilizer. He rode through swaying hollyhocks, past slaves and artisans at work, while his sheep and cows groaned. Glittering beyond was the blue and silver Potomac, speckled by ducks.

Martha was glad to be gone from Philadelphia, where the mandatory social life made her feel "like a state prisoner." She had financed much of Mount Vernon (thanks to an inheritance from her late first husband) and people called her "Lady Washington." But Abigail Adams found the President's wife "modest and unassuming," with "not the Tincture of ha'ture about her."

During the summer of 1795, smarting from her husband's vilification, the sixty-five-year-old Martha Washington felt "Infirmities of Age and lowness of spirits."

Soon the fracas over Jay's Treaty thundered into Washington's Mount Vernon paradise.

Retiring to his study, he donned spectacles and read the fevered reports from Philadelphia. "The cry against the Treaty is like that against a mad dog," he recorded. People were "running it down" with "the most abominable mis-representations," and "working like bees to distill their poison," fighting for "victory more than truth."

He found a letter from New Jersey "too rude to merit a reply." Of one from Petersburg, Virginia: "Tenor indecent. No answer returned." Of still another, he wrote that a "Solomon" was "not necessary" to understand the author's malign intentions.

Writing to those he deemed worthy of response, Washington asked for faith in his personal character: "In every act of my administration, I have sought the happiness of my fellow citizens" by ignoring "personal, local and partial consideration" in favor of the "permanent interests of our country" and the "dictates of my conscience."

---

* Jefferson privately carped that the leisure hours employed by other men for reading were used by Washington to record tiny observations about his fields and stables.

George Washington enjoying his Mount Vernon "paradise"

The President had yet to make up his mind about Jay's Treaty. He wrote Randolph that his current feeling was still "what it was: namely, not favorable to it." But, he went on, if Britain canceled its Provision Order and the "obnoxious" Article Twelve, it was probably "better to ratify it than to suffer matters to remain as they are, unsettled."

After a week at Mount Vernon, Washington was so agitated by the political storm beyond his gates that he decided to return to Philadelphia.

With the country in "violent paroxysm," he wrote that "a crisis is approaching," threatening "anarchy," if not "arrested."

With George Hammond sailing back to London in mid-August, the President felt he had to give the British his verdict on the treaty.

Edmund Randolph had offered to "run down" to Mount Vernon and provide his counsel. But with his sense of ritual and precedent, Washington felt that a matter of "such vast magnitude" should be resolved in Philadelphia, with the advice of his full Cabinet.

The President informed Randolph that "to leave home so *soon* will be inconvenient" but he would "never suffer private convenience to interfere with . . . my official duties."

Bracing for the struggle ahead, Washington was "preparing my mind for the obloquy which disappointment and malice are collecting to heap upon my character."

Whatever the brickbats, he would not "quit the ground I have taken." He saw "but one straight course, and that is to seek truth and pursue it steadily."

As the President's bags were packed, he received a baffling, ominous letter ("for your eye alone") from his Secretary of War, Timothy Pickering.

"Return with all convenient speed," it begged. "On the subject of the treaty I confess I feel extreme solicitude; and for a *special reason* which can be communicated to you only in person." Until then, "I pray you to decide on no important political measure."

Washington left Mount Vernon at the first moment the rains lifted, noting "the suddenness of my departure." The roads had been "miserably torn up" by the storms, "and the mills, dams, bridges, etc., almost universally carried away."

Reaching Philadelphia on Tuesday afternoon, August 11, 1795, he invited Randolph to his residence for dinner. He also summoned Pickering, who noted that Randolph looked "cheerful" dining with the President.

Taking a glass of wine, Washington rose from the table and winked at Pickering. Leaving Randolph behind, he led the Secretary of War into another chamber and shut the door. Referring to Pickering's strange message, he asked, "What is the cause of your writing me such a letter?"

Pointing at the closed door, Pickering replied, "That man in the other room is a *traitor!*"

As Washington's second Secretary of State, Edmund Randolph was no Thomas Jefferson.

With Jefferson and Hamilton gone, Washington was glad to be rid of their backbiting, but he missed what he called the "first characters" of his original Cabinet—men of Revolutionary stature. He had always liked Randolph, but knew he was ultimately a trimmer and errand boy.

Son of a royal Attorney General of Virginia, scion of one of the commonwealth's most respected dynasties, Randolph had used family connections—including Thomas Jefferson, his third cousin—to join General Washington's Revolutionary staff, drafting letters and documents. After independence, Randolph took his father's old place as Virginia's Attorney General, serving also as Washington's personal lawyer.

By 1787, Randolph was Governor of Virginia. When the Constitutional Convention was called for Philadelphia, he helped persuade Washington to attend. (The General, with his usual pointed modesty, conceded that "my friends . . . seem to wish for my attendance.") After the Constitution was finished, Randolph refused to sign it, but once he saw the wind blowing in its favor, he campaigned for its ratification.

In 1789, the newly elected Washington asked Randolph to be his Attorney General. Other, more august figures were delighted to join the great man's Cabinet. But the tone-deaf Randolph complained the salary was too small and only accepted the offer after the President reminded him that being Attorney General "would confer pre-eminence" on any lawyer.

When Hamilton and Jefferson squared off during Washington's first term, Randolph pleased the President by trying to conciliate the two men.

After Jefferson resigned as Secretary of State, he suggested Randolph as his temporary successor, warning that with his financial problems Randolph was not independent enough to have the job for good.

But Washington did not want to eject the last remaining non-Federalist in his Cabinet. Halfheartedly he made Randolph his Secretary of State.

Now, as Randolph waited in the other room of Washington's house, Pickering told the President why he thought his Secretary of State was guilty of treason.

Two weeks earlier, he explained, George Hammond had shown Wolcott a packet of dispatches from the French minister in Philadelphia,

Joseph Fauchet, captured when a French battleship, the *Jean Bart*, was seized in the Atlantic. The Frenchmen had hurled the pouch into the sea, but a British sailor had grabbed it.

Pickering told Washington the documents showed that Randolph had divulged state secrets to Fauchet and asked him for a bribe to tilt American foreign policy toward France. He said they also showed that Randolph had secretly helped to incite the Whiskey Rebellion of 1794, against a federal liquor tax in Pennsylvania, which the President had quashed with fifteen thousand troops.*

Half-fluent in French, Pickering had scrawled out a rough English translation of Fauchet's messages, which he now handed to the President.

Washington gave Pickering no hint of his reaction to his astonishing charge. Solemnly he said, "Let us return to the other room to prevent any suspicion of the cause of our withdrawing."

Late that night, after Randolph and Pickering were gone, Washington was alone in his darkened mansion, except for the servants. Staggered by Pickering's revelations, he had to decide by himself whether his top appointee was a new Benedict Arnold.

Like Randolph, Arnold had been an ambitious young man with financial problems whom Washington had promoted. As Philadelphia's wartime military governor, Arnold had resided in this very house before taking the secret British bribes that led to his treason against the Patriot cause.

In the fall of 1780, after Arnold disappeared from his Hudson River headquarters, it was Alexander Hamilton who handed the incriminating dispatches to the General.

"Arnold has betrayed us!" replied the trembling Washington, blinking back tears. "Whom can we trust now?"

---

* Fauchet's reports said that during the Whiskey Rebellion, Randolph had asked for a large French bribe to mobilize Philadelphians against Washington's use of force, boasting of his influence over an ineffectual President. Acidly Fauchet wrote, "Thus the consciences of the pretended patriots of America have already their prices." Fauchet claimed that, of course, he had refused Randolph's bribery demands.

*   *   *

Tonight at the President's House, Washington was determined to keep his quandary secret. He did not call for expert advice, or even for a better translation of Fauchet's dispatches. Instead he was one man, deliberating alone.

In the absence of some magic document that would clear Randolph, Washington had to assess the damage of throwing him into a long, public trial. Even if Randolph were found innocent, many Americans and Europeans would suspect that Washington's chief diplomat had sold himself to a foreign power: for all Washington's pretensions about republican virtue, the U.S. government would have revealed itself as no cleaner than the Old World regimes.

Already rocked by the national commotion over Jay's Treaty, Washington knew his administration might not survive such a scandal.

Two centuries later, it is still impossible to establish whether Randolph was guilty. Like many diplomats, Fauchet may have exaggerated for the home office his craftiness in squeezing secrets out of the Secretary of State. While talking to Fauchet, trying to build a relationship, the clumsy Randolph may have also exaggerated his eagerness to help France.

Missing from the French documents was Dispatch Number Six, which supposedly proved that Randolph had sold himself for cash.

Washington knew that the British had the motive to fabricate a case against Randolph, who did not share the Federalists' Anglophilia and was advising the President to go slow on Jay's Treaty.

But Washington also realized that Randolph had ample motive to solicit a bribe. Feeling more cash-poor than ever, the man had recently complained he could no longer entertain or use his carriage.

The President darkly noted how Randolph had been dragging his heels on Jay's Treaty. The Secretary of State's insistence that the treaty be renegotiated would mean no deal with the British for at least a year, which would delight the French—and the Jeffersonians who supported France.

Before the morning light shone into Washington's upstairs bedroom, he made two important decisions.

First, he would sign Jay's Treaty immediately. If the Randolph scandal was about to explode, he did not want to leave the treaty hanging. But he would insist that the British drop the despicable Article Twelve.

Second, he would fire Edmund Randolph, but not yet. If provoked, the Secretary of State would be in a position to scuttle Jay's Treaty. Better to keep Randolph ignorant of the President's suspicions against him. Only after Randolph sent the executed treaty to London would Washington pounce.

CHAPTER THREE

THE DAMNEDEST LIAR

On Wednesday morning, August 12, 1795, exhausted from lack of sleep, Washington called in his Cabinet secretaries and asked their formal advice on Jay's Treaty.

Backed by Wolcott and Attorney General William Bradford, Pickering advised him to ignore the "detestable and nefarious" protests and sign it.

But Randolph told the President he must not sign until the British canceled their Provision Order. "Combining" with Britain to "starve" the French might risk war.

Washington overruled him: "I will ratify the treaty." Randolph reacted with "unutterable astonishment."

During the next five days, using his considerable dramatic ability, Washington gave Randolph no hint anything was amiss. While quietly scrutinizing the Secretary of State for signs of guilt, he twice had Randolph to dinner and even ignored protocol—a President should call on no one—to take some papers over to Randolph's house.

On Tuesday, August 18, Washington put his elegant signature on Jay's Treaty and had Randolph send it to Minister Hammond. The next morning, he summoned Randolph to the President's House.

Strolling to his meeting with Washington, Randolph was stopped by one of the General's stewards, who asked him not to arrive for ninety minutes.

When he was finally admitted to Washington's presence, Randolph was startled to find him talking gravely with Wolcott and Pickering. The

President gave him one of Fauchet's dispatches: "Make such explanations as you choose."

Schooled in French, Randolph studied the document while the others watched. As Pickering later recalled, the President "desired us to watch Randolph's countenance" and "fixed his own eye on him." Pickering had never seen Washington's eye "look so animated."

After more than half an hour, Randolph denied saying anything "improper" to Fauchet, or taking any money from him. If allowed to examine the dispatch further, he could "throw my ideas on paper."

"Very well," said Washington. "Retain it." He asked Randolph to leave the room.

Wolcott and Pickering told him Randolph had looked embarrassed but showed no clear sign of guilt.

When Randolph rejoined them, having absorbed the full impact of his plight, he shrieked, "I could not continue in the office one second after such treatment!"

He ran down the stairs and out of the Presidential mansion.

With Randolph lashing out, Washington knew he was in danger of a messy public scandal. He looked shocked and apprehensive.

The next day, Randolph sent him a scorching resignation: "Your confidence in me, sir, has been unlimited. . . . My sensations then cannot be concealed when I find that confidence so immediately withdrawn without a word or distant hint being previously dropped to me!"

Randolph warned that he would not stop trying to clear his name: "No, sir, far from it!" He wanted Fauchet to show him Dispatch Six and other papers. Until then, the President, "as one piece of justice due me," must keep his accusations "in secrecy."

Anxious to contain the scandal, Washington was happy to oblige.

Writing a fellow Jeffersonian, James Madison, Randolph compared the President to a Roman tyrant: "I feel happy at my emancipation from attachment to a man who has practiced on me the profound hypocrisy of a Tiberius and the injustice of an assassin."

The next scene was picaresque. Fauchet had gone to Newport, Rhode Island, where the French frigate *Medusa* was ready to take him home. But the *Medusa* was trapped in Newport Harbor by the British cruiser *Africa*,

Edmund Randolph

whose crew hoped to kidnap Fauchet or at least steal a few seamen from nearby U.S. ships.

When the breathless Randolph caught up with Fauchet in Newport, the French minister pledged to clear his name in writing.

But storms forced the *Africa* out to sea, and the *Medusa* escaped, with Fauchet aboard.

By the time Randolph came to Fauchet's lodgings to pick up the promised statement, the Frenchman had already sailed.

Frantically Randolph hired a boat but could not catch up with the *Medusa*. Instead he announced an "appeal to the people of the United States," which would reveal why he had resigned as Secretary of State.

Randolph asked Washington by letter for a copy of his written advice not to sign Jay's Treaty until the British canceled their Provision Order.

To show he had nothing to hide, Washington replied that Randolph could "publish, without reserve, *any* and *every* private and confidential letter I ever wrote you; nay more, every word I have ever uttered in your presence." He was sure Americans would "appreciate my motives," even if they condemned giving Randolph such "unlimited license."

Eager to trap the President into confessing he had dirty secrets, Randolph replied that he wouldn't "exhibit to public view *all* and *everything* which is known to me."

Furious at Randolph's insinuation, Washington wrote a "rough Draught" of a scalding reply, saying that he couldn't "see what relation there is between the Treaty with G. Britain" and "the intercepted letter of Mr. Fauchet."

On second thought, the President decided that Randolph's letter was too "full of innuendoes" to deserve any reply. From that day forward, Washington never communicated with Edmund Randolph again.

Before Christmas 1795, Randolph tried to have the last word with a 103-page pamphlet, which he called *Vindication*.

In it, he admitted asking Fauchet for money, but dubiously claimed that his purpose had been to help flour merchants holding evidence that Great Britain had secretly instigated the Whiskey Rebellion.

Foreshadowing some aides fired by later Presidents, Randolph tried to destroy his old boss. He wrote that beneath Washington's "exterior of cool and slow deliberation" was a small mind that "rapidly catches a prejudice and with difficulty abandons it." He claimed that Washington had signed Jay's Treaty so abruptly because he was growing senile and over-ambitious to give selfish advantage to the Federalists.

Disgusted, John Adams found Randolph's broadside "a Piece of Revenge against the President but for what Injury or Offence I cannot discover. . . . His Logic is better for a Comedian than a Statesman."

Washington was incensed by Randolph's charge that "my *final* decision" on Jay's Treaty was the result of "party-advice." For the President, being called partisan was almost the worst insult.

Thumping a table, Washington cried (according to one witness) that Randolph, "by the eternal God," was "the damnedest liar on the face of the earth!" He bemoaned his stupidity in appointing Randolph—and now "he has written and published this!" Bursting with epithets, he hurled his copy of *Vindication* at the floor.

The obtuse Randolph had hoped his pamphlet might restore his political stardom. He did not understand that, however much Americans might oppose Jay's Treaty, you could not expect to battle the Hero of the Revolution over personal honor and expect to win.

Gleefully Wolcott plunged a knife into Randolph's back, announcing that the former Secretary of State had taken official money. Barred from evidence that might have cleared him, Randolph had to pay the government fifty thousand dollars.*

Forced to borrow the money from a relative, Randolph and his wife were reduced to what they considered semipoverty. When America's second Secretary of State died in 1813, he was so forgotten that his hometown, Richmond, paper reported his death in only four sentences.

Back at Mount Vernon in the fall of 1795, Washington consoled himself that "the great body of Yeomanry" had no real opinion about Jay's Treaty.

With the "abominable misrepresentations" being published, who should wonder that "uninformed minds" thought it "diabolical"? The "voice of malignancy" was trying "to wound my character and deceive the people."

But one of Jefferson's Virginia Republicans wrote a friend that Washington had been unmasked "as the head of a British faction, and gratitude no longer blinds the public mind."

The *New York Daily Gazette* published the old forged British claims that General Washington had secretly conspired with King George. The forgeries used information about the General's private life that Washington suspected had been provided by the Anglo-servile father of Edmund Randolph.†

Ben Bache's *Aurora* charged that the President had overdrawn his official salary. Unfortunately for Washington, this was at least technically true: although he had asked Congress for no salary, he had repeatedly exceeded the stipend given him. Wolcott told Washington that Bache had probably been fed the information by Edmund Randolph.‡

The President privately resolved "(for the present time at least) to let my calumniators proceed, without taking notice of their invectives myself."

---

* About a million dollars today.

† Washington greeted the forgeries with his usual public silence, but he was embarrassed enough to write an exonerating letter to his new Secretary of State.

‡ Who may have been trying to divert public attention from his own problems with public funds.

*   *   *

Next came an ugly display of what Washington called Britain's "dominating spirit."

A British consul in America ordered some British sailors on shore leave hunted down like criminals.

Outraged by Britain's contempt for U.S. law, the President threatened military retaliation. He warned John Jay that such British high-handedness would "sour the minds of those who are friends to peace, order and friendship."

In December 1795, Washington arrived at Congress Hall to deliver the annual report required by the Constitution.

Thanks to the battle over Jay's Treaty, it was the first time the President addressed the House and Senate "without a full assurance of meeting a welcome."

He insisted that Jay's pact would keep "external discord" from disrupting "our tranquility." Then "how precious a foundation will have been laid for accelerating, maturing and establishing the prosperity of our country!" This was "a fervent, and favorite wish of my heart."

Caught off guard by the commotion over Jay's Treaty, powerful Federalist tycoons rolled into gear.

New York firms stopped issuing ship insurance until the treaty was enacted, making the Atlantic safer. Maryland Federalists drew up petitions, crying, "It is time for Baltimore to save the republic!"

In Philadelphia, debtors were pressured by their banks to support the treaty. James Madison complained it was "like a Highwayman with a pistol demanding the purse."

Taking his nom de plume from the Roman truth-teller Camillus, Alexander Hamilton wrote passionate essays against the Republican "war party." * Should America attempt to fight England now, "our trade, navigation and mercantile capital would be essentially destroyed."

---

* Hamilton did not limit himself to writing as Camillus. Soon he published, in the same Republican paper, more essays—under the pseudonym "Philo Camillus"—that praised what Camillus was writing.

Knowing the identity of the hidden writer, Washington wrote Hamilton of his "pleasure" in reading the arguments "under the Signature of Camillus."

Thomas Jefferson lamented that Hamilton's intellectual fireworks were so much brighter than the "middling performances" of his own Republicans.

CHAPTER FOUR

━━━◦⊙◦━━━

HE MAY RETIRE WITH
UNDIMINISH'D GLORY

By early 1796, the tide had turned in favor of Jay's Treaty. Britain scrapped its Provision Order and accepted the President's version of their deal.

Washington's envoy to Spain, Thomas Pinckney, won major concessions to the United States with the Treaty of San Lorenzo.

Afraid that Jay's Treaty would spur an Anglo-American attack on Spaniards in North America, Spain had recognized the Thirty-first Parallel as America's southern border. Americans could now navigate the Mississippi River unharmed and trade from New Orleans.

Nevertheless, Republicans made a final attempt to kill Jay's Treaty. The House, which they controlled, tried to withhold the ninety thousand dollars required to enact it.

John Adams feared a Constitutional crisis. He wrote Abigail that if the House denied the money, it was "difficult to see how we can avoid war" with Britain, which might lead to an American "civil war" between the Anglophile Northeast and Southern Francophiles.

Muscle-flexing House Republicans now refused to recognize Washington's Birthday, which they derided as the nation's "Political Christmas." Bache's *Aurora* said that previous such celebrations had encouraged the President to behave "with all the insolence of an Emperor of Rome."

Washington wrote Hamilton that an "Era of strange vicissitudes" was unfolding with "a sort of irresistible fatality." He added, "I shall not be surprised at any event that may happen."

Hamilton agreed: "In these wild times, every thing is possible."

At Congress Hall on Wednesday, March 2, 1796, a young Jeffersonian from New York, Edward Livingston, demanded that President Washington surrender all documents related to the diplomatic bargaining over Jay's Treaty.

Spitting tobacco and quaffing fine Madeira, the House debated the issue for two weeks, then backed Livingston—with the proviso that Washington could conceal any papers that might damage future diplomacy.

Hamilton warned the President that Jay's documents were "a crude mass that will do no credit to the administration." What might their enemies find while picking through them? If Washington surrendered, the House might try to grab more power from the President and the Senate.

Hamilton advised standing tough: "whatever may happen," such fortitude would "elevate the character of the President and inspire confidence abroad."

Washington agreed: "These are unpleasant things, but they must be met with firmness." He told Hamilton that the House Republicans had "brought the Constitution to the brink of a precipice," endangering the "peace, happiness and prosperity of the Country." If they succeeded, they would make its treaty-making provisions an "absolute absurdity" and "reflect disgrace" on the Founding Fathers.

The President knew his belligerence would "set a host of Scribblers to work," but he would simply have to tolerate more "abuse" from "Mr. Bache and his correspondents."

The showdown came on Wednesday, March 30, 1796. One Congressman observed, "Anxiety is on the tiptoe." John Adams predicted that both sides would "bite like savages and tear like lions."

In a message read aloud, Washington reminded the House that the Constitution gave responsibility for treaties to the Senate, whose fewer members were more likely to protect national secrets.

He said the only way the House could claim wholesale access to executive documents was to impeach him, adding that "no part of my conduct" had shown a desire "to withhold any information" required by the Constitution.

Republicans were outraged. John Adams felt "a few outlandish men" in the House were "determined to go all lengths."

Congressman Albert Gallatin, a Swiss-born Republican from Pennsylvania, said Jay's Treaty had "pusillanimously" tarnished U.S. "honor." Uriah Tracy of Connecticut responded by asking why Gallatin had sailed "all the way from Geneva" to lecture true Americans about "pusillanimity."

Then, with petitions and subtle threats, the Federalist machine pushed Maryland's Samuel Smith and other House Republicans to reverse themselves, citing harm to the Constitution.

Watching from Monticello, Thomas Jefferson wondered whether secret British bribes were behind his fellow Republicans' cowardice.

Since the Revolution, Jefferson had been hyperalert for signs that the British were subverting patriots who had once fought valiantly for freedom. He now wrote a friend, "It would give you a fever were I to name to you the apostates who have gone over to these heresies, men who were Samsons in the field and Solomons in the council, but who have had their heads shorn by the harlot England."

On Thursday, April 28, 1796, Federalist Fisher Ames limped onto the House floor.

Confined to his house in Dedham, Massachusetts, by severe infection, Ames had been presumed near death. Members gasped as he pulled up his wasted frame.

Ames said in a quavering voice, "Mr. Chairman, I entertain the hope—perhaps a rash one—that my strength will hold me out to speak for a few minutes."

Without notes, he delivered a ninety-minute tour de force later remembered as one of the most powerful speeches in American history. One witness recalled that Ames "threw a spell over the senses, rendering them insensible to every thing but himself."

Ames acknowledged that critics found Jay's Treaty "bad—fatally bad." But a "treaty is the promise of a nation. . . . Shall we break our faith?"

If the British kept conspiring with the Indians, American frontiersmen would stay vulnerable.

Addressing those settlers, Ames warned, "The wounds, yet unhealed, are to be torn open again. In the daytime, your path through the woods will be ambushed. The darkness of midnight will glitter with the blaze of your dwellings.

"You are a father? The blood of your sons shall fatten your corn-field! You are a mother? The war-whoop shall wake the sleep of the cradle! . . . While one hand is held up to reject this treaty, the other grasps a tomahawk. . . . I listen to the yells of savage vengeance and the shrieks of torture."

If Jay's Treaty were passed, Americans would be free to trade across the Atlantic, protected by the British navy, and settle the West unmolested.

Not long ago, people had "deemed war nearly inevitable." Now, "like a rainbow on the edge of the cloud," this treaty promised sunshine. "If we reject it, the vivid colors will grow pale. It will be a baleful meteor portending tempest and war."

With his death's-head face, Ames said, "Those who see me will believe that the reduced state of my health has unfitted me . . . for some exertion of body or mind." But "when I come to the moment of deciding the vote, I start back with dread from the edge of the pit into which we are plunging."

Exhausted, he fell into his chair. The chamber was silent but for the weeping of both Republicans and Federalists.

A Supreme Court Justice turned to John Adams and cried, "My God, how great he is! . . . Bless my stars, I never heard anything so great since I was born!"

Adams felt the only dry eyes in the House belonged to the Republican "Jack Asses" who had made Ames's speech necessary. Fearing its impact, they "grinned horrible ghastly smiles."

Later one Federalist Congressman told Ames he should have ended his speech by dropping dead. Never again would he have "an occasion so glorious."

When the House finally voted on funding Jay's Treaty, the result was a 49 to 49 tie. Chairing a Committee of the Whole, the tiebreaker would be Republican Frederick Muhlenberg, a German-speaking Lutheran pastor from Pennsylvania.

Republicans were jubilant. The previous summer in Philadelphia, when a copy of Jay's Treaty had been burned on Minister Hammond's doorstep, Muhlenberg was one of the protestors.

But now Muhlenberg shocked everyone by supporting the treaty. He knew he was committing political suicide. His district included many German-Americans who hated England. After his vote, Muhlenberg's German-American brother-in-law stabbed him.

Some Republicans explained that Muhlenberg had been black-mailed—not for money but love. The Federalist father of his son's fiancée supposedly told him, "If you do not give us your vote, your son shall not have my Polly."

Bursting with gratitude, Washington thanked Fisher Ames over dinner at his residence and had his private secretary escort the ailing Congressman to recuperate at Mount Vernon.

The President wrote his plantation overseer to expect "a respectable member of Congress (traveling for his health)," insisting that Ames be "well treated while he stays."

Many Congressmen who had heard Ames's bravura speech were certain it would be his last. But in fact, Ames found his performance cathartic.

Soon he felt better than he had for a long time. Ames lived for twelve more years, surviving many of the colleagues who had thought him a goner.

John Adams found it "mortifying" that "five Months have been wasted upon a Question whether National Faith is binding on a Nation. Nothing but the Ignorance and Inexperience of this People can excuse them."

Adams noted that Washington, approaching the end of his career, had been looking "worried and growing old faster than I could wish." But now, with his triumph over the treaty, the Hero "may retire with undiminish'd Glory."

Washington wrote John Jay he had ridden out "the Storm" but could never forget the "pernicious" figures "dissiminating the poison" against him. The experience had "worn away my mind," making "ease and retirement indispensably necessary."

[29]

Washington was informed that "certain Jackasses" were predicting that "the President, sensible of his declining popularity," would not risk running for a third term in the fall of 1796.

Washington confided to Jay that unless some crisis made it "dishonorable," he would not seek reelection. He was eager to stop being "buffitted in the public prints."

Quietly working with Hamilton on a farewell message, Washington showed how deeply he had been hurt by the battle over Jay's Treaty—the "malicious falsehoods" and "virulent abuse" designed "to wound my reputation and feelings" and "weaken, if not entirely destroy" confidence in the President.

He insisted that he had never been "ambitious." He had known that the Presidency might risk his reputation.

Public service had not fattened his coffers—in fact, "the reverse." He would leave the Presidency with "undefiled hands" and "uncorrupted heart."

After working on this draft, deciding that such "egotisms" were "undignified," Washington deleted his *cri de coeur.* He did not wish to show "self-distrust and mere vanity."

Modest to the end, Washington sent his Farewell Address not to Congress but a friendly newspaper, as the "counsels of an old and affectionate friend."

In the published version, he predicted that by offering "greater security from external danger," Jay's Treaty would bring Americans "everything they could desire" by "confirming their prosperity."

With Washington removed from politics, grateful editorials and correspondence descended on the President's House. Daniel Jones of Pennsylvania sent his wish that the wounds "cruelly inflicted on your feelings as a man" might "be entirely healed." Hoping that his son might "inherit your virtues," Jones had named him "Washington."

Still doing business at the same old stand, the *Aurora* claimed that Washington had quit politics merely to escape defeat: "Every heart" should beat "with exultation" that "the name of Washington" would no longer license "political iniquity" and "corruption."

The struggle over Jay's Treaty had destroyed Washington's dream that America might forever be governed by national consensus—no parties, no factions, just patriots.

By the fall of 1796, the country was bitterly divided between Federalists, derided by their foes as the "British party," and Republicans, lampooned as the "French party."

Washington's final Cabinet included not a single Republican. He scarcely spoke to his old Founding brother Thomas Jefferson.

When Federalists asked the House to praise Washington and his Farewell Address, a just-elected young Tennesseean named Andrew Jackson voted no. Jackson was angry at Washington for Jay's Treaty, which he called "the insulting Cringing and ignominous Child of aristocratic Secracy."

Other Republicans were willing to honor Washington for the Revolution and Constitutional Convention, but not for his Presidency. Raising glasses in Philadelphia, they cried, "George Washington—down to the year 1787. *And no farther!*"

By fighting for Jay's Treaty, Washington gave his country a gift that was almost as important as his victorious Revolutionary command—the gift of peace. No other leader could have pushed the treaty through Congress. Even the great Washington almost fell short.

The old man had the thankless job of dispelling many Americans' illusions that they had the strength to stand up to the British once again. Like a prophet, he warned that the country must not "prematurely embarrass" itself in war "for the attainment of trifles, comparatively speaking."

But after "twenty years' peace, with such an increase of population and resources as we have a right to expect," Americans would be ready, "in a just cause, to bid defiance to any power on earth."

Under Jay's Treaty, the British evacuated their posts in the Northwest Territory, allowing Americans to discover the rich possibilities of the new West. As Washington had dreamt, the country could seize "command of its own fortunes."

And just as he had predicted, by the time Americans fought England in the War of 1812, they were powerful enough to win.

*　　*　　*

Washington always knew there was "scarcely any part of my conduct" as the first "President of the U. States" that would not set a precedent for his successors.

The precedent Washington set with his leadership on Jay's Treaty was that a President should not merely preside. He must use his unique standing—even if it made him unpopular or cost an election—to convince Congress and the American people to accept unpopular notions that may be in their long-term interest.

The Constitution did not include this conception of the Presidency. But by his deeds, Washington encouraged Americans to measure his successors against his standard of self-sacrifice, risking his good name to fight for a much-reviled treaty that he thought essential for his young country to survive.

Had Washington simply bucked the British problem to his successor, he might have remained the man who "unites all hearts" and spared himself the hounds of hell. Martha Washington later insisted that Jay's Treaty hastened his death.

Washington once wrote, "I am *sure* the mass of Citizens in the United States *mean well,* and I firmly believe they will always *act well* whenever they can obtain a right understanding of matters." By sponsoring a treaty with Britain, he practiced what he preached.

Content to let history provide his reward, he wrote, "I have a consolation within that no earthly efforts can deprive me of, and that is, that neither ambitious nor interested motives have influenced my conduct.

"The arrows of malevolence, therefore, however barbed and well pointed, never can reach the most vulnerable part of me."

In November 1796, when John Adams was elected the second President of the United States, General Washington yearned to retire under "the shade of my Vine & Fig tree."

Shaken by the tumultuous "closing scenes" of his two Presidential terms, he wrote an old friend, "I have not a wish to mix again in the great world or to partake in its politics, yet I am not without regret at parting with (perhaps never more to meet) the few intimates whom I love."

At sixty-five, Washington expected to survive only "a few years." After retiring to Mount Vernon, he would "seclude myself as much as possible from the noisy and bustling crowd."

In the House of Representatives, on Saturday, March 4, 1797, he oversaw his nation's first transfer of Presidential power to "my Successor to the Chair of government." Reminding people he was now just a citizen, the hatless General arrived at the ceremony alone.

John Adams had known that with Washington present, he would not be the cynosure of his swearing-in. But he had not expected all those "streaming eyes" for his predecessor, the "grief for the loss of their beloved."

Before leaving Philadelphia by coach with Martha and their grandchildren, parrot and dog, the man who now called himself "Farmer Washington" walked to a hotel reception honoring the new President.

Turning to wave from the front steps, he heard people roaring and clapping "like thunder." They were astonished to see that the cheeks of their old hero were glistening with tears.

CHAPTER FIVE

RIVALRIES IRRITATED
TO MADNESS

John Adams insisted that "popularity was never my mistress," but it wounded him to know that when Americans saw him as President, they dreamt of George Washington.

Adams appreciated Washington's virtues. He understood the benefits of having a hero as the first President. He envied the General's intuition about people. "Talents of a very Superior kind," Adams told Abigail. "I wish I had as good."

He felt that Washington had shown him respect—not by asking much for advice, but by including the Vice Presidential couple in formal dinners, plays and ceremonies.

Adams privately did not accept the Washington legend. "I loved and revered the man," he later wrote, but "in his divinity I never believed."

He complained that Washington was so "very superficially read in the history of any age, nation or country" and "could not write a sentence without misspelling some word." Adams once even called the General "Old Muttonhead."

Starting his Presidency, Adams faced two heavy burdens left by Washington. First was his Cabinet, all appointed by the General. Adams feared that firing any of them would "turn the World upside down."

The second was Alexander Hamilton. Adams felt that Washington had "puffed" the cagey adviser "like an air balloon," serving at times like a "viceroy under Hamilton." He knew that in 1796, Hamilton had implored electors to give the Presidency not to Adams but Thomas Pinckney, whose strings Hamilton had a better chance to pull.

Abigail warned her husband against Hamilton's hidden, malevolent influence on the Cabinet. She thought Hamilton's "wicked eyes" were "lasciviousness itself." She called him "Cassius," the chief plotter against Julius Caesar.

Adams had also inherited from Washington his biggest challenge as President—the danger of war with France.

Before leaving office, Washington had gently warned Congress that French ships were "inconveniences and embarrassments." But most Federalists considered the problem far more perilous.

France's newest revolutionary regime, called the "Directory," had found Jay's Treaty a hostile act. French privateers were ordered to seize and plunder U.S. ships on the Atlantic and Caribbean. American sailors were beaten and tortured.

Adams resented the assaults and feared they would stop American trade. "Those Treaty breaking Frenchmen take every vessel," Abigail wrote him. "What is to be done with them?"

Like Washington, Adams knew that his young nation was ill-prepared to fight Britain or France. He was for "neither John Bull nor Louis Baboon."

But Federalist papers were inciting the public against France. *Porcupine's Gazette* asked why Americans must tolerate French "insults and robberies."

Adams feared that if the anti-French fever rose, America's modest Army would have to be transformed into a "many bellied Monster" that might "tyrannize the people" and draw the country into unnecessary wars.

He agreed with his old friend Elbridge Gerry of Massachusetts, who thought a large standing army was like a swollen penis, providing "an excellent assurance of domestic tranquility, but a dangerous temptation to foreign adventure."

In Paris, the new French leaders refused the newly appointed U.S. envoy, Charles Cotesworth Pinckney.*

---

* Brother of Thomas Pinckney, architect of the San Lorenzo Treaty.

Adams wrote his son John Quincy, U.S. Minister in Prussia, that he would try to "reconcile" the "misunderstanding with France." But if the French demanded "infidelity, dishonor or too much humiliation," they would find that "America is not SCARED."

To replace Pinckney in Paris, Adams wished to send Thomas Jefferson, his new Vice President. Having once succeeded Benjamin Franklin as minister to France, Jefferson was a devout Francophile.

In the system of the time, Jefferson was Vice President because he had won the second most electors in 1796. Adams hoped that giving him a serious role would help to overcome the interparty bitterness inflamed by Jay's Treaty.

Elected over Jefferson by three electoral votes, Adams insisted to friends he was no knee-jerk Federalist: "I am of no party."

The new President's offer to Jefferson was not wholly altruistic. If Jefferson's mission failed and the U.S. had to fight France, it would be much more difficult for the Vice President to oppose it.

Spotting the trap, Jefferson told Adams he was "sick of residing in Europe" and thought a Vice President should not be so long out of the country.

Jefferson knew his nation was nearing a crisis with France: Washington had been lucky to leave "just as the bubble is bursting."

In the spring of 1797, Adams asked his Cabinet what to do about France. Following old habit, Pickering, Wolcott, and Secretary of War James McHenry wrote Hamilton in New York for advice.

Hamilton suggested that Adams "exhaust the expedients of negotiation" but "prepare *vigorously* for the worst." On the edge of war, *"real firmness* is good for everything. *Strut* is good for nothing."

On Tuesday, May 16, 1797, the new President addressed Congress on the "half-war with France." Members noted his false-tooth lisp and the nervous tremor in his hands.

Adams said the French had inflicted a "wound in the American breast" by insulting Pinckney, attacking U.S. ships, and trying to create "fatal divisions among the American people." Pledging a "fresh attempt at negotiation," he asked Congress to strengthen American defense.

The House and Senate voted to build twelve new frigates and fortify the Eastern coast. But they refused to arm more than a few merchant vessels against French assaults or to impose an embargo against hostile ships.

Abigail Adams told her husband that Congress was full of timid imbeciles.

The ultra-Federalists trumped the President by demanding a fifteen-thousand-man Army. Cranking up his rhetoric, Hamilton said that France was now ruled by the most "horrible tyrants that ever cursed the earth," and the Republicans wanted to "lick" their "feet."

From Monticello, Jefferson warned that Adams was conspiring with the "English faction" to wage a war against France in order to help the Federalists at the polls.

The hypersensitive Adams felt that Jefferson's mind had been "eaten to a honeycomb with ambition." He wrote his son John Quincy, "However wise and scientific as a philosopher, as a politician he is a child and the dupe of party!"

Adams feared the escalating conflict between Republicans and Federalists. Soon he told Abigail, "Rivalries have been irritated into madness."

The President decided to send a new three-man mission to Paris. Bowing to Cabinet members who threatened to quit if he chose a non-Federalist, he settled on Ambassador Pinckney, John Marshall of Virginia and his crony Elbridge Gerry.

Adams knew that Gerry would loyally protect his interests. He considered himself and Gerry "the two most impartial men in America."* Gerry was "an honest and firm man on whom French acts could have no effect."

The President wrote Abigail that Gerry's "Constancy and Fidelity" were different from the "weathercockism" and "Hypocrisy" of people like Hamilton: "Gerry is Steady, while so many prove as Slippery as Eels."

But Adams's Federalist Cabinet complained that Gerry was a maver-

---

* After the 1796 election, Gerry had vainly tried to broker a deal between Adams and Jefferson that would have the new Vice President cooperate with Adams in exchange for Adams's promise to support him as his successor.

ick. In Philadelphia in 1787, he had refused to sign the new Constitution because it lacked a Bill of Rights.*

Fearing to split his party, Adams backed down and chose a more orthodox Federalist. But when the substitute proved too sick for Paris, Adams decided not to be the Cabinet's "slave" and sent Gerry's name to the Senate.

Impudently, Adams's inherited Secretary of State, Timothy Pickering, asked Federalist Senators to scotch Gerry's appointment, but he failed.

McHenry consoled himself by speculating that Gerry's presence would ensure the mission to Paris collapsed: "It is ten to one against his agreeing with his colleagues!"

Pickering was not the only high official undercutting the President. In Philadelphia, Thomas Jefferson secretly advised the French consul that when Adams's envoys reached Paris, the Directory should "drag out the negotiations."

Jefferson insisted that Adams would be ousted after a single term. Then in 1801, the French could bargain with a Republican President who was a trusted friend of France.

---

* Gerry is remembered today for his later efforts as Governor of Massachusetts to reshape a Congressional district to maximize his party's chances. The word "gerrymander" is a combination of Gerry's name (he pronounced it with a hard 'G') and salamander, which the reshaped district resembled.

CHAPTER SIX

—◆—

OH, THAT I WAS A SOLDIER!

On Sunday evening, March 4, 1798, an angry Timothy Pickering rushed to the Presidential mansion, which Adams had taken over for the same rent as General Washington's.

The Secretary of State brought a message from the three-man mission in Paris. The diplomats had not been heard from for six months. Washington had written McHenry to ask if they had been "guillotined."

By candle, Adams read the dispatch with mounting fury. On arrival in Paris, the three envoys had been received by Charles Talleyrand, the notoriously duplicitous Foreign Minister.

Talleyrand told friends he had no fear of America—a nation of "debaters" who could not even build a serious navy.

Demanding amends for Adams's "insults" to France, he shunned the Americans for a week. Then four of his agents asked them for a formal apology from Adams, a large U.S. loan to France and a gratuity of fifty thousand pounds sterling—presumably for Talleyrand.*

Pinckney told the Frenchmen, "No, no, not a sixpence!" Before long, American political culture would transform his reply into a bracing slogan: "Millions for defense, but not one cent for tribute!"

Outraged by Talleyrand's "arrogance," Adams asked his Cabinet whether he should demand "an immediate declaration of war."

Pickering said all *"real Americans"* should be happy to fight France: it

---

* The requested amount equaled almost seven million dollars today.

was time to consider a formal military alliance with Britain, which John Quincy Adams called the last "bulwark against the universal domination of France." Attorney General Charles Lee felt it was war or "national ruin."

Abigail Adams was so certain war was coming that she ordered twenty-five pounds of coffee and a hundred of brown sugar.

In the President's House, Adams scrawled out a truculent speech to Congress, asking for a war declaration. Without naming them, Adams's text excoriated the Jeffersonians whose "unqualified devotion" to the French had encouraged French aggression.

But when Adams laid down his quill, his passions had cooled. He had never shared the ultra-Federalists' zeal to face down the French. He also realized that Congress would not go to war unless he revealed Talleyrand's outrageous bribery demands. But such a revelation might provoke the French to send Pinckney, Marshall and Gerry, still in Paris, to their deaths.

Therefore Adams simply told Congress that the three-man mission had failed and that all U.S. merchant vessels must be fully armed.

The *Aurora* responded by defaming the "bald, blind, crippled" President. Told of the insult, Abigail Adams chuckled that she should be consulted by anyone who doubted her husband's manhood.

After Adams's speech, House Republicans overplayed their hand. Presuming the President had concealed facts favorable to the French, they demanded a look at his secret correspondence with his three envoys.

Although still worried about their safety, Adams duly sent Congress the secret evidence of Talleyrand's shakedown attempt, referring to the French agents as "W, X, Y and Z." For Republicans who thought he was exaggerating the French danger, here was "proof as strong as Holy Writ."

Kept informed by Pickering, Hamilton predicted that the Directory's "abominable corruption" would "shock every reasonable man."

As soon as they read the file, House Republicans knew it would provoke a war against France and voted to keep it quiet. But the Federalist Senate, hoping to spread the fever of war, published fifty thousand copies.

*   *   *

From Maine to Florida, shocked by what they called the "XYZ Affair," Americans clenched their fists against France. Some burned effigies of Talleyrand.

Abigail Adams found public opinion changing "very fast." One New York Federalist felt the XYZ revelations had the "most magical effects." Fisher Ames observed that Americans were dropping out of the undecided camp "like windfalls from an apple tree."

Thomas Jefferson felt the XYZ report had shocked the nation like nothing "since our Independence," but only because of the three envoys' "artful misrepresentations." Francophile to the end, he thought the Directory "above suspicion," with the bribery charges "neither proved nor provable."

Conceding that Talleyrand was a diplomat of "most noted ill fame," Jefferson said the "great obstacle to accommodation" was John Adams.

He insisted the Federalists were fabricating a war scare to bolster their dwindling popularity. Just as Hamilton had once called Republicans the "war party," Jefferson now applied the same epithet to the Federalists. Coining a term that would survive through American wars in Vietnam and Iraq, Jefferson denounced the "war hawks."

The chasm between the two parties was growing. Jefferson noted that "men who have been intimate all their lives cross the street to avoid meeting, and turn their heads another way, lest they should be obliged to touch hats."

As war hysteria spread, the president of Yale University warned that French invaders might force American "wives and daughters" into "legal prostitution." According to rumor, before the French attacked the Eastern Seaboard, French agents would murder President Adams and urge American slaves to throw off their chains.

Adams ordered muskets so that he and his servants could defend the President's House. He expected such "treachery" from a Directory known for its "reign of terror." Adding a new term to the American language, he called such tactics "terrorism."

In a proclamation, he asked Americans to assume a "warlike character" and observe a national day of "humiliation, fasting and prayer."

Thus in the spring of 1798, John Adams became a war leader, and he found that he enjoyed it.

Since youth, he had tried to sharpen his own "true *martial* qualities." Prone to judge other men on their "manly" or "effeminate" qualities, he felt the one figure of "true manliness and grandeur" was the soldier. During the French and Indian War and the War of Independence, he had longed "ardently to be a Soldier" and feared that others might think him a "coward."

During the Revolution, Adams once confessed that if the British marched on Philadelphia, he and most of the Continental Congress would probably "run away" because they were "too brittle . . . to stand the Dashing of Balls and Bombs." *

One of Adams's many jealousies toward Washington was the General's battlefield reputation. Adams once exclaimed to himself, "Oh, that I was a soldier!"

Now, given the opportunity to cut a dashing military figure, Adams could not resist. At public events, he began wearing a dress commander's uniform, a gleaming sword hanging from his waist.

When he traveled, he was greeted by patriotic throngs. One Federalist praised Adams's boldness toward France by saying that no American had "greater luster. . . . I will not even except *George Washington*."

The Revolutionary hero Henry Knox said, "The President Shines like a God."

Toasting John Adams, some High Federalists predicted that "like *Samson*," he would "slay thousands of Frenchmen with the *jawbone* of Jefferson!"

Hamilton was demanding a fifty-thousand-man army against the "TYRANTS of France." †

But Adams remained unnerved by so large a possible army. "I have always cried Ships! Ships!" he later wrote. "Hamilton's hobby horse was Troops! Troops!"

Splitting the difference, Congress called for a "Provisional Army" of twenty thousand men, and a new Department of the Navy to oversee new

---

* When the British took Philadelphia in 1777, Adams was proven correct.
† Revealing his private self-image, Hamilton now wrote under the pseudonym of the Roman military hero Titus Manlius.

American frigates—the "wooden walls" that would shield the nation's coast.

A new property tax was imposed to pay for it all. Congress also abrogated the 1778 treaty with France, which the Directory had exploited to pit Americans against the British.

And in the "warlike" spirit that Adams had proclaimed, it passed the notorious Alien and Sedition Acts.

Knowing that new U.S. citizens were inclined to vote Republican, the Federalists extended the waiting time for citizenship to fourteen years. The President was also empowered to deport enemy aliens or anyone else he considered dangerous.

Long afterward, Adams claimed that he had merely "consented" to these draconian acts as a war measure. But Abigail hailed the Sedition Act for stopping the "wicked and base, violent and calumniating abuse" of her husband in Republican gazettes.

The law let Pickering decide whose articles were seditious, and he did so with gusto. Ben Bache's Federalist competitors reminded Pickering that the *Aurora* publisher was one of the "desperadoes" prone to "vomit" against the government. But before Bache's trial began, Bache died.

Republican Congressman Matthew Lyon of Vermont—known as the "Spitting Lyon" for spitting at one Federalist—was arrested for anti-government writings, fined a thousand dollars and thrown into a prison cell used for fugitive slaves.

Thomas Jefferson rightly complained that the Alien and Sedition Acts had unleashed a "reign of witches."

Congress had authorized Adams to choose the Provisional Army's commander. Hamilton insisted that George Washington be the man on horseback. Who could disagree?

Having finally stuck his pudgy toe outside the Hero's shadow, Adams was not eager to have the General galloping back onto the public stage from Mount Vernon. He knew that Washington would wish to make Hamilton his number two, giving Adams's enemy a splendid position from which to destroy him.

Adams hoped that if he lent his imprimatur to the Provisional Army, Washington would not meddle too much in military affairs.

Thus in July 1798, Adams carefully wrote the General that since he himself, of course, had "no qualifications for the martial part" of the Presidency, he hoped that Washington would be willing to lead the new army: "I must sometimes tax you for advice. We must have your name, if you will, in any case, permit us to use it."

Washington replied that only "in case of *actual* invasion" by France would he leave the "shades of Mount Vernon" and the "smooth paths of retirement" for the "thorny ways of public life." Although it was the "Age of wonders," he thought the French were not foolish enough to invade America.

But Adams had been so eager to wrap himself in Washington's cloak that without waiting for the General's reply, he had already barged ahead and sent Washington's nomination to the Senate.

Eager to pit his old boss against Adams, Hamilton wrote Washington that he was "much surprised" that the President would send his name to Congress "without any previous consultation of you." Nevertheless he advised Washington to accept, since Adams's "prepossessions on military subjects" were so clearly "of the wrong sort."

When the Senate confirmed Washington as commander, Adams asked McHenry to carry the official documents to Mount Vernon. Still nervous about putting Washington in command, he assured McHenry that if the General felt he could not accept, "all the world will be silent and respectfully acquiesce."

As Secretary of War, McHenry had his own qualms about Adams, so he wanted to ensure Washington would take the command. Before leaving Philadelphia, he wrote the General that "in a crisis so awful and important," the country needed "its ancient pilot." Knowing how to spur the old man, McHenry implored, "You alone can unite all hearts and all hands."

Washington "finally determined" to accept the command but refused to be "called into the field until the Army is in a situation to require my presence."* He also wished to "make observations" to President

---

* Still suffering from the revelations about his Presidential stipends, Washington pointedly insisted that he did not want the government to pay him "before I am in a situation to incur expense."

Adams on who should serve under him. Translation: he wanted his own people, starting with Hamilton.

Adams wrote that Washington's advice would, of course, be "extremely desirable," but when the President suggested fifteen names to serve under him, Hamilton's was well down his list.

Pickering warned Washington that Hamilton "will gladly be *Your Second* in command," but nothing else. Thus the General insisted to Adams that Hamilton be Number Two "at *almost* any price."

Adams was thunderstruck. Not only was Washington demanding Hamilton, but until France invaded, he would stay at Mount Vernon and let Hamilton run the Army himself!

To forestall this, Adams tried a painfully obvious ruse: generals in the new army must be ranked by seniority during the Revolution, which would put Hamilton in fifth place.

Ganging up on their boss, Pickering, Wolcott and McHenry told Adams that Hamilton must be Washington's deputy, with the rank of Major General: Washington's "reasonable wishes should be gratified."

For the summer of 1798, Adams had returned to Peacefield, his beloved home in Quincy, Massachusetts. There he agonized over Abigail's "dangerous sickness."

The President wrote that her "precarious destiny" had "thrown my mind into a state of depression, agitation and anxiety."

Abruptly he decided that "there has been too much intrigue in this business with George Washington and me."

He drafted a letter to Wolcott: "If I should consent to the appointment of Hamilton as second in rank, I should consider it as the most irresponsible action of my whole life."

But after rereading the letter, Adams had second thoughts and put it back in his desk drawer.

From Mount Vernon, fed up with his successor's foot-dragging on Hamilton, Washington sent Adams the most belligerent letter that ever passed between them.

Bluntly he complained that Adams had thrown him into a "delicate situation" by sending his appointment to the Senate "without any previous consultation of my sentiments." Now he would "respectfully ask" why Adams had not "complied" with his conditions for taking the command.

Washington conceded that Hamilton was thought to be "an ambitious man and therefore a dangerous one. That he is ambitious I readily grant, but it is of that laudable kind which prompts a man to excel in whatever he takes in hand."

Writing McHenry, Washington threw down the gauntlet. He would resign the Provisional Army command if there should be a "violation of the terms" of his acceptance. If Adams broke his promises, "the Public must decide which of us is right, and which wrong."

Adams was informed that Washington was about to quit and blast him in public. Feeling "no more at liberty than a man in prison," he gave the number-two job to Hamilton, fuming that Washington had forced him to promote "the most restless, impatient, artful, indefatigable and unprincipled intriguer in the United States, if not the world."

CHAPTER SEVEN

━━◆━━

ROCKS AND QUICKSANDS
ON ALL SIDES

Like a man waking up with a head-splitting hangover, Adams shud-
dered at what he had done.

In his new guise of military leader, he had finally managed to feel that
Americans truly loved him. And there were a thousand reasons to
strengthen the country's defense.

But by caving in to the ultra-Federalist war hawks, he had mortgaged
his Presidency to the very leaders of his party who thought him too weak
and unpredictable, letting them exacerbate the differences with France
for "electioneering purposes."

He had always pledged to help both the "simplemen" and the "gentlemen." But in backing High Federalist taxes and military spending,
he was helping the richest Americans make even more "monstrous
fortunes."

As a new President, Adams had been exhilarated to be his own man,
finally unbeholden to Washington and Hamilton. By creating a new
army with those two leaders at its pinnacle, however, he had made them
almost co-Presidents.

Full of remorse and apprehension, Adams wondered whether
Hamilton and the ultra-Federalists were planning to use the Provisional
Army to wage a coup d'etat against him.

The President warned a friend that some High Federalists were plotting to "proclaim a Regal Government" under Hamilton, who would make the United States "a Province of Great Britain." *

Most important of all, by the autumn of 1798, Adams had privately concluded that the French would not invade: "There is no more prospect of seeing a French Army here than there is in Heaven."

But how could he tell Americans that it had all been some terrible mistake?

Despite Pickering's shrill orders to come home at once, Elbridge Gerry had lingered in Paris after the XYZ Affair to try and avert war with France.

Pickering felt that by staying in Paris, Gerry had proven himself a traitor. Railing at Gerry's *duplicity and treachery,* Pickering wished the French had done America a "favor" by sending the "contemptible animal" to the guillotine.

When Gerry finally returned to Boston, Federalist fanatics in the inky night circled his home with torches and shouted crude insults at his wife.

Adams empathized with his old friend. He knew that the French had threatened Gerry with war if he did not remain in Paris.

In October 1798, Adams invited Gerry to see him at Peacefield. There in the President's parlor, Gerry assured him that the French wanted peace.

By November, Adams's wife was well enough for him to leave for Philadelphia. As his carriage bounced along, nervous and underweight from months of worry, he suffered from colds, headaches and toothaches.

Reinstalled in the President's House, he summoned his Cabinet. Even the pugnacious Pickering confessed that Congress was not ready to declare war against France. But Adams was told that bargaining with the French would be an "act of humiliation."

Later, Adams had tea poured for a Quaker doctor, George Logan,

* Adams was also learning of what he called Hamilton's "mad" dream to let U.S. soldiers and British sailors "liberate" Spanish Florida and Louisiana. He said, "I do not know whether to laugh or weep."

who had seen Talleyrand in Paris after the XYZ Affair. Like Gerry, Logan insisted that the French wanted to talk.

When Logan gave the same message to the Secretary of State, the latter kicked him out of his office. Incensed at Logan's "meddling," Pickering and other High Federalists got Congress to pass the Logan Act, which to this day bans U.S. citizens without official sanction from bargaining with foreign governments.

Adams was also deeply affected by a series of dispatches from his young envoy in The Hague, William Vans Murray.

A close friend of John Quincy Adams, Murray cited his talks with a young French diplomat to argue that the French were afraid of a war that might threaten their American holdings and push the United States into Britain's full embrace.

The last straw was when the President learned that after two years of "quasi-war" on the Atlantic the French were still causing U.S. vessels less trouble than the British.

On Saturday, December 8, 1798, Adams went to Congress Hall. Bowing to Generals Washington and Hamilton, who were there planning the Provisional Army, he told the Senate that France now seemed "averse to a rupture" with America.

If the French sent "determinate assurances that he would be received," he would send a new envoy to Paris.

Federalists did not complain about Adams's peace offer because they were sure Talleyrand would never send such assurances.

But they cited the warning by the *Gazette of the United States*: "Talleyrand is like a cat—he retires from the hole to encourage the mouse to come out, and . . . arranges his bloody paws to spring upon us."

Adams's youngest son, Thomas, had been serving in Europe under his brother John Quincy. Returning to Philadelphia in January 1799, Thomas beseeched his father to bargain with the French.

William Vans Murray sent the President a letter Talleyrand had written someone pledging to receive a U.S. envoy "with the respect due the representative of a free, independent and powerful country."

In early February, George Washington sent Adams a letter from Joel

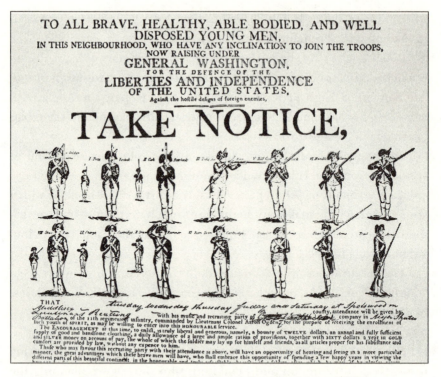

Recruiting poster for John Adams's Provisional Army, 1798

Barlow, a poet and ex-diplomat living in Paris, reporting that Talleyrand would not demand money or "apologies" from any American who came with goodwill.

Washington offered to respond to Barlow "with pleasure and alacrity" if it would bring an "open, fair and honourable" negotiation. He felt "Peace and tranquility" were the "ardent desire of all the friends of this rising Empire."

Privately Adams considered Barlow a worthless "Wretch." But he was delighted by Washington's letter. It suggested that if he sent an envoy to Paris, the old Hero would help him mollify the ultra-Federalists by publicly blessing the mission.

Adams scrawled out a new message to Congress announcing that he would send William Vans Murray to Paris. If the French gave an "unequivocal" promise to receive him cordially, Murray would try to end "all controversies" with France.

Fearing they would sabotage his peace mission in advance, Adams did not divulge his intentions to his Cabinet.

On Monday, February 18, 1799, when the President's message was read aloud to the House of Representatives, one flabbergasted Federalist asked, "Is the man mad?" Another hoped that one of Adams's carriage horses would run wild and break his neck.

Disgusted by Adams's reversal, *Porcupine's Gazette* lectured that "a statesman must act with vigor, steadiness and consistency." A Federalist citizen ("a ruined merchant, alas! With ten children!! Made beggars by the French") sent the President an anonymous wish that *"Assassination shall be your lot."*

Pickering wrote friends that like "every *real patriot,"* he felt Adams deserved the "torments of the damned."

Insinuating that some French secret agent had blackmailed or bribed the President, Pickering wrote Hamilton, "I beg you to be assured that it is *wholly his own act."*

Hoping to jaundice Washington against the peace mission, Pickering wrote the old General, "Confidence in the President is lost. . . . The *honor* of the country is prostrated in the dust—God grant that its *safety* may not be in jeopardy."

Pickering informed Washington that Adams's "real friends and the friends of his country" had all condemned his "dishonourable and disastrous" surprise. What better proof of Adams's infamy than the "slaver of praise" from the "filthy press of the *Aurora*"?

Adams assured Washington by letter that he had not buckled to the Republicans' "babyish and womanly blubbering for Peace." He noted that "those who Snivell" for peace "were hot for War against Britain a few Months ago, and would be now if they Saw a Chance."

Washington was unpersuaded. He later wrote, "I was surprised at the *measure,* how much more so at the manner of it!"

He suspected that the myopic Adams had been tricked by the French, writing Pickering that "a very intelligent Gentmn (immediately from Philadelphia)"—his nephew, Supreme Court Justice Bushrod Washington—had reported that Adams had actually received "no *direct* overture" from France.

General Washington felt Talleyrand was playing "the same loose and round-about game" as in the XYZ Affair.

On Saturday night, February 23, 1799, Senator Theodore Sedgwick of Massachusetts and a gaggle of Federalist colleagues rapped on the front door of the President's House.

When Adams had them let in, Sedgwick was so furious that he shouted. The "foulest heart and the basest head" could not have imagined such an "embarrassing and ruinous caprice" as sending callow Murray to Paris.

Sedgwick felt the problem was Adams's "vain, jealous, half-frantic mind."

His own fuse lit, Adams threatened to resign and let their detested Jefferson be President. He defended Murray as "a gentleman of talents, address and literature," who was already on the scene.

Nevertheless, as a sop to the Senators, Adams agreed to augment Murray with two seasoned Federalists—Chief Justice Oliver Ellsworth and North Carolina Governor William Davie. Adams tried to appease the angry Pickering by letting him draft the team's negotiating instructions.

Behind the President's back, Pickering promised fellow High Federalists to make the terms so stringent that the French could never accept them.

Peering into the night from a frost-filigreed window of his mansion, Adams could hear the clopping of horses' hooves and fishmongers calling out their wares.

Suffering from one of his "great Colds," he longed for his "talkative Wife," still recovering in Massachusetts. That winter he wrote her that he had "a Peck of Troubles."

With the Federalists at his throat, he wondered whether he would "be chosen President a second time." Some people were saying he would never have announced the peace mission had his "old woman" been in Philadelphia to advise him.

"This was pretty saucy," Abigail replied, "but the old woman can tell them they are mistaken." She had "revolved the subject on my pillow" and decided her husband's peace mission was a "master stroke."

*   *   *

In March 1799, the President left the capital to rejoin his wife in Quincy.

Told that Adams was leaving for another long respite, George Washington warned that the President's foes would chuckle. While in office, he had never left the capital for more than three months. Adams haters insisted the President must have fled in shame to Canada.

Ultra-Federalists were plotting how to "get rid" of him in 1800. The governor of Connecticut begged General Washington to save the country by seeking a third term as President.

Still aching from the struggle over Jay's Treaty, Washington sadly replied he was "thoroughly convinced I should not draw a single vote" from the anti-Federalist side.

Arriving at Peacefield, with his own Federalists turning their backs, Adams fell into one of his depressions. He could not eat and told his family he was nearing the end of his life.

Losing his temper, he upbraided servants and mistreated guests. When three friends arrived for a visit one warm day, the President kept his nose behind his papers and offered them nothing to drink.

During one of his morning rides, several officers from the USS *Constitution* came to invite him to a ceremony. Adams told them to go away.

Abigail's heart sank when she saw the shock and disappointment on the officers' faces. She started withholding her husband's official papers so that he would do nothing rash.

Adams once called himself the "most open, unsuspicious man alive," and during that summer of 1799, he showed it.

He could not imagine why Pickering was taking so long to draft the peace mission's orders.

As Adams recalled, "I was uneasy because our Envoys ought to be upon their passage." Talleyrand had sent his direct assurance that they would be welcomed. The President wrote Pickering to get going, but the Secretary of State ignored him.

Adams's loyal Secretary of the Navy, Benjamin Stoddert, implored him to come back to Philadelphia, but Adams pooh-poohed the appeal.

Stoddert wrote again to warn that "artful designing men" were conspiring to "make your next election less honourable than it would otherwise be."

Adams replied to Stoddert that he had "read over and over again your letter." He would return to the capital, "if no fatal accident prevents," by mid-October.

Assuming his preferred pose as a statesman unsoiled by politics, Adams told Stoddert he had "only one favor to beg, and that is that a certain election may be wholly laid out of this question."

After a storm-soaked journey, Adams disembarked in Trenton, New Jersey, the temporary seat of the U.S. government while yellow fever raged through Philadelphia.

In Trenton, Adams occupied the bedroom and parlor of a house owned by two maiden sisters named Barnes, who were tickled to host the President.

Hoarse and shivering from his travels, Adams wrote Abigail that his "kind" landladies had managed to "keep me warm" with "a bed of down, the finest Thing in the World," and dosed him with "Rhubarb and Calomel."

Abigail felt a tinge of jealousy that John seemed to think the Barnes sisters' home remedies rivaled her own.

Receiving Pickering, Wolcott and McHenry in the Barnes parlor, Adams would not be dissuaded from his peace mission.

Pickering tattled to Washington that Adams had said he had *"made up his mind."* Pickering was praying for God to "save our country" from the President's *"fatally erroneous"* choice.

In his own private report to Mount Vernon, McHenry warned that in the 1800 elections, Adams's peace mission could cost the Federalists all "the fruits of their past labours."

He told the General that Adams "suffers from those who flatter him. . . . I see rocks and quicksands on all sides, an administration in the attitude of a sinking ship." He could not predict "whether she is to weather the storm or go down."

Washington wrote McHenry that his letter had left him "stricken dumb."

Frustrated by the Cabinet's inability to budge Adams, Alexander Hamilton called on the President.

"I heard him with perfect good humor," recalled Adams, "though never in my life did I hear a man talk more like a fool."

Hamilton insisted that the peace mission be postponed until the political upheavals in Paris cleared. He predicted the French might reinstall their old king, Louis XIII.

Adams retorted that the "sun, moon and stars" were more likely to "fall from their orbs." He was amazed that the excited "little man" showed such "total ignorance" of the French Revolution.

Grasping at another straw, Hamilton warned that Adams's peace mission might provoke England, just as Jay's Treaty had inflamed the French.*

The President told him not to worry about the British: they knew that renewing their conflict with the U.S. would only push Americans toward France.

When Hamilton departed, Adams knew he had better act before his enemy did more damage. He ordered Ellsworth and Davie to sail at once for Europe, where Murray was waiting to join them.

Rolling out his biggest cannon, Hamilton asked the Hero of Mount Vernon to denounce Adams's peace mission.

Washington agreed that "this business seems to have commenced in an evil hour, and under unfavorable auspices." As someone "not behind the curtain" or "acquainted with the secrets of the Cabinet," he found it "quite incomprehensible" that Adams had not exploited the new chaos in Paris to cancel his *"faux pas."*

But the General was too tired to join the Federalist family feud. In November 1799, a month before his death, Washington wrote McHenry that it was "anxious and painful" for him to watch his cherished country moving "by hasty strides to some awful crisis." But "considering myself as a Passenger only, I shall trust to the Mariners whose duty it is to watch, to steer it into a safe Port."

In a last-gasp attempt to stop the mission, Hamilton accosted Ellsworth and warned him to stay home. But that month, Ellsworth and Davie boarded the new American frigate *United States* and sailed for Europe.

---

* An odd argument for the champion of Jay's Treaty to make.

*   *   *

In December 1799, back in Philadelphia, Adams learned of General Washington's death from a respiratory illness at Mount Vernon.

The President's genuine grief did not dampen his outrage over Federalist obituaries saying that Washington's true heir was not Adams but Hamilton. He fumed that High Federalists were claiming that "Washington was the painted wooden head of the ship and Hamilton the pilot and statesman."

Assuming his place as chief official mourner, Adams orchestrated a memorial service for the old General in Philadelphia and a funeral banquet at the President's House, with the ladies wearing white dresses and black corsages.

Abigail Adams was astonished that some of the Federalist wives were clearly trying to enjoy themselves. They obviously expected her husband to lose the next election and presumed they would not be back in the Presidential mansion for a very long time.

—————◉—————

CHAPTER EIGHT

THE MOST SPLENDID DIAMOND
IN MY CROWN

In the spring of 1800, with Washington dead, John Adams finally felt empowered to expel from his official family, one by one, the men who wished him harm.

With Washington's passage from politics into history, Americans were turning against the General's old party. They were sick of high Federalist taxes, contempt for civil liberties, snobbish patricians who boasted, as Fisher Ames did, that their party was "the wise, the rich and the good."

Even the self-absorbed Hamilton realized that American politics was evolving into a struggle "between the Rich and the poor."

That May, Republicans broke the Federalist hold on the New York legislature, which would decide the state's twelve electoral votes in the fall's Presidential election. Federalist mandarins reacted with "rage and despair."

From the New York results, Adams knew that Jefferson was likely to be elected President that fall. He always insisted he was above the partisanship of lesser men, but he realized that breaking with the discredited ultra-Federalists might peel off electoral votes that might salvage his reelection.

Thus he now swung his axe against his Cabinet enemies—and Hamilton, their furtive instigator, whom Adams condemned as the "Sovereign Pontiff of Federalism."

*   *   *

At the President's House, Adams accused McHenry of conspiring to give the Provisional Army to Hamilton, who, he claimed, had also secretly abetted the New York Federalist defeat in order to hurt the President.

"I have heard no such conduct ascribed to General Hamilton, and I cannot think it to be the case," replied the War Secretary.

"Hamilton is an intriguant," cried Adams, "the greatest intriguant in the world—a man devoid of every moral principle—a Bastard. . . . You are subservient to Hamilton, who ruled Washington and would still rule if he could. Washington saddled me with three secretaries who would control me, but I shall take care of that!"

Lacerating McHenry for incompetence, the President said, "You cannot, sir, remain longer in office."

McHenry thought Adams sounded "insane." He found it "a most mortifying scene," with "insults which I will never forget."

Adams next turned on Pickering, "an Idolater of Hamilton," qualified only for being "a good collector of customs." With Hamilton's "secret aid," the Secretary of State had "obstructed" the peace mission and "embarrassed me to the utmost of his power."

But Pickering flatly refused to quit. He condescendingly wrote the President that Adams could not cope without him: "I do not feel it to be my duty to resign."

Purple with indignation, Adams wrote back, "You are hereby discharged from any further service as Secretary of State."

Unwilling to offend Federalist voters in Wolcott's home state of Connecticut, Adams did not fire his Treasury Secretary.

But on the same day as Pickering's sacking, the President fatally undermined Hamilton by abolishing the Provisional Army, which Adams considered one of the "wildest extravagances" of that "knight-errant."

Hamilton responded to the news by saying Adams was not only "mad" but "wicked."

Despite his talent for concealing emotion, even Hamilton could not feign nonchalance. He had lost what he called the "Aegis" of General Washington and the Federalist foothold in New York. Now he had just been stripped of his last source of national influence.

Although still in Adams's Cabinet, Wolcott warned friends that, given a second term, the President would grow even more "violent and vindictive" against his foes, with his "passions and selfishness" overcoming him like "leprosy."

As the fall campaign approached, Hamilton tried to prevent that gruesome prospect. No longer working through others, he lunged at the President with both hands by writing a vicious pamphlet, under his own name, exposing Adams's "defects"—the "distempered jealousy," the "extreme egotism" and "ungovernable temper." *

Showing how he had lost his old touch, Hamilton published his indictment too late to affect the voters. Federalist leaders charged him with emotionalism and betrayal.

Adams insisted that Hamilton's real problem was not emotional but biological: he suffered from "a super-abundance of secretions which he could not find whores enough to draw off!"

The President's final hope for reelection was that his diplomats in Paris would achieve a peace treaty that would show Americans his wisdom and foresight.

But little had been heard from his envoys. From the trio's few cryptic messages, the new Secretary of State, John Marshall, told Adams that France seemed to be stalling until the more congenial Jefferson could be elected President.

Morose, Adams replied that if the mission failed, America would have to "fight the French Republic alone."

Marshall should not have been so pessimistic. Murray, Ellsworth and Davie had been welcomed at Tuileries Palace by the new French supreme leader, Napoleon Bonaparte. Impressed by Adams's military buildup and the Anglo-American detente, Napoleon had showed he was earnest by choosing his brother Joseph as chief bargainer.

Murray complained to his diary that his fellow U.S. envoys were "exceedingly rude and raw . . . ignorant of the world and its manners" and "too conceited" to accept a young man's advice. He disdained Ellsworth's references to logic, "as if Logic had much to do with the courts of Europe."

Loyal to Adams, who had honored him with such responsibility, Murray wanted a quick agreement that would help the President win the fall

---

* Hamilton recognized such qualities, having all of them himself.

election. He wrote John Quincy Adams that he was trying hard, "but events have been very much against speed and success."

Nevertheless in September 1800, the two sides made a deal: the French would not compensate America for the treasure seized from U.S. ships, but they would stop their naval assaults.

The exhilarated Napoleon wanted it called not a treaty but a convention, which sounded more permanent.

At his brother's country château, Mortefontaine, he signed the convention at a banquet lit by fireworks. To celebrate their achievement, Napoleon offered the U.S. envoys gold Roman coins, but they declined in order to avoid bribery charges back home.

Unfazed, Napoleon raised his goblet of champagne: the "family quarrel" with the United States was over!

"Toasts to perpetual peace . . . and to the successor of Washington were drunk to the sound of cannon," Murray wrote. He could imagine the "pleasure" with which Adams "and the vast majority of the nation will receive the treaty."

On Friday, November 7, 1800, a Baltimore paper reported the "Glorious News" that Adams's peace mission was a success.

Learning of the Convention of Mortefontaine should have made the day one of the happiest of Adams's life. Instead he was crushed.

At almost the same moment, Adams heard that Republicans had won the South Carolina legislature, which chose the state's electoral votes, meaning that he would almost certainly lose the Presidency.

Adams's son Thomas decried "the insolent triumph and exultation of these vulgar dogs who have got the day."

American voters had learned of Adams's peace treaty a month too late to be moved in his favor. For all they knew when they cast their ballots, the President's audacious gamble with France had been a flop.

William Vans Murray wrote John Quincy Adams that he would "always regret that it could not have been sooner." *

---

* Nevertheless Adams was grateful to Murray. Three years later, told of Murray's premature death at forty-three, the sentimental Adams scrawled on the young envoy's last letter to him, "In my memory and hopes his existence will cease but with my own."

*   *   *

In November 1800, the President and Abigail had left their Philadelphia mansion and taken up residence in the new American federal city of Washington, D.C.

Holed up in the cold, damp, unfinished Executive Mansion, Adams counted the days until he was once again a farmer, gone from the "intrigues" and "passions that agitate the world." Physically and psychologically spent, he later averred that "had I been President again, I am certain I could not have lived another year."

That December, Adams proudly held the first American copy of the Convention of Mortefontaine. To ultra-Federalists who reviled him for destroying their party, it was "another chapter in the Book of Humiliation" that, for them, was the Adams Presidency.

Before dawn on Wednesday, March 4, 1801, Adams rose in darkness and boarded a public stagecoach heading out of Washington, D.C.

Out of bitterness or reluctance to blot the new President's day, he declined to witness the swearing-in of Thomas Jefferson, elected by the House of Representatives after an electoral deadlock with Republican Aaron Burr of New York.

Since the Sedition Act had expired, the Adams-hating press was back in action. Resuming its old invective, the *Aurora* insisted that God had thrown Adams out of the Presidency like "polluted water."

When Adams climbed into the stagecoach, he faced another sign of his vanished luck. Like some evil practical joke, his coachmate for the long journey back to Massachusetts was his arch-foe Senator Sedgwick, who had lately opined that Adams's humiliating defeat was "sufficient notice to quit" public life.

For the quarter-century of his existence that remained, John Adams rarely left the commodious old house in Massachusetts that he and Abigail had built.

He complained that his Presidency had been "condemned" to "infamy." Americans had worn him out "with hard service, and then turned me adrift like an old Dray horse." Unlike Washington at Mount Vernon, few young Americans came to Peacefield to sit at his knee: "I am buried and forgotten."

Adams claimed not to be shaken by the fizzling of his career: "all my life," he had "expected" to end in failure. Convincing no one, he insisted that it did not matter how history described him: "I am not, never was, and never shall be a great man."

The ex-President said he had "little faith" in written history—he read it "as I do romance"—but he could not "keep my Eyes off it." Mentioning no names, he hoped that "some characters now obscured under a cloud of unpopularity will come out with more luster."

As Vice President, Adams had watched George Washington walk through fire to enact Jay's Treaty and grant his country an essential peace with England. Always measuring himself against the Hero, Adams dared hope that future scholars might recognize his own greater personal sacrifice in making peace with France.

Irked by how Washington outshined him, he wondered why Americans were not grateful for what he had done: one day, such a book must be written, "if ever an Historian should arise fit for the investigation."

Adams insisted that his peace mission was "the most splendid diamond in my crown; or, if anyone thinks this expression too monarchical, I will say, the most brilliant feather in my cap." * Americans must realize that "great is the guilt of an unnecessary war."

In 1809, a newspaper friend innocently referred to Adams's renown for making peace with France. The ex-President's bile came flowing out.

"You speak of the fortunate issue of my negociation with France to my Fame!!!" Adams replied. "I cannot express my astonishment. No thanks for that action, the most disinterested, the most determined and the most successful of my whole life.

"No acknowledgment of it ever appeared among the Republicans, and the Federalists have pursued it with the most unrelenting hatred and my Children too, from that time to this. . . . My Fame!!! It has been the systemical policy of both parties . . . to conceal from the people all the services of my life."

*   *   *

---

* Adams's reference to "monarchical" was tongue-in-cheek. Although Washington was far more rich and patrician, Adams had long been criticized for his aristocratic airs, insisting that the President and Vice President be addressed by semiroyal titles, and reports that he and John Quincy wished to establish a political dynasty.

Allowing for overstatement, Adams was right. After he left office, Federalists thought of him mainly as a renegade who cost them the Presidency. To Republicans, he was the scourge of their hero Thomas Jefferson.

But in retrospect, Adams deserves lasting credit for his political sacrifice. Had he, as President, remained silent and played the front man for the arch-Federalists' war program, he might have kept his party together and won a second term.

But Adams knew that had he done so, he would have loathed himself. He had long argued that a leader "must run the risk" of incurring "people's displeasure sometimes, or he will never do them any good in the long run."

Adams's personal tragedy was that he did not need to forgo a second term to make peace with France. Had he handled his Cabinet, Congress, his rivals and the public with more finesse, he could have saved his career.

The President's constant need for reassurance and praise deafened him to the shortcomings and hidden treacheries of those who flattered him. Just as he had once described Jefferson, Adams was more talented as political philosopher than working politician. His inability to fathom complex men like Washington and Hamilton would have been comic were the result not so painful.

Insisting that he must "preserve my Independence," Adams often behaved as if the only independent leader was one with no real political friends. Thus when his peace mission brought on the storm, he had few allies who could help him ride it out.

Adams did so little to avert his great act of political suicide that one suspects that, at some level of his mind, he actually courted defeat to persuade himself once and for all that he was a good and moral man.

In his youth, he had agonized about whether he was "Scheming for Power" or advancing the "Welfare of my Country." For a man so racked by insecurities and self-doubt, perhaps the best way for Adams to convince himself he was truly virtuous—a leader of General Washington's caliber—was to refuse the masses' acclaim and give up a second term.

For the rest of his life, having made his dramatic sacrifice, Adams boasted that his conscience was "clear as a crystal glass." He had "made Peace with France at the expense of all my consequence in the World, and their unanimous and immoral hatred."

* * *

Adams's treaty with France spared his tender young country a confrontation that might have threatened its survival. In that sense, it gave him the right to expect that history would link his name to Washington's.

The cordial relationship that Adams began with Napoleon led, under President Jefferson, to the Louisiana Purchase, which made America a truly continental nation.

None of this would have happened had Adams been too timid to defy his own party. As Adams insisted, he had indeed brought the American ship "into a peaceable and safe port," with "its coffers full" and "all the world smiling in its face." He would "defend my missions to France as long as I have an eye to direct my hand, or a finger to hold my pen."

So rudely evicted from office, Adams lived long enough to see his son John Quincy elected in 1824 as the sixth President of the United States. On hearing the news, the eighty-eight-year-old man wept with joy and thanksgiving.

Adams died at Peacefield on Independence Day 1826, a few hours after Thomas Jefferson at Monticello. Among his last words were "Independence Forever!"

The death of the two Founders, "hand in hand, ascending into heaven," on their country's fiftieth birthday, was not the only miracle that day. Adams's relatives insisted that as soon as their patriarch was gone, "a clap of thunder shook the house" and "a splendid rainbow arched immediately over the heaven."

Politely circumnavigating his doomed Presidency, most of the newspapers predicted that future Americans would most honor Adams for his role in waging the Revolution.

But that was not Adams's hope. Long before his death, the ex-President had dreamt that his tombstone might say, "Here lies John Adams, who took upon himself the responsibility of peace with France in the year 1800."

CHAPTER NINE

I WILL KILL IT!

Before going to sleep, President Andrew Jackson took off the cameo of his late wife, Rachel, that hung near his heart and propped it on a bedside table so that he could see it first thing in the morning. While reading Rachel's favorite Bible passages, he sometimes wept.

Jackson blamed Rachel's death, a month after his election in 1828, on his political foes. Noting that she had not been properly divorced before marrying Jackson, they had issued handbills suggesting she was an adulteress and whore.

Jackson was called Old Hickory because he was tough as a hickory branch. Americans recalled his heroism in 1815 at the Battle of New Orleans.

For this man of honor, the worst offense of all was to have slandered his wife. He had once killed a man in part for that, and the symbol of his chivalry was the avenging pistol, which he displayed above his White House bedroom fireplace.

On the sultry Sunday evening of July 8, 1832, Jackson looked up from his pillows at his new Vice Presidential running mate, Martin Van Buren of New York. Van Buren found the ailing President "a spectre in physical appearance, but always a hero in spirit."

Brushing aside a few strands of white hair, Jackson reached for Van Buren's hand and ranted against the Second Bank of the United States and its supercilious president, Nicholas Biddle.

Jackson viewed the Bank as a "hydra-headed monster," buying editors and Congressmen "by the Dozzen" to corrupt the "morals of our people."

Despite its official-sounding name, the Bank was a federally chartered quasi-private corporation with influence so vast that Biddle's whim could send the economy into a tailspin.

Jackson felt the Bank profaned America's Revolutionary ideals with its excessive power over farmers, mechanics, and the others unconnected to the Eastern "moneyed aristocracy."

By 1832, Biddle was openly siding with the President's enemies—the same ones who had dogged Rachel to her grave—turning a political conflict into a battle to the death.

With hoarse defiance, Jackson now told his running mate, "The Bank, Mr. Van Buren, is trying to kill me. *But I will kill it!*"

As the seventh American President, and the first nonaristocrat, Jackson had acquired his class antagonism early.

Born in South Carolina in 1767, he lost his parents and brothers by the age of fourteen and lived on family charity. The melancholy Andrew would not be trod upon. Shaken by a gun's recoil, he told friends, "By God, if one of you laughs, I'll kill him!"

As the "law of my life" Jackson always cited his mother's final words: defend his "manhood" and vindicate "wanton outrage," but "do it calmly."

In 1796, the young lawyer was elected the newly admitted Tennessee's first Congressman, arriving in Philadelphia with his ponytail wrapped in eelskin.

Jackson had little affection for the patrician early Presidents. He felt that Washington deserved every punishment he got for Jay's Treaty. Jackson wished the humiliating document could be "removed Erased and obliterated from the archives of the Grand republick of the united States."

He abhorred John Adams's willingness to have civil liberties crushed under the pretense of almost-war against France. Jackson turned against President Jefferson when he refused to make him governor of the new Louisiana Territory.*

Jackson had hoped that "before I get too old," his country would "fight England again." With the War of 1812, he got his wish. From his victories at New Orleans and later, driving the Spanish from Florida, Jackson became the most idolized American since General Washington.

---

* Jackson lampooned Jefferson as "the best republican in theory and the worst in practice."

*   *   *

Prodded by millions of citizens, Jackson agreed in 1824 to run for President. With Presidential electors increasingly chosen directly by the voters, the humbly born hero had a huge advantage over the patricians of old.

Jackson's appeal gave him the popular vote, but he lacked an Electoral College majority. When the election was bucked to the House, the General's chief opponents, John Quincy Adams and Henry Clay, closed their "corrupt bargain"—so the Jacksonians insisted—making Adams President and Clay his Secretary of State.

Jackson decried Clay as "the *Judas* of the West" and Clay's "bare-faced corruption" as "bribery."

Clay retorted that he had thrown his electoral votes against Jackson because a mere "military chieftain" should not be President.

Jackson told Americans that the "Military Chieftain" would refer the question "to the Judgment of an enlightened patriotic and uncorrupted electorate."

In 1828, under the banner "Jackson and Reform," the General defeated John Quincy Adams by a landslide, which he called a "triumph" over aristocratic "intrigues."

In February 1829, Jackson arrived in Washington wearing a black mourning ribbon around his tall beaver hat. With Rachel dead, he told a friend, "My heart is nearly broke," his "least hope of happiness" gone.

Recalling how Adams's and Clay's "midnight assassins" had tried to "destroy me" and "snatched from me" his cherished wife, Jackson wanted "retribution and vengeance."

He insisted that Biddle and the Bank of the United States had dispensed their "golden favors" across the twenty-five States of the Union to help Adams.

He saw Biddle's Bank, largely owned by foreign "Lords, Dukes and Ladies," as an ugly emblem of the corruption he had been elected to stop. He was repelled by the Congressmen and Senators who shamelessly took cash from corporations and people like Biddle: "I weep for the liberty of my country."

Injured long ago by land speculation in Tennessee, Jackson felt that debt, bankers and paper money—"ragg money"—were all the devil's work. As he wrote a friend, he had "always been opposed to the United States Bank, nay all banks."

Most of Jackson's advisers did not share Jackson's hostility toward Biddle and worried about the banker's power to harm him. They restrained the General from confronting the Bank in his inaugural address.*

In Philadelphia, perched in his white temple modeled on the Parthenon, Nicholas Biddle assured aides that Jackson would never be so daft as to set the "country afloat" by harming the Bank: he may have carped about it in private, soon he would no doubt realize what the Bank meant to the nation.

From a genteel Philadelphia family, with his wavy hair and delicate cheekbones, Biddle looked like a blowsy Romantic poet. As a young man, he had gained minor renown when family friend William Clark asked him to edit the lyrical journals he and Meriwether Lewis had written on their pathfinding trek to the Pacific.

After marrying a mogul's daughter, Biddle dabbled in state politics before President James Monroe elevated him to the Bank. Though elitist to the core, he loved the architecture of the world's oldest democracy. On his wife's country estate, Andalusia, he built a Greek Revival mansion that looked quite like his Bank.†

Biddle's Bank had a troubled lineage. With Jeffersonian anxiety about an unaccountable powerhouse, Congress had refused to renew the charter of the First Bank of the United States in 1811.

Then, confessing error after financial chaos ensued, Congress in 1816 established a Second Bank with a twenty-year charter and an exalted place in American life. The U.S. government chose only a fifth of its directors, but the new Bank became its fiscal agent, holding public funds, paying public bills, charged with maintaining a sound American currency.

Biddle claimed that he did not meddle in Presidential politics. "The

---

* Emulating his father, John Quincy Adams became the second of the only two Presidents in American history to shun their successors' inaugurations.

† Two centuries later, Andalusia is often considered the most splendid Greek Revival house in America. Biddle descendants own it and live there.

Bank is neither a Jackson man nor an Adams man," he said. "It is only a Bank." But since the Bank's charter would expire in 1836, even the self-intoxicated Biddle could not ignore his need to retain the goodwill of the President and Congress.

Thanks in part to the Bank's lavish loans to members of Congress, Biddle did not worry about the House and Senate. He knew that should he ever have trouble with Jackson, he would have an ally—the new President's Tennessee friend William Lewis, who occupied a White House bedroom and venerated the Bank.

During Jackson's first year in office, Biddle sent Lewis an unctuous letter for the President's eyes: "There is one glory which I should rejoice to see General Jackson possess. . . . In the history of the world, no nation has ever paid off its debt."

The President, "in his independent and energetic way," could "pay off the last dollar in person" in 1833, on the anniversary of his victory in New Orleans: "What a day of Jubilee that would be for him. . . . It depends only on General Jackson to say that it shall be."

Lurking within Biddle's offer was a golden fishhook. Before paying off the debt, Jackson would have to endorse a new charter for Biddle's Bank. Without such a commitment, Biddle warned, Americans would be consumed by "confusion and anxiety and speculation."

When Jackson read Biddle's letter, he must have thought the Bank chief regarded him as a gullible backwoodsman. In the fall of 1829, he asked Biddle to the White House.*

When visitors walked into the mansion's entrance hall, lit by glowing oil lamps, they passed a huge portrait of Andrew Jackson. With his democratic instinct, the President tried to receive any American who stopped by and asked, but if he could not, the portrait let visitors feel his powerful presence.

Jackson hosted East Room receptions standing under a triumphal arch newly spangled with twenty-five stars, representing the American states. Elegant ladies mixed with clerks, Indians in warpaint and "rag-a-muffins," who climbed in through the windows. Jackson equipped the

---

* The formal name of the residence would be the "Executive Mansion" until 1901, but Americans were already calling it the White House.

room with twenty gold spittoons, which made the Capital's dowagers cackle.

Sensitive to those who thought him too rough-hewn, the President made sure his public attire and manners were of military quality. When a U.S. diplomat—future President James Buchanan—came to announce a British noblewoman, he was chagrined to find Jackson unshaven, wearing rumpled clothes, his feet atop his desk.

Buchanan noted the lady's high station. Jackson told him to mind his "own business." By the time she arrived, he was handsomely dressed, and she said she had never met a gentleman with better manners.

When Nicholas Biddle came to the White House, Jackson showed the famous banker both courtesy and steel.

He told Biddle he must "be perfectly frank." From his reading of the Constitution, he doubted that Congress had the right to establish any bank outside the "ten-mile square" of Washington, D.C.

Genially the President assured Biddle, "I do not dislike your Bank any more than all banks." But he feared another "South Sea Bubble." Since reading about the panic that swept England after the corrupt South Sea Company collapsed, he had been "afraid of banks."

———◦❖◦———

CHAPTER TEN

NOT A MAN TO BE FORCED

Jackson planned to declare himself against Biddle's Bank in his first annual message to Congress.*

Secretary of State Martin Van Buren thought it was too dangerous. But eager to win Jackson's blessing as his Presidential successor, he did not want to risk annoying the President. Famed for political sleight-of-hand—his nickname was "the Little Magician"—Van Buren instead sent one of his advisers to help Jackson draft his message.

His choice was inspired—the late Alexander Hamilton's son James, whose father had engineered the First Bank.† A New York lawyer, James knew that Jackson privately hated the Bank. Allowing his emotions to distort the most obvious history, the General had once bizarrely assured James, "Your father was not in favor of the Bank of the United States."

When Hamilton came to the President's private quarters, Jackson was writing his annual message among busts and portraits of himself. Shown one of the drafts, James was appalled to read an attack on the Bank, rendered "in a loose, newspaper, slashing style."

Assigned to a bedroom adjoining Jackson's, Hamilton worked through the night. While stoking his fireplace, he accidentally woke up the President, who appeared in a long, white nightgown and offered him his body servant George, who slept on a rug next to Jackson's bed.

---

* Presidents had not given annual messages in person since Jefferson shirked the practice, finding it too similar to the British monarch's speech from the throne. Such self-restraint ended with Woodrow Wilson, who understood how a live annual message could enhance Presidential influence on Congress.

† The elder Hamilton had perished in his duel with Aaron Burr in 1804.

By dawn, Hamilton was done. Jackson asked him, "What have you said about the Bank?"

"Very little," said Hamilton.

Jackson said, "Oh, my friend, I am pledged against the Bank."

He wanted, at least, to reform the institution. When he issued his annual message in December 1829, it denounced the Bank as unconstitutional and unable to keep the currency sound.*

He later explained to Hamilton that his conscience had told him "now was the proper time." He "could not shrink" from restoring "the safety and purity of our free institutions. . . . I have brought it before the people and I have confidence that they will do their duty."

Pretending that his tender feelings had been bruised, Biddle wrote William Lewis that the President's criticism had "exceedingly hurt and pained" him.

Privately Biddle regarded Jackson as a child. He told aides to treat his complaints as the "honest though erroneous notions of one who intends well. . . . If our currency is not sound and uniform, I do not know what is."

Biddle was glad to hear from Washington friends that Jackson's Cabinet did not share his hostility toward the Bank. Thus the President's annual message had merely been his "personal . . . opinion."

Biddle had his own Hamilton—Alexander Hamilton, Jr., who warned him that Jackson would not halt his crusade against the Bank: "The die is now cast."

Alexander advised Biddle not to question Jackson's "fairness and integrity." If he goaded members of Congress to oppose the President's "avowed sentiments," he would suffer the Jacksonians' "cunning intrigues," which would be "ruinous."

Rejecting Alexander's excellent counsel, Biddle ordered Congressional leaders he controlled to rebut Jackson's complaints about the Bank. With doglike obedience, they assigned the writing of the official report to Biddle himself, who spent Bank money to publish it across the country.

*　　　*　　　*

---

* By contrast, the Supreme Court had ruled that the Bank was constitutional in *McCulloch v. Maryland* (1819).

Biddle wrote William Lewis that he had never "abused" the Bank's power "for political purposes" and that he was treating the President "fairly and cordially."

Unfooled, Jackson escalated his battle against the "hydra of corruption" that threatened "our liberties." He demanded that sympathetic papers like the *United States Telegraph* do more to "defend" his crusade: Duff Green, the *Telegraph*'s editor, claimed he was "heart and soul" against the Bank, but you wouldn't know it from his editorials.*

Jackson was delighted when his close adviser Amos Kendall joined Francis Preston Blair, a fellow Kentuckian, to found a Jacksonian paper called the *Globe*.

From now on, when Jackson wished to send official word to his legions, he would say, with his country accent, "Send it to Blahr!" He lavished government printing contracts on Blair, and ordered political allies to "patronize the *Globe*."

Soon Blair had so much cash that he bought a mansion across from the White House on Pennsylvania Avenue, which locals started calling the "Blair House."†

Grateful to his patron, Blair took fresh pails of milk from his own cows to the Executive Mansion by hand to bolster the President's flagging health.

One of Biddle's Washington pawns warned him that Jackson was privately vowing to pull the Bank's "damned head off."

In December 1830, the President asked Congress to merge Biddle's Bank with the U.S. Treasury and bar it from lending money or buying property. Then the Bank could no longer manipulate the people's "hopes" and "fears."

Biddle believed that Jackson by now sought "the destruction of the Bank." He predicted "a great struggle" but had "too much confidence in the sense of my Countrymen" to fear Jackson would prevail. Americans would not "cut their own throats to please anybody."

---

* Green's hesitation may be explained in part by his request of a twenty-thousand-dollar loan from Biddle.

† Since 1942, Presidents have used Blair House as an official guest mansion. In 1950, Harry Truman was nearly murdered there by Puerto Rican separatists.

Some of Biddle's friends warned him that by paying editors to defend the Bank, he was only antagonizing the President.

But Biddle retorted that Jackson was using his "whole influence," including "the presses subservient to his government," to "break down the Bank." What was wrong with paying editors for their trouble? "If a grocer wishes to apprize the public that it has a fresh supply of figs, the printer . . . never thinks of giving its labor for nothing."

"Disgusted" by the "wicked" opposition's "depravity" and "slanders," Jackson longed for "retirement to the peaceful shades" of his beloved Tennessee home, the Hermitage.

Still he wanted another term as President. Departing without "the Bank question settled" would mean being "driven" out "by my enemies." He declared, "I cannot retire now."

Jackson would have preferred to delay a final showdown with Biddle until he was safely reelected. Wary of the Bank's "magic power" to warp Presidential elections, he did not wish to fully ire the "monster" now.*

In the fall of 1831, Jackson sent his Treasury Secretary, Louis McLane, to Philadelphia, proposing an armed truce. The choice was not casual: Biddle regarded McLane as a "known friend."

Sitting in the Greek temple, McLane reported that Jackson was "now perfectly confident" of reelection. Biddle must not do anything that the President might consider "interference in the peoples' decision." For example, if Biddle persuaded Congress to renew the Bank's charter before the 1832 election, Jackson would retaliate by veto.

McLane pledged that if Biddle held his fire until after Jackson's reelection, he would advise the President to accept a new charter. To save face, Jackson could simply tell the House and Senate he would let them decide the Bank's future.

Biddle was delighted by the olive branch. McLane left the office presuming that they had a deal.

---

* Jackson had another consideration: as Biddle had suggested, Jackson hoped to repay the national debt as early as 1833, selling the government's seventy thousand shares of Bank stock. If Americans thought the Bank was doomed, those shares would plummet in value.

But when the Bank-hating Attorney General, Roger Taney, heard what McLane had done, he warned Jackson that if he accepted the deal, Americans would wonder what secret enticement had turned the President soft.

Jackson replied that if Congress voted to recharter the Bank, he would still retain his right to veto. But to mollify Taney, he assured Congress in his annual message of December 1831 that he still opposed the Bank.

The day after Jackson's statement, however, McLane publicly called for the Bank to be rechartered.

The President explained to friends that McLane's opinion was only his own: he liked it when Cabinet secretaries "openly" challenged him, as long as it was with "proper decorum."

But Jacksonians like the President's gravely sick old friend Virginia Senator John Randolph read McLane's statement with "pain and mortification." *

Randolph wrote Jackson that since he was dying, subsisting on "asses' milk and Sarsaparilla," he could speak the truth: opportunists like McLane "who differ so essentially from you" were putting Jackson "in a *false* position." †

When Frank Blair criticized McLane for siding with the Bank, the Treasury Secretary tried to have him removed from the *Globe*. One astute Congressman observed that by stupidly attacking Jackson's crony, McLane had just "ruined himself."

Jackson was angry at McLane, but let him stay for now. He did not want to rock his official household during an election year.

Even more than during the time of George Washington and John Adams, the Capital was rife with suspicions of bribery and betrayal. Jackson may have wondered whether McLane had been secretly taking cash or favors from Biddle all along.

---

* Randolph was the nephew of the ill-fated Edmund Randolph, under whom he had studied law.

† Randolph went on to compare himself to Hephestion, the adviser and homosexual lover of Alexander the Great—"although you are not Alexander (that would be fulsome flattery) and I boast that I am something better than his minion (the nature of their connexion, if I forget not, was *Greek* Love)."

*   *   *

As Jackson's opponent for 1832, the National Republican party chose Senator Henry Clay of Kentucky, the great champion of Biddle's Bank.* Delegates denounced Jackson as "by education and character wholly unfit" for the Presidency.

While a member of the House, Clay had been a well-paid director and counsel for the Bank. He now claimed "no connexion" with the Bank for a decade, but in fact, Biddle had just given him a quiet five-thousand-dollar loan.

Convinced that the Bank issue could win him the Presidency, Clay urged Biddle to apply at once for a new charter. Jackson would, no doubt, veto, and the Bank would become the "controlling question" of the 1832 campaign.

But Biddle was nervous: if Jackson vetoed and was reelected, the Bank would be in critical danger.

Clay speculated that if Jackson had to decide now, he would not risk a veto, which might jeopardize his reelection. But if Jackson won a second term, he would be unconstrained.

Others warned Biddle that Jackson was "not a man to be forced" and that he should not drive the President "into a Corner."

Biddle's political tactician, Thomas Cadwalader, advised that a "general alarm ring through the Nation" would compel Congress to override any Jackson veto: if Biddle took charge of the battle and exploited the Bank's influence, he would "overcome the scruples of those weak people" on Capitol Hill "who dare not act from fear of offending the President."

Biddle decided that a reelected Jackson would be "ten times more disposed" to veto the charter: "Now he has at least some check in public opinion."

Thus at the start of 1832, Biddle threw down his gauntlet. At his behest, Congress was formally asked to recharter his Bank.

Biddle threatened one Jacksonian that if the President waged "war upon the Bank," he would "awaken a spirit which has hitherto been . . . reined in." If Jackson blocked the Bank's recharter, "it will destroy him. . . . Moreover, I think it ought to."

------
* Clay was chosen by the first American major party nominating convention, which met in Baltimore.

CHAPTER ELEVEN

I WAS BORN FOR THE STORM

Steeling himself against Biddle and his allies, Jackson now said, "I will prove to them that I never flinch."

Old Hickory always felt most alive while struggling for a noble cause: "I was born for the storm, and calm does not suit me."

Jackson's friends marveled at how the old man's impending war against Biddle had revived his spirits. He told them that they "need not fear my energy." The "corrupting monster" must be "shriven of its ill-gotten power." If Congress chartered the Bank, "my veto will meet it frankly and fearlessly."

From Philadelphia, Biddle vowed that "no child in the United States" would miss the President's "great error." Roger Taney felt that Biddle was clearly saying, "Beware of our power!" One Senator wrote it was now "a trial of strength between General Jackson and the Bank."

Van Buren wrote the President that he admired his courage against the Bank: "few men" had "more fortitude" to "resist the torrents of calumny." The ailing John Randolph wrote Jackson that he had a "Sisyphean labor to perform. I wish I were able to help you roll up the stone."

Recalling Solomon's admonition that "there is a time for all things," Jackson yearned to expose Henry Clay, with "his duplicity and hypocrisy unveiled and naked to the world."

Leading the President's fight in the Senate was Thomas Hart Benton of Missouri, who was once his enemy.

In 1813, Jackson was shot during a struggle with Benton and his brother in a Nashville hotel.* Having long ago mended fences, Benton was now eager to "display the evil" of Biddle's Bank. With his rural accent, he insisted that "Bane-ton and the people" were "one and the same, sir. Synonymous terms, sir!"

Benton pledged to "attack incessantly, assail at all points" and "rouse the people," forcing the Bank's defenders in the Senate to tell voters why they were siding with a "mammoth moneyed aristocracy."

Nearly burnt down by the British in the War of 1812, the U.S. Capitol had been rebuilt and crowned with a new copper-veneered wooden dome. Looking down from crimson swag in the Senate chamber was a newly acquired portrait of George Washington.

From the Senate floor, Tom Benton bellowed that, if given twenty more years, Biddle's Bank would establish a permanent American nobility: "Duke of Cincinnati! Earl of Lexington! Marquis of Nashville!" Farmers and merchants would have to "crook the pregnant hinges of the knee."

Jacksonians in the House investigated Biddle's use of Bank funds to buy editors and Congressmen. Roger Taney chuckled when he learned of how a sweetheart loan had switched one Member to the Bank's side: perhaps the beneficiary felt that an institution that treated him "with so much kindness" couldn't injure the public!

Jackson found himself "shedding a tear over the immorality of our Congress."

Cadwalader told Biddle that "our life depends" on getting the nation "roused" before the November elections. Moving to Washington to command the Bank's forces, Biddle told his branch officers in every state to pressure the Congress and public.

Nervous about his prospects, he wondered whether he should compromise with Jackson and "let him write the whole charter with his own hands."

---

* When the bullet was finally extricated from Jackson's arm in 1832, he offered it to Benton, but the Senator joked that from decades of ownership, Jackson deserved to keep it.

But by now, the President felt that compromise equaled surrender. Without warning, Biddle had forced him into this struggle. If some part of the "hydra-headed monster" were left intact, the whole reptile would grow back to menace the American people.

Jackson now felt that the Bank could never be tamed. It had to be killed.

Before Independence Day 1832, the Senate and House voted to recharter the Second Bank of the United States.

Grinning, Biddle walked onto the House floor and shook hands. One ally told him that if "Jacksonism" survived now, "we may as well give up the rule to vulgarity and Barbarism at once."

Henry Clay promised that if Jackson vetoed the charter, "I will veto him!"

The President knew the dangers of a veto. It might harm his reelection, especially in vote-rich Pennsylvania, which was so tied to the Bank's fortunes. The opposition would no doubt paint him with "slanders."

Jackson knew that Biddle would use any available weapon against him. Convinced of the Bank's invisible power over all areas of American life, Old Hickory could not predict what those weapons might turn out to be. But if death—political or otherwise—was the price for stopping the Bank, he would pay it.

That summer, Jackson wrote his daughter-in-law, "Knowing that we have to die, we ought to live to be prepared to die well."

He told Amos Kendall that Providence had given him the chance to "preserve the Republic" from the Bank's "thralldom and corrupting influence."

Jackson's talk of Providence was not just rhetoric. Encouraged by the departed Rachel, he drew strength from his religious belief and Bible reading.

If a veto cost him reelection, that did not faze him. He had survived defeat before, and he would still be Andrew Jackson. Since Rachel's death, he had been so numb to happiness that returning to the Hermitage held no terrors for him.

But Jackson did not expect to lose. He felt that he and the American people understood each other. With his mastery of public psychology, he knew how to dramatize a Bank veto for his own political benefit—Jackson and the People versus Biddle, Clay and the Bank.

Most of Jackson's Cabinet was still urging him to avoid all-out war with Biddle, so he turned to his wordsmith-tactician Amos Kendall.

Born on a hardscrabble Massachusetts farm, Kendall had gone by stagecoach and horseback to Lexington, Kentucky, where he tutored the children of Henry Clay. As editor of the influential *Argus of Western America*, Kendall abandoned Clay for Andrew Jackson. He admired Old Hickory's common touch but was also punishing Clay for letting a federal printing contract that was vital to the *Argus* be canceled.

After Jackson's victory in 1828, the wizened, sallow Kendall, with his migraines and asthmatic cough, came to Washington and worked his way into the President's confidence. He cultivated the image of a semi-recluse, which reinforced the public impression that he had Jackson's ear.

Using the term for the first time, Washingtonians referred to advisers like Kendall and Frank Blair as the President's "Kitchen Cabinet." Nicholas Biddle carped that the "Kitchen" would always "predominate over the Parlor."

To work on his veto message, Jackson installed Kendall in the upstairs White House bedroom, reeking of oil paint, that was occupied by his resident portrait artist. Kendall drafted the lion's share of a hellfire message announcing the President's veto of the Bank's recharter.

Pleased with the result, on Tuesday, July 10, 1832, Jackson sent it to Congress.

In the message, Jackson complained that the House and Senate had violated the Founders' Revolutionary spirit by granting a "gratuity of many millions" to the Bank's rich shareholders, robbing "the humble members of society."

All Americans should "tremble" before the perils of the Bank. During peace, it threatened "our liberty and independence." In war, with so many foreign owners, it might be used to aid "hostile fleets and armies."

Government must "shower its favors alike on the high and the low." Renewing the Bank would "make the rich richer and the potent more powerful." Jackson said the people would decide whether his veto was right.

Jackson's veto of the Bank recharter has rightly been called the most important in American history, establishing vast new authority for himself and future Presidents.

Since George Washington, Presidents had rarely used their veto: for them, it was mainly a sanction against bills they deemed radical or unconstitutional. By contrast, Jackson's innovation would empower Presidents to stop measures they simply did not like.

Jackson's veto message was daubed with demagoguery. It came close to declaring a national class war, and gave no hint of the economic dangers facing the country if the Bank were abolished without some kind of substitute.

But Jackson had addressed Americans' souls. The Pittsburgh *Manufacturer* said, "With one voice, with one arm, mighty and just as that which placed the Hero of New Orleans in the Presidential Chair, let us rise in our might and sustain his veto on this vampire (misnomered the U.S. Bank) of our country's prosperity."

Frank Blair had written language for Jackson's veto message but felt free to praise it in his *Globe*. He wrote that the evil Bank was getting "its death-blow." *

With his tin ear for public opinion, Nicholas Biddle presumed that other Americans would be as repelled by Jackson's "manifesto of anarchy" as he was.

To him Jackson's message sounded like "a chained panther biting the bars of his cage." He predicted to Henry Clay that public revulsion against it would liberate the nation from "the dominion of these miserable people. . . . You are destined to be the instrument of that deliverance, and at no period of your life has the country ever had a deeper stake in you."

---

* Understanding the lasting potency of Jackson's appeal, President Franklin Roosevelt told voters while running for reelection in 1936 that "government by organized money is just as dangerous as government by organized mob." FDR said those forces were "unanimous in their hate for me and I welcome their hatred."

Certain it would help Clay's candidacy, Biddle had thirty thousand copies of Jackson's veto message sent to the voters.

On the Senate floor, the famed Daniel Webster of Massachusetts rose to defy Jackson's veto.

As a young man, Webster had taught himself oratory by memorizing Fisher Ames's stirring address of 1796 defending Jay's Treaty. Now he answered what he called the *"trash"* in Jackson's "monstrous long paper."

While Senators mopped their brows from the heat, Webster warned that the "despotic" President was launching "experiments" that were "fearful and appalling." Unless Congress overturned Jackson's veto, there would be "a complete change in our government," with the President seizing the "power of originating laws." If that happened, the Constitution would not survive "to its fiftieth year."

Lucky for Webster, Americans did not know that he had just asked Biddle for a twelve-thousand-dollar loan.

With his Kentucky drawl that filled the Senate chamber "as an organ fills a great cathedral," Henry Clay condemned Jackson's "perversion of the veto power."

Rising to Old Hickory's defense, Tom Benton denounced Webster and Clay as "duplicate Senators," both "indecorous and disrespectful to the President." By scheming with Biddle and his corrupt "mercenaries," they were using the Bank as a "battering ram" to "destroy a hero and patriot."

Benton warned that if Congress let the Bank choose the next President, it would be the end of the American republic. Clay and Biddle would run the country as political "cousins," leaving "their thrones to their descendants."

Benton said, "This Bank is now the open—as it long has been the secret—enemy of Jackson. . . . It is impossible to be in favor of this power and also in favor of him. . . . Choose ye between them!"

Frowning with his narrow lips, Clay mentioned Benton's ancient gunfight with Jackson. Unlike the Senator from Missouri, *"I* never complained of the President beating a brother of mine after he was prostrated and lying apparently lifeless."

Clay said Benton had once warned that if Jackson became President, members of Congress would be forced to defend themselves with guns and knives. Benton sprang up: "That's an atrocious calumny!"

Clay asked, "Can you look me in the face, sir, and say that you never used that language?" Benton did. Clay went on, "Then I declare before the Senate you said to me the very words!"

"False, false, false!" cried Benton. As the floor erupted, the presiding officer banged his gavel. Benton apologized to the Senate, "but not to the Senator from Kentucky."

Clay too made amends, but "to the Senator from Missouri, *none!*"

Neither Senate nor House mustered the two-thirds vote required to overturn Jackson's veto. The President departed for the Hermitage in triumph.

Henry Clay insisted that the nation's "redemption" was at hand. He pledged to "heal the wounds of our bleeding Country, inflicted by the folly and madness of a lawless Military Chieftain!"

Clay felt the "tyrant's" veto was "in everybody's mouth" and would be "seriously felt in the purse" before Election Day.*

Tom Benton expected Biddle's Bank to threaten Americans that if Jackson were reelected, "suits, judgments and executions shall sweep like the besom of destruction."

One pro-Clay newspaper warned, "Constitution is gone! It is a dead letter, and the will of a DICTATOR is the Supreme Law!" A Boston journal said "Jacksonism" meant "ANARCHY."

But Biddle left nothing to chance. Back in Philadelphia, he flung open his cash drawer, spending a hundred thousand dollars to topple the President.†

Blair's *Globe* exposed the "shower of gold" flowing from Biddle's Bank to journalists and civic leaders, demanding that "every Bank agent who offers a bribe" be prosecuted. If Biddle decided the election, then "nothing remains of our boasted freedom except *the skin of the immolated victim.*"

* Indeed some American banks, citing the danger of a depression should Jackson be reelected, discounted their holdings. That fall factories laid off workers and livestock prices dropped.
† About $2.3 million today.

The *Globe* cited one New York editor who had switched from Jackson to Clay after a fat loan from Biddle. The "two-legged, strutting, mouthing, bullying animal" now sat "perched on the United States Bank, chanting his cock-a-doodle-doos."

Blair argued that Clay, the "leader of the aristocratic party," was irrelevant. The real struggle was between Old Hickory and Biddle: "Down with bribery—down with corruption—down with the Bank!"

Agents for Biddle and Clay retaliated by carping that Jackson's appointees were abusing their free mailing privileges by sending out the *Globe*. "A lie!" replied Blair.

From the Hermitage, Jackson assured a friend that "the virtue of the people will meet the crisis and resist all the power and corruption of the Bank." He was delighted Blair's feisty paper was out there punching for him: "The *Globe* revolves with all its usual splendor."

Jackson did not have to rely purely on the *Globe*. Using his inside knowledge of Clay's private habits, Senator Isaac Hill of New Hampshire published a warning in the journal he owned that the Kentuckian "spends his days at the gaming table and his nights in a brothel."

Amos Kendall organized "Hickory Clubs" across the nation to honor the "Man of the People" and "counteract the power of money." Jackson workers did not demand the two dollars a day that the Bank was allegedly paying people to campaign for Henry Clay.

At Jackson rallies, under banners decrying "Emperor Nicholas," local speakers exhorted their flocks to "Stand by the Hero." With fife and drum, children pranced around hickory poles and sang,

> Here's a health to the heroes who fought
> And conquered in Liberty's cause;
> Here's health to Old Andy who could not be bought
> To favor aristocrat laws!

In mid-September 1832, a well-rested Jackson left the Hermitage for the month-long journey back to Washington. Along the way, he paid for his room and board in gold: "No more paper-money, you see . . . if I can only put down this Nicholas Biddle and his monster Bank!"

Even in Clay's hometown of Lexington, Jackson was greeted by a cheering throng, some on horseback, waving hickory bushes in the air. He wrote, "Never have I seen such a gathering. . . . The political horizon is bright as far as we have seen or heard."

Based on his soundings in the West, he found that the Bank veto "works well." Some had predicted "that the veto would destroy me," but instead, "it will crush the Bank." He predicted that Clay "will not get one electoral vote west of the mountains or south of the Potomac."

When Jackson reached Virginia, climbing off a boat on the Ohio River, he assured Isaac Hill that the election would be "a walk": "If our fellows didn't raise a finger from now on, the thing would be just as well as done. In fact, Isaac, it's done now."

That November, Jackson and his running mate, Martin Van Buren, won fifty-five percent of the popular vote. Except for Kentucky, Clay was shut out of the South and West, just as the President had forecast.

The Kentucky Senator could not understand how he, one of America's finest gentlemen, could be defeated by its "refuse." Jackson was "ignorant, passionate, hypocritical, corrupt and easily swayed by the basest men." Under Jackson's "dark cloud," Clay wondered whether the nation would "ever see light and law and liberty again."

Though downcast over Clay's defeat, Nicholas Biddle was by no means ready to let his Bank expire. If he had to wreck the whole economy to teach Americans how much they needed him, he would do it.

CHAPTER TWELVE

WHO WOULD HAVE HAD THE COURAGE?

Before Jackson's second inaugural in March 1833, James Hamilton warned him that despite everything, Nicholas Biddle still "counts on" getting his Bank rechartered: "The serpent is scotched, not killed."

Hamilton reported that Biddle was planning a "run" on all "moneyed institutions." Then the public would demand the Bank's renewal "as the only means of restoring sound currency." Biddle did not care that such a scheme would cause "immense injury to the whole nation."

By the summer of 1833, Jackson decided to cripple Biddle's Bank by removing the huge deposits kept there by the federal government: otherwise Biddle would use the money to "buy up all Congress" and win a new charter.

Amos Kendall advised Jackson that it was "better to fail" while trying to "put down corruption" than "enjoy ease and office under a heartless Bank government."

William Lewis asked how the President would react if Congress passed a bill to restore the deposits. "Why, I would veto it," said Jackson.

Lewis warned that if Congress overrode his veto and the President kept on withholding the deposits, the House might impeach him.

"Then sir," Jackson said, "I would resign the Presidency and return to the Hermitage!"

Preparing a secret plan, Jackson had Kendall scout for state banks that could absorb the deposits. They had to be friendly to Jackson and willing to brave Biddle's certain retaliation.

By now, Jackson had replaced McLane at the Treasury with William Duane, whose maverick father had succeeded the late Ben Bache as editor of the *Aurora*. Jackson presumed that Duane would be "a chip of the old block" who, unlike McLane, would be happy to help him yank the federal deposits from Biddle's Bank.

But Duane refused, warning the President that Biddle would crush the "pet banks" that would inherit the deposits. Panic and "chaos" would follow.

Jackson was furious. For him, Duane had just shown him why he should pull the deposits immediately. Otherwise, until its old charter expired in 1836, Biddle would retain the ability to cause "bankruptcy and distress," leaving Americans "enslaved."

The President told Duane, "My object, sir, is to save the country, and it will be lost if we permit the Bank to exist."

Except for the Bank-hating Roger Taney, Jackson's Cabinet sided with Duane. Outraged, the President asked them, "How shall we answer to God, our country or ourselves if we permit the public money to be . . . used to corrupt the people?"

Jackson wrote his adopted son, "My conscience told me it was right to stop the career of this destroying monster." He asked Duane to resign. When Duane refused, Jackson fired him.

Before now, Senators had insisted that since the Constitution required them to confirm Cabinet appointees, they must also approve dismissals. By axing Duane without serious opposition, Jackson once again enhanced the power of the Presidency.

To expose Duane's disloyalty, Jackson let the *Globe* publish snippets of their private correspondence, suggesting that Duane had been manipulated by Biddle and the "Golden vaults of the Mammoth Bank."

Indignant at the *Globe*'s "persecution," Duane asked Jackson's nephew and secretary, Andrew Donelson, why the President had "opened a battery on me." Unmollified by Donelson's claim that Jackson did not control the *Globe*, Duane threatened to put embarrassing information about the President "before the public eye." *

---

* In an unsent letter, Duane asked why Donelson would "patiently" witness "the assassination of an unarmed man."

Instead, in the tradition of the bounced Edmund Randolph, Duane tried to exculpate himself with a published memoir, insisting that Jackson had grown "intoxicated with power and flattery," wanting "adulation from everybody, plain truth from nobody."

Jackson told his new Treasury nominee, the stalwart Roger Taney, to remove the federal deposits from Biddle's Bank "as tho Mr. Duane had never been born." He vowed himself "ready with the screws" to pull out the Bank's "every tooth"—and if necessary, "the stumps." Then Biddle would be "as quiet and harmless as a *lamb.*"

When the deposits were pulled, the *Boston Post* said Jackson was like Jesus expelling the money-changers from the temple. Thanks to him, the evil Bank had been "BIDDLED, DIDDLED, AND UNDONE."

But Biddle stood tough: Jackson was mistaken if, "because he has scalped Indians and imprisoned judges," he expected to "have his way with the Bank." Biddle insisted, "The Bank of the United States shall not break."

Biddle no longer claimed that his Bank stayed out of politics. Using language he would have earlier eschewed, he privately boasted that "in half an hour, I can remove all the Constitutional scruples in the District of Columbia" by offering "a dozen cashierships, fifty clerkships, a hundred directorships" to people with "no character and no money."

Claiming he had to reduce the Bank's exposure, Biddle called in loans and tightened credit, hoping that public "suffering" would break Americans' strange "allegiance" to Jackson. With financial panic and widespread layoffs, James Hamilton reported that New York merchants were "in very great distress." A Virginia Senator found bankruptcy "almost general."

On the Senate floor, Henry Clay said it was Jackson's "experiment" against the Bank that had created so many "helpless widows" and "unclad orphans," leaving the country "bleeding."

As presiding officer, Vice President Van Buren showed his contempt for Clay's charge by ignoring it. Stepping off the rostrum, he merely asked Clay for a pinch of his fabled aromatic snuff.

One of Biddle's lackeys in the House attacked Jackson's character by questioning his claim that a British officer had once slashed his forehead.

When Blair informed Jackson of the slander, the President noted his scar and said, "Put your finger there." Blair fit his entire finger into the gash.

Jackson warned that God would "punish" Americans if they kept bowing to Biddle's Bank, just as the Israelites had "sorely suffered" for the Golden Calf: "As for myself, I serve the Lord."

New Yorkers came to the White House, imploring Jackson to bring back prosperity by restoring Biddle's deposits and his charter.

The President stormed that he would never "sign a charter for any bank, so long as my name is Andrew Jackson!" He would sooner "cut off my right hand."

When other visitors begged for relief, Jackson blustered, "Go to the monster! . . . Go to Nicholas Biddle! We have no money here. . . . Biddle has all the money!" *

Heeding Jackson's admonition, they sought out Biddle in Philadelphia. But tipped off in advance, the Bank chief had fled to his country estate.

In the winter of 1834, Henry Clay mobilized the eight-vote Senate majority held by his party, now reconstituted as the Whigs, against the man they called "King Andrew the First." †

Clay demanded Jackson's censure for withholding a document he had read to his Cabinet before pulling the deposits.‡ Jackson had shown "utter contempt" for Congress. Should "the sword and the purse be at once united in the hands of one man?"

Clay had turned his fire on Jackson's usurpation of Congressional power because the Bank issue had proven such an albatross for him and his party.

He explained to the touchy Biddle that it was Jackson's "lawlessness" that "convulsed" the country. Once the Senate bearded him for that, Americans would demand that Biddle get his deposits back.

Biddle agreed that their "first purpose" must be to break Jackson's "gang" and drive "these miserable people from the high places which they dishonor."

---

* Jackson's intimates later insisted that the President had simulated anger, asking after his visitors left, "Didn't I manage them well?"

† The ever-sparring *Globe* gibed that a Whig was merely "a cover for bald Federalism."

‡ No matter that its contents were already public, having appeared in the *Globe.*

Whigs claimed that Jackson would try to avert censure by abolishing the House and Senate by bayonet: if he tried it, two hundred thousand patriots would rush to Washington and stop him.

Jackson carped that Clay had become as "reckless and as full of fury as a drunken man in a brothel."

Defending the President, Tom Benton told the Senate that Clay was trying to avenge the "private griefs" of his defeat in 1832. He said if the Whigs wished to upbraid the President, they must impeach him, and the Constitution gave that job to the House, not the Senate.

Nevertheless on Friday, March 28, 1834, Senators voted by 26 to 20 to censure an American President.

Jackson did not take it lying down. With Kendall's help, he issued an angry message of "Protest." He found himself, "without notice, unheard and untried," charged with "the high crime of violating the laws and Constitution of my country." He said the Constitution made no provision for censure.

Henry Clay shown trying to silence Andrew Jackson, 1834

More controversial, Jackson claimed that, unlike Senators, who were chosen at the time by state legislatures, a President was "the direct representative of the American people." He was "responsible to them."*

Clay assured a friend that Jackson's "Protest" would be the last nail "driven into the coffin—not of Jackson, may he live a thousand years!—but of Jacksonism." Now it was "the will of one man" against "twelve millions of people."

Riding high, Clay's Whigs rejected Roger Taney's nomination as Treasury Secretary, the first time the Senate had ever refused a Cabinet appointee. Upping the ante, Jackson named Taney to the Supreme Court, but the Whigs killed that too.

Jackson cried, "Nicholas Biddle now rules the Senate, as a showman does his puppets!"

With midterm Congressional elections ahead, Jackson moved to outfox the Whigs. He ordered Biddle to turn over the pension money held by his Bank for veterans of the Revolution.

When Biddle refused, the government stopped paying the pensions. Veterans were told to blame Biddle's Bank—and the Whigs who defended it.

Fury at the Whigs raged so high that a mob sacked and burned their headquarters in Philadelphia. Frightened that they would torch his city house, Biddle had it secured with muskets and took his wife and children to Andalusia.

That November, indignant about the nation's financial chaos and the veterans' abuse, the voters turned the Whigs out of control in the Senate. Confounded by the defeat, Clay told his son of his "despondency."

A Whig paper in Albany, New York, said it was time for the Whigs to

---

* Later Democratic Presidents embraced Jackson's argument. In 1962, President John Kennedy told the United Auto Workers that only fourteen or fifteen million Americans "have the resources to have representatives in Washington. . . . The interests of the great mass of other people—the hundred and fifty or sixty million—is the responsibility of the President of the United States." Lyndon Johnson and Bill Clinton made similar appeals.

dump Biddle: "After staggering along from year to year with a doomed Bank upon our shoulders, both the Bank and our Party are finally overwhelmed."

Once again commanding the Senate, Jackson sent up Roger Taney's name to become Chief Justice of the United States.

With the Whigs gone from power, Biddle abandoned hope of renewing his charter before it expired in 1836.

All he could do now was vent his spleen. He told fellow Jackson haters that America's government had been stolen by a vulgar "gang of banditti" who pandered to "the passions of the people."

To replace his federal charter, Biddle acquired one from his home state and founded a new "Bank of the United States of Pennsylvania."

Biddle wrote his friend John Quincy Adams, now a Congressman from Massachusetts, that the new state bank should be a "chrysalis" for a new "smart butterfly"—a Third Bank of the United States, once Americans awoke from their Jacksonist nightmare.

In January 1837, Jackson had only three months left as President. Knowing he had the votes, Tom Benton asked the Senate to "expunge" the censure imposed by "a few Senators and . . . their confederate, the Bank of the United States."

Benton vowed to keep his motion before the Senate until it passed. To fortify colleagues through the night, he ordered in steaming coffee, cold beef, ham, turkey and pickles. Wood-burning stoves warded off the winter cold.

Dressed in black, as if mourning the Constitution, Henry Clay said Jackson had behaved like "Caesar," and Senators must not "bow" at his feet. "Like the bloodstained hands of the guilty Macbeth, all ocean's waters will never wash out" Jackson's offenses. Then, realizing his cause was hopeless, Clay muttered, "Why do I waste my breath?"

In the bitter climate, worried that someone might kill her husband, Benton's wife joined him on the Senate floor. One Jacksonian Senator armed himself with pistols.

Benton's resolution passed by 24 to 19. Whigs stalked out of the chamber. The Senate secretary opened the official journal for 1834, found Jackson's censure and scrawled, "Expunged."*

When Benton gave Jackson the pen that was used, the President pledged that when he died, he would bequeath him the "precious" relic "used in this righteous act." Then Jackson held a feast for the "expungers" who had rescued his good name.

Clay sputtered to friends that Jackson was "the tyrant to the last." The Senate was "no longer a place for any decent man." He would "escape from it as soon as I decently can, with the same pleasure that one would fly from a charnel-house."†

On Friday night, March 3, 1837, smoking his long-stemmed pipe, Jackson signed his Farewell Address. Deliberately echoing George Washington, whose final message had once offended him, Jackson now looked toward history.

Jackson warned that had Biddle's Bank been allowed to pursue its "war upon the people," Americans would have lost the "living spirit" of their Constitution. He said, "My own race is nearly run." Soon he would "pass beyond the reach of human events." He thanked God for granting him "a heart to love my country with the affection of a son."‡

The next morning, after watching Van Buren sworn in to succeed him, Jackson told Frank Blair that his finest act as President had been to vanquish Biddle's Bank. With dark humor, he added a wish that he had also shot Henry Clay.

Traveling by train and carriage back to Tennessee, Jackson was welcomed by some of his old soldiers and their sons, who declared themselves "ready to serve under his banner."

The General bowed his head and wept: "I could have stood all but this. It is too much, too much!"

---

* In 1998, some Democrats seeking to avert President Bill Clinton's impeachment suggested censure instead. Republicans replied a censure would be too lenient, because some future Congress, as with Jackson's, might expunge it.

† Clay got over his indignation. He did not finally leave the Senate until 1852.

‡ In a breach of the separation of powers doctrine that modern Americans would not tolerate, Chief Justice Taney helped Jackson write his final message.

*   *   *

After Jackson's retirement came the Panic of 1837. Nicholas Biddle told friends that Van Buren should fix it by making "peace" with his Bank. With his blinding ego, Biddle said that "for the sake of the country," he would accept "a general amnesty," to begin when he got his federal deposits back.

Biddle even hallucinated that the Panic had so changed the public's mood that he might be elected President. Hadn't he exercised more power than some who had held the office? "I stand ready for the country's service."

But for Biddle, there was only calamity. His Pennsylvania-chartered bank went bust, and fingers were pointed at him. Sued by angry shareholders, Biddle "got out of the scrape just in time," escaping to his country mansion "with an immense fortune."

After the Bank was shuttered in 1841, the British novelist Charles Dickens toured Philadelphia and spied "a handsome building of white marble, which had a mournful ghostlike aspect. . . . I hastened to inquire its name and purpose, and then my surprise vanished. It was the tomb of many fortunes, the great catacomb of investment, the memorable United States Bank."

Biddle beat a criminal indictment but died at fifty-eight. The Jackson-loving poet William Cullen Bryant carped that Biddle's "elegant retirement" should have been "spent in the penitentiary."

During his war with the Bank of the United States, Andrew Jackson was by no means unflawed. He took on the Presidency largely ignorant of economics and made little effort to learn. Too often he was ruled not by reason but vindictiveness and fight.

By destroying Biddle's Bank without some more accountable replacement, Jackson peddled the dubious notion that America did not need a central bank to preserve a sound currency. Through eighty years of boom and bust, until Congress established the Federal Reserve in 1913, millions of Americans suffered.

The Founders had worried about demagoguery, but Jackson did not hesitate, distorting complex banking issues into a stark public choice between the rich and the poor. We are lucky that few of his successors tried to emulate this part of his appeal.

Nevertheless had Old Hickory acceded to the Bank, Biddle and his heirs might have kept on expanding the untrammeled influence of the mock Parthenon in Philadelphia.

Jackson's audacity gave later Presidents more power. Had he not redefined the veto and broadened expectations of what Presidents owed the people, the American future would have been very different.

Had Jackson been terrified of losing reelection or of Biddle's threats against him, he would have been immobilized. Instead, as a Tennessee friend declared, Jackson's "awful *will* stood alone, and was made the will of all he commanded."

What braced him was his conviction that his crusade against the Bank was right, his faith in Providence, and the grim knowledge that, with his cherished Rachel gone, there was little his foes could take from him.

Warned that some decision of his would risk a public clamor, Jackson once said, "I care nothing about clamors, sir! . . . I do precisely what I think just and right."

At the start of Jackson's second term, one voter wrote a Senator that the country was lucky to have him: "Who but General Jackson would have had the courage to veto the bill rechartering the Bank of the United States? And who but General Jackson could have withstood the overwhelming influence of that corrupt Aristocracy?"

Despite his advancing maladies, Andrew Jackson lived until 1845. At the Hermitage, the dying General murmured that "all would be well" if Americans stayed free of "monopolies and privileged classes."

But still he feared for his country. On the evening of his reelection as President, he had been tortured by the possibility that South Carolina, followed by other Southern states angry about tariffs, might secede.

That danger was avoided, but Jackson suspected that the "slave question" would some day "blow up a storm," with Southern leaders forming a "southern confederacy" that would "destroy the Union."

CHAPTER THIRTEEN

I AM GOING TO BE BEATEN

On Tuesday morning, August 23, 1864, President Abraham Lincoln was leading the fight against the Southern confederacy that Andrew Jackson had dreaded.

Lincoln had to face the voters in November, and he feared he would lose reelection. Exhausted after three and a half years of civil war, many Northerners were turning to the Democratic aspirant, General George McClellan, who was pledging a quick peace with the Rebels.

Lincoln's political advisers told him that his Emancipation Proclamation was dragging him down: millions of Northerners were willing to shed blood to restore the American Union, but not to abolish slavery.

Some told Lincoln that if he continued to make abolition a condition for peace with the South, he would be drubbed even in his home state of Illinois. Why not pull out of the race in favor of someone who could win?

But Lincoln refused to withdraw or back down, and he knew the consequences. He told one visitor, "You think I don't know I am going to be beaten, *but I do*—and unless some great change takes place, *badly beaten.*"

Disgusted by the disloyalty of Lincoln's political allies, his young aide John Hay wrote, "If the dumb cattle are not worthy of another term of Lincoln, then let the will of God be done and the murrain of McClellan fall on them."

With the morning sun high over the Capital city, Lincoln emerged from his fourteen-room stucco cottage at the Soldiers' Home, where he decamped each summer with his wife, Mary, and youngest son, Tad. Mary

[96]

found it a "very beautiful place" where they could be "as secluded as we please."

This morning, the First Lady was not there in nightcap and gown to wave "Mr. Lincoln" goodbye. She was vacationing with Tad and their oldest son, Robert, at the New Jersey shore and the mountains of Vermont.

With only his servants to bid him farewell, Lincoln rode three miles downhill to the White House. Sitting in the same chair and office as Jackson's—the walls were now papered in forest green and gold stars— the President did not know that a big overhead gaslight was leaking, threatening him with asphyxiation.

When Lincoln's tall windows were open, he braved the annual Washington plague of insects. His aide John Nicolay wrote, "They are buzzing about the room and butting their heads against the window panes."

Lincoln also smelled the summer stench of the dismal canal and swamps that lay south of the White House. John Hay found the odor like "twenty thousand drowned cats."

This morning, Lincoln felt even more melancholy than usual. In a strange private ritual, he took out "Executive Mansion" letterhead, dipped his fountain pen in black ink and scrawled out a dark message:

> This morning, as for some days past, it seems exceedingly probable that this Administration will not be re-elected. Then it will be my duty to co-operate with the President elect, as to save the Union between the election and the inauguration *; as he will have secured his election on such ground that he cannot possibly save it afterwards.

Lincoln signed and dated this last political testament. Then, using the skills learned as the young postmaster of New Salem, Illinois, he pasted it shut.

That afternoon, with an air of mystery, the President asked his seven Cabinet secretaries to ratify the sealed document by signing the outside, sight unseen.

---

* Mimicking his Kentucky accent, Lincoln misspelled the word.

*　　*　　*

During her vacation, Mary Todd Lincoln tried to escape her fear that her husband would be driven out of office. She wished she could go "down on my knees to ask votes for him."

Mrs. Lincoln confided to Lizzie Keckly, her African-American dress-maker, "There is more at stake in this election than he dreams of."

Behind the President's back, she had run up enormous bills for dresses, fur coats and jewelry befitting a First Lady.* Because she came from the West, "the people scrutinize every article I wear."

She told Keckly that Lincoln had "little idea" how much a wardrobe cost. Glancing at her "rich dresses," he presumed she had paid for them with the "few hundred dollars" he gave her: "He is too honest to make a penny outside of his salary."

Keckly asked, "And Mr. Lincoln does not even suspect how much you owe?"

With a "hysterical sob," Mary said, "God, no! If he is reelected, I can keep him in ignorance of my affairs. But if he is defeated, then the bills will be sent in and he will know all!"

Disturbing her sleep, the First Lady imagined herself and her husband exiled by the voters to Illinois in humiliating bankruptcy.

Mary also had premonitions that an assassin would murder her husband. In her absence that August of 1864, her fears might have come to pass.

One late evening, Lincoln rode his favorite horse, Old Abe, from the White House back to the Soldiers' Home. According to his sometime bodyguard, Ward Hill Lamon, a bullet pierced and knocked off the President's stovepipe hat.

Startled by the rifle crack, with Lincoln still astride him, Old Abe took off for the cottage at breakneck speed.

By Lamon's account, Lincoln said he wanted his brush with violent death "kept quiet." During a no-holds-barred Presidential campaign, his foes might cite it to show the public anger he evoked. After learning that the President had almost been killed, someone else might now be in-spired to finish him off for good.

As Lamon recalled, Lincoln tried to minimize the incident, speculat-

---

* The term entered common usage during the Lincoln years.

ing that "some foolish gunner" had fired off his rifle after a "day's hunt." Of himself and his horse, Lincoln joked that "one of the Abes was frightened" but "modesty forbids my mentioning which."

Nevertheless Lamon insisted on cavalry protection for the President's late-night rides to the Soldiers' Home: otherwise, "we shall have no Lincoln."

Sudden, unexpected death was a black thread that ran through Lincoln's life. As a boy, he lost his mother and sister; as a man, his sons Eddie and Willie. Through the Civil War, hundreds of thousands of Americans had perished by his order.

The President asked a friend, "Doesn't it strike you as queer that I, who couldn't cut the head off a chicken, and who was sick at the sight of blood, should be cast into the middle of a great war, with blood flowing all around me?"

Sighing that the war was "eating my life out," he watched from his cottage at the Soldiers' Home as thousands of Union graves were dug across the road.

In 1864, Mary was not the only Lincoln who imagined the President's sudden death. Her husband told a reporter of his own "presentiment" that he would "never live to see the end" of the Civil War.

After his election in 1860, Lincoln had received such disturbing death threats that his advisers forced him to enter Washington secretly, at nighttime, in disguise.

When reporters discovered the scheme, they chided him for cowardice, which made him furious. One cartoon showed a terrified Lincoln skulking into the city under a Scottish cloak and tam-o'-shanter.

The new President told frightened Illinois relatives not to be afraid: "I never injured anybody. No one is going to hurt me."*

But the prospect of murder was clearly on his mind. While traveling by train to Washington, he had told a crowd at Independence Hall in Philadelphia he would "rather be assassinated on this spot" than surrender the federal Union.

---

* Still one cousin refused an invitation to Lincoln's inauguration, fearing the scene would be "dangerous." Back in Illinois, Lincoln's stepmother, Sarah, "felt it in my heart" that "something would befall Abe and that I should see him no more."

*   *   *

Born in the 1809 Kentucky wilderness, the young Lincoln had matured with only about a year of formal education. When his illiterate, struggling father, Thomas, moved the family to Pigeon Creek, Indiana, neighbors noted Abe's "deep earnestness," his desire to "outstrip and override" the other boys.

It was said that when Abe teased local girls, they asked what would ever become of him, and he flippantly answered, "Be President of the United States!"

Lincoln's stepmother, Sarah, recalled how Abe "read all the books he could lay his hands on"—the Bible, Shakespeare, political and military histories, reciting passages that moved him.

The young Lincoln was excited by Mason Locke Weems's vastly read small life of George Washington. Weems's semi-fable advised American boys, "Though humble of birth, low thy fortune and few thy friends, still think of Washington and HOPE." If they emulated the Hero's virtues, they too could "stand before Kings." *

Well into his political career, Lincoln's image of a President was Washington. Leaving Springfield as President-elect in 1861, he told fellow townsmen that his task would be "greater than that which rested upon Washington." From the White House, Lincoln asked Americans to read Washington's "immortal Farewell Address," insisting that Washington's Birthday be a national holiday.

But the President who dominated most of Lincoln's adult life was Andrew Jackson. A boyhood Lincoln friend recalled, "We were all Jackson boys and men."

But soon after Old Hickory's first election as President, Lincoln's cousin was startled when Abe "turned Whig." For Lincoln, Whigs like John Quincy Adams and Henry Clay embodied the rational intellect,

---

* Lincoln's Springfield law partner, William Herndon, said Lincoln told him most biographies were "false and misleading," with their "hero" painted as a "perfect man"—"an injury to the living and to the name of the dead." Caustically Lincoln suggested that "book merchants and sellers have blank biographies on their shelves ready for sale" so that the dead man's relatives and friends could fill in the blanks "eloquently and grandly . . . thus commemorating a lie."

Jackson the "burning appetites" of the mob—people like his father, who thought reading was loafing.

Lincoln was also enchanted by his "beau ideal" Clay's dream of federally sponsored roads, schools and canals across the United States, all financed by Nicholas Biddle's Bank.

As President, Lincoln was touched when Clay's son sent him his father's famous aromatic snuff box. The son implored Lincoln to embrace his father's old motto, "I'd rather be right than President."

Mary Todd Lincoln, daughter of a Lexington, Kentucky, merchant and banker, had known Clay since girlhood. Early in Lincoln's political career, Jacksonian foes needled him about his "marriage in the Aristocracy."

Lincoln retorted that such an indictment would "astonish, if not amuse" the "older citizens" of New Salem, who had known him as a "strange, friendless, penniless, uneducated boy." He said he was still "the same Abe Lincoln that I always was," adding that the only in-law who ever sought him out had been "accused of stealing a Jew's-harp."

Elected to Congress in 1846, Lincoln gibed on the House floor that even with Jackson dead, the Democrats still stuck to "the tail of the Hermitage lion" like "a horde of hungry ticks."

Lincoln's complaint had a kernel of envy. He knew the voters wanted down-to-earth candidates like Jackson who could touch their hearts. Thus in 1860, Lincoln let himself be presented not as the well-to-do lawyer he had become, but instead as "Honest Abe the Rail Splitter."

By the time he was Commander-in-Chief against the Southern rebellion, Lincoln embraced two key tenets of Jackson's legacy—Old Hickory's ardor to keep the Union whole and his expansion of Presidential power. In 1861, when Lincoln took over Jackson's old White House office, he hung a portrait of the Hero of New Orleans over the fireplace.

Lincoln's Postmaster General, Montgomery Blair, was the son of the old Jacksonian editor of the *Globe*. Young Blair and his wife gave sparkling dinner parties at the same mansion across from the White House where his father had once milked his cow for Andrew Jackson.

Despite the passage of time, Old Frank Blair remained so influential that Lincoln had asked him to vet his inaugural address.

Throughout the Civil War, Lincoln, like Jackson, relied on the people's wisdom. He told a friend that "the voice of the people in our emergency" was the "next thing to the voice of God."

In 1864, a Lincoln admirer sent the President a copy of Old Hickory's letter warning that the Southern states might secede over the "pretext" of slavery. In it, Jackson sputtered that "ambitious men who would involve their country in civil wars" should be sent to "Haman's gallows."

Despite his self-effacing manner, Lincoln resembled Jackson most of all in the strength of his personal will. Lincoln's wife recalled how "none of us—no man or woman—could rule him" when he "put his foot down."

Querulous editorials he dismissed by saying, "I know more about that than any of them." John Hay noted that Lincoln's rivals were rankled by his "intellectual arrogance and unconscious assumption of superiority." Hay later said, "It is absurd to call him a modest man. No great man was ever modest."

Lincoln once declared that the "chief gem of my character" was his "ability to keep my resolves when they are made." He could not recall a single time he had erred as President by following his own judgment. By contrast, when he "yielded to the views of others," he usually regretted it.

Lincoln looked back to his courageous predecessors for strength. Beseeched at the start of the Civil War to make peace at almost any price, he was outraged: "There is no Washington in that—no Jackson in that!"

CHAPTER FOURTEEN

TOO ANGELIC FOR THIS DEVILISH REBELLION

By the summer of 1864, many Northerners feared that Lincoln's armies could not win the Civil War.

General William Tecumseh Sherman was stalled in his march toward Atlanta. Moving Union troops "in blood and agony" across Virginia's Rapidan, General Ulysses Grant lost sixty thousand men. With blow after blow, Lincoln cried, "I cannot bear it!"

Then, that July, the President witnessed Washington, D.C., under military attack for the first time since the War of 1812.*

Led by the scraggly, foul-mouthed General Jubal Early, the Rebels had launched a surprise raid against the weakly defended Union capital. The Confederate president, Jefferson Davis, hoped that Early's raid would spur Northern voters to oust the militant Lincoln in favor of a more pliable adversary.†

Told of Early's attack, Lincoln ordained, "Let us be vigilant, but keep cool." Still the President feared that Washington would be sacked. One Union general thought his Commander-in-Chief looked "almost crushed."

Secretary of War Edwin Stanton ordered Lincoln and his family to flee the Soldiers' Home for the better-protected White House.

---

* And the last, until terrorists flew a plane into the Pentagon on September 11, 2001.
† Early also hoped to divert Union troops and liberate Confederate prisoners held in Washington.

Lincoln was irked to discover that Stanton had also moored a gunboat on the Potomac. If the Rebels captured the city, the President would have to evacuate.

As they marched toward Washington, General Early and his deputy, John C. Breckinridge, stopped their horses at Frank Blair's farm, Silver Spring, just north of the city. Blair and son Montgomery were off on a fishing trip.

Breckinridge had been Vice President under Lincoln's predecessor, James Buchanan. Running as a pro-slavery Presidential candidate in 1860, the Kentuckian had won more electoral votes than Lincoln's Democratic opponent, Stephen Douglas.

In his falsetto voice, Early now told Breckinridge that when they took Washington, he would personally escort him back to the U.S. Senate and install him in his old chair as presiding officer. The plans of some of their soldiers were less grandiose: storm the U.S. Treasury and fill knapsacks with greenbacks and gold bullion.

Having plundered their way through Maryland, Early's troops guzzled the superb Blair wines and "cleaned out larder and poultry." One drunken soldier donned Mrs. Blair's British riding clothes and performed a joyous dance.

The troops did not know that Breckinridge was a Kentucky cousin of the Blairs, or that he considered Silver Spring his second home. He was furious to find them pawing through the family's valuables and stealing a piano cover to use as a horse blanket.

Breckinridge stopped them, but he could not save Montgomery Blair's nearby mansion, Falkland, which the Rebels burned to the ground. The culprits would have been horrified to know that the owner of the home they had just destroyed was related by marriage to their commander, General Robert E. Lee.*

---

* Frank Blair's Silver Spring mansion and his son's rebuilt Falkland were both torn down in the late 1950s and replaced by a dismal shopping mall, called "Blair Plaza."

*   *   *

Soon Early's troops reached the fortifications around "Mr. Lincoln's City." Eager to show he was not afraid, the President, wearing frock coat and stovepipe hat, rode uphill to one of the city's northern defense outposts, Fort Stevens.

From a parapet, Lincoln peered through field glasses at the onrushing Rebels, with bullets whizzing past his ears. It was the only time in history that a sitting American President has subjected himself to such combat. By legend, a young Union captain—and future Supreme Court Justice—named Oliver Wendell Holmes did not recognize Lincoln and called out, "Get down, you fool!"

Lincoln was joined in this show of bravado by his wife. According to one account, Mary Lincoln collapsed when she mistook a wounded surgeon for her husband.

In the end, thanks to belated Union reinforcements and Early's tactical mistakes, the Confederates failed to seize the Capital. "We haven't taken Washington," cried Early, "but we've scared Abe Lincoln like hell!"

Shaken by the spectacle of Rebel soldiers approaching the city, Northern voters wondered whether their President knew what he was doing.

Lincoln was furious when he learned that Early's men had been al-

Lincoln under Rebel fire, Washington, D.C., July 1864

[105]

lowed to escape unscathed. He bitterly complained that his generals hadn't bothered to chase the Rebels because they might "actually catch some of them."

After Early's raid receded, a woman disguising herself as "Lizzie W. S." sent Lincoln a warning: The Rebels invading Washington had been aided by "hordes of Secesh-sympathizers" in "our *very midst.*" *

Lizzie apologized for her "woman's whining"—"women have *no* business with politics." But "even should I offend you, Mr. Lincoln . . . I cannot help but warn you!" Rebel plotters were "biding their time" to kill the President.

Soon thereafter, the celebrated Shakespearean actor John Wilkes Booth was playing billiards in the Capital. A staunch Confederate, Booth told his fellow players, "Abe's contract is nearly up, and whether he is reelected or not, he'll get his goose cooked!"

Early's raid on Washington increased Northern pressure on Lincoln to make peace with Jefferson Davis, abolition or not.

The bombastic *New York Tribune* editor Horace Greeley published an open letter to the President: "Our bleeding, bankrupt, almost dying country . . . shudders at the prospect of fresh conscriptions . . . and of new rivers of human blood."

Claiming that two Confederate envoys were waiting in Canada "with full and complete powers for peace," Greeley asked Lincoln to see them.

At the White House, Lincoln scoffed, "While Mr. Greeley means right, he makes me almost as much trouble as the whole Southern Confederacy." Still if he slammed the door in Greeley's face, the *Tribune* would charge that a callous Lincoln had spurned a serious chance to save Union lives.

Thus Lincoln wrote Greeley that if "any person anywhere" could provide Jefferson Davis's written pledge both to restore the Union and end slavery, "say to him he may come to me with you."

Greeley replied that as an editor, he must not join in such talks, but the President must *"somehow"* let the South know he was willing to "seek a peaceful solution" to the war.

---

* Meaning secession sympathizers.

Toying with Greeley, Lincoln wrote back that he was "disappointed" at his response. He had expected the editor to "bring me a man," not "send me a letter."

Accepting Lincoln's challenge, Greeley went to Niagara Falls and sent a message across the Canadian border to the Confederate agents that if they had official credentials, he could take them to Washington. Overeager for success, Greeley did not confide Lincoln's demand for Davis's written assurance of reunion and abolition.

Greeley discovered that the Rebel agents did not even have bargaining authority. But he wired Lincoln that he was sure they could get it if the President would only signal Davis he was willing to talk.

At the White House, Lincoln handed the problem to John Hay. The self-possessed, discreet young aide with the "peach-blossom face" had been a Springfield law clerk before joining Lincoln, whom he came to honor as a "backwoods Jupiter."

Upstairs in the Mansion, Hay slept across the hall from the Bavarian-born John Nicolay, his Illinois boyhood friend. When Lincoln could not sleep, he would arrive in his nightshirt and talk with his two aides late into the night.

Hay's wry humor made the troubled President feel like a boy again. During working hours, Lincoln called Hay to his office to repeat a new joke. Petitioners waiting in the corridor raised eyebrows at the "uproarious peal of laughter."

The President and his young aide read Shakespeare aloud and took meals together, especially in the absence of Mary, whom both Hay and Nicolay called "the Hellcat."*

Hay and Nicolay ultimately came to consider their boss "the greatest character since Christ." They squirreled away notes for the momentous biography they would publish thirty years hence. When the President was out of earshot, they called him "the Ancient," "the Premier," "the Tycoon," or more simply, "the American."

*   *   *

---

* Mary resented the two young men as rivals for her husband's attention. They would not let her drain White House expense accounts, which Lincoln had prudently assigned to their care.

Directed by Lincoln, Hay took the train to Niagara Falls with a letter from the President. Addressed "To Whom It May Concern," Lincoln's message pledged to weigh any high Confederate proposal "which embraced the restoration of peace, the integrity of the whole Union and the abandonment of slavery."

Hay refused Greeley's insistance that Lincoln drop his preconditions. Crossing into Canada, Hay and Greeley gave the letter to one of the Rebel agents, James Holcombe, whom Hay found "a false-looking man, with false teeth, false eyes and false hair."

The next day, Holcombe used the press to blast Greeley for failing to warn him that Lincoln demanded such stiff concessions. Rival papers denounced Greeley's "bungling" and "cuddling with traitors."

Embarrassed by his public flogging, Greeley blamed the President. "No truce!" he wrote Lincoln. "No mediation! Nothing but surrender! . . . I never heard of such fatuity before."

Standing on the veranda under the White House South Portico, a Senator complained to Lincoln that Greeley had not proven "a very good ambassador to Niagara."

Lincoln explained that the *Tribune* editor had "kept abusing me" so "I just thought I would let him go up and crack that nut for himself." Later the President told his Cabinet that the "rotten" Greeley was "not truthful" and "good for nothing."

Despite Greeley's follies, Lincoln remained so sensitive to the charge of prolonging the Civil War that he sanctioned another peace expedition. Union Colonel James Jaquess, a Methodist preacher, and his novelist friend James Gilmore, who sometimes wrote for Greeley's *Tribune,* were allowed to cross Northern lines to see Jefferson Davis in Richmond.

First the two men were submitted to what Gilmore called the "keen black eye" and "Jewish face" of Davis's Secretary of State, Judah Benjamin.

When they saw Davis himself, he gave them his own precondition for talks—the "permanent independence" of the South! The struggle would grind on "till the last man of this generation falls in his tracks. . . . We are fighting for independence. And that, or extermination, we will *have!*"

Jaquess and Gilmore reported to Lincoln that nothing remained but "war to the knife."

Rebel propagandists exploited Lincoln's two failed peace explorations in an effort to turn Northern voters against him.

One of Greeley's Confederate agents declared, "The stupid tyrant who now disgraces the Chair of Washington and Jackson could, any day, have peace and restoration of the Union—and would have them, only that he persists in the war merely to free the slaves."

Lincoln had not become President demanding to free the slaves. He had tried to entice the seceded states back into the Union by pledging to leave slavery intact where it was already in force.

The radical abolitionist Senator Benjamin Wade of Ohio said the new President's weakness was that he was "born of poor white trash and educated in a slave state." Repulsed by Lincoln's caution, Wade wrote him he was "murdering your country by inches."

In the summer of 1862, Congress passed a bill to free any slave who escaped from the South to Union-held territory. Lincoln proposed paying money to Southern states in exchange for slowly phasing out slavery, but was rebuffed.

Instead that July, he summoned his Cabinet and read them his draft of a preliminary Emancipation Proclamation. On New Year's 1863, "all persons held as slaves within any state" would become "forever" free.

Lincoln called his proclamation a "military measure" to stop hundreds of thousands of slaves from helping the Confederacy and get them to "come bodily over" to the Union side.

If the Negroes were to risk their lives for the Union cause, "they must be prompted by the strongest motives," Lincoln later explained. "Why should they do anything for us if we will do nothing for them?"

Secretary of State William Seward asked the President to postpone his proclamation until the Union won a major new victory. Otherwise it might seem like a public confession of weakness.

Lincoln agreed. He did not want his order to be heard as "our last shriek, on the retreat."

During his debates with Stephen Douglas in 1858, Lincoln said he opposed moving toward "the social and political equality of the white and black races."

Since then, he had not changed his mind. Hoping to blunt the con-

servatives' anger when they realized that hundreds of thousands of Negroes would now enter the North, the President revived his old idea that
the best solution to the race problem might be to encourage the Negroes to depart for some colony elsewhere, perhaps in Latin America.

To appease the reactionaries, he called African-American leaders to
the White House in August 1862 and reminded them that they were suffering injustice in America. Negroes suffered from living with whites,
while the whites "suffer from your presence." It was "better for both" to
separate. Lincoln said there would have been no Civil War "but for your
race among us."

The African-American leader Frederick Douglass was not present,
but when told of Lincoln's message, he demanded to know why the President would wallow in "Negro hatred." Didn't he understand that Douglass and his people were Americans too?

That September, with the Union's bloody triumph at Antietam, Lincoln felt it was time to announce his proclamation. He had told his Cabinet that "if God gave us the victory" at Antietam, he would consider it a
Providential sign to "move forward."

Gauging the public's reaction to his Emancipation Proclamation,
Lincoln called in his old fellow Illinois circuit-rider Leonard Swett, a
close enough friend to tell him the truth, "Am I doing anything wrong?"
Swett said no. Lincoln cried, "Well, then, get out of here!"

Signing the document, he had "never" felt "more certain that I was
doing right." Still he worried about Northerners who were passionate for
the Union but not abolition. To mollify them, he had declared that if he
"could save the Union without freeing *any* slave, I would do it."

Despite such efforts, the voters punished Lincoln's party in the
midterm elections of 1862.

Lincoln solaced himself by reading Henry Wadsworth Longfellow's
The Song of Hiawatha:

> I am weary of your quarrels,
> Weary of your wars and bloodshed,
> Weary of your prayers for vengeance,
> Of your wranglings and dissensions;
> All your strength is your union.

*   *   *

Despite the Emancipation, Radical Republicans like Ben Wade thought Lincoln was "too angelic for this devilish rebellion." Although hurt by the Radicals' criticism, Lincoln comforted himself by saying, "After all, their faces are set Zionwards."

Radicals in Congress wanted a Union victory to be followed by scorched earth, with the South "laid waste and made a desert."

In July 1864, worried by Lincoln's far more lenient plans for Reconstruction, they passed the Wade-Davis Bill, which would keep a former Rebel state out of the Union until at least half of its prewar voters pledged to support the U.S. Constitution. High Confederate officials and military officers would be tried as criminals and banned from U.S. citizenship.

Lincoln let the Wade-Davis measure die without his signature. Strolling out of the U.S. Capitol, with the gleaming new white dome behind him, he predicted to John Hay that the Radicals would retaliate, but explained, "I must keep some standard of principle fixed within myself."

Wade and his co-author, Maryland Congressman Henry Winter Davis, responded to the President's pocket veto with the most scalding denunciation Lincoln ever heard from fellow Republicans: the "rash" and "dictatorial" President was trying to rush seceded states into the Union to improve his reelection chances.

Lincoln sadly told Seward that "the most grievous affliction" was to be "wounded in the house of one's friends."

Crowing at the party split, a Richmond paper said, "The obscene ape of Illinois is about to be deposed . . . and the White House will echo to his little jokes no more."

Wade and Davis demanded that Lincoln be ditched in favor of some candidate who "commands the confidence of the country"—like General Grant.

The worried Lincoln sent an emissary to discover whether Grant had political ambitions. Slapping the leather strap arm of his camp chair, the General cried, "They can't compel me to do it!" He said Lincoln's reelection was "important for the cause."

*   *   *

That same July, Lincoln bought himself more political trouble by asking that half a million more men be drafted into the Union Army—a signal that the war would not be over soon.

General Sherman warned the President that if he reduced the draft call "by one man," it would endanger the men at the battlefront and turn the crucial soldiers' vote against him that November.

For much of the conflict, a Northerner could duck the fighting by paying three hundred dollars for a substitute. Such legal draft dodgers included a future President, Grover Cleveland of Buffalo, and the father of one—Theodore Roosevelt, Sr., of New York City.

Residing in Washington early in the war, Roosevelt had shared a church pew with the Lincolns, gone hat shopping with Mary and befriended John Hay. Insisting that his work counseling soldiers on keeping their families afloat was vital to the war effort, Roosevelt paid an immigrant to risk his life for him.

One of his daughters later said he knew "he had done a very wrong thing." Embarrassed by his adored father's abstention from the Civil War, son Theodore hoped to throw himself one day into military combat.*

By 1864, Congress had stopped letting anyone but conscientious objectors pay for substitutes. Anti-Lincoln agitators warned Northern men that the President's marshals would "drag you from your home" and "tear you from your loved ones to die under the torrid Sun of the South."

An Ohio editor predicted that if Lincoln didn't cancel his menacing new draft call before the November election, he would be "deader than dead."

"I am quite willing that people understand the issue," said the President. "My reelection will mean the Rebellion is to be crushed by force of arms."

Party managers begged him to postpone the new draft. Lincoln refused—"even if I am defeated." He asked, "What is the Presidency worth to me if I have no country?"

---

* Culminating when T.R. led his Rough Riders up Kettle Hill during the Spanish-American War.

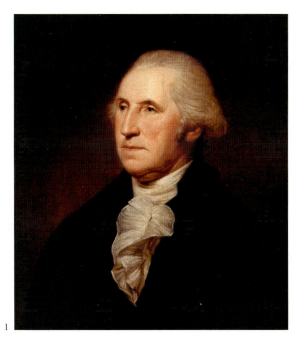

1

President George Washington in 1795 was agonized by the public outcry against his treaty with Great Britain. Some Americans were demanding his impeachment or murder.

2

Martha Washington felt like a "state prisoner" as First Lady in even the best of times.

3

Chief Justice John Jay, who negotiated Washington's hated treaty with England, joked that he could see his way at night by the light of his burning effigies.

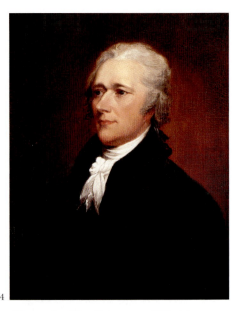

4

Alexander Hamilton urged Washington to stand firm.

5

Fighting Ohio Indians at the Battle of Fallen Timbers, 1794. Washington insisted that until peace was made with England, the American frontier would never be safe.

President John Adams
envied General
Washington's military
reputation and allowed
himself to be drawn
into the "quasi-war"
against France.

6

Abigail Adams, the second
President's "dearest
partner." When political
enemies lampooned her
husband for impotence,
she gibed that she could
prove them wrong.

7

8

Elbridge Gerry of Massachusetts, Adams's eccentric old friend, beseeched him not to battle France.

9

Adams's envoys sign a treaty with Napoleon at Mortefontaine, France, 1800. Adams hoped it would save his reelection.

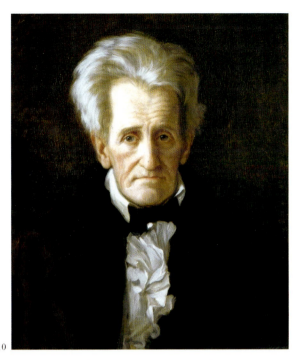

10

President Andrew Jackson boasted, "I was born for the storm."

11

Old Hickory thought his wife, Rachel, was driven to her grave by his political enemies. Around his neck, he wore a miniature of her image.

12

Nicholas Biddle, the vainglorious chief of the
Second Bank of the United States, who considered
himself at least the equal of American Presidents.

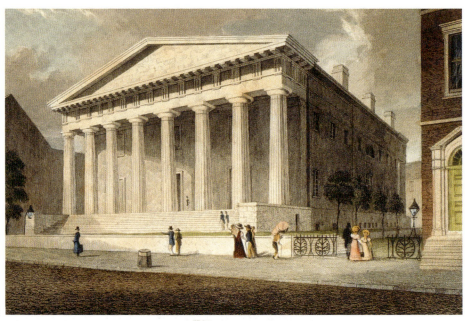

13

Biddle's bank in Philadelphia, whose corrupt power Jackson sought to destroy.

President Abraham Lincoln scrawled out a secret prediction in the summer of 1864 that he would lose reelection.

14

Mary Todd Lincoln, despondent over the Civil War and the death of their cherished son Willie. She worried that if her husband lost the 1864 election, he would have to pay off the large debts she had run up for clothes and furniture behind his back.

15

16

Lincoln writing the Emancipation Proclamation, 1863. The sixteenth President knew that by making himself the historic "liberator of a race," he had alienated millions of Northerners unwilling to fight a civil war to free the slaves.

17

General George McClellan, Lincoln's 1864 opponent, and his Copperhead running mate, George Pendleton.

CHAPTER FIFTEEN

A WELL-MEANING BABOON

Compounding Lincoln's political dilemmas in the summer of 1864 was his likely Democratic opponent. Who could better argue that the President had botched the Union cause than the popular General he had fired two years earlier?

Old Frank Blair warned Lincoln that he needed the soldiers' vote to win a second term, and "McClellan is dear to them."

Born to a Philadelphia surgeon and his patrician wife, McClellan had studied at West Point and served under General Winfield Scott in the Mexican War. As an Illinois Central Railroad executive, he had attended one of the Lincoln-Douglas debates and was jarred by Lincoln's "disjointed" storytelling.

After the Union defeat at Bull Run in July 1861, Lincoln called McClellan to command the Army of the Potomac. "By some strange operation of magic, I seem to have become *the* power of the land," the General wrote his wife, Ellen.

"I almost think that were I to win some small success now I could become Dictator . . . but nothing of that kind would please me. . . . Admirable self denial!" He insisted his job was to "save the country" and surmount "anything that is in the way."

McClellan was delighted to find the President "much under my influence," because he felt that Lincoln was "not a man of very strong character . . . certainly in no sense a gentleman." Among friends, he called his Commander-in-Chief "a well-meaning baboon."

McClellan made little effort to conceal his feeling of superiority. One evening Lincoln and Seward called at McClellan's rented mansion near the White House, but the General did not bother to rush home from a military wedding.

When he finally returned, with the President and Secretary of State still in his parlor, the tired General did not greet them and climbed the stairs to bed.

John Hay felt McClellan's "unparalleled insolence" was "a portent of evil to come."

From almost the start, Lincoln complained that McClellan suffered from the "slows," regarding the Army of the Potomac as his personal "bodyguard."

By the fall of 1862, the President said McClellan would be "a ruined man" if he did not move his soldiers more quickly. When the General said he needed fresh horses, Lincoln caustically asked "what the horses of your Army have done since the Battle of Antietam that fatigue anything."

By then, the President wondered whether McClellan "did not want to hurt the enemy." After his party lost the midterm elections, Lincoln fired him.

"A great mistake," wrote McClellan. "Alas for my poor country."

The General wrote Ellen that on bidding his soldiers farewell, he hadn't realized "how much they loved me. . . . Gray haired men came to me with tears streaming down their cheeks."

Even while commander, McClellan had vented his spleen against the President in private talks with anti-Lincoln editors and Democrats.

Informed that Lincoln was planning an Emancipation Proclamation, McClellan told friends he would not "fight with the South to free the slaves." Citing "prejudice in favor of my own race," he did not "like the odor of either Billy Goats or niggers."

After he was fired, McClellan moved his family to New York City, where he was embraced by the wealthy Democrats he considered the "best people." Hoping to groom the General against Lincoln for 1864, they gave him a furnished townhouse and railroad equities that brought him almost twenty thousand dollars a year.*

---

* About $309,000 today.

Many party leaders felt only McClellan could unite the Copperheads, who wanted peace now, and the War Democrats, who were willing to fight on but skeptical of Lincoln's aims and tactics.

The Democratic editor of the *New York World*, Manton Marble, assured McClellan that "the people's eyes are turned all one way in their search for the candidate who will win in 1864."

Knowing McClellan would be trouble for Lincoln's reelection, Edwin Stanton tried to clip the General's wings. Discovering that McClellan had been asked to speak at West Point, the War Secretary had those who invited him punished or fired.

McClellan found his movements "dogged" by Stanton's detectives. Certain that his mail was being intercepted, he used couriers and coded his telegrams, vowing to give Stanton and the other "wretches" the "punishment they so richly deserve."

While Stanton used the stick with the General, Montgomery Blair tried the carrot. He assured a McClellan crony that if the General stayed out of the Presidential race, Lincoln would give him a big military job.

Blair's father held a private meeting with McClellan at a New York hotel. Having performed such partisan errands for Andrew Jackson, the old fixer told McClellan that returning to the Union Army was his "duty."

But McClellan said no. Why should he do otherwise? His backers were already on the verge of calling him "Mr. President."

That summer, with booming cannons and fireworks, McClellan's claque staged a "monster" nighttime rally on New York City's Union Square—"A Hundred Mass Meetings Rolled into One."

Under a banner showing a Southern hand grasping McClellan's in friendship, speakers denounced Lincoln's "nigger administration," which stole people's liberties in the name of the Civil War and "perverted" the Union cause into a struggle for abolition.

One speaker asked, "What has Abraham Lincoln done to recommend him?" From the darkness came the reply: "Made smutty jokes!" *

---

* Referring to the canard circulated by Lincoln haters that while touring the corpse-strewn Antietam battlefield, the President had told jokes.

* * *

Then at the start of August 1864, Lincoln made a costly mistake. He approved Horace Greeley's request to publish the President's "To Whom It May Concern" letter, which conceded that peace was impossible unless the Rebels agreed to free the slaves and remake the Union.

When the letter appeared, Democrats said it was proof Lincoln had hijacked the war effort "in the interest of the black race." A Green Bay, Wisconsin, editor named Charles Robinson wrote the President that his letter to Greeley "takes us War Democrats clear off our feet."

When Lincoln read Robinson's complaint, brought to him by Wisconsin Governor Alexander Randall, he was shaken: if Robinson was a bellwether of millions of War Democrats, he would surely lose to McClellan.

Groping for language that might retain their support, Lincoln reacted like a cagey lawyer. In a draft reply to Robinson, he wrote that "saying re-union and abandonment of slavery would be considered" was different from "saying that nothing *else* or *less* would be considered."

Lincoln wrote, "If Jefferson Davis wishes . . . to know what I would do if he were to offer peace and re-union, saying nothing about slavery, let him try me."

The President knew that if he signed and sent such a letter, he would be taking a large step back from his previous insistence that slaves be freed before the War Between the States could stop—even though he knew that Davis would not relax his demand for the full independence of the South.

Justifiably nervous about the political dangers such a letter might unleash, he asked Governor Randall to the Soldiers' Home. Greeting his guest, he wore black carpet slippers embroidered with a flowery gold "A.L."

He reminded Randall that the Emancipation had spurred almost two hundred thousand slaves to bolt the Confederacy to serve the Union side. Without them, "we would be compelled to abandon the war." If he tried to please the South by returning them "to their masters," he would be "damned in time and eternity."

The President said, "My enemies condemn my emancipation policy. Let them prove . . . that we can restore the Union without it."

Lincoln also tried out his draft letter on Frederick Douglass, who told him it was "a complete surrender of your anti-slavery policy."

With that, Lincoln knew there was no magic formula to make the War Democrats happy. If his stubbornness cost him the election, he would have to accept it.

For the wartime campaign of 1864, the Republicans had recast themselves under the more welcoming style of the "National Union Party."

That August, like Grim Reapers, its leaders called on Lincoln in "obvious depression and panic." One New York boss said the President was politically "gone," adding that therefore "the country's gone too."

"Weak-kneed d—d fools," wrote John Nicolay. "Everything is darkness and doubt and discouragement."

Perhaps the most painful such visit was from Leonard Swett, who knew Lincoln as "intimately" as "any man in my life," since their Illinois circuit-riding days. Swett had been an engineer of Lincoln's dark-horse nomination in 1860.

In the parlor at the Soldiers' Home one evening, Swett mournfully told his friend that the politicians had thrown up their hands "in despair." As of that night, Lincoln could not even carry three states.

Hating himself for conveying so bitter a message, Swett asked Lincoln to consider dropping out of the race after McClellan's nomination.

As Swett recalled, the "anxious" President "understood fully the danger of his position" and asked him to "try to stem the tide bearing him down."

On Thursday, August 25, Lincoln's party chairman, Henry Raymond, led another funereal delegation to the White House. The President called Raymond, owner-editor of the *New York Times*, his "lieutenant-general in politics."

Raymond implored Lincoln to make a peace offer "at once" to Jefferson Davis, asking only one concession—"the supremacy of the Constitution."

Raymond said if Davis accepted, Northern voters would keep the trusted Lincoln in power to do the bargaining. If not, Lincoln would "dispel" the widespread notion that he didn't want peace. Whatever happened, it would "take the wind completely" out of the Democrats' sails.

Exasperated, Lincoln replied that crawling to Davis "would be worse" than losing the Presidency: "It would be ignominiously surrendering it in advance."

To show Raymond the problem, Lincoln scrawled out a draft letter asking Raymond to "obtain, if possible, a conference for peace with Hon. Jefferson Davis": if Davis agreed to restore the Union, "the war shall cease at once." The slavery question would be settled "by peaceful means."

Lincoln warned Raymond that such a gambit would bring the "utter ruination" of the United States.

In the late summer's heat, Lincoln poured himself a tumbler of water and jerked his head back, frontier-style, before downing the contents.

With so many friends pronouncing him politically dead, he painfully recalled losing to Stephen Douglas for the U.S. Senate in 1858. Ever the realist, he had expected almost everyone "to desert me."

When Lincoln's friend General Carl Schurz came to the Soldiers' Home at twilight, the President was at the end of his tether.

Moist-eyed, despondent, Lincoln told Schurz, "God knows, I have at least tried very hard. . . . And now to have it said by men who have been my friends . . . that I have been seduced by . . . power, and that I have been doing this and that unscrupulous thing . . . only to keep myself in office!"

He said that politicians were asking him, in "almost violent language," to pull out in favor of a better man. "Perhaps some other man might do this business better than I. . . . But I am here, and that better man is not here."

Angrily Lincoln scoffed at the Republicans' lip service to the Union cause: "Have they thought of that common cause when trying to break me down? *I hope they have!*"

———=•()•=———

CHAPTER SIXTEEN

THE COUNTRY WILL BE SAVED

Worried about Lincoln's mental exhaustion, one visitor to the Soldiers' Home told the President he should "play hermit for a fortnight."

Lincoln said, "Ah, two or three weeks would do me no good. I cannot fly from my thoughts." The inescapable fact was that "things look badly and I cannot avoid anxiety."

With his wife and sons gone on vacation, he was facing his political crisis alone.

Before they came to Washington, which now seemed a million years ago, Mary had fired his ambition and bolstered his self-confidence. In 1860, when Lincoln fretted that he was unfit to be President, she told him, "You've got no equal in the United States!"

But their son Willie's passing in 1862 and the pressures of the war had broken her. Lincoln implored his "child-wife" to "control your grief or it will drive you mad."

Dressed in permanent black, Mary feared that critics would compel Robert, who was destined for Harvard Law School, to be drafted, captured and killed. She could not shake her obsession that an assassin would take her husband's life.

"All imagination!" he told her. "Don't worry about me, Mother, as if I were a little child."

More mercurial than ever, the First Lady was blind to her husband's bone-crushing worries. In 1864, a White House overnight guest heard, through a wall, Mary saying to Lincoln, "Need to be taught a lesson—yes, sir! Promise me what I asked you, or I won't leave go of them!"

Lincoln's voice replied, "Ma—come now! Be reasonable. . . . How do you reckon I can go to a Cabinet meeting—without my *pants?*"

When Lincoln spoke at a fair that year, Mary said within strangers' hearing, "That was the worst speech I ever listened to. . . . I wanted the earth to sink and let me go through!"

Lizzie Keckly winced at how Mary "wounded" her husband "in unguarded moments."

Brushing off such incidents, the First Lady wrote a politician who had heard them squabble, "Notwithstanding our opposite natures, our lives have been eminently peaceful." Had she and Mr. Lincoln been unable to "have a laugh together," life would "have broken our hearts."

The President felt lonely at the Soldiers' Home that August. But Mary's absence was not without benefits. One evening the President took John Hay to a "Sacred Concert of profane music" at Ford's Theatre. As Hay recorded, Lincoln "carried on a hefty flirtation" with some of the "girls."

Lincoln's relative calm on the edge of political defeat drew in part on his religious faith, which had steadied him through the war's sadness and chaos.

Abe's father and stepmother had taken him to a Primitive Baptist church, but the shrill, uneducated preachers predisposed him against organized religion.

As a young man in New Salem, Lincoln allegedly wrote an essay questioning the divinity of Jesus Christ and the notion that God's purposes were revealed in the Bible.* When he ran for Congress at thirty-seven, he had to deny that he was "an open scoffer at Christianity." But the deaths of two sons and the Civil War's traumas no doubt changed him.

He told friends, "I have been all my life a fatalist." But his fatalism did not keep him from relentlessly trying to comprehend God's will. As President, he considered himself "an humble instrument in the hands of the Almighty and of this, his almost chosen people."

Lincoln once said that when God wished him to do something, "He

---

* No such Lincoln writing survives. A storekeeper friend, fearing that it would end Lincoln's political future, supposedly burned it.

Lincoln's summer cottage at the Soldiers' Home, Washington, D.C.

finds a way of letting me know it." Before issuing the Emancipation, he had waited for that sign of "Divine Will."

In a note probably written during the painful summer of 1864, which was later found in his desk, Lincoln scrawled that while "the will of God prevails," he was struggling to understand His attitude toward the Civil War.

The Almighty "could have either saved or destroyed the Union" without a civil war: "And, having begun, he could give the final victory to either side any day. Yet the contest proceeds."

Lincoln observed that it was "quite possible" that "God's purpose is something different" from that of either North or South.

Marching into the chasm of the Civil War, Lincoln immersed himself in the Bible, which he called "the best gift God has given to man."

During the summer of 1864, Lincoln's old Springfield roommate Joshua Speed stayed overnight at the Soldiers' Home. Before departing for Kentucky in 1841, Speed had been Lincoln's closest friend.

Recalling Lincoln's old complaints about religion, Speed was now startled to find the President in his bedroom, absorbed in his Bible. He told Lincoln, "If you have recovered from your skepticism, I am sorry to say that I have not."

"You are wrong, Speed," replied Lincoln. "Take all of this book upon reason that you can, and the balance on faith, and you will live and die a happier and better man."

Suddenly, at the end of that excruciating summer, Lincoln regained his political balance.

When the Democrats convened in Chicago on Monday, August 29, the Copperheads—John Hay called them "Peace Snakes"—rammed through a platform demanding an immediate end to Lincoln's "experiment" of war. The South need not even pledge to reenter the Union.

After nominating McClellan, the delegates forced him to take an egregious Copperhead, Ohio Congressman George Pendleton, as his running mate.

McClellan's New York sponsor William Aspinwall told the General that not even he could support him unless he disowned the party platform.* Another McClellan backer warned that the platform seemed "concocted to destroy" his candidacy.

The General declared that he would not embrace his party's platform "for a thousand Presidencies." If peace were not contingent on restoration of the Union, he could not "look in the face of my gallant comrades" and tell them that "the sacrifice of so many of our slain and wounded brethren had been in vain."

But Northern voters could not ignore the platform—or McClellan's running mate. Summing up the General's problems, one cartoon showed a Union soldier saying, "Goodbye, 'little Mac'—if that's your company, Uncle Abe gets my vote."

For Lincoln, the Democratic crack-up at Chicago was only the start of his good news.

After midnight on Thursday, September 1, 1864, rockets lit the Atlanta skies as General Sherman's army marched into the city. One citizen

---

* Aspinwall was the great-uncle of future President Franklin Roosevelt.

recalled, "The houses rocked like cradles, and on every hand was heard the shattering of window glass and the fall of plastering and loose bricks."

Sherman cabled the President, "So Atlanta is ours, and fairly won."

Leonard Swett, who had been so mortified to ask Lincoln to quit the Presidential contest, now wrote his wife, "God gave us the victory at Atlanta, which made the ship right itself, as a ship in a storm does after a great wave has nearly capsized it."

"The dark days are over," wrote Lincoln's old sponsor Joseph Medill, owner of the *Chicago Tribune.* "Thanks be to God! The Republic is safe!"

At the White House, two weeks after Sherman's Atlanta victory, Lincoln learned that General Philip Sheridan had scoured Jubal Early's troops from the Shenandoah.

Chuckling at how his fortunes had somersaulted, Lincoln said it looked as if "the people wanted me to stay here a little longer."

A Lincoln man wrote him from Illinois, "The September victories have changed all, and as we reason here, your reelection is certain."

On Tuesday, November 8, 1864, Tad Lincoln tugged his father to a White House window to watch Union soldiers lining up to vote for him.

Through the rain that evening, the President walked next door to the War Department's Telegraph Office, where he had spent so much time reading bulletins from the battlefront.

By midnight, Lincoln knew it was an electoral landslide.* General Grant wired him that his reelection was "worth more to the country than a battle won."

When supporters arrived to serenade the victor, Lincoln said, "If I know my heart, my gratitude is free from any taint of personal triumph."

Lincoln's bodyguard Ward Lamon knew the people's verdict would make the President even more of an assassin's target. After Lincoln went to bed, Lamon drank some whiskey, armed himself with pistols and Bowie knives, and slept outside the President's bedroom door.

---

* Lincoln received 212 electoral votes to McClellan's 21. His popular margin was closer: 2,213,665 votes to McClellan's 1,802,237.

*   *   *

Had the War Democrats and Copperheads elected McClellan as President, they would now have demanded that he shut down the war, which would probably have meant the end of the eighty-eight-year-old United States of America.

Lincoln would have gone back to Illinois one of the great losers in history, a President who had spent untold American lives to restore the Union, then destroyed it by transforming the Union cause into a hopeless crusade against slavery.

As Ralph Waldo Emerson wrote a friend in Europe, "Seldom in history was so much staked on a popular vote—I suppose never in history."

Emerson was not the only American of letters to cheer Lincoln's election. The fervent abolitionist Henry Wadsworth Longfellow responded to the victory by saying, "The country will be saved."

Lincoln loved Longfellow's work and thought it "a wonderful gift to be able to stir men like that."

But the poem that stole the President's breath was "The Building of a Ship," in which an abolitionist of the 1840s fears the slavery question will destroy the sacred Union:

> Sail on, O Ship of State!
> Sail on, O *Union*, strong and great!
> Humanity with all its fears,
> With all the hopes of future years,
> Is hanging breathless on thy fate! . . .
>
> Our hearts, our hopes, our prayers, our tears,
> Our faith triumphant o'er our fears,
> Are all with thee—are all with thee!

When a young man recited the verse at the White House, Lincoln wept.

Startled by Lincoln's political comeback, some Americans of the time explained it as sheer luck—the well-timed Union victories, the Democrats' self-destruction.

But this ignored the President's shrewdness and fortitude. Had Lincoln revoked his half-million-man draft call, the soldiers might have angrily concluded that he was playing politics with their lives. Instead the crucial soldiers' vote went for Lincoln by almost eighty percent.

Had he caved in to the Radicals, on one side, or the War Democrats, on the other, Lincoln would have shattered the coalition that ultimately brought him victory. Instead, although fleetingly tempted to backpedal, he stuck to his conviction that slavery must vanish before there could be peace.

Lincoln had clung to his belief that the Emancipation was a military necessity. But more important, by 1864, that document had become a pillar of his conception of himself, and he would not knock that pillar over. He told a Union officer it was "a momentous thing to be the instrument, under Providence, of the liberation of a race."

Born in oblivion, Lincoln had always aspired to write his name in history. As a young politician, he wished to be Illinois's "DeWitt Clinton," transforming his state with roads and canals. During his single term in the U.S. House, he had tried to become a national spokesman against President James Polk's Mexican War.

Lincoln had launched his Presidency eager to be the leader who restored the Union. But by 1864, he realized that if the North won the war, that would not be his chief claim to immortality. He told a portrait artist that his Emancipation Proclamation was "the central act of my administration and the great event of the nineteenth century."

On Friday, November 11, 1864, it was time for Lincoln to close the books on his summer's fear that he would not be reelected.

He summoned his Cabinet, along with John Hay, and took a sealed document from his desk drawer: "Gentlemen, do you remember last summer, I asked you all to sign your names to the back of a paper, of which I did not show you the inside? This is it. Now, Mr. Hay, see if you can get this open without tearing it."

For the first time, the Cabinet secretaries saw Lincoln's August prediction that he would lose the Presidency. They knew that another kind of politician would have pretended that all along he had been certain of victory.

Lincoln told them, "You will remember that this was written at a time when . . . we . . . seemed to have no friends."

Had McClellan been elected President, he would have told him, "General, the election has demonstrated that you . . . have more influence with the American people than I. Now let us get together . . . and . . . try to save the country."

William Seward piped up: "The General would answer you, 'Yes, yes!' . . . and so on, forever, and would have done nothing at all."

Knowing McClellan so well from the hurtful disappointments of the early war, Lincoln agreed. But "at least," he told Seward, "I should have done my duty and have stood clear before my own conscience."

CHAPTER SEVENTEEN

I SEE DYNAMITE

By this Sunday morning in October 1904, the young John Hay who had beguiled Abraham Lincoln was old John Hay. Sallow and fretting about his various ailments, Hay was now Secretary of State to President Theodore Roosevelt.

After Lincoln's murder, Hay wrote editorials for Lincoln's old irritant Horace Greeley at the *New York Tribune*. Then he married a Cleveland heiress and returned to Washington in style, building a Romanesque revival mansion on Lafayette Square, facing the White House.

The boy from Warsaw, Illinois, marveled that with "so little ability and so little power of sustained industry," he had won "great prizes": a rich wife, a literary reputation, prestigious jobs under Presidents, even a well-born mistress, the wife of the Brahmin Senator from Massachusetts, Henry Cabot Lodge.

This morning, President Roosevelt bounded into Hay's house for one of his Sunday visits after church.

T.R.'s face was scraped and bruised. During a ride the previous day, his horse had stumbled and threw him down. Second in the line of succession, Hay realized that he had come close to a "fatal elevation" to the Presidency.*

Hay wished his boss would not take such physical risks. He told his

---

* With no Vice President after Roosevelt succeeded William McKinley in 1901, the Secretary of State was the Constitutional successor-in-waiting. In 1947 this role was given to the Speaker of the House.

diary, "The President will, of course, outlive me, but he will not live to be old."

Two weeks from now, T.R. would face the voters and, despite his fearless reputation, he was nervous. He had his job only because William McKinley had been murdered, and he knew that no President-by-succession had won election on his own.

Comforting troubled Presidents was Hay's specialty. To reassure T.R., he gave him a copy of Abraham Lincoln's gloomy letter of August 1864, predicting his own defeat for reelection.

Roosevelt took his oath in September 1901 in Buffalo, where McKinley had died of his bullet wounds.

T.R. insisted that had he been the man shot, the assassin "wouldn't have gotten away so easily. . . . I'd have guzzled him first." But his worried wife, Edith, exclaimed, "My husband is so young!"

John Hay reminded the new President of "my old-time love for your father," dating back to the Civil War. He wished Theodore Sr. "could have lived to see where you are!"

After boarding the funeral train from Buffalo to Washington, T.R. sent an invitation to McKinley's "political prime minister," Ohio Senator Mark Hanna, to dine in his car.

Although he had once joked about McKinley's "selfishness," Hanna loved the martyred President. Leaning over the comatose, dying leader, he had piteously asked, "Mr. President, can't you hear me? William! Don't you know me?"

After leaving the deathbed, Hanna "cried like a child." Campaign manager to the very end, Hanna chose McKinley's casket and wired the Pennsylvania Railroad to arrange his funeral train.

But Hanna's loyalties did not extend to Roosevelt, whom he considered a "madman." On receiving T.R.'s invitation, he said, "That damn cowboy wants me to take supper with him alone, damn him!"

Hanna used their dinner to send the new President a warning. As Eastern towns rolled past the train's windows, he unwrapped an expensive Cuban cigar and advised "Theodore" not to seek another term as President in 1904.

*   *   *

An Ohio mining-shipping-banking tycoon, Hanna in 1896 was McKinley's chief promoter, pamphleteer and fund raiser, puffing his chest and joking, "Me big Injun!"

Hanna portrayed his candidate as the nation's "Advance Agent of Prosperity," offering the "Full Dinner-Pail." T.R. gibed that Hanna sold McKinley like a "patent medicine."

As a speaker, McKinley was no match for his opponent, William Jennings Bryan, "Boy Orator of the Platte." Thus Hanna fashioned a "front-porch campaign," with "dinner-pail brigades" flocking to McKinley's home in Canton, Ohio.

Hoisting the scarecrow of a "communistic" Bryan, Hanna prodded big businessmen to fork over a quarter percent of their corporate assets to the McKinley campaign. Breaking all records, he collected seven million dollars.*

McKinley won in a landslide, but Hanna had paid a heavy toll to be his handler. In political cartoons, he was "Dollar Mark," McKinley's fat, greedy ventriloquist, covered with dollar signs.

Less hard-boiled than he appeared, Hanna wept over the acid caricatures. When friends told him he should be Treasury Secretary, Hanna replied that the press would have him "selling the White House kitchen stove."

Displeased that people saw him as Hanna's monkey, McKinley kept his distance from Hanna by offering no better reward than Postmaster General, traditional refuge of party hacks.

But even the icy McKinley knew that Hanna deserved something better. By naming the almost senile Ohio Senator John Sherman as his Secretary of State, he created a vacancy, allowing Hanna to be named to the Senate.

In 1900, McKinley ignored Hanna's warning that T.R. was "crazy" and chose the New York Governor as his Vice Presidential running mate.

---

* Equal to about $143 million today. In 1972, Maurice Stans adopted Hanna's approach—akin to direct taxation—while finance chairman of Richard Nixon's notorious Committee to Re-elect the President. Many of those approached by Stans took his demands as a veiled threat of federal retaliation—especially since, unlike Hanna in 1896, Stans was representing an incumbent President who could immediately exact federal retribution upon those who refused him.

"Dollar Mark" Hanna, 1896

Hanna wrote McKinley, "Your *duty* to the Country is to *live* for four years from next March."

Now, during their private dinner on McKinley's funeral train, Hanna warned the new President not to stray from the dead man's pro-business conservatism: "I am sure we will agree on a proper course to pursue. Meantime, go slow."

Bristling at the condescension, Roosevelt complained that "Hanna treats me like a boy."

In December 1901, T.R. showed the nation he was no McKinley.

He wrote Congress that the Constitution's framers had not foreseen the "startling" rise and "grave evils" of corporate monopolies. Since the trusts crossed state lines, the U.S. government should oversee them—especially the railroads, "through which the crucial lifeblood of this nation flows."

Before sending his message to Capitol Hill, Roosevelt had politely shown his decree to Hanna, who warned, "I see dynamite in it."

* * *

Having fired his fusillade, T.R. ordered his Attorney General, Philander Knox, to sue the Northern Securities Company, the biggest trust on earth.

Just created by J. Pierpont Morgan, the world's most powerful capitalist, and the railway barons Edward Harriman and James J. Hill to end their "battle of titans," Northern Securities controlled all U.S. train traffic from Chicago to the Northwest.

Collier's Weekly said, "You can now ride from England to China . . . without once passing from the protecting hollow of Mr. Morgan's hand."

Mark Hanna thought the new behemoth wonderful. James J. Hill, a close friend, had helped him raise New York money for McKinley. Hanna asked a Morgan partner to sell him some stock, writing, "I wish you would look 'a little out' for me."

Having ranched in the Dakota Badlands and loving the West, T.R. knew how many Americans resented Eastern banks and corporate trusts, whose dictates on railroad rates and routes could destroy towns and farms.

He had told his friend Cabot Lodge that working men were "sullenly grumbling that McKinley is under Hanna's dictation," adding, "The trusts are crushing the life out of the small men."

Roosevelt yearned to discipline the "great law-defying corps of immense wealth." He hated the "swinish indifference" of the "Pierpont Morgan type" and the "unscrupulous politicians" they bought. He wrote a friend that if his "soul" did not "rise up" against such malfeasance, "why, then, naturally you are out of sympathy with me."

An old friend of his father, Pierpont Morgan had given T.R. money to become New York Governor in 1898 but felt stung when he demanded a corporate income tax.

Roosevelt tried to make up by throwing Morgan a dinner in New York. Tongue in cheek, he asked "encouragement" from a friend for his effort "to become a conservative man, in touch with the influential classes."

As President, T.R. knew that fighting Morgan would please the masses who blamed him and his kind for their troubles, but that he would be risking the hatred of the Republican establishment, which called Morgan a "statesman."

In February 1902, before the Northern Securities lawsuit was filed, T.R. asked Hanna to breakfast. Worried about leaks that would cause "violent fluctuations" in the stock market, he cryptically asked the Senator what he thought of Morgan's mammoth new trust.

Hanna said it was the "best thing" that could happen to the Northwest.

Two days later, riding a train from Manhattan to Washington, Hanna asked why so many trust lawyers were aboard. He was staggered to be told that President Roosevelt had just sued to break up Northern Securities.

In Washington, Henry Adams, the acerbic historian, great-grandson of the second President, told his diary that the "stormy petrel" in the White House had just "hit Pierpont Morgan, the whole railway trust, and the whole Wall Street connection, a tremendous whack square on the nose."

Pierpont Morgan heard the shocking news while hosting a dinner party in New York. Morgan's son Jack was incensed that "Teddy" had not bothered to consult "someone interested" in the subject before flailing at Northern Securities.

Pierpont felt that Roosevelt should have done "the gentlemanly thing" and privately asked him to resolve any problems caused by the new trust. He damned him for demagoguery.

As the news spread through Wall Street, Morgan bought up stock in his own gigantic trust to avert a financial panic.

Convinced he could talk the President out of his ill-conceived caprice, the tycoon rushed through a heavy blizzard to Washington and dined with Mark Hanna and a dozen friends at a house on Lafayette Square.

The guests were lions of politics, finance and industry who by summer sailed on Morgan's yacht *Corsair* and called themselves the "Corsair Club."

Morgan had met Hanna during McKinley's first Presidential campaign. When someone said later that Wall Street had put Hanna in the Capital to "look out for us," Morgan retorted, "We did nothing of the kind. He sent himself. We did not know how to spell his name in '96!"

Morgan now asked Hanna why he had not warned him of the Northern Securities suit. The Ohio Senator confessed that T.R. had blindsided him too.

Describing the Corsair Club dinner, Henry Adams wrote that the "whole party" was "bleak," and that Pierpont "sulked like a child."

To soften Morgan up before their confrontation the next day, Roosevelt called to ask all the diners to the White House. As Adams recorded, "Pierpont refused, but they made him go."

When Morgan went to the White House the next morning, he took Hanna and New York Senator Chauncey Depew, who, by the looser ethics of the time, was also board chairman of the New York Central Railroad.

Imperiously, Morgan told the President, "If we have done anything wrong, send your man to my man and they can fix it up."

"That can't be done," said T.R.

"We don't want to fix it up," said Philander Knox. "We want to stop it."

Unused to such audacity, Morgan asked, "Are you going to attack my other interests—the Steel Trust and the others?"

"Certainly not," said Roosevelt. "Unless we find out . . . they have done something . . . wrong."

After the meeting, Roosevelt told Knox that Morgan's response was "most illuminating": he "could not help regarding me as a big rival operator" who wished to "ruin all his interests" and with whom he could make a deal to stop it.

Back in his hotel suite, Morgan was furious. Only his lawyers kept him from sending the President a "violent" protest.

Unwilling to let Morgan leave Washington feeling completely enraged, Roosevelt invited him to a dinner for the German Kaiser's visiting brother.

Morgan refused, but his lawyers made him put on his white tie and tailcoat and pushed him out the door.

In March 1902, before Attorney General Knox filed the formal papers against the "great triumvirate" that owned Northern Securities, Morgan's partners asked the President to protect the nation's financial stability by leaving out Morgan's name.

Knox told Roosevelt he would not sign the lawsuit if Morgan's name were removed.

Watching the struggle from his stone house, adjoining his friend John Hay's on Lafayette Square, Henry Adams wrote, "Theodore's vanity, ambition, dogmatic temper and cephalopodic brain are all united on hitting everybody, friend or enemy." *

Adams felt that Roosevelt, "blind-drunk with self-esteem," was like a "naughty boy who breaks china when his mother isn't looking."

After attending a White House dinner, Adams noted that "Theodore absorbed the conversation, and if he tired me ten years ago, he crushes me now," lecturing about history "as though he were a high-school pedagogue."

Chagrined by how America had strayed from the romantic past he imagined, Adams felt that he and John Hay had become "sages": it was time for their generation to "scuttle gracefully, and leave Theodore to surround himself with his own rough-riders."

Roosevelt chortled to Knox that thanks to their lawsuit, the New York rich would now "cross themselves at the mention of our names."

John Hay teased the President about his "dangerous" hostility toward business, calling him the "Enemy of Property." He wished T.R. were not so harsh on his Wall Street friends.

Mark Hanna carped that the Northern Securities lawsuit was killing his steel business: customers would not place a single order beyond November.

But Roosevelt had no tolerance for such complaints. He said the Northern Securities suit would harm the U.S. economy about as much as New York's prosperity would be damaged by "a raid on Canfield's," a Manhattan gambling den.

He wrote a friend, the British historian and politician George Otto Trevelyan, that his "chief fight" as President was against the new plutocracy, "as unattractive now as in the days of Carthage."

He found the "typical American multimillionaire" an "unlovely being," with little resemblance to Washington, Lincoln and other heroes

---

* On the old site of the Hay and Adams houses now stands the Hay-Adams Hotel.

who "founded this government, conquered this continent, and fought to a finish the great war for Union and for liberty."

Roosevelt knew that posing as the "incorruptible foe of the great and the wealthy" held "attractions for the demagogue." But he genuinely thought of himself as a gladiator against evil. Resembling John Adams, making people angry made him feel principled.

Like both Adams and Andrew Jackson, he was taking a large risk by challenging the citadels of wealth and power.

Since the 1870s, big business had owned the Republican Party. As T.R. wrote, with their "enormous sums of money," tycoons and their "agents" had controlled "a portion of the public press . . . men in public life . . . men in the pulpit, and most melancholy of all . . . a few men on the bench."

Roosevelt knew that if the power elite got angry enough, they would try to stop his nomination in 1904. Like Nicholas Biddle and his allies in the Bank War, they might also try to destroy his character.

But T.R. felt that the only men "fit to live" were those "who do not fear to die." Exulting both physical and political risk, he felt both life and death were "parts of the same Great Adventure."

Such words were not just empty rhetoric. Every day of his adult life, he fought to overcome his memories of being a weak, asthmatic child.

He knew it was "rather absurd for a president to appear with a black eye or a swollen nose or a cut lip," but he sparred with famous boxers in the East Room. One punch left him almost blind in one eye.

Edith Roosevelt felt that if the bland McKinley had been murdered, her controversial husband must be next: "The horror of it hangs over me, and I fear for Theodore."

To this, T.R. shrugged: if some assassin wished to trade his life for the President's, no one could stop him.*

Nevertheless before running around the Washington Monument at midnight, he mollified his wife by packing a pistol. Slapping his hip pocket, he said, "They would have to be mighty quick to get the drop on me!"

---

* President John Kennedy uttered the same sentiment just before his assassination in 1963.

CHAPTER EIGHTEEN

———=◦◦(◦)◦◦=———

BLACK STORM

Long before he was President, Roosevelt began writing popular history—in part to make back his considerable losses from ranching in the Dakotas. Working fast, he knew it was probably a "mere dream" for him to "write some book" of the "very first class."

T.R.'s subjects were usually great Americans and their struggles—the Revolutionary leader Gouverneur Morris, Andrew Jackson's ally Tom Benton, Americans settling the Western frontier.

Showing his predilection for Presidents who put themselves on the line, he praised George Washington for approving Jay's Treaty while knowing it would subject him to a "perfect torrent of wrath."

T.R.'s account of a horseback ride to Mount Vernon was poetic: "The woods were green and lovely, the roads soft for the horse's feet."

Like himself, Andrew Jackson had fought the plutocracy, but Roosevelt could not bring himself to praise the Democrats' icon. Though willing to concede Jackson's courage and that the "unscrupulous" Nicholas Biddle had "too much power," he deplored Old Hickory's "narrow mind" and "bitter prejudices."*

By contrast, T.R. felt an emotional connection to Lincoln that emerged from his childhood.

In the tragic spring of 1865, when Lincoln's funeral train moved

---

* But when Roosevelt broke with the Republican establishment in 1912 to run for President as a Progressive, he wrote a friend that "for all his faults," he had become "a great admirer of Andrew Jackson."

from Washington to Springfield, major cities along the way held mourning parades. The six-year-old Theodore gazed down from his grandfather's New York City townhouse, chin on the windowsill, as the martyr's coffin passed below.

As President, T.R. had the rosewood "Lincoln bed," carved with ornate birds and grapes, moved into his and Edith's bedroom.* Living in the Mansion made him "think of Lincoln, shambling, homely, with his strong, sad, deeply-furrowed face, all the time."

He wished "to Heaven" he shared Lincoln's calm: "Sometimes I do get deeply irritated."

T.R. said that "so far as one who is not a great man can model himself upon one who was," he tried to follow Lincoln. By seeking a "square deal" for what Lincoln called the "plain people," he hoped to rescue his party from the "commercial conservatism" that "culminated in Hanna."

He boasted to Trevelyan that the "farmers, mechanics, small tradesmen, hard-working professional men" all considered him "their President."

That much was true. But unlike Lincoln, T.R. feared "the tyranny of the mob." He felt leaders like him, elegantly raised and schooled, knew better than the proletariat what was good for them.

Roosevelt once told a sister that fifty-one percent of the time, the people's voice was "the voice of God," but the rest of the time, it was "the voice of the devil . . . or a fool."

Despite his misgivings about Andrew Jackson, T.R. said he belonged to the "Lincoln-Jackson school" of Presidential power.

With his crusades for conservation, workers' rights, a Panama canal and U.S. global influence, he tried to reendow the Presidency with the glory and power it held in Lincoln's time. Roosevelt believed a President must "do anything" the country needed, as long as it was legal.

Speaker Joe Cannon complained Roosevelt went further than that: T.R. had "no more use for the Constitution than a tomcat has for a marriage license!"

---

* Lincoln apparently never slept in the great bed with its cathedral-shaped headboard, although his son Willie died there. Used in an upstairs guest room during Lincoln's time, the bed occupies the Lincoln Bedroom of today's White House—the chamber used by Jackson and Lincoln as their office.

[137]

*　　*　　*

Roosevelt also wished to make his official residence worthy of a world leader.

The White House, with its dark Victorian walls and garish-patterned carpets, reminded him of the seamy New York hotel ballrooms of his earlier political life. Its entrance hall, now a depressing olive-drab, had been sealed off by a red, white and blue Tiffany glass wall with the monogram "U.S."

When Edith Roosevelt discovered that the President's office was upstairs, next to the family bedrooms, she was aghast that she and her children would have to make their way through visiting politicians and favor-seekers.

To banish all of this, Roosevelt hired the fashionable New York architect Charles McKim to restore the Mansion to the elegance "planned" by Washington—and do it "quickly and cheaply."

He asked McKim to "smash" the glass greenhouses protruding from the Mansion, replacing them with a West Wing including offices for himself and his staff. The front hall and East Room were repainted in gleaming ivory.*

While his family repaired to Sagamore Hill, their barnlike house at Oyster Bay, Long Island, T.R. tried to tough it out at the White House, but the suffocating plaster dust forced him into a townhouse on Lafayette Square.†

There, in the fall of 1902, he tried to stop an anthracite coal strike that threatened, more than any event since the Civil War, to divide the country.

Over a hundred thousand Pennsylvania workers had been striking for months, resulting in sabotage, riots and murder.

Across the United States, organized labor was threatening a sympathy strike that would bring daily life to a halt. The Northeast was already short of coal, with children shivering in their beds.

---

* McKim had the Tiffany screen auctioned for $275, less than a tenth of its 1883 purchase price. Fortunately the auction, along with that of other White House furniture and artifacts, was the last time such important pieces of the Mansion's heritage were sold.

† Now called 736 Jackson Place, the building houses the President's Office of National AIDS Policy and the USA Freedom Corps.

Alarmed by the "black storm" in the coalfields, Roosevelt was at his "wits' end." He feared a national "revolution" jeopardizing "the whole system of private management."

T.R. complained to a friend that the "big moneyed men" wouldn't settle the strike. In the wake of the Northern Securities suit, they wouldn't "grant favors to me."

Roosevelt did not wish to emulate the cowardly James Buchanan, "striving to find some Constitutional reason for inaction." Presidents did not normally meddle in work stoppages, but the potential "catastrophe" was too dangerous.

In October 1902, T.R. called the anthracite and coal-road barons and their nemesis, John Mitchell of the United Mine Workers, to his upstairs parlor on Lafayette Square, determined to knock some sense into them.

The previous month, in Pittsfield, Massachusetts, a streetcar had struck Roosevelt's open carriage, bouncing him onto the street.*

Boasting it took "more than a trolley accident to knock me out," T.R. suffered from blood poisoning and shin injuries. He thus had to greet John Mitchell and the coal barons from a wheelchair.

Repelled by the coal men's "arrogance" and "gross blindness," he found Mitchell the finest gentleman in the room. He liked the union leader's suggestion to solve the strike by Presidential commission.

But the railroad man George Baer refused to bargain with "instigators of violence and crime." He asked the President, "Are you asking us to deal with a set of outlaws?"

Roosevelt was furious. He later said if it weren't for his "high office," he would have "chucked" Baer out the window. He wrote a friend that the coal barons were "putting a very heavy burden on us who stand against socialism, against anarchic disorder."

Hoping to scare them into action, T.R. warned their fellow mining magnate Mark Hanna that if they didn't come to their senses, he might try a "radical experiment" and sue them all for antitrust.

*　　　*　　　*

---

* The accident killed Roosevelt's Secret Service man, Bill Craig, the first agent to die while guarding a President.

Roosevelt feared that if the strike wore on, there would be "the most terrible riots the country has ever seen," requiring him to impose "drastic, and perhaps revolutionary measures."

To prevent such chaos, he quietly called in the seventy-two-year-old John Schofield, ex–Commanding General of the U.S. Army, who had marched toward Atlanta under General Sherman.

T.R. obtained Schofield's commitment to seize the mines, if necessary, using ten thousand troops. He was pleased that the General, with his outdated black skullcap and side whiskers, did not look like a "military dictator."

He told Schofield he knew the assault might be unconstitutional, but if it came to that, the General must ignore "any authority . . . except mine."

From his history, Roosevelt knew that Lincoln had played fast and loose with the law during the Civil War.

He recalled the Union General Benjamin Butler's tough tactics after capturing New Orleans in 1862. When Confederate ladies spat and cursed at Butler and his troops, Butler had them jailed as prostitutes.

Roosevelt felt that if he stormed the coalfields, no Member of Congress "would have raised his voice against me"—so long as nationwide coal famine seemed imminent. But once the fear receded, his foes would unleash their furies.

This didn't scare him. All they could do was impeach him—and "they would not have ventured to try."

But, unwilling to test the Constitution without some kind of Congressional sanction, he whispered about seizing the mines to a few House and Senate leaders, including his party's House Whip, James Watson.

By Watson's account, he asked the President, "What about seizing property without due process of law?"

Clutching Watson's shoulder, T.R. cried, "The Constitution was made for the people, and not the people for the Constitution!"*

Before turning to the Army, T.R. persuaded John Mitchell to back an arbitration board, whose rulings would be enforced by the President.

---

* In 1952, when President Harry Truman aimed to prevent a steel strike during the Korean War by seizing the mills, government lawyers cited T.R.'s plans to seize the anthracite fields. Federal Judge David Pine replied that "with all due deference and respect for that great President," Roosevelt's plans did not "comport with our recognized theory of government."

Then he turned to J. P. Morgan, still fending off the Northern Securities suit.

Morgan's holdings gave him great power over the anthracite barons. By letter, the President asked him to ignore their differences for the "sake" of "our nation." He told Morgan he was "full of anxiety."

T.R. warned Morgan's partner Bob Bacon, an old Harvard classmate, that Democrats wanted him to seize the coal chiefs "by the throat" and nationalize their industry.

He asked Bacon, "Have you ever read Hay and Nicolay's Lincoln?" Like the sixteenth President, he had to "guard" against the "extremists of both sides."

Roosevelt sent his Secretary of War, Elihu Root, to meet Morgan aboard the *Corsair*, moored off Manhattan. Root may have promised Morgan that if an arbitration board failed, the President would send the Army into the coalfields.

Morgan went to Roosevelt's townhouse to report that the coal barons would accept such a board, so long as they could name five of its seven members, including an "eminent sociologist."

Mitchell proposed that his two members be a Catholic priest (in respect to the largely Catholic miners) and Edgar Clark, chief of the railroad conductors' union.

Certain the debacle was over, the President celebrated over dinner at the mansion of John Hay, who later wrote Henry Adams that the jubilant Theodore "began talking at the oysters, and the *pousse-café* found him still at it. When he was one of us, we could sit on him—but who . . . can sit on a Kaiser?"

After dinner, Roosevelt returned home to a "screaming comedy"— Morgan's partners Bacon and Perkins, "nearly wild," warning that George Baer wouldn't truckle to any "labor man."

Disgusted by the "woodenheaded" Baer's "stupidity," T.R. proposed calling Clark an "eminent sociologist." Certainly Clark must have thought "deeply" about the subject. The coal barons agreed.*

Pocketing his victory, the President felt like "going to the circus."

---

* In March 1903, the arbitrators recommended that the anthracite workers receive a ten percent wage hike and a nine-hour working day, but they refused Mitchell's plea to certify his union as their exclusive bargaining agent.

Sharing the country's feeling that "a nightmare had been lifted," he insisted that the strike would have spun out of control "had I not interfered."

The Constitution hadn't "required" him to settle the strike. But "being for the moment the head of the Nation, I obeyed the supreme law of duty to the Republic in acting as I did."

T.R. wrote his sister Bamie, "Heavens and earth, it has been a struggle!"

CHAPTER NINETEEN

A ROUGH-AND-TUMBLE MAN

In November 1902, impressed by T.R.'s dexterity, voters gave Republicans their best midterm showing since the Civil War.

The President felt he was being "overpraised by everybody," which made him apprehensive.* He predicted to his British friend Trevelyan that the moguls to whom "I gave mortal offense" would soon retaliate.

If they did, he would "fight it out . . . win or lose." He would "much rather be a real President for three years and a half than a figurehead for seven years and a half."†

While battling his political dragons, Roosevelt felt the security of an adoring wife and family—the boys throwing a snake onto a Congressman's lap, pasting spitballs onto General Jackson's portrait.

"I love all of these children and have great fun with them," he wrote, "and I am touched by the way in which they feel I am their special friend, champion and companion."

After voting at Oyster Bay in the 1902 election, the President wrote son Kermit, "Mother and I took a walk accompanied by all six dogs. . . .

---

* One skeptic of T.R.'s performance was the twenty-year-old Franklin Roosevelt, a Harvard junior, who wrote his mother that their cousin had "made a serious mistake in interfering—politically, at least. His tendency to make the executive power stronger than the Houses of Congress is bound to be a bad thing, especially when a man of weaker personality succeeds him in office."

† In April 1970, President Richard Nixon, a close student of T.R., borrowed Roosevelt's observation without identifying his source. Announcing his invasion of Cambodia, Nixon said he would "rather be a one-term President and do what I believe is right than to be a two-term President at the cost of seeing America become a second-rate power."

The unfortunate [kitten] Tom Quartz . . . was clasped affectionately in Archie's arms . . . which . . . gave him a strong feeling as to the weariness of life." Five-year-old Quentin "fell asleep."

He told a sister he had "the happiest home life of any man whom I have ever known."

Characteristically T.R. extrapolated his good fortune into a moral lesson for everyone. In the fall of 1902, he wrote that the "highest of all joys" came only from having and raising "many healthy children." Anyone who "deliberately" shunned marriage or who had "a heart so cold . . . and a brain so shallow and selfish" to avoid having children was committing "a crime against the race."

Roosevelt confessed he had "the morals of a green-grocer, they are so old-fashioned." As a young rancher, he had priggishly turned his back when cowboys told off-color tales. He and Edith would not entertain "loose living" people. Easy divorces were dragging the country into the "barnyard."

His wayward younger brother Elliott had once jeopardized the family name by impregnating a housemaid called Katy Mann. Denouncing his brother as a "flagrant man-swine," T.R. paid her ten thousand dollars to disappear, along with her son, who was named Elliott Roosevelt Mann.*

Dissipated by anisette and brandy, Theodore's brother died in 1894, leaving a son and a sad, sweet and lonely little daughter called Eleanor.

In November 1902, Roosevelt moved his family into the newly restored White House. T.R. found his new Mansion "the ideal house for the head of a great democratic republic." He insisted that the house be forever "unchanged and unmarred."† Anyone who disliked his improvements was a "yahoo."

Looking down on guests in the newly expanded State Dining Room were a dozen stuffed buffalo, antelope, and other animal heads—

---

* Over a luncheon at his New Jersey home in 1992 with the author of this book, ex-President Richard Nixon noted a new Woodrow Wilson biography that recounted how Wilson's friends apparently bought silence from a Wilson paramour to protect Wilson's political future. The President who had tried to contain the Watergate scandal with hush money went on to say, "Of course, they paid her off—as they should have!"

† A wish mainly fulfilled. The Mansion's public rooms today—especially the entrance hall and East Room—are essentially what Theodore Roosevelt envisaged.

theater props for the President to gasconade about his Dakota adventures. Edith Roosevelt was quietly horrified by the "awful open mouths and shining eyes."

The President was shocked to find two lions' heads on the dining room's new fireplace. Scorning the British symbol, he ordered them replaced by American bison.

T.R. loved his new burlap-papered Presidential office, only fifteen feet square, with slightly bowed windows facing a new tennis court on the South Grounds, which he used strenuously and often. Edith kept the room supplied with purple heliotrope, a symbol of marital bliss.

Over the fireplace, Roosevelt hung a Lincoln portrait. While wrestling with a problem, "I look up to that picture, and I do as I believe Lincoln would have done."

The President also posted a photograph of a bear and a John James Ingalls sonnet called "Opportunity," which began,

> Master of human destinies am I
> Fame, love and fortune on my footsteps wait.

From that new West Wing office in 1903, Roosevelt asked Congress to establish a Department of Commerce, assigned to scrutinize American business. A new Bureau of Corporations would investigate corporate malfeasance.

To make sure the Senate passed his Commerce bill, T.R. personally leaked a false report that Standard Oil's John D. Rockefeller was strong-arming Senators against it.

Deferring to big business, the House renamed Roosevelt's entity as the "Department of Commerce and Labor," ensuring that unions were scrutinized as closely as corporations.

T.R. sought opportunities to show he was just as tough on tycoons as on the workers. He boasted that John Mitchell had "been to see me quite as often as Pierpont Morgan." His doors would "swing open as easily to the wageworker as to the head of a big corporation—*and no easier.*"

In the fall of 1903, the American Federation of Labor got the U.S. Government Printing Office to fire a foreman who spurned the union. T.R. had him reinstated, giving the union's famous chief, Samuel Gompers, a "good jolt."

The President warned that if Gompers responded with a strike, "not one man jack of them will do another stroke of government work while I am President."

T.R.'s demand for a tough Bureau of Corporations did not expand his Wall Street fan club. His New York fund-raisers were "decidedly blue."

One of the conservative moguls unsettled by Roosevelt was the white-bearded chief of Chicago's Pullman Palace Car Company, Robert Todd Lincoln, the late President's last surviving son, who complained years later that T.R. had "perverted" the Great Emancipator's ideas to push "radical" and "revolutionary doctrines" his father "would abhor."

Roosevelt told friends he wished to be elected President in his own right more than "anything tangible." But Hanna and "the whole Wall Street crowd" were against him: "The big New York and Chicago capitalists—and both the criminal rich and the fool rich—will do all they can to beat me."

If Hanna and his friends wished a "knockdown and dragout fight," he would provide "all the fighting they wish." He was "a rough-and-tumble man, and in the long run, I reckon on giving more punishment than I receive."

T.R. felt he should "stop shilly-shallying" and tell Hanna that he would not crawl to him as his "suppliant" for the Republican nomination. "Better to have a fight in the open at once than to run the risk of being knifed secretly." Hanna must be forced to show his hand.

In May 1903, Roosevelt's friend Senator Joseph Foraker called on fellow Ohio Republicans to declare their support for the President's reelection.

Hanna cabled Roosevelt that he must decline: "When you know all the facts, I am sure you will approve my course."

The President wired back that Hanna's silence would be interpreted as opposition. Put on the spot, just as Roosevelt intended, Hanna had to respond that, of course, he backed the President's reelection.

Exhilarated by his own deftness, T.R. told a friend that cornering Hanna had "entirely revived me."

Still he could not take Hanna's response at face value. T.R. heard that Hanna was "sufficiently equivocal" about 1904 that wealthy Republicans would not open their checkbooks for the President.

When a Roosevelt aide asked Hanna to formally endorse the President, the Ohio Senator said it would not be "dignified." He was "tired of going to the White House every morning" and "swearing allegiance."

T.R. felt that despite his public stigma as "Dollar Mark," the old man was "half" convinced he could be nominated for President himself in 1904.

The Republican party's treasurer, Cornelius Bliss, later said that if Roosevelt had stumbled, "Hanna would have been nominated, hands down."

More likely was that Hanna might lead an anti-Roosevelt cabal. At sixty-six, he suffered from painful rheumatic attacks and heart disease, carping to friends that "too much blood" was flowing to his brain.

Distressed by Hanna's pallor, a Cleveland friend begged him to "get on a steamer and sail to someplace" for a rest. But Hanna told him, "I can't do it. . . . I must be in the Senate."

Hanna was not Roosevelt's only problem for 1904. T.R. feared the Democrats might haul ex-President Grover Cleveland out of retirement.

He wrote his friend Senator Lodge that Cleveland could appeal across party lines to the "big Wall Street men who resent the Northern Securities suit and the settlement of the anthracite coal strike, as well as . . . the Bureau of Corporations."

T.R. felt Cleveland would be the "most formidable Democrat" to beat. He predicted that "Morgan and other Wall Street men" would "support Mr. Cleveland against me with all their power."

Cleveland declined to run, but Roosevelt feared that "the wealthy capitalists who practice graft . . . will give my opponent, whoever he may be next year, unlimited money."

In November 1904, Pierpont Morgan had Mark Hanna to a private Thanksgiving feast at his Manhattan home and said it was his "duty" to save the nation from Roosevelt: it would be "easy" to nominate Hanna for President, if he "would only give the word."

Citing his wife's concerns about his health, Hanna demurred, but Morgan's allies kept up the pressure. One Senator warned, "If we renominate Roosevelt, it means defeat."

T.R. wrote a friend, "I cannot tell you at length all the intrigues that have been going on." With support from lawless "big moneyed men," the "intoxicated" Hanna thought he could be the 1904 nominee—or dictate his own man. Roosevelt said if he went down, it would be "with colors flying and drums beating."

In February 1904, just as Roosevelt prepared to flash his sword, Mark Hanna collapsed at his hotel apartment with typhoid fever.

With the Senator too sick to see outsiders, Roosevelt crossed Lafayette Square to console Hanna's wife, Charlotte.

The old king-maker scrawled him a note: "You touched a tender spot, old man. . . . I may be worse before I can be better but all the same such 'drops' of kindness are good for a fellow."

"Indeed it is your letter from your sick bed which is touching, not my visit," T.R. replied. "May you soon be with us again, old fellow, as strong in body and as vigorous in your leadership as ever."

But Hanna's weakened heart gave out. Told of the Senator's death, Roosevelt said, "I am very, very sorry." He asked a Cabinet member, "Did I tell you that the last letter he wrote was one to me?"

He beseeched his daughter Alice to go to the Hannas' apartment and comfort their daughter Ruth.

The independent Alice, whose mother was the President's late first wife, loved to gamble at racetracks and cavort with Newport socialites who hated T.R. and his politics. At the end of her long, largely self-absorbed life, she called her father "much more of a poseur than a man of substance."

When T.R. asked her to see Hanna's bereaved daughter, Alice replied that the girl couldn't possibly wish to receive someone she knew "so slightly," but for this one occasion, she acceded to her father's wish.

With Hanna no longer a threat, the President turned sentimental. Rereading Hanna's final message, his "eyes swam with tears." He told an aide, "I shall not give that note away. I shall keep it and hand it down to my children."

With hindsight, T.R. said, "He was a fine old boy!" He knew how much trouble Hanna, with his "burly strength," could have made by going public against the President's policies.

But as Roosevelt recalled, "He stood by them just as loyally as if I had been McKinley. Thank Heaven, before he became sick, the whole opposition to me collapsed."

A Morgan partner wrote Pierpont Morgan's son Jack that Hanna's death was "a blow to your father" because it probably made "Roosevelt's nomination certain."

CHAPTER TWENTY

I UPSET THEM ALL

In March 1904, the Supreme Court gave T.R. a monumental victory, ruling by 5 to 4 to dissolve Northern Securities.

Irritated that his own appointee, Justice Oliver Wendell Holmes, had opposed the decision, Roosevelt said he could carve "a judge with more backbone than that" from a "banana."

Vindicated by the Court, the President declared an election-year truce with Wall Street. His Attorney General pledged not to run "amuck" against other corporations.

When Republicans met in Chicago that summer, one delegate raised his glass: "Here's to Roosevelt, whom nobody wants!"

Under a huge Mark Hanna portrait, six times as big as the President's, speakers could not conceal their uneasiness about their nominee.

One Senator said, "We love . . . our young leader" for his "impulsiveness" and "rashness." In his nominating speech, New York ex–Governor Frank Black conceded that T.R. "does not claim to be the Solomon of his time."

For Vice President, against Roosevelt's will, the delegates chose a McKinley conservative, Senator Charles Fairbanks of Indiana, hoping he would dampen the President's "radicalism."

Through the summer and fall of 1904, T.R. held on to the luck that began with Mark Hanna's well-timed death.

Hoping to drain conservative votes from Roosevelt, the Democrats chose a New York judge, Alton Parker, whom William Jennings Bryan lambasted as "the muzzled candidate of Wall Street."

Parker's running mate was a rich, eighty-year-old ex–West Virginia Senator, Henry Davis, whose chief virtue was his willingness to finance the Democrats' fall campaign.

Rushing onto T.R.'s bandwagon, with nowhere else to go, were the big moneyed rich who resented and feared him. Pierpont Morgan gave Roosevelt's campaign $150,000 in cash. Edward Harriman outbid him with $250,000.

For all of the President's moral pretensions, T.R. let his campaign manager, George Cortelyou, remain as Secretary of Commerce and Labor, which gave him the power to reward and punish the same business titans he was begging for large contributions.

In October, the *New York World* complained that big businessmen took T.R.'s "acceptance" of their money as an "implied promise of protection" from future lawsuits and regulation.

Roosevelt had always inveighed against the "lies" in the press, "as foul and dirty . . . as ever was made by any dog."

Outraged that the *World* should question his character, T.R. told his campaign manager to "hit back as savagely as possible." But knowing that the *World* had a point, Cortelyou simply announced that Roosevelt would be elected without "a single promise."

Still the whiff of scandal did not abate. Another report had it that a Standard Oil man had given the Republicans money after being told he would be sorry if he didn't pony up.

T.R. defended himself by asking Cortelyou, in view of his troubled "past relations" with John D. Rockefeller and Standard Oil, to return "any such donation."

Cortelyou's money man, Cornelius Bliss, shielded the President by claiming that no money had been raised from Standard Oil, but in fact, the company had given $125,000 in cash.

Judge Parker denounced Republican efforts to "blackmail" captains of industry.

Roosevelt was incensed about Parker's "monstrous" and "infamous falsehoods." But as he later confessed to a friend, he couldn't really be "certain" someone in his campaign hadn't done "something foolish or wicked."

*   *   *

T.R.'s sister Corinne felt that for Theodore, this was not just an election, but a test of his personal "merit."

Before he began campaigning that fall, the President had told Cabot Lodge he felt inexplicably depressed.

The Massachusetts Senator replied that inactivity had "something to do with depressing you." It was hard to "sit by and watch the fight go on with others doing all the fighting."

Now, "in the last hours of the campaign," Lodge reported to his friend that "everyone is tired and nervous, and the air is thick with rumors." He told T.R., "Everybody thinks you are one of the most sanguine of men. I . . . know better."

The President admitted, "I am lying still under shell fire, and I mortally hate the experience." Edith too felt "anxious" and "uneasy."

Roosevelt "never permitted myself to regard the election as anything but doubtful." He wrote his friend Rudyard Kipling that "if beaten I shall be sorry," but he would have had "a first class run for my money, and I have accomplished certain definite things."

On Election Day, after voting in Oyster Bay, he took the railroad back to Washington. "It makes no difference how it goes," he assured his wife. "I have had a vision on the train, and it was of you and the children. Nothing matters as long as we are well and content with each other."

Despite his forebodings, T.R. won the biggest Presidential mandate since 1872, all of the forty-five states outside the Democratic South. To Edith he exulted, "I am no longer a political accident!"

He noted that the only states opposing him were those in which "no free discussion is allowed" and "fraud and violence have rendered the voting a farce."

He cabled Lodge, "Have swept the country by majorities which astound me." He had "no idea that there would be such a sweep." He told son Kermit that it was his "day of greatest triumph" and he felt "very proud and happy."

But on victory night, T.R. made what he came to consider a huge mistake. Overreacting to gibes about his "personal ambition" to "perpetuate myself in power," he announced he would not seek another term in 1908.

The next day, writing his novelist friend Owen Wister, Roosevelt gave the credit for his mandate to "Abraham Lincoln's 'plain people.' " As for the "criminal rich" who had tried to oust him from the White House, "I upset them all."

T.R. said that of his domestic actions during his first term, he was "proudest of" the Northern Securities lawsuit and settling the anthracite strike. For all future Presidents, he had established the government's right to scrutinize great corporations and mediate between management and labor.

Why couldn't Wall Street understand that he had amended capitalism to save it? "I am on their side. I believe in wealth," he told Wister after the 1904 election. Better to take reform from him than "some Bryan" who would "ride over them roughshod."

With his pulsing ambition, his sense of history and moral purpose, Roosevelt felt that great Presidents were those who took noble risks. The politician who cared "only for his own success" was a "curse."

In the most famous utterance of his life, T.R. lauded the "man in the arena," who, if he failed, at least did so "while daring greatly."

Roosevelt had the freedom to so dare because there was more to his life than politics. He loved boxing, wildlife, poetry, his family and his many friends, including Mark Twain, Bat Masterson and Buffalo Bill. When an old Western roughneck pal couldn't get into the White House, Roosevelt advised him to "shoot through the windows."

Roosevelt's patrician reluctance to wear religion on his sleeve concealed the importance of his faith. Taught by his pious Dutch Reformed father, he had started memorizing the Bible at age three.

T.R.'s religion had little of Lincoln's self-criticism. Instead it gave him the moral certainty to make bold decisions. He once told a Bible study group, "It is a good and necessary thing to be intelligent. It is a better thing to be straight and decent and fearless."

For Roosevelt, a good Christian must not be greedy for earthly rewards. He told a son that if he lost the Presidency in 1904 and "felt soured at not having more," he would "regard myself as having a small and mean mind."

On the eve of his inauguration in March 1905, T.R. received an extraordinary gift from his old family friend, Secretary of State John Hay—a heavy gold ring, including six strands of hair mounted under a tiny oval pane of glass.

With the ring came a handwritten note from Hay:

> The hair in this ring is from the head of Abraham Lincoln. Dr. Taft cut it off the night of the assassination, and I got it from his son—a brief pedigree.
>
> Please wear it to-morrow; you are one of the men who most thoroughly understand and appreciate Lincoln.
>
> I have had your monogram and Lincoln's engraved on the ring.
>> Longas, O utinam, bone dux, ferias
>> Praestes Hesperiae.*

Hay had had the ring engraved with the initials "A.L." and "T.R." He knew how proud T.R. would be to have his name joined with that of his hero.

The President's sister Corinne felt he had never received "a gift for which he cared so deeply."

Roosevelt pledged that the Lincoln ring would remind him to "put human rights above property rights." With "love and gratitude," he wrote Hay, "Surely no President, on the eve of his inauguration, has ever received such a gift from a friend. . . . I shall think of it and you as I take the oath tomorrow."

Roosevelt did not know it, but, in fact, an earlier President had indeed received such a gift.

Before McKinley's inauguration in 1897, Hay, always the courtier, had given the President-elect a ring with the intertwined monograms "G.W." and "W.M." He asked McKinley not to reveal who had given him the talisman suggesting that he was George Washington's heir.

Delighted by the ring, McKinley soon sent Hay to London as Ambassador to the Court of St. James's.

By 1905, the poetic old Hay longed to "lie in the orchard and eat the

---

* A quotation from the Roman poet Horace's *Odes*, translated as "Mayest thou, Good Captain, bring long peace to Hesperia!" The strands of hair on the ring had been cut away by a doctor just after Lincoln's shooting to look into his open wound. Charles Taft, another physician who treated Lincoln, willed the strands to his son, who had sold them to Hay for one hundred dollars a month before Roosevelt's inauguration.

sunny side of peaches." Before his death that summer, he dreamt of going to the White House to see President Lincoln, who was "sympathetic about my illness."

While dreaming, Hay had not been surprised that Lincoln was still alive and in power. But he felt "overpowering melancholy."

On Saturday morning, March 4, 1905, as sun and snow pierced the clouds, Roosevelt took his oath on the East Front of the Capitol.

With delight, he spied anthracite miners holding a banner: "WE HONOR THE MAN WHO SETTLED OUR STRIKE."

Glowing from the day's festivities, he proudly wrote Trevelyan that the revelers were "old friends with whom I had lived on the ranches . . . Puerto Ricans and Philippine Scouts . . . Indians in their war paint . . . sixty or seventy cowboys . . . farmers clubs . . . mechanics clubs—everybody and everything." *

A fortnight later, T.R. gave his beloved niece Eleanor's hand in marriage.

She was the daughter of the President's hard-drinking dead brother, Elliott, and the groom was her fifth cousin, once removed, Franklin, of the Roosevelt branch at Hyde Park on the Hudson River.†

The Hyde Park Roosevelts were Democrats, but the President liked young Franklin so much "I'd be shot for him." He wrote the groom he was "as fond of Eleanor as if she were my daughter," and "I like you, and trust you, and believe in you."

Indulging his penchant for philosophical aphorism, T.R. assured Franklin that "no other success . . . not the Presidency, or anything else" could equal "the joy and happiness" of marriage. He wrote Eleanor that she and her "sweetheart" were "worthy of one another."

Since T.R. had to be in New York City for the annual parade, the wedding was set for St. Patrick's Day. At a relative's brownstone, marchers outside sang "The Wearing of the Green" while bride and groom took their vows.

The President chortled, "Well, Franklin, there's nothing like keeping

---

* T.R.'s description echoed the written accounts of Andrew Jackson's first inaugural—not likely by accident, since Roosevelt had studied the Jackson years so closely.
† The late Elliott had been Franklin's godfather.

the name in the family!" When he repaired to the dining room, other guests followed, leaving the bridal couple almost alone.

The young FDR venerated his uncle, but he was irked not to be the centerpiece of his own wedding. He was further annoyed when friends congratulated him on landing a President's niece.

At twenty-three, Franklin Roosevelt was already seeking to emulate Cousin Theodore. While at Harvard, he had bought himself a gold-rimmed pince-nez that looked just like T.R.'s.

Now, with the President's favorite niece at his side, FDR dreamt of following his cousin upward to become Assistant Secretary of the Navy and Governor of New York, which gave him "a good chance to be President."

With his spacious view of his destiny, young Franklin already looked on his Oyster Bay cousin as both model and rival. Decades later, one of his sons told the author of this book, "My father spent his whole adult life competing with T.R."

CHAPTER TWENTY-ONE

———=◦《◎》◦=———

WE MUST PROTECT THE CHIEF!

On Tuesday night, November 5, 1940, in his mother's Victorian dining room at Hyde Park on the Hudson, a shirtsleeved Franklin
Roosevelt, with open collar, necktie slung loose, saw signs that voters
were turning him out of office.

He was seeking a third term as President—a goal that Cousin
Theodore had never achieved.

Studying the tally sheets, FDR drew on a cigarette in its trademark
ivory holder. His face broke out in sweat. With friends and relatives pop-
ping in, he told his Secret Service man, Mike Reilly, "I don't want to see
anybody in here."

"Including your family, Mr. President?"

"I said *anybody!*"

Never before had Reilly seen the iron-willed Roosevelt lose his com-
posure. He guessed that the President was unsettled by early returns
from New England, which showed his opponent, Wendell Willkie, running stronger than expected.

With Adolf Hitler crushing Europe, FDR was worried about losing
more than just an election. The FBI and other intelligence services had
told him things that made him "shudder." Lurking behind Willkie were
Nazi agents slipping money to Senators and others who wanted him to
push Winston Churchill into a quick peace with Hitler.

FDR was grimly certain that Willkie, the amiable political neophyte,
lacked the experience and mettle to resist such pressures.

After hearing "so many sinister stories," the President's wife, Eleanor, felt "really alarmed." She feared that Willkie's backers were "a greater menace than many of us were willing to believe."

If Roosevelt were defeated tonight, he would have lost because people had been scared by his warnings against Hitler and his calls to rebuild America's military machine. They did not want to be dragged into Europe's war.

Just before the election, the *New York Times* reported that a sudden "anti-war psychology" had brought Willkie "within easy striking distance of victory."

The biologically competitive Roosevelt did not want to lose the Presidency. But he knew that by catering to Americans' overwhelming isolationism, he would have done them no favors. If war came, the people would have been left fatally vulnerable to Hitler and the imperial Japanese.

By the late 1930s, most Americans felt that Woodrow Wilson's decision to enter World War I had been a ruinous mistake.

They had been shocked by Senate hearings exposing the bankers and arms merchants—the "merchants of death"—who had profiteered from the war. One Senator said if "the Morgans" wanted another war, they should join the Foreign Legion.

Asked by the Gallup Poll why the U.S. had entered World War I, people replied most frequently that their country had been "the victim of propaganda and selfish interests." And less than thirty years later, Europe was sliding into conflict once again.

To keep FDR from repeating Wilson's errors, Congress tied his hands by making neutrality the law of the land.

House isolationists tried to go further. They almost passed a Constitutional amendment saying that the only ones who could take America to war should not be Roosevelt or Congress but the people themselves, by national referendum. The Ludlow Amendment, named for its sponsor, Louis Ludlow, an Indiana Democrat, had support from 73 percent of Americans.*

As Wilson's Assistant Secretary of the Navy, Franklin Roosevelt had

---

* According to the Gallup Poll. The Ludlow Amendment would have exempted cases of foreign attack.

We Must Protect the Chief!

been even more interventionist than his boss. Thus as Europe sank into another great war, he was being carefully watched for signs that he was secretly plotting to plunge the United States into the mess.

Roosevelt knew that his country might one day have to help keep Hitler from conquering the world. But he knew also that rebuilding the nation's defense and edging toward aid to Britain could risk him unpopularity, defeat and conceivably, impeachment.

After Britain declared war against Hitler in September 1939, Roosevelt opened a secret correspondence with Winston Churchill, the new First Lord of the British navies, whom he had met during World War I while Assistant Secretary of the Navy.

FDR's move immediately raised the suspicions of the U.S. Ambassador in London, Joseph Kennedy. Kennedy was determined to stop another fruitless war that would threaten the lives of his elder sons—Joe, Jack and Bobby.

Why would the President cast out a secret line to a subordinate British official—especially one so notorious for his zeal to fight Hitler? Perhaps he was scheming to help Churchill become Prime Minister, Kennedy thought, after which he would enter Britain's war.

Kennedy's first meeting with the new First Lord increased his suspicions. As he wrote in his diary, when Churchill spoke of "keeping the war away from U.S.A.," the Briton "kept smiling."

Kennedy insisted that Churchill would "blow up the American Embassy and say it was the Germans if it would get the U.S. in. . . . I just don't trust him."

Furious that FDR had not consulted him, Kennedy told his diary that Roosevelt's Churchill ploy revealed his "conniving mind. . . . It's a rotten way to treat his Ambassador. . . . I am disgusted."

As the secret exchanges accelerated by transatlantic telephone and cable, Kennedy recorded his outrage at Roosevelt's "complete lack of understanding. . . . He calls Churchill up and never contacts me. A rotten way to win men's loyalty. . . . I'll have my say some day!"

Before Christmas 1939, Kennedy lunched with King George and Queen Elizabeth at Buckingham Palace.

Determined to prove his immunity to royalty, Kennedy had once told the matronly Elizabeth that in a recent newsreel, she looked "much better" than "that last horrible picture."

As Kennedy told his diary, the Queen now took the "high moral tone" of claiming that her kingdom was defending Western civilization from Hitler.

The Ambassador did not buy it. He felt that England was "fighting for its life" and so were the royals, who were no doubt worried that they "might lose their thrones if this war goes on too long." He felt that despite her lofty rhetoric, the Queen was just as practical as he was: "She doesn't fool herself."

Returning to Washington, Kennedy called on FDR, who was lying regally in bed, pouring himself coffee. Face-to-face, he asked why the President was cozying up to Churchill.

Knowing Kennedy's suspicions, Roosevelt said he had "always disliked Churchill." During their first meeting at a London dinner in 1918, Churchill had "acted like a stinker, lording it all over us."

The President said he was paying Churchill attention because he might become Prime Minister, "and I want to get my hand in now."

As a fund-raiser and strategist, Kennedy had grown close to FDR during his first Presidential campaign in 1932. He was startled to note that Europe's crisis had left his old friend so exhausted and drawn. He told his diary that the President "didn't flash the way he used to."

"What about this third term?" Kennedy asked. "You'll have to run."

"Joe, I can't. I'm tired. I can't take it. What I need is one year's rest. That's what you need too. You may think you're resting, but the subconscious idea of bombings, wars and all that, is going on in your brain all the time. I just won't go on—unless we are in war."

Realizing that he had just told Kennedy that America might fight for England, Roosevelt quickly corrected himself: "Even then, I'll never send an army over. We'll help them, but with supplies."

Back in London on the eve of spring 1940, Kennedy called on Churchill, who was "reading the evening paper, smoking a cigar."

Churchill told him that the "only hope for civilization" was the "absolute defeat" of Hitler: "It will be hell for us, but we will, of course, win the war. . . . For goodness' sake, don't let the President come out with a peace plan! It will just embarrass us, and we won't accept it."

Churchill made it clear that he wanted FDR to stay on for a third term. Kennedy suspected that the First Lord would "stir things up by July in the war, so that Roosevelt would run. He is plenty warlike."

The Ambassador told his diary, "I can't help but remember what Roosevelt said to me over a year ago. He would be a bitter isolationist, then help with arms and money, and then, depending on the state of affairs, get in. I'm very leery."

On Friday, May 10, 1940, with Hitler marching through Europe, the old British bulldog became Prime Minister.

When Kennedy arrived with congratulations, he found Churchill "drinking a Scotch highball, which I felt was indeed not the first one he had drunk that night."

The new Prime Minister offered a cocktail. Annoyed, Kennedy reminded Churchill, "I don't drink."

"My God," replied Churchill. "You make me feel as if I should go around in sackcloth and ashes!"

Churchill had just asked Roosevelt by secret cable for "forty or fifty of your older destroyers"—or else "you may have a completely subjugated, Nazified Europe."

Knowing that Kennedy would influence FDR's decision on the desperately needed aid, Churchill tried to charm the U.S. Ambassador.

He modestly told Kennedy that he wouldn't have made Prime Minister had there "been any meat left on the bone." Describing his work habits, he said he preferred the night. For Churchill, an afternoon nap, putting "my belly on the sheet," was the same as three hours after dark.

As Kennedy told his diary, the Prime Minister conceded that "within a month, there would be bombs and murder and everything terrible happening to England." But he insisted that whatever Hitler attempted, "We shall never be beaten!"

Kennedy was not impressed. He detected "a very definite shadow of defeat" over Churchill.

Realizing that Kennedy had left his office still skeptical, the Prime Minister telephoned him after midnight and implored him not to be "too depressed" about Hitler's might.

By Kennedy's account, Churchill told him that they all had to "put on a good front." He told the Prime Minister that he had "no trouble putting on a front" but couldn't discard "my inner thoughts, based on the facts."

When FDR responded to Churchill's appeal for destroyers, Kennedy was furious at what he considered the President's duplicity.

In writing, Roosevelt icily reminded Churchill that offering military aid was Congress's responsibility. But by telephone, he told Kennedy to assure the Prime Minister that he would do everything he could.

Kennedy carped into his diary that in his passion for war, FDR would stop at nothing short of "complete violation of the law."

Deep inside Kennedy's Embassy was a young code clerk named Tyler Kent, who saw the secret messages between London and Washington and was "shocked" by the "barefaced conspiracy between Churchill and Roosevelt."

To Kent, here was proof the two leaders were covertly dragging an innocent United States into the war on behalf of Soviet Communists and Jews. Kent believed that "all wars" were inspired by international banks "largely controlled by the Jews."

In an effort to stop it, Kent took home copies of the Roosevelt–Churchill messages and shared them with a secret agent named Anna Wolkoff, who had ties to Nazis and Italian Fascists.

Descendant of an old Virginia family, Kent had big plans for himself. Before the 1940 Presidential election, he would present his incriminating secret cache to the U.S. Senate and American press. Scandalized by Roosevelt's hidden machinations, voters would no doubt evict him from office, with Kent a national hero.

But on Monday morning, May 20, 1940, detectives from Scotland Yard pounded on Kent's door. Wearing pajamas, he cried, "Don't come in!"

Smashing into his seedy flat, they accused Kent of stealing U.S. government property. As one of the agents advanced toward his bedroom door, he said, "You can't go in. There's a lady!"

The "scantily attired" lady was Kent's mistress, and she was Jewish. The code clerk's anti-Semitism did not stop him from sleeping with Jewish women.

The detectives ransacked Kent's rooms, including a filing cabinet emblazoned, "THIS IS A JEW'S WAR." They found almost two thousand documents, including a penciled message that Churchill had asked Kennedy to send Roosevelt that very morning.

The day Kent was arrested, Kennedy was relaxing at his rented house near Windsor Castle with the beautiful Clare Boothe Luce, the histrionic, Roosevelt-hating wife of the *Time-Life* magnate Henry Luce.

That spring, Kennedy had been almost as angry as Kent about Roosevelt's secret steps toward war. But when told of Kent's treachery, he worried that people would blame him for the security breach in his Embassy.

Even worse, he realized that when British diplomats pawed through the secret messages they had carried off from Kent's flat, they would learn how vehemently Kennedy had been warning the President against Churchill's warmongering.

Steaming at Kent's insolence, the Ambassador returned to his embassy, where the prisoner was brought to explain himself. Kennedy cried, "Send the traitorous bastard in!"

As Kennedy recalled, the "contemptuous and arrogant" clerk showed "no remorse" and issued "an anti-Semitic blast." Kennedy later insisted that had his country been at war, he would have ordered Kent to be shot.

Instead he approved Churchill's request to have Kent tried in London under the Official Secrets Act, which would allow the whole case to be hushed up.

The Prime Minister warned Kennedy that if Kent were tried in the United States, it would be hard to conceal his secret correspondence with FDR, which might alarm Americans by showing that the two of them had "too close a connection."

Back in Washington, an Assistant Secretary of State, Breckinridge Long, recorded that thanks to Kent's villainy, "our every diplomatic maneuver was exposed to Germany."

Long feared that with access to Kent's documents, Hitler would do what Kent had only hoped. If the evidence of Anglo-American collaboration were published at the height of a close Presidential campaign, it might help depose FDR in favor of someone who would "play ball with Germany or surrender America."

Horrified by that prospect, Long told colleagues, "We must take immediate action to protect the Chief!"

But Franklin Roosevelt was too self-protective to leave his political fate—and the world's—to some mid-level official.

On the same day Tyler Kent was handcuffed and photographed in London, the President happened to be pondering whether to authorize secret, warrantless wiretapping of suspected plotters against the United States.

The Supreme Court had lately declared such surveillance illegal, so Attorney General Robert Jackson had ordered the FBI's Director, J. Edgar Hoover, to stop it.

Furious, Hoover complained to Roosevelt that Jackson's order had kept his agents from listening in on Nazi saboteurs planning to blow up the *Queen Mary*.

Since the President realized that the Germans might use Tyler Kent's stolen treasure in an effort to destroy him, the question of warrantless wiretapping now took on an additional dimension. Such surveillance could offer useful advance warning of such a political assault.

We do not know how much FDR was affected by this consideration, but he signed a secret order giving Hoover blanket authority to "secure information by listening devices."* He told Jackson he was sure that the Court didn't really want the country's "enemies" exploiting its communications system to harm Americans.

Jackson felt that Roosevelt's secret order was probably illegal, but he did not resign. He later wrote that the President usually acted in terms of "right and wrong," not "legal and illegal." Convinced "that his motives were always good," FDR bridled at the notion "that there should be legal limitations on them."

At Roosevelt's instruction, Jackson quietly informed House leaders that he had changed his mind about warrantless wiretapping.†

The President's closest Cabinet friend, Henry Morgenthau, Jr., of the Treasury, noted how FDR would say, "If you are a good Attorney General,

* The instruction specified that such efforts should be kept "to a minimum" and used "insofar as possible" against hostile aliens.
† Jackson did insist that such evidence must not be divulged in court.

tell me how I can do it." As Morgenthau observed, "They always give him a silly laugh, and go out and tell him how to do it."

A strong civil libertarian, Jackson soon came to regret his decision, which gave Presidents almost carte blanche to wiretap anyone they pleased. For the next thirty years, through Richard Nixon, they used Jackson's ruling to have Hoover's FBI pursue their political critics and other enemies of the state, real or imagined.*

Despite his absolute victory over the Attorney General, Hoover pursued his grudge to the end of Jackson's life—and beyond.

In 1954, when Jackson, by then a Supreme Court Justice, died of a heart attack, the FBI Director had his agents tell reporters that the married Justice had salaciously died in the arms of his private secretary and mistress.

In the unbroken cycle of American history, the late Justice's family had to dispense with his Potomac River estate, Hickory Hill, which had served as General George McClellan's military headquarters during the Civil War.

Jackson's heirs sold Hickory Hill to Joe Kennedy's son Jack, a young Senator from Massachusetts, and his pregnant wife, Jacqueline, who created a nursery there. But when the infant died, Jackie found it too painful to remain at Hickory Hill, so the estate was resold to Jack's younger brother Bobby.

---

* In 2005, revelations about President George W. Bush's program of warrantless wiretapping against terrorists opened a similar debate over civil liberties versus national security.

CHAPTER TWENTY-TWO

GLOOM PERSONIFIED

In the wake of his secret wiretapping order, Franklin Roosevelt warned Americans about the hostile agents among them.

On Sunday night, May 26, 1940, in a radio speech from the White House, he predicted that "spies, saboteurs and traitors" with "clever schemes" would try to foment "political paralysis and eventually, a state of panic."

When some listeners responded with vicious letters and telegrams, the President asked J. Edgar Hoover to investigate them. Eager to please the Boss, Hoover widened his net to include anti-Roosevelt Senators and the bitter isolationist Charles Lindbergh.

The icon of the *Spirit of St. Louis* had denounced the President's alarums about Hitler as "hysterical chatter." Joe Kennedy thought that Lindbergh's views were "honest." But privately FDR told friends he was "absolutely convinced" that Lindbergh was a Nazi himself.

Despite Roosevelt's public optimism about stopping Hitler, his wife found him to be "gloom personified." He told her what a "terrible world" it would be if the Nazis prevailed, adding that he and Eleanor would probably be the first Americans sent before the firing squad.

The First Lady's assistant, Malvina Thompson, told her that if Hitler's navies reached the East Coast, she would "kick, scream, pull their hair."

Most Americans would have been shocked to know that in private FDR was so pessimistic about Europe. They saw him as he presented himself—a jovial extrovert, just like Cousin Theodore. In fact, behind his grinning T.R. mask, the second President Roosevelt was a loner.

At a time when most people took First Families at face value, Americans would have been surprised to know that in 1918, the Roosevelts had almost divorced, after Eleanor discovered Franklin's love letters to her social secretary, Lucy Mercer.

The marriage that survived had severe limits. As the First Lady confided to a friend in 1936, she realized "more and more that FDR is a great man" and "he is nice to me, but as a person, I'm a stranger."

The President appreciated his wife's help as a kind of roving Cabinet member without portfolio. But he wished she would be more sensitive about when to give him advice.

Their daughter, Anna, later described how during cocktails with friends, her mother once stormed in with a sheaf of papers, saying, "Now, Franklin, I want to talk to you about this."

As Anna recalled, "He blew his top. . . . He wanted to tell stories and relax and enjoy himself—period."

FDR had grown up accustomed to his mother's constant adoration. With his wife unwilling to provide that and no close male friends, by 1940, he was increasingly relying on two women.

The first was Margaret "Daisy" Suckley, his plain, bookish distant cousin, who smilingly gazed at "My Franklin" while he dictated letters and drove her around the Hyde Park hills in his open Ford Phaeton with special hand controls.

Clearly Daisy hoped for something more. "The President is a MAN—*mentally, physically and spiritually*," she told her diary. "What more can I say?" After driving to a Hyde Park crest they called "Our Hill," Daisy cut out a poem called "Eros" and pasted it into her journal.

The other was Lucy Mercer Rutherfurd, now married to an elderly squire. Despite his pledge to Eleanor never to see his old paramour again, by the early 1940s, FDR was talking to Lucy by telephone as often as twice a week.

Upstairs at the White House, with Eleanor gone, one of Roosevelt's sons once walked in as Lucy was rubbing his father's polio-afflicted legs. The President suavely introduced her as an "old friend."

When FDR died in 1945 while signing documents at his cottage in Warm Springs, Georgia, the faces of Daisy and Lucy were probably the last he saw on this earth.

*   *   *

Roosevelt's emotional and physical need to have admiring women around did not end with these two women. He persuaded Dorothy Schiff, the wealthy young owner of the *New York Post*, to build a hilltop cottage at Hyde Park, next to his own.

Much later Schiff recalled the President as a "warm, sexy guy," and said that "in a rather sweet way, he was fairly bold, and everything about his body—except his legs—were so strong." *

At least one Roosevelt son later insisted that his father had been intimate with his gregarious secretary, Missy LeHand. Joe Kennedy thought so too. When FDR once asked him to give up a too prominent lady friend, Kennedy allegedly retorted, "Not until you get rid of Missy LeHand!"

But by 1940, Daisy and Lucy were probably the only human beings to whom the President really opened himself. Feeling bruised by public life, he once scrawled to Daisy,

> I found this the other day—by A. Lincoln during some of the difficult days of the war:
>
> > "If I were trying to read, much less answer all the attacks on me, this shop might well be closed. . . . I do the best I know how, the very best I can. . . . If the end brings me out all right, what is said against me will not amount to anything. If the end brings me out all *wrong,* then angels swearing I was right would make no difference." †
>
> All the same—no matter how philosophic he was in public— these attacks did hurt A. Lincoln. . . . But he kept his peace—that was and is the great lesson. . . .
>
> Did you know that you alone have known that I was a bit "cast down" these past weeks? I *couldn't* let anyone else know it—but somehow I seem to tell you all these things and what I don't happen to tell you, you seem to know anyway!

---

* In 1978, Schiff told the current author she was annoyed at a biographer who suggested that she and the President had sexually gone further than "the edge of the ledge."

† Lincoln was referring in 1864 to Congressional complaints about his military "blunders." In 1969 and 1974, President Nixon used the famous quote to defend himself from attacks over the Vietnam War and Watergate.

*   *   *

Like Cousin Theodore, FDR enjoyed reading and telling Lincoln stories.

One favorite was how the Great Emancipator rescued a British diplomat who had locked himself inside Lafayette Park during a tryst with the Spanish ambassador's wife. As the tale was told, William Seward helped Lincoln find a ladder, which they used to pull the couple over the iron fence.

Roosevelt had also been amused to find that his press secretary, Steve Early, was the grand-nephew of the Confederate general who had raided Lincoln's Washington in 1864.

Appalled like Cousin Theodore at how Lincoln's party exploited his legend while they "repudiated" his beliefs, FDR called on fellow Democrats to claim the sixteenth President as "one of our own."

In June 1940, Roosevelt was absorbed in Carl Sandburg's popular new history of Lincoln's Presidency. Sandburg had written FDR that he was the "best light of democracy" as President "since Lincoln," and warned him to "expect me some day at the White House door with a guitar." Roosevelt thanked Sandburg for his "fine sense of justice."

Now, during an off-the-record meeting with young people in the State Dining Room, FDR compared Lincoln's war troubles to his own.

When one guest accused Roosevelt of dropping his New Deal reforms to attend to the war in Europe, he replied, "Young man, I think you are very sincere. Have you read Carl Sandburg's Lincoln? . . . Lincoln was one of the unfortunate people called a 'politician.' . . . He was sad because he couldn't get it all at once. And nobody can!"

Despite his old hero worship, FDR rarely mentioned Theodore Roosevelt. He did not wish to build up a Republican, and he privately felt that his achievements had long ago surpassed T.R.'s.

He wrote a journalist friend in 1935 that while his cousin could do "superficial" things like stir people's "enthusiasm," he never aroused their "truly profound moral and social convictions."

By the end of his second term, FDR's Hyde Park branch of the Roosevelts was no longer on speaking terms with those from Oyster Bay. Frustrated in his ambitions to follow his father to the White House, Theodore Roosevelt, Jr., and most of his siblings had responded to Franklin's political rise with disbelief, envy and anger.

By 1940, Ted and his sister Alice Longworth were both leaders of the isolationist lobby America First, campaigning against their cousin's re-election. Alice cried, "I'd rather vote for Hitler!"

Ted wrote Alice he was sure Franklin was "itching" to get into Europe's war—both "as a means of bolstering himself" and because of his "megalomania."

The plainspoken Alice later insisted that her motives in joining the isolationist league were more basic: "Mischief and dislike of Franklin. . . . Anything to annoy Franklin!"

The one gap in the Oyster Bay clan's opposition was T.R.'s son Kermit, whom FDR was always prodding to switch parties and become a Democrat. When Kermit once disappeared, FDR asked J. Edgar Hoover to find and contact his mistress for information, so that Kermit could be located and treated for his drinking and venereal disease.*

In June 1940, just before the opposing party's Philadelphia convention, FDR drove most of his Oyster Bay cousins wild by putting two T.R. Republicans in his Cabinet—ex–Secretary of State Henry Stimson for the War Department, and Frank Knox, the 1936 Republican Vice Presidential nominee, for the Navy.

With the growing world emergency, Roosevelt wanted to make his Cabinet more bipartisan. But he also knew that with two of the biggest Republican stars on his side, it would be more awkward for the opposition to vilify his foreign policy.

That month, Hitler stunned Americans by conquering France. Responding to the gravity of the hour, Henry Luce wanted Republicans at Philadelphia to choose the man they considered to be their biggest internationalist.

Wendell Willkie was a New York utilities man who had until recently been a Democrat. With Luce's encouragement, *Time* insisted that Willkie was saying "what many a U.S. citizen believed."

In a well-orchestrated campaign, powerful Northeastern Republicans eager to aid England made sure the convention floor was deluged

* Kermit sadly took his own life in 1943. After Pearl Harbor, his brother Theodore Jr. became an Army Brigadier General and died of a heart attack in France after landing there on D-Day.

by pro-Willkie telegrams and pro-Willkie shouts from the balconies. (One shouter was a future President, Gerald Ford.) Delegates surprised even themselves by choosing the dark horse big businessman on the sixth ballot.

Estranged from his Indiana wife, Billie, Willkie was conducting a romance with the *New York Herald Tribune*'s book editor, Irita Van Doren, that was almost a marriage.

After his nomination, Willkie convinced his lawful wife, who still loved him, to campaign with him and share his hotel rooms. Not devoid of humor, Billie told him, "Politics makes strange bedfellows!" *

---

* Mrs. Willkie's witticism was soon repeated within political circles. The novelist-playwright Gore Vidal used it in his 1960 drama *The Best Man*. In Vidal's play, the remark is made by the wife of an adulterous Presidential aspirant who is once again cohabiting with him. When Senator John Kennedy read the script of the play in 1960, he asked, "Is Gore writing about me?"

CHAPTER TWENTY-THREE

SALUTE YOUR CAESAR?

Franklin Roosevelt was unsettled by Willkie's nomination, and to those around the President, it showed. Unlike his earlier opponents, Herbert Hoover and Alf Landon, Willkie would be difficult to marginalize as a mossback.

Revealing his anxiety that Willkie might win, FDR told Eleanor that despite his sterling public image, his challenger was really a "crook." Willkie reminded him of "the sleight-of-hand fellow at the Dutchess County Fair."

During a Presidential fishing trip, when someone caught an eel, Roosevelt ordered it named "Wendell Willkie."

The President asked his Cabinet to tie Willkie to the "corporate state" as the "original idea" of the Italian Fascist dictator Benito Mussolini.

Taking care to use a middleman, Roosevelt asked J. Edgar Hoover to investigate Willkie's history. Rumor had it that Willkie's paternal forebears were Polish, and that he had changed his family name to disguise it. If true, millions of Polish-American voters would be offended by such bigotry.

Possibly worried that Willkie might be elected and discover the FBI's complicity in such a smear campaign, Hoover refused.*

* * *

* Willkie turned out not to be Polish.

Since George Washington forswore a third term in 1796, no other President had dared to violate his unwritten law.* Thus Roosevelt felt that his best strategy for 1940 would be to feign extreme reluctance, with Democrats demanding that he stay at his plow to guide them through the world emergency.

On Tuesday evening, July 16, 1940, in Chicago, FDR's third-term "draft" was overseen by his aide Harry Hopkins, wearing pajamas, shouting into his hotel bathroom telephone. On the convention floor, a Soviet witness noted the delegates' "cries of ecstasy" when Roosevelt's name was mentioned.

From his hidden eyrie, Hopkins had warned party leaders that the President would decline the third-term prize if he should be opposed by more than 150 of the delegates.

Amid growing worry that Roosevelt wanted to join the European war, when the first and only ballot arrived, the opposition numbered 148. Among the delegates who turned thumbs-down on the President was young Joe Kennedy, Jr., defying heavy White House pressure.

To thwart public anxiety about Roosevelt's intentions, the party's proposed platform included a pledge to stay out of "foreign wars." Working through Hopkins, FDR added the phrase "except in case of attack."

The platform writers thought the addition anodyne, but the President privately considered this a loophole that would let him, if necessary, take the country to war. Privately he said, "If someone attacks us, it isn't a foreign war, is it?"

Roosevelt remembered that McKinley and Wilson had used such attacks to go to war. He also knew that such presumed "aggression" was not always what it appeared. For example, the much ballyhooed "assault" on the USS *Maine*, which McKinley cited to enter the Spanish-American War, was later found to have been just a boiler room accident.†

---

* T.R. sought the Presidency on the Bull Moose ticket in 1912, but he had only been elected President once, in 1904.

† In 1964, when Lyndon Johnson mistook alarming signals from the Gulf of Tonkin for a North Vietnamese "offensive," he got Congress to approve military retaliation, almost unanimously. For the next nine years, LBJ and his successor, Richard Nixon, used the Tonkin Gulf Resolution as license to wage and expand their war in Indochina. In 2003, citing evidence of Saddam Hussein's possession and impending use of weapons of mass destruction, which later proved mistaken, President George W. Bush and leaders of an international coalition went to war against Iraq.

*   *   *

After midnight on Friday, July 19, Roosevelt addressed the Chicago convention and the nation by radio from the Diplomatic Reception Room.

Before such appearances, FDR slipped a bridge into the gap between his lower teeth to avoid making a whistling sound. The Mansion's air-conditioning system had been shut off in deference to the President's troubled sinuses, so his shirt was drenched with sweat.

He told the radio audience that "lying awake, as I have many nights," he had decided that his "conscience" would not let him refuse a third term.

Interior Secretary Harold Ickes thought the Boss was overdoing it: such "undignified playacting" would not "fool" people.

Girding for a brutal autumn campaign, Roosevelt went on to denounce "appeaser fifth-columnists"* who charged him with "hysteria and warmongering."

Roosevelt's warning about enemies inside America was not offhand. He was reading confidential reports that secret hordes of foreign agents were working to oust him.

"You can't say that everyone who is opposed to Roosevelt is pro-Nazi," he told visitors to the Oval Office. "But you *can* say . . . that everyone who is pro-Hitler in this country is also pro-Willkie." There was "no question" that the Axis "would give anything in the world to have me licked."

Hitler's chief diplomat in Washington, the unctuous Hans Thomsen, was funneling money to isolationists on Capitol Hill, publishing houses and advertising agencies. Thomsen wanted Americans to know that Roosevelt was plotting the early deaths of their husbands and sons.

Suspicious about the fast-growing influence of America First, FDR once wrote Early, "Will you find out from someone—perhaps the FBI—Who is paying for this?"

He knew that during an overheated campaign, even a false rumor—echoed by what he termed the "eighty-five percent" opposition press—could provoke the whole electorate.

Bitterly he remembered how a Senator had falsely claimed after a

---

* Meaning secret followers of Hitler within America.

meeting in 1939 that FDR had secretly confided that he would defend Western Europe all the way to the Rhine. The result was a national furor.

Now, to prevent more such damaging misquotations during his contest with Willkie, Roosevelt had a secret recording machine installed under the Oval Office.

Most mornings at the Mansion, the President swung himself into his wheelchair—an armless kitchen seat fitted with bicycle wheels—and wheeled himself at high speed down Jefferson's outdoor colonnade to the Presidential office.

His office was not the one created by Cousin Theodore. Early in his term, styling himself an architect, FDR had sketched on paper how the West Wing must be rebuilt—a new upper floor, an indoor swimming pool for his polio therapy and a new Oval Office, relocated to the southwest.

With tall windows overlooking the South Grounds, the Presidential chamber was painted gray-green and hung with dark green curtains and U.S. eagle cornices, which FDR designed.

In that Oval Office in August 1940, the President sat talking with a political aide, Lowell Mellett, about the fall campaign. He would have been aghast to know that with his secret recorder running, he was making a permanent record of his hidden-hand efforts to sling mud at Wendell Willkie.

Referring to his foe's affair with Irita Van Doren, Roosevelt said, "Now you'd be *amazed* at how this story about the *gal* is spreading around the country."

Noting that a President shouldn't soil himself with "dirty politics," he asked Mellett to get voters murmuring about Van Doren: "Spread it as a word-of-mouth thing. . . . We can't have any of our principal speakers refer to it, but the people down the line can get it out."

Ridiculing the fact that Willkie's wife was campaigning with him, FDR went on, "Now, Mrs. Willkie may not have been *hired,* but in *effect* she's been hired to return to Wendell and smile and make this campaign with him. Now whether there was a *money* price behind it, I don't know."

The President told Mellett that Willkie should be compared with the corrupt, womanizing ex–New York Mayor Jimmy Walker, who was "openly living with this gal. . . . An extremely attractive little tart. . . . Jimmy and his wife had separated."

FDR recalled that when Walker was put on trial in Albany, "Jimmy goes and hires his former wife for ten thousand bucks. . . . Lives with him—ostensibly—in the same suite in the hotel, and on Sunday, the two of them go to Mass at the Albany cathedral together. Price? Ten thousand dollars!"

Having set an anti-Willkie whispering campaign in motion, Roosevelt soon had his own scare. The Republicans discovered strange, dreamy letters from his 1940 running mate, Henry Wallace, to a guru and a fortune-teller whom FDR's handlers called "Madame Zenah."

Once again the President turned to Bob Jackson: "You've got the FBI. Can't you find Henry in bed with this woman? . . . Everyone would understand that, but nobody would understand the writing of this kind of letters without any romance in it."

Waiting for a Wallace scandal to break, Roosevelt's aide Dave Niles felt as if he lost "fifty pounds in three weeks." By Niles's account, the scandal was contained by blackmail:

"We went out and dug some dirty stuff on Willkie, with photographs showing that Willkie's father had been buried in potter's field as a drunkard with whom Willkie would have nothing to do. . . . We let the Republicans know that if they used the Wallace stuff, we were going to use the stuff on Willkie."

Turning from low politics to high, Roosevelt in August 1940 read a new appeal from Churchill: "It has now become most urgent for you to let us have the destroyers, motor boats and flying boats for which we have asked. . . . Mr. President, in the long history of the world, this is a thing to do now."

In London, the Prime Minister bluntly warned Joe Kennedy that if FDR denied his request, "we will all go down the drain together" and "you will be taking orders from the Germans."

FDR privately conceded that Britain's survival "might very possibly depend on their getting these destroyers."

His new Navy Secretary, Frank Knox, suggested offering fifty World War I–era destroyers and the other ships Churchill wanted in exchange for long-term rights to British bases from Newfoundland to the West Indies.

FDR liked the idea, but the timing was awful. On the eve of the fall campaign, isolationists would howl that such a gift would pull America into Britain's war—and that if Hitler vanquished the British, he would use the U.S. ships against America.

Roosevelt had already heard this complaint from the Democratic chairman of the Senate Foreign Relations Committee, Key Pittman of Nevada. As Harold Ickes recalled, when Pittman came to see FDR, he was "so drunk that he could hardly navigate" and "pawed the President, much to his disgust."

Roosevelt explained to Pittman he couldn't order the British fleet to do anything. For a moment, he feared that the Senator would blab the comment to the newspapers. Then he realized that Pittman was "too drunk to do that."

To mollify the isolationists, the President insisted that any destroyers-for-bases deal include a pledge from Churchill that if Hitler captured England, the vessels would "sail for North America or British Empire ports" for use by the United States.

Knowing that Joe Kennedy might try to sabotage any destroyer deal, FDR did his secret bargaining through the British Embassy in Washington.

Furious that the "inconsiderate" President was cutting him out of the action, Kennedy warned Roosevelt's aides that such secret negotiations might subject FDR to charges that he was "deceiving the U.S. people" by concealing his dealings with Britain.

The Ambassador was happy to suggest he might soon make such accusations himself—in public. He told his diary that by now, he was almost certain that Roosevelt "wants to get us into war."

Before taking his Destroyer Deal to Congress, Roosevelt tried to get Willkie to remove it from politics by blessing it.

But Republican leaders warned Willkie that the President would exploit any such cooperation to harm him.

FDR sent a mutual friend, the Kansas publisher William Allen White, to intervene with his opponent, but White failed. He cabled Roosevelt, "I can't guarantee either of you to the other, which is funny, for I admire and respect you both."

White explained that Willkie was feeling a "natural diffidence" about defying his party's establishment "before his ears are dry."

With Willkie refusing to play ball, Democratic Senators warned the President that a Destroyer Deal would have "no chance" in Congress. Therefore Roosevelt leaned on Robert Jackson for a written opinion that the President could send the destroyers to Churchill without Congressional approval.

As with warrantless wiretapping, Jackson gave the Boss what he wanted. The grateful FDR told him that when the Republicans "knocked off" his head for sidestepping the House and Senate, "they will get into a row over *your opinion*, instead of *my deal*. . . . After all, Bob, you are not running for office!"

Nevertheless Roosevelt remained anxious that his Destroyer Deal might cause his defeat or even impeachment. He told aides, "Congress is going to raise hell about this, but even another day's delay may mean the end of civilization."

On Tuesday, September 3, 1940, while returning by train from a "defense tour" of West Virginia, Roosevelt announced the Destroyer Deal to the traveling press.

Straining for historical precedents, he called it "probably the most important thing that has come for American defense since the Louisiana Purchase." He noted that when Jefferson bought Louisiana, he did not bother the Senate for "any two thirds vote."

Hoping to use the deal against FDR, Willkie called it "the most dictatorial and arbitrary act of any President in the history of the United States." *

But Americans accepted the President's argument that he had made a "good trade"—the equivalent of exchanging fifty muzzle-loading Civil War rifles for "seven modern guns." Eleanor wrote daughter Anna, "Pa is thrilled over acquiring the naval bases."

---

* Later Willkie said he regretted that comment more than any other he made during the campaign.

Henry Stimson told his diary that by steeling the British to stave off Hitler, the Destroyer Deal might prove "the turning point in the tide of the war."

But Roosevelt was not given even a moment to savor his accomplishment. At the end of September 1940, imperial Japan joined Hitler and Mussolini in their effort to dominate the globe.

FDR warned his country by radio that "never before, since Jamestown and Plymouth Rock, has our American civilization been in such danger as now."

With his secret recorder running in the Oval Office, Roosevelt told his two House leaders, Sam Rayburn and John McCormack, that a President Willkie couldn't cope with such ominous news.

The "trouble with Willkie," he explained, was that "he will say *anything.*" His opponent was borrowing "the tactics of Hitler." (FDR pronounced it "Hit-lah.") Willkie was saying "the same thing so often that after a while, people are going to believe it."

Acidly FDR speculated that Republicans might bribe George Gallup with a "good round sum" to "do the greatest harm to the Democratic ticket." If Gallup wished to "sell out," this was probably his "best chance."

Roosevelt assured Rayburn and McCormack that "crooked" Republican pollsters would claim that Willkie was gaining momentum.

After showing the challenger in a "bad slump" in September, "they're going to start Willkie pickin' up, pickin' up, pickin' up. . . . You know what a horse race is like. . . . Three lengths behind, coming around into the stretch. And then . . . he gains a length. . . . Gives people the idea that this fellow can still win!"

In October 1940 came the Republican surge that Roosevelt had feared.

During the summer, when voters felt that Hitler was about to seize England, they had embraced the President to defend them against the storm. But now that Hitler seemed to be stalled, the ambitious Willkie was gaining traction from Republican charges that Roosevelt was making "secret deals" with Britain that would take the country into an unnecessary war.

Decrying "Mr. Third-term Candidate," Willkie said, "If his promise to keep our boys out of foreign wars is no better than his promise to balance the budget, they're already almost on the transports!"

The powerful union leader John L. Lewis warned Americans by radio that a "scheming" Roosevelt would make "cannon fodder" of their sons: "You who may be about to die in a foreign war—created at the whim of an international meddler—should you salute your Caesar?"

Assuming his statesman's mantle, the President had pledged not to campaign, except to correct "falsifications of fact." Now in the face of the Willkie riptide, Roosevelt's managers implored him to go out and answer the charges. Eleanor told him that he "simply *must* make some speeches." There was "so much scurrilous stuff."

Roosevelt agreed to make five major addresses. He wrote political friends that the European crisis required him to be "within twelve hours by rail of the Capital." Flying was "impossible, because with my large group, it would take a whole squadron of planes to move me."

FDR's Secret Service man Mike Reilly noted that the crippled President also "must have realized that he had no chance of crawling from a plane wreck."

Reilly and Roosevelt's protective detail were anxious about his decision to campaign before open crowds. But the President had long ago braced himself for that kind of physical danger.

As President-elect in 1933, he had almost been killed by a gunman in Miami. Cousin Theodore had warned him that if he stayed in politics, he might one day face an assassin and had better prepare for it.

On Wednesday, October 23, 1940, before a vast Philadelphia crowd, Roosevelt offered his "solemn assurance" that there was "no secret treaty . . . no secret understanding in any shape or form" to enter "some foreign war."

But to Joe Kennedy, FDR's "assurance" was a provocation. Certain that the President was hiding the truth, Kennedy was the single American with the credentials, the evidence and the motive to warn voters that Roosevelt was secretly conspiring with Churchill for war.

Kennedy's relationship with his old friend was fast unraveling. From London in August, he had complained to the President by telephone, "I am not doing a damn thing here that amounts to anything."

Roosevelt replied that it helped British "morale" to have Kennedy in the British capital—a whopper, since FDR knew that Kennedy was rattling his British friends with warnings that Hitler would soon trounce them.

Roosevelt politely asked whether the Ambassador was optimistic about British survival. Kennedy replied, "Yes, if you mean they are willing to fight with broken bottles!"

Kennedy wrote a friend back in America that he had been "damned fresh" with FDR, but that the President had to take it. If he quit his Embassy in protest before the election, it "would be quite embarrassing to him."

Kennedy added that "every conversation I have is tapped," and that Roosevelt would use his private comments against him, "should some showdown occur." He complained that the columnist Joseph Alsop, a Roosevelt cousin whom Kennedy called "that little pimp," was already using access to his secret cables to embarrass him.

A friend at the State Department asked Kennedy if he knew where Alsop was getting his "inspiration." Referring to FDR, Kennedy replied, "I suspect!"

Lying in bed as German bombs lit the London skies, Kennedy wondered whether he would ever be reunited with his wife and nine children, now returned to safety in America. Feeling "damned sick and disgusted," he told his diary he would "resign today" but for fear of being charged with cowardice under the Blitz.

In October 1940, Kennedy told British diplomats that he would fly back to America and issue a "sensational" broadside against the President. Noting that fellow Irish-Americans had no love for their British oppressors, he said he was ready to "put twenty-five million Catholic votes behind Wendell Willkie to throw Roosevelt out."

Worried about what havoc Kennedy might create in the United States, Winston Churchill beseeched the Ambassador to remain at his Embassy. Lying boldly for his country, Churchill told Kennedy, "I don't want a new man over here."

But Kennedy told the Prime Minister his appeal was no use. He was "having a row with Roosevelt" and he was going home.

CHAPTER TWENTY-FOUR

WE HAVE AVOIDED A PUTSCH

With his acute eye for people's vulnerabilities, Roosevelt explained to his son-in-law that Joe Kennedy was "terrifically spoiled at an early age by huge financial success, thoroughly patriotic, thoroughly selfish and thoroughly obsessed with the idea that he must leave each of his nine children with a million dollars apiece. . . .

"To him, the future of a small capitalist class is safer under a Hitler than under a Churchill. . . . Sometimes I think I am 200 years older than he is!"

FDR felt that Kennedy was so gloomy about England's chances because he distrusted democracy. If Joe ever became President, he would "give us a fascist form of government," ignoring Congress in favor of a "powerful committee under himself as chairman."

But Roosevelt knew that his reelection might now hinge on the "temperamental Irish boy" who was returning from London aboard Pan American's great new flying boat, the *Atlantic Clipper*.

Worried that Willkie or his people might get at Joe before he could, Roosevelt sent the Ambassador a cable at each of his stops across the Atlantic, asking him to come "immediately after your arrival" in New York to the White House.

As Kennedy told his diary, Roosevelt's obvious efforts to capture him made him feel all the more "indignant."

On Sunday, October 27, 1940, Kennedy's plane skidded onto the water off La Guardia Airport's Marine Terminal. He called the President, who was lunching with Speaker Rayburn and Rayburn's young Texas protégé, Congressman Lyndon Johnson.

FDR said, "Ah, Joe, it is so good to hear your voice." He hoped that Kennedy and his wife could be at the White House that evening "for a little family dinner. I'm dying to talk to you."

Johnson never forgot that as Roosevelt spoke those words, he drew his fingers across his neck as if slitting Kennedy's throat.*

Besieged by reporters at La Guardia, Kennedy said, "Nothing to say until I've seen the President. . . . I'll talk a lot after I'm finished with that!"

Kennedy knew how Roosevelt could overwhelm him, especially in the presence of his wife, Rose, who felt the President had "more charm than any man I ever met."

Thus before their confrontation, he armed himself by scrawling notes. For example, "You can't say you don't want to go to war if you listen with great intolerance to somebody like Col. Lindbergh who points out what he thinks are the dangers."

That evening, when the Kennedys walked into the Mansion's upstairs Oval Room, they found the President behind his desk. As Rose recalled, he was "shaking a cocktail shaker and reaching over for a few lumps of ice with his powerful hands."

The massive oak desk was a symbol of British-American friendship. U.S. sailors in the Arctic had discovered the abandoned HMS *Resolute,* which was returned to the British. As a thank-you gesture, Queen Victoria had some of its timbers made into a desk, which she presented to President Rutherford Hayes.†

To "butter up Joe," the President had also invited Kennedy's friends Missy LeHand and South Carolina Senator James Byrnes—"proving," Kennedy felt, "that Roosevelt didn't want to have it out with me alone."

---

* In 1998, ex-Senator Eugene McCarthy told the current author that when he met with President Johnson in the Cabinet Room in April 1968, LBJ assured McCarthy that he would not block him or any other Presidential aspirant—even his bitter foe Robert Kennedy. McCarthy recalled that as Johnson gave him this assurance, he pantomimed slitting Kennedy's throat. McCarthy did not know that LBJ had watched FDR perform the same act at the White House in October 1940.

† In the early 1960s, the desk became famous after President John Kennedy moved it to the Oval Office, where his son John Jr. was photographed crawling out through the knee-hole door added by FDR to hide his leg braces.

After finishing the Sunday night repast of scrambled eggs and sausages, Kennedy blurted out, "Since it doesn't seem possible for me to see the President alone, I guess I'll just have to say what I am going to say in front of everybody."

He told FDR, "You have given me a bad deal." He was "damn sore" at being shut out of the destroyer bargaining, forcing him to "smash my way through" by warning Churchill that if he were not cut in, he would be "most unfriendly" to Britain.

Roosevelt blamed it all on the State Department. He told Joe he hadn't known that his old valued friend had been so mistreated. ("Which isn't true," Kennedy thought. "Someone is lying . . . and I suspect the President.")

FDR insisted that behind the campaign rhetoric, there was no serious difference between Willkie and himself on the war. Willkie's supposed isolationism was merely "a ploy that worked too well."

Roosevelt praised the "good speeches" that Kennedy's son Joe was making for the Democratic ticket. By Joe Senior's later account, the President suggested that if the Ambassador stayed on his reservation in 1940, he would back young Joe for Governor of Massachusetts in 1942.

He also dangled the prospect of a new prestigious job for the elder Kennedy, telling Rose that she shouldn't let Joe "think he is going to get away from me and loaf."

Some later speculated that FDR threatened Kennedy with embarrassing information collected by American and British intelligence. Lyndon Johnson insisted that during their showdown, Roosevelt threw "the red meat on the floor," warning Kennedy, "Give me public support or I'll throw you to the public as a pro-German bastard!"

If such a threat was made, it was probably issued elsewhere, and by others. It was hardly Roosevelt's style to threaten a dinner guest personally in front of his wife.

Finally Roosevelt asked Kennedy to endorse him on the radio. "All right," said Kennedy. "But I will pay for it myself, show it to nobody in advance, and say what I wish."

Before he could change his mind, Missy LeHand grabbed a telephone and asked the Democratic National Committee to sell its existing Tuesday night broadcast time to Kennedy.

Kennedy left Rose behind to spend the night. Once again he had succumbed to the man who had given him honors and office.

Still he left the White House convinced "that deep down in his heart, Roosevelt had a decidedly anti-Catholic feeling."

He later noted that Alice Roosevelt Longworth had told a friend that T.R. too "was anti-Catholic," and that the prejudice was "firmly embedded in the Roosevelt family."

During the final week of the campaign, emotions ran high.

At a Washington cocktail party, Roy Howard of the Scripps Howard newspapers bloviated that "Roosevelt wants to get us into war," but that the "real danger" was the Communists, not the Nazis. Howard boasted that his candidate, Wendell Willkie, if elected, would bargain with Hitler.

Charles Lindbergh's close friend and adviser, Colonel Truman Smith, agreed. He told Howard and other guests that the "syphilitic son of a bitch" in the Oval Office was "more paralyzed from the waist up than he is from the waist down."

When Harold Ickes heard about Smith's comment, he demanded that the insolent colonel be driven out of the Army.

On Monday evening, October 28, FDR greeted twenty-two thousand cheering supporters at Madison Square Garden. Looking up at him from the front of the throng was the smiling Lucy Rutherfurd, escorted by several New York City detectives.

By now running neck and neck with Willkie, the President needed the comfort and reassurance of Lucy's presence. Normally he did not risk having her sitting so prominently at a public event.

The next day in Washington at high noon, Roosevelt went to the War Department and presided over a lottery starting the first peacetime draft in American history. Sixteen million men, aged twenty-one to thirty-five, would have to register.

During the summer of 1940, the isolationist Burton Wheeler of Montana had warned that fellow Senators who voted for the draft would be "driving nails in their coffins."

An Ohio Democrat warned the President that his draft bill was "fraught with political disaster." Roosevelt retorted that if Lincoln had authorized an earlier draft, the Civil War would "in all probability have ended by the end of 1862."

Recalling that FDR had supported "peacetime conscription or compulsory military training" after World War I, the perennial Socialist Presidential candidate Norman Thomas accused the President of lurching toward "fascism."

Roosevelt demanded that Thomas withdraw his "grossly unfair" insinuation that he would grab political power by drafting young men.

To the President's immense relief, Wendell Willkie scuttled the opposition to a draft by endorsing "some form of military service." But a columnist predicted that "when men are actually called to the colors," it would start a "strong emotional current" against Roosevelt.

Democratic leaders begged the President to stay away from the opening ceremony at the War Department, broadcast on radio, that could ultimately send young Americans to their deaths.

FDR felt that staying away would be "cowardly." He reminded the audience that the "muster" was an "old and accepted principle." Nine of the original thirteen states had required every man to serve, bringing "his musket and his powder horn."

Donning a linen blindfold made from a chair used when the Declaration of Independence was signed, Henry Stimson took the first blue capsule from a large goldfish bowl and gave it to Roosevelt, who personally read the draft number aloud.

Radio listeners could hear a woman scream. Across the country, Democratic precinct captains bit their nails. The election was only a week ahead.

That Tuesday evening, Joe Kennedy was scheduled to announce his Presidential endorsement on nationwide CBS Radio. To build suspense, he had refused any hint of who it was going to be.

His friend Clare Boothe Luce, who knew him so intimately, was sure FDR must have taken Joe into camp.

Holed up writing his speech at the Waldorf-Astoria in New York, half-ashamed and unwilling to face her, Kennedy refused her calls. Finally Clare sent him a letter that struck him where it hurt:

Clare Boothe Luce, 1940

Joe dear: —

I've tried all day to get you. . . . I want only for you to know, when you make that radio address tomorrow night, throwing as you will, all your prestige and reputation for wisdom . . . into the scales for F.D.R., you'll probably turn the trick for him. . . . I believe with all my heart and soul you will be doing America a terrible disservice.

I know too well your private opinions not also to know that half of what you say (*if* you say it) you *really* won't believe in your heart. . . . Perhaps I will deserve to be smacked for doubting you, but I'm so *terribly* frightened for this country. . . .

Please remember that the rift that the election of F.D.R. will drive through the national heart is the same rift your speech in support of a third term is going to drive through mine tomorrow.

Gee, Joe, I know I don't know from nuthin' about great political problems, but I know good guys and great guys and patriots when I see them. Our friend Willkie is all three. And I've *always* believed you were all three. And if ever there was a time when we didn't need "smart politicians" and all the rest of that nonsense but *good* men . . . this *is* the time.

Well, *these* are the good old days now. At least they are until you speak tomorrow. And sure we won't know the difference a hundred years from now, but I'll know it tomorrow and for many years thereafter.

Love, Clare

Holy God, the thing I can't bear is everybody telling me . . . "See, what we told you about Kennedy is true!" *

That evening, Kennedy gave his radio address endorsing the President. Complaining that Republicans were accusing FDR of "trying to involve this country in the world war," he insisted "such a charge is *false.*"

Having heard all he needed to, Roosevelt wired him, "I have just listened to a great speech. Thank you."

Listening in London, Kennedy's air attaché, who had heard his private fulminations against Roosevelt's warmongering, carped that the Ambassador had proved he was "exactly the opportunist that everyone now thinks he is."

That final week of the campaign, FDR's managers implored him to reassure "American mothers." The President replied that the platform had already ruled out "foreign wars, in case of attack." But a speechwriter told him, "You've got to say it—again and again and again."

Thus on Halloween Eve, Roosevelt brought a Boston Garden crowd to its feet by declaring, "I have said this before, but I shall say it again and again and again: *Your boys are not going to be sent into any foreign wars!*"

---

* For months, Luce's friends had warned her that Roosevelt would ultimately buy off the craven Kennedy's support. Luce told the current author in 1978 that Joe's speech for FDR remained such a sore subject that she did not ask him why he had caved in until the summer of 1956, while they sunned themselves near Kennedy's rented villa on the Côte d'Azur. As she recalled, Kennedy gave her his explanation "with a Cheshire cat smile—like Jimmy Carter's."

This pledge was technically honest. Roosevelt took refuge in his private contention that no war would be "foreign" if America were attacked.

But it was scarcely the President's noblest moment. In years to come, Republican agitators like Clare Luce would cite the speech as evidence that FDR had "lied us into a war because he did not have the political courage to lead us into it."

When Willkie heard Roosevelt's Boston pledge, he told his aides, "That hypocritical son of a bitch! This is going to beat me!"

Like a little boy trying to top himself, the President went to Buffalo and offered a more blanket pledge that would later be even harder to defend: "Your President says this country is not going to war."

Now it was Election Night 1940. After his nervous moment sitting at his mother's mahogany dining table, the political trends turned against Willkie. FDR had the doors flung open, and jubilant friends and family flowed in with congratulations.

Although victory was in his pocket, the President remained haunted by the country's near-conquest by the ominous forces behind the well-meaning Willkie. Before going to bed, he said, "We seem to have avoided a *putsch*."

Hitler's diplomats in Washington informed the Reichschancellery in Berlin that Roosevelt's reelection was horrendous news. With his "irreconcilable hostility" to Germany, FDR would now mold the "easily excitable character" of his fellow Americans to bring the United States into the war.

That very same week, after a secret London trial, Tyler Kent was jailed on the Isle of Wight.

Released after World War II, the ex–code clerk returned to America and wed a rich, older divorcée who, despite his verbal abuse, bought him yachts and expensive clothes and a weekly newspaper in northeastern Florida, which Kent turned into a "hate sheet," lambasting Jews, blacks and Franklin Roosevelt.

After squandering his wife's fortune on libel suits and currency schemes, Kent fled to Mexico, then finally settled in a house trailer in Mission, Texas.

Six years before his death in 1988, Kent emerged from seclusion to attend a Chicago meeting of Holocaust deniers, where he fulminated that "supposed Nazi atrocities" were Jewish rants about "the hoax of the twentieth century."

Had Franklin Roosevelt bowed to the polls in 1940, he would not have dared push public opinion toward aiding Britain while trying to win a third term. On the eve of that election year, when Gallup asked Americans what problem was "most important," forty-seven percent—by far the largest number—had said, "Keeping out of war."

But Roosevelt knew that, especially in crisis, a President's job is not to follow the public but lead it. Part of his genius was framing events like the fall of France for Americans in ways that advanced his cause.

Another part was his feline sensitivity to how far he could change people's minds at a given time. As King George wrote FDR in 1941, "You have led public opinion by allowing it to get ahead of you."

To those who complained that rearmament and helping England would, in fact, drag America into the war, FDR cogently replied that, on the contrary, it was the best way to keep America out. With such political jujitsu, Roosevelt turned potentially unpopular decisions like the Destroyer Deal, which would have doomed less talented politicians, to his own advantage.

Roosevelt took strength from his Episcopalianism, which espoused an eternal divine order that even Hitlers could not overturn, and from his ferocious self-confidence. It rarely occurred to him that he might fail at anything. He reminded family and aides that he had "broad shoulders," boasting, "I am a tough guy!"

One danger in Roosevelt's approach was his deception and secrecy. By vowing in 1940 that Americans would fight in no "foreign war" and that he had no "secret understanding" with Churchill, he made himself vulnerable to the Tyler Kents and Joe Kennedys who had powerful evidence to the contrary.

Any President with dangerous secrets is hostage to those who know them. Kent and Kennedy both came close to tattling everything they knew. Had they done so, FDR might have been voted out of office.

But instead, with considerable thanks to Roosevelt's leadership, the world survived Hitler, Mussolini and the imperial Japanese. The *New*

York Times was right when it predicted after FDR's death that Americans of the future would "thank God on their knees" that he had been President in the 1940s.

Roosevelt was inspired by an almost mystical belief in the glory and power of Presidential leadership, which he shared with a nighttime throng in Cleveland at the end of the 1940 campaign:

> There is a great storm raging now . . . that makes things harder for the world. And that storm . . . is the true reason that I would like to stick by those people of ours. . . . until we reach the clear, sure footing ahead. . . .
>
> We will make it before the next term is over. . . . When that term is over, there will be another President* . . . And I think that in the years to come, that word "President" will be a word to cheer the hearts of common men and women everywhere.

After the 1940 election, Joe Kennedy went to the White House and offered his resignation. FDR politely asked his advice on a successor in London. Kennedy joked that it didn't matter: "If there is a Chinese nigger, Churchill would talk to him now if you sent him!"

Turning more serious, Kennedy warned Roosevelt he was gambling by moving the country toward war: "You will go down either as the greatest President in history—greater than Washington or Lincoln—or the greatest horse's ass!"

"There is a third alternative," said FDR. "I may go down as the President of an unimportant country at the end of my term."

To keep Kennedy from publicly denouncing his growing efforts to aid Britain, the President received him again two months later, this time in his upstairs White House bathroom.

Wearing gray pajamas, Roosevelt sat in his wheelchair and shaved while Kennedy inveighed against the President's "hatchetmen" in the press.

FDR told Joe he shouldn't complain. The press was as tough on him

---

* When the crowd heard the words "another President," they shouted, "No! No!" Fearful that radio listeners would think he planned to be President-for-life, FDR drowned them out by pressing his lips to the microphone and raising his voice.

and his family: "I don't call them 'sons of bitches,' because that reflects on someone else. They're *bastards*!"

Working to keep the Ambassador friendly, Roosevelt asked about his children. Kennedy reported that his twenty-three-year-old son, Jack, had abdominal problems.

Citing his own sons, Roosevelt insisted that the "stomach troubles of these kids" came from drinking. Kennedy replied that his boys did not drink. "Well, that explodes that theory," said the President.

Returning to his obsession, Kennedy told FDR that Americans were still "not sure that you want to keep out of war."

Roosevelt replied, "I have said it a hundred and fifty times, at least. . . . I have no intention of going to war!"

But Kennedy noticed that since the election, the President's promises to eschew war were more hedged: he "didn't sound as convincing" as before.

After the Pearl Harbor attack and Hitler's war declaration thrust Americans into World War II, Joe Kennedy felt he deserved a vital wartime job. He told friends that FDR had "admitted" to Churchill "that I was an important factor in his reelection." He didn't "enjoy being a bum in these troubled days of war."

But with Kennedy's old reputation for anti-Semitism and pro-appeasement of Hitler, the President kept him at arm's length. Asked to the White House in December 1942, Kennedy was furious to find his noontime appointment reduced to a mere ten minutes.

Roosevelt's appointments secretary, Edwin "Pa" Watson, explained to Kennedy that Rabbi Stephen Wise of New York and "several other Jews" were waiting in the Oval Office. To make sure the Jewish leaders did not cross paths with Kennedy, Watson ensured that the President saw him in another room.

As Kennedy told his diary, Roosevelt tried to filibuster with the usual irrelevant stories, and he "stunned" the President by saying, "You haven't appointed a Catholic to any important post since Election 1940!" As FDR fumbled for a response, Watson arrived "to get me out."

After Kennedy's departure, Roosevelt wheeled himself into the Oval Office for an important moment in history. Rabbi Wise warned him of the assault on the Jewish people that later generations would know as the Holocaust.

By 1944, Kennedy was agonizing over his eldest son, Joe's, heroic death in the skies above the English Channel. He told a friend that "for a guy who did his God-damnedest to keep out of war," he had certainly had "the crowns of suffering on my soul."

Kennedy blamed the man he endorsed in 1940. This fall, he asked the President's new running mate, Senator Harry Truman of Missouri, why he would help "that crippled son of a bitch that killed my son Joe." Truman asked him to stop "throwing rocks at Roosevelt."

Although privately resolved to support FDR's opponent, Thomas Dewey, Kennedy went to the White House and told the President that Irish-Americans feared he was "Jew-controlled." He carped that his Jack had been "recommended for a medal by all of his officers" for bravery in the South Pacific aboard the *PT-109*, but had lost the award "because I was persona non grata to the powers that be in Washington."

After World War II, Kennedy was sitting at the Hialeah racetrack in Florida when told that ex–Prime Minister Churchill was in the stands. Bitter at Churchill, he stalled before going to the old lion's box.

By Kennedy's written account, Churchill told him he felt "so sad for you. . . . You had a terrible time during the war. Your losses were very great."

Still smoldering at Churchill's old eagerness to fight Hitler, Kennedy confronted him: "After all, what did we accomplish by this war?"

Churchill replied, "Well, at least we have our lives."

Kennedy turned to stone: *"Not all of us!"*

But in January 1941, all of this was in the future. On the day before his third inaugural, Franklin Roosevelt invited Wendell Willkie to the Oval Office, hoping to enlist his public support to help England.

Some of Willkie's rich supporters were threatening him. Roy Howard warned him that if he planned to mouth "British propaganda," the Scripps Howard papers would "tear your reputation to shreds." *

---

* Willkie later said, "If Howard wasn't such a little pipsqueak, I'd have felt like knocking him down!"

Others assured Wilkie that the world crisis could be "fixed up" if only Roosevelt would bargain with Hitler. They carped that if war came, they would have to "pay big taxes" and they might lose their businesses.

Feeling "hurt and worried," Willkie now wished to help the President, as if in penance for his more outlandish antiwar statements of the campaign. At the suggestion of Irita Van Doren, with whom he had resumed his romance after Election Day, he planned to visit London to get "firsthand information."

Waiting for his guest at the White House, FDR worried that his clean desktop might suggest he was lazy. He asked aides for "any papers" they had, so that he could look busy when "Wendell" arrived.

During their visit, Roosevelt gave him a handwritten letter to Churchill, reporting that Willkie was "truly helping to keep politics out over here."

He had included from memory a verse that, he wrote, "applies to you people as it does to us":

> Sail on, Oh Ship of State!
> Sail on, Oh Union strong and great,
> Humanity with all its fears
> With all the hope of future years
> Is hanging breathless on thy fate.

FDR did not know that this Longfellow poem had moved Abraham Lincoln to tears when he heard it read aloud at the White House during the Civil War.

At Buckingham Palace, referring to Joe Kennedy, Willkie told the Queen she had charmed him more effectively than she had a "certain person." Elizabeth replied, "It wasn't because I didn't try on him!"

Over luncheon, Willkie gave Churchill the handwritten letter from FDR. Afterwards Churchill wrote the President he was "deeply moved" and would frame it as "a souvenir of these tremendous days" and of "our friendly relations, which have been built up telegraphically under all the stresses."

In a radio speech, Churchill, seeking Lend-Lease aid, proudly cited Roosevelt's letter as a symbol of the growing Anglo-American partnership. "Give us the tools," he told the President, "and we will finish the job!"

Carl Sandburg published a poem lauding FDR for sending Churchill the Longfellow verse "that made President Lincoln cry."

As Roosevelt prepared himself for a task as great as that facing Lincoln, the Lincoln biographer wrote FDR to pay him his highest compliment:

"In these hours of ordeal you command loyalties that no one could. I'm glad you are cunning—as Lincoln and Jackson were cunning."

NO PEOPLE EXCEPT
THE HEBREWS

If you walked into the Oval Office on Wednesday, May 12, 1948, you would know that Franklin Roosevelt was no longer President. The armless wheelchair and naval prints were gone.

Instead, there was a large DuMont console television, crowned by an ear of corn mounted in Lucite. Atop the President's desk was a 4-H Club paperweight and a plaque copied from that of an Oklahoma prison warden: "The buck stops here!"

On the previous Saturday night, President Harry Truman had been floored when his Secretary of State, George Marshall, architect of victory in World War II Europe, attended his small sixty-fourth birthday dinner.

Truman revered Marshall as "the great one of the age," and knew he almost never went to parties.

What was more, when Marshall toasted the President, he praised Truman's "integrity" and "courage" in making decisions with only the country's "best interest" at heart.

The President was so choked up that all he could do was point at Marshall and say, "He won the war!"

Truman was emotional because few Americans were praising him that political season, let alone the great General Marshall.

Disgruntled by postwar adjustments and Truman's stumbles after FDR's death, voters in 1946 had given Congress to the Republicans ("Had enough?") for the first time in eighteen years.

By the spring of 1948, Truman's approval ratings had dropped to the mid-thirties.* Most pollsters forecast he would lose the fall election.

Now as the Wednesday afternoon sun slanted through the tall windows of the Oval Office, General Marshall took a chair beside Truman's.

Sitting in front of the President's desk, befitting his more junior position, was Truman's White House counsel, Clark Clifford of St. Louis, whose well-groomed wavy blond hair and deliberate manner suggested a silent film actor.

On Friday at midnight, two days from now, the British would withdraw from their Palestine protectorate. The United Nations had resolved to divide the region into one Jewish state and one Arab state, with ancient, holy Jerusalem as an international city.

Despite the U.N. plan, five Arab armies were ready to kill the fledgling Jewish state.

American Jewish leaders and others implored Truman to recognize the new nation as soon as it was declared. If the U.S. granted legitimacy, so would its allies, allowing the Jewish state to survive.

But Marshall advised Truman to keep his distance, warning that the Jews could never stave off Arab legions who far outnumbered them. If they came "running to us for help," the U.S. would have to say no.

Clark Clifford insisted that the President recognize the Jewish state immediately.

Clifford argued that Americans had always felt "a great moral obligation" to stop persecution. Jews deserved the same rights as "other people who have their own country." U.S. recognition might make up, "in some small way," for the "atrocities" of the Holocaust.

Clifford noted that Truman was trying to stop the Soviet Union from conquering the world. A democratic Jewish state would be a reliable American friend in the "unstable Middle East."

Marshall could not contain himself: "Mr. President, I don't even know why Clifford is here!"

"He's here because I asked him to be here," said Truman.

---

* Today's equivalent might be the mid-twenties. In 1948, a President was still regarded with sufficient awe that some voters were probably too embarrassed to tell pollsters they disapproved of Truman.

No longer lauding his "integrity," Marshall upbraided the President (in what Clifford found "a righteous Goddamned Baptist tone") for playing politics with the Middle East to attract Jewish voters.

Piping up, Marshall's deputy, Robert Lovett, warned Truman that if he pandered to "the Jewish vote," it would hurt his "prestige." Recognizing a Jewish state would be "buying a pig in a poke." Who could guarantee that the new nation wouldn't turn Communist? The Russians had already sent Jewish "Communist agents" into Palestine.*

Like a vengeful prophet with Arctic blue eyes, Marshall told the President, "If you follow Clifford's advice and if I were to vote in the election, I would vote against you."†

Shaken to be so condemned by "the great one of the age," Truman adjourned the meeting.

Having never seen his Secretary of State "so furious," he warned Clifford, "I can't afford to lose General Marshall!"

In April 1945, as Harry Truman became President and Allied soldiers liberated the death camps of Europe, Americans were learning about the terrible reach of the Holocaust.

For many American Jews, the Holocaust showed that they must never again depend on the kindness of strangers: only a Jewish state could protect their people from another Hitler.

They feared that the small-town Missouri Baptist in the White House could not possibly understand their predicament. They did not know that Truman had grown up knowing Jews or that he had studied their history since boyhood.

For two years in Independence, a Jewish family called the Viners lived next door to Truman's family. As Sarah Viner much later recalled, her brother Abe was "very close friends" with the future President: "Harry was always over at our house. . . . I think this was his first contact with Jewish people."

Sarah recalled being startled at how Harry's frugal mother used

---

* For a Jewish state, Lovett's "pig" metaphor was ill-chosen. Clifford correctly thought Lovett's argument about Communist infiltrators was "ridiculous."
† Marshall believed that as an Army professional, he should not vote.

an old tin can lid for a chopping knife. (Sarah used the Yiddish term "*hackmesser.*")

The Viners introduced the young Truman to kugel, matzoh and gefilte fish. On the Sabbath, when observant Jews could not do household chores, Harry served as the Viners' "Shabbos goy."

While a sixteen-year-old student at Independence High School, young Truman was assigned to write about Shylock, Shakespeare's Jewish villain in *The Merchant of Venice.*

Truman's essay was discovered in 2000. Given the anti-Semitism of his time and place and the vast potential for indulging in it when writing of Shylock, Truman viewed the Jewish people with considerable sympathy:

> The Jews soon found that money was a great factor in the Christian world's makeup (although their religion, as far as I can see, doesn't teach a love of gain) and that they might bring the world to their feet by means of it. This was not hard to do with the Jew's great business ability.
>
> We cannot blame Shylock for getting money as a means for revenge upon those who persecuted him. He was not a miser, and if one of his own nation had been in trouble, he would have helped him as quickly as a Christian would help a Christian. . . .
>
> Who can blame a Jew for getting revenge when his religion as good as teaches it? I never saw Jew, Christian or any other man who, if he had the chance, wouldn't take revenge. . . .
>
> The Christians teach, "Love to enemies." They love them, don't they? Who instituted . . . that very Christian institution, the Inquisition? . . .
>
> Now if the Christians carry not out their teachings, who's to carry them out? Not China, nor Turkey and surely not the Jews, when their religion (if they wish to interpret it that way) teaches "an eye for an eye and a tooth for a tooth."

Truman went on to insist that no one "except the Hebrews" had "ruled" the world, then "when they fell," remained "a distinct people." He wrote that after two thousand years, the Jews were "a nation apart from nations . . . persecuted for their religion," still "waiting for a leader" to gather their "scattered people." *

As an adult, Truman privately used anti-Semitic slurs that were too common in that era. He described New York City as a "Kike town" and said that a greedy poker player "screamed like a Jewish merchant."

As President in the spring and summer of 1945, even as he learned the full horrors of the Holocaust, Truman used private epithets like "Jew boys," writing in his diary, "The Jews claim God Almighty picked 'em out for special privilege. Well, I'm sure He had better judgment."

Such private gibes belied Truman's genuine distress about hundreds of thousands of stateless Holocaust survivors incarcerated in Europe. Some of them suffered in the same camps, with barbed wire and death ovens, where millions of Jews and other victims had perished.

Truman told an aide, "Everyone else who's been dragged from his country has somewhere to go back to. But the Jews have no place to go."

When the Big Three met at Potsdam in the summer of 1945, Truman asked the British to let Jewish Holocaust survivors into Palestine, but he refused to pledge U.S. military force to protect them against angry Arabs.

The Zionist patriarch Chaim Weizmann bitterly explained to his diary that Truman's "phony" offer was undermined by his thirst for Arab oil: "He will never jeopardize his oil concessions for the sake of the Jews, although he may need them when the time of election arrives."

By the fall of 1945, with many Jews dying in their European camps, Truman infuriated Jewish leaders by saying he would let an Anglo-American committee study the problem.

Eleanor Roosevelt, feeling bereft that she and her late husband could not have saved more Jews, warned the President he was being "used" by England, which was "always anxious to have someone pull her chestnuts out of the fire."

She asked Truman to help the "few Jews remaining in Europe" settle either in Palestine or else one of the Allied nations that won the war.

---

* Reflecting his own Christianity, Truman lamented that the Jews "know not that their leader has already come."

[200]

Then "we would not . . . have on our consciences the death of at least fifty of these poor creatures daily."

Groucho Marx, whom Truman had loved watching as a young usher at Kansas City's Orpheum Theatre, sent the President a scathing *Life* editorial asking why "in God's name" the U.S. was "doing nothing" to help the poor refugees.

Groucho wrote Truman, "Even a President at times can be confused."

In April 1946, British Foreign Minister Ernest Bevin told a Labour party conference that Americans wished to send the Jews to Palestine "because they do not want too many of them in New York."

Truman was shocked by Bevin's "raw, ignominious" comment—and by the Foreign Minister's about-face after years of Labour party pledges to ensure the Jews a home in Palestine. Truman said, "Today they are cheating the Jews, and where is the assurance that they won't cheat us tomorrow?"

The Anglo-American committee recommended letting a hundred thousand Jews into Palestine by the end of 1946—but only if the Arabs accepted them—and ruled out a Jewish state there.

When Truman pronounced the report "fair," the Zionist leader David Ben-Gurion darkly concluded that the President was urging "the elimination of Zionism."

In the wake of the Holocaust, many American Jewish leaders blamed themselves for not having demanded that their government do more to stop it.

Believing now that the survival of the European detainees and their entire people was at stake, they cast off the polite deference that leaders now derided as "court Jews" had once used around Franklin Roosevelt.

In July 1946, the emotional Rabbi Abba Hillel Silver, an Ohio Republican who thought American Jews were too dependent on the Democrats, bellowed at Truman about the Anglo-American committee report, pounding on his desk. Furious, the President thenceforth banned Silver from the White House.

That same month, the two Democratic Senators from New York and a pro-Zionist ex-diplomat, James McDonald, came to complain about the report. His back up, Truman told them that he thought it was "mar-velous."

McDonald warned the President he was "scrapping" the Jewish cause in Palestine and would "go down in history as anathema."

Truman erupted: "You cannot satisfy the Jews anyway. . . . They are not interested in the United States. They are interested in Palestine and the Jews. . . . The Jews aren't going to write the history of the United States—or my history!"

Tactlessly McDonald noted that FDR had understood the "impon-derables" of the issue.

"I am not Roosevelt!" cried Truman. "I am not from New York. I am from the Middle West. I must do what I think is right."

He told another group of New York Democrats who opposed the re-port, "This is all political. You are all running for reelection." He was "tired" of Jews, Poles, Irishmen, Italians and Armenians all pushing their own interests. Why didn't he ever hear from "Americans"?

At a Cabinet meeting that summer, the exhausted Truman displayed some of the angry cards and telegrams descending on him, adding he was "put out" with the Jews:

"Jesus Christ couldn't please them when he was here on earth, so how could anyone expect that I would have any luck?"

One of the undercurrents of Harry Truman's Presidency was his con-stant private braying about the pressures of the Zionists and the Jews.

Granted, it was no pleasure to have the wild-eyed Rabbi Silver thump-ing his desk. But with his considerable knowledge of U.S. history, Tru-man knew that the Zionist lobbying did not rival the assaults against Jackson by Nicholas Biddle and his Bank—or against FDR by the ap-peasers and isolationists of 1940.

As President of the United States, proprietor of the world's only atomic weapons, Truman was easily the most powerful man on earth. The problem was that he didn't feel that way.

As a boy, "blind as a mole," Harry had been forced to avoid bruising sports and bullies because his parents could not easily afford to replace his eyeglasses if he broke them. A first-grade teacher noted that Harry "just smiled his way along."

Arriving in Washington as a Senator in 1935, Truman was overralert to potential snubs by FDR and his Cabinet, certain that the President thought him "the representative of the devil" as the handpicked candidate of the Kansas City machine boss Tom Pendergast.

When he ran for reelection in 1940, Truman was flabbergasted when, despite his loyal support of the New Deal, Roosevelt seemed to favor his wealthy primary opponent, Lloyd Stark. Sensing a conspiracy against him by two fellow elitists, Truman defeated Stark but sighed, "I'll never be the same again." He had lost his old reverence for FDR.

During his seventy-three days as Roosevelt's Vice President, Truman was kept at a distance. Reduced to writing truckling letters to FDR ("Hate to bother you"), he wished he had stayed in the Senate.

Truman had always been hypersensitive to any efforts to bulldoze him—and determined to show that it couldn't be done. His aides were startled at how, after an apparently friendly talk with some visitor, the President would boast, "I certainly set him straight" or "I let him have it."

With his chip on the shoulder against the arrogant and powerful, Truman thus bridled at the intense, well-financed Zionist apparatus. He complained to Eleanor Roosevelt that "Jews are like all underdogs. When they get on top, they are just as intolerant and cruel as the people were to them when they were underneath."

Truman ignored the irony that the "powerful" Jews he denounced were still one of the chief targets of American bigotry and discrimination—or that the Jews in Europe and Palestine for whom they were fighting included some of the most helpless people on earth.

THE RIGHT PLACE
AT THE RIGHT TIME

Since the end of World War II in Europe, desperate Holocaust survivors had slipped onto all manner of vessels, hoping to make their way to Palestine.

Then the British lowered the boom. In July 1947, the old steamer *Exodus 1947*, owned by the Palestine Jewish underground Haganah, left Marseilles with over four thousand refugees, many of them children.

As the ship neared Palestine, British destroyers attacked it, wounding thirty people. The British sent other passengers back to Germany, provoking worldwide outrage.*

Henry Morgenthau, Jr., who had been FDR's close friend and Treasury Secretary, called Truman to complain about British handling of the *Exodus*.

Once an unobservant Jew, Morgenthau had been moved on learning of Hitler's growing atrocities to urge Roosevelt to do more to save his people. After the war, he had become chairman of the United Jewish Appeal.

But Truman was feeling so dyspeptic about the Zionists that he complained into his diary (in a passage discovered in 2003),

---

* In 1960, Otto Preminger adapted Leon Uris's novel about the poignant episode for his three-and-a-half-hour epic *Exodus*, starring Paul Newman and Eva Marie Saint.

[Morgenthau had] had no business whatever to call me. The Jews have no sense of proportion, nor do they have any judgment on world affairs. . . . The Jews, I find, are very, very selfish.

They care not how many Estonians, Latvians, Finns, Poles, Yugoslavs or Greeks get murdered or mistreated . . . as long as the Jews get special treatment. Yet when they have power—physical, financial or political—neither Hitler nor Stalin has anything on them for cruelty or mistreatment to the underdog.

By now, Truman was telling his aides that he didn't want to see one more Zionist.

Anxious about their exclusion, Jewish leaders searched for some new way to reach the President.

A Kansas City attorney named A. J. Granoff got a call from a national official of the Jewish fraternal organization B'nai B'rith: "Do you know a man by the name of Jacobstein . . . who is supposed to be a very close friend of President Truman?"

"You mean Eddie Jacobson," said Granoff. "Sure, I ought to! I'm his friend and lawyer."

Eddie Jacobson was born on New York's Lower East Side to Yiddish-speaking Orthodox Lithuanian Jews. The family settled in Kansas City, where young Eddie dropped out of school to help his father, a shoemaker, support their large family.

In 1917, the genial, quiet Private Jacobson clerked in an Army canteen at Camp Doniphan, Oklahoma, under Lieutenant Harry Truman. Truman wrote his girlfriend, Bess Wallace, back in Independence, that he had a "Jew clerk" running his canteen and that Jacobson was "a crackerjack."

The canteen sold apples, tobacco, near-beer and woolen sweaters. Truman later insisted that its success was the reason he was promoted to be "Captain Harry" of his beloved Battery D.

Praising his "Jewish ability" in business, other soldiers told Truman that he must be a "lucky Jew" himself and called him "Trumanheimer."

The nickname allowed Truman to feel the sting of anti-Semitism. He wrote Bess that one "very pretty girl" had shunned him after "someone told her my name was Trumanheimer."

After fighting the Germans in France, the two friends opened a men's store in Kansas City, with Harry as salesman-bookkeeper, Eddie as buyer, and many old Battery D pals as customers. "Those were happy years," recalled Jacobson.

Then came the postwar depression. "I lost all I had and all I could borrow," said Truman. "Our creditors drove Eddie into bankruptcy, but I became a public official, and they couldn't do that to me."

The friendship survived. During Senator Truman's visits to Kansas City, the ex-partners drank bourbon, played poker, told off-color stories and joked about "losing our asses in that store."

In June 1945, Jacobson and other Battery D veterans went to the White House, where the new President showed them the jewel-encrusted baton once brandished by the Nazi Marshal Hermann Göring.

Eddie had just opened his own men's shop in Kansas City. Truman said he was "pleased to death you are back in the game again."

Eddie told Harry that his ascension to the Presidency "gave me a lot of publicity that really helped." He did not want to "ride along on your coattails, but what could I do?"

During Truman's first trip home as President that summer, he beat Eddie at poker. The next morning, with flash photographers, he called at Jacobson's new store to buy three white shirts: "I thought you'd need this sale, after what we did to you last night!" *

That evening, glowing from his Presidential visit, Eddie joked to his wife and daughters, "Well, all you peons, bow down!"

Before joining B'nai B'rith in 1945, Jacobson had belonged to no Jewish group but his Reform synagogue. "We never discussed Jewish questions," said Granoff. "It would be just like having discussed Greece or Babylonia with him."

---

* Jacobson had no white shirts in Truman's size, but gave him eighteen pairs of socks and "some red hot bowties." Despite Truman's demand to pay at least the wholesale price, Jacobson would not charge him.

*   *   *

In the summer of 1947, Jacobson sat down at Kansas City's Hotel Muehlebach with Granoff and Frank Goldman, the national president of B'nai B'rith.

He told them he would never ask Truman for a personal favor, but would "always be glad" to discuss with him "my suffering people across the seas." He had endless faith in Harry's "kindly heart."

Granoff said the problem was getting more Jewish refugees into Palestine. Eddie said, "Harry Truman will do what's right if he knows all the facts. . . . But I'm no Zionist, so first I need the facts from you."

Before now, in his friendship with Truman, Eddie's Judaism was a sidelight. He had once told Harry, "You know that I am not the praying type." But now he schooled himself to beseech the President for a Jewish homeland in Palestine.

Jacobson's daughter Gloria much later recalled, "My Dad always said that he was *besheret*, which is a Yiddish word meaning that it was just his fate to be at the right place at the right time."

Arriving in Washington, Eddie called the President's appointments secretary, Matt Connelly, who gibed, "What the hell are you doing here without his permission?"

When Jacobson and Granoff were ushered into the Oval Office, Truman said, "Sit down, you bastards!"

As Eddie recalled, after Truman signed dollar bills for their children and asked about business in Kansas City, he and the President talked *"takhles"*—a Yiddish term that meant "with serious purpose."

Making their case for a Jewish homeland, Granoff and Jacobson insisted they would never ask Truman to act against America's best interests.

"You guys wouldn't get to the front gate if I thought any differently," said Truman. "You bastards are the only ones that never tried to embarrass me in any way."

In the fall of 1947, when Britain said it was leaving Palestine, a U.N. committee proposed the land's partition into Jewish and Arab states, joined by economic union.

Loy Henderson, Assistant Secretary of State, warned his superiors that if the U.S. had anything to do with founding a Jewish state, it would jeopardize oil supplies in Iraq and Saudi Arabia, and the "whole Arab world" would become the "enemy" of the United States.

Born in rural Arkansas, the mustachioed, Anglophile Henderson was happy to exploit George Marshall's military penchant for delegating authority. He claimed the Arab world as his personal province.*

Henderson was outraged by the "Zionist juggernaut" now demanding a Jewish homeland. He later recalled, "I was attacked by the Zionists and their allies in such a vicious and effective manner that my name became almost synonymous with anti-Semitism."

Truman had never liked the State Department's "striped-pants boys."

His Senate Majority Leader, Alben Barkley of Kentucky, once told him of meeting a U.S. diplomat in Cairo, who "carried a cane, wore a cap and talked with an Oxford accent." When Barkley asked where he came from, the envoy said, "Topeka, Kansas."

Truman cracked that if the guy ever "dared go back" to Topeka looking and sounding so foppish, he would last "about ten minutes."

As Truman recalled, after FDR's death, the State Department boys had warned him that the Palestine issue was "highly complex" and that he should "watch my step." He complained that "nobody seemed to think I was aware of anything."

Emboldened by politics and personal conviction to fight for a Jewish state, Clark Clifford played to Truman's resentment of Henderson's kind.

In September 1947, he had Henderson summoned to the White House and asked him to defend his hostility to a Jewish refuge in Palestine before the President and senior aides.

Like a prosecutor, Clifford asked Henderson if he was motivated by anti-Jewish "prejudice or bias." Fuming at Clifford's effort to "humiliate and break me down," Henderson insisted that all of State's experts on Palestine felt the same as he did.

On this rare occasion, Clifford overplayed his hand. Annoyed by his

---

* When Henderson served in Moscow during the late 1930s, one of his code clerks was the soon-to-be-treacherous Tyler Kent.

Harry Truman and Clark Clifford during a Presidential vacation, Key West, Florida

counsel's rough questioning, the President stood up and cried, "Oh, hell, I'm leaving!"

That fall, Truman was boiling over at the ferocious lobbying for a Jewish state. He claimed to one Senator that if it weren't for "the unwarranted influence of the Zionists, we would have had the matter settled a year and a half ago."

Truman boasted that he had gathered all the "mail and propaganda from the Jews" and "struck a match to it."

As Truman recalled, almost every night, he and his wife, Bess, talked in his upstairs oval White House study about "everything that came up."

Truman had fallen in love at age six with the "little blue-eyed, golden-haired girl" he met in Sunday School. He thought Bess Wallace "the most beautiful and sweetest person on earth."

But Bess's mother considered Harry's family of "dirt farmers" beneath the Wallaces' stature as local gentry. Even when Truman became

President, Madge Wallace couldn't understand what all the fuss was about.

During Truman's first year in office, he was understandably absorbed by the last chapters of World War II, the Bomb and the first tremors of the Cold War. But as daughter Margaret recalled, Bess was "very, very angry" that she had become "a spectator rather than a partner" in her husband's career.

When Truman flew back to Independence on Christmas Day 1945, Bess told him, "I guess you couldn't think of any more reasons to stay away. As far as I'm concerned, you might as well have stayed in Washington."

He later wrote her, "You can never appreciate what it means to come home . . . and have the only person in the world whose approval and good opinion I value look at me like I'm something the cat dragged in."

As Margaret recalled, her father made amends by consulting the First Lady "each night for a long, quiet discussion of the issues, the problems and the personalities with which he was grappling."

During these nightly conversations, it is unlikely that Bess urged the President to support a homeland for the Jews.

Eddie Jacobson's wife, Bluma, noted that the Trumans never asked her and her husband to the White House, or to their house in Independence, inherited from Bess's mother: "The Wallaces were aristocracy in these parts, and . . . the Trumans couldn't afford to have Jews at their house."

Jacobson's daughter Gloria recalled, "We met and knew the President, but not his family." *

While staying in Independence to interview Truman for a TV series on his Presidency in 1961, the talk show host David Susskind asked the ex-President why he never asked him into his home.

By Susskind's account, Truman replied, "You're a Jew, David, and no Jew has ever been in the house. Bess runs it, and there's never been a Jew inside the house in her or her mother's lifetime."

---

* Gloria recalled that her docile father did not object to his family's exclusion, saying that he understood the President's "problems."

HOW COULD THIS HAVE HAPPENED?

For Truman, the White House was a glorious hall of history. He could "almost smell the big hunk of cheese" at General Jackson's farewell reception. He regaled visitors with how Old Hickory had "dolled up" the East Room with "twenty spittoons" and how "Jefferson designed the original outhouses."

As he once wrote Bess, he could "just imagine old Andy" arguing with "Teddy" Roosevelt about FDR. He thought the whole "damn place" was "haunted" by the ghosts of Presidents past.

Before retiring at night, Truman donned a green eyeshade and put his hawklike nose in a history book. He had "tried to increase my knowledge all my life by reading and reading and reading"—especially biography and history, insisting, "There's nothing new in human nature. . . . The only thing new in the world is the history you don't know." *

As a nearsighted boy in Independence, Harry devoured a gold-trimmed, four-volume history called *Great Men and Famous Women*—from Nebuchadnezzar to Sarah Bernhardt.

---

* Like John Adams and Lincoln, Truman distrusted written history. In 1950, he scrawled a note to his aide George Elsey: "The truth is all I want for history. If I appear in a bad light . . . that's just too bad. . . . But I don't want a pack of lying so-called historians to do to me what the New Englanders did to Jefferson and Jackson." In 1959, when his own historical stock was low, Truman complained that historians had become "propagandists," like the "Madison Avenue boys," which made him wonder "whether the ancient historians told the truth or not."

From the tales he read, he always remembered Cyrus the Great, the Persian king of the sixth century B.C., who enabled the Jewish people to leave their exile and go back to Palestine.

Of the American Presidents, Truman thought George Washington was "probably the greatest" because without him, "there would have been no United States."

By Truman's time, few Americans were aware of the Hero's struggle to enact Jay's Treaty. But Truman knew that when confronted by the "damn fools" of the Senate, Washington had "got up and told them they could go to hell."

When under fire, Truman comforted himself by recalling that President Washington "wasn't as popular" as people later supposed: "He was abused constantly by the press, by the Congress and a lot of individuals like that bastard son of Ben Franklin's."*

Truman's affection for Andrew Jackson ran so deep that as Jackson County judge in Missouri, he had insisted that the new courthouse feature a statue of the great man and drove all the way to the Hermitage to measure one of Jackson's uniforms personally.

As with other Presidents he admired, Truman tried to see himself in Old Hickory. He felt that Jackson was "afraid of absolutely nothing" and that he had to endure "a lot of snobbery" but that "it didn't bother him very much" because "he was as good as everybody else."

Truman admired Jackson for doing "what was right," even when it "wasn't very popular." For him, Jackson's lesson was that "when a leader senses what the people want and need . . . they'll always stay with him."

Truman believed that like Jackson, Abraham Lincoln had the "guts" to do "the right thing" against "a great big opposition." Had Lincoln failed, "we would have been divided into half a dozen countries."

But as Truman recalled, his mother and other border-state relatives thought Lincoln probably deserved his assassination. Union soldiers had burned his grandmother's barn, taking "everything loose that they could carry."

When Truman's mother came to the White House, she admonished

---

* Truman actually meant Franklin's grandson Ben Bache, the *Aurora* publisher.

her other son, "You tell Harry if he tries to put me in Lincoln's bed, I'll sleep on the floor!"

To the romantic legend of Theodore Roosevelt, Truman was immune, carping that the great trust-buster "didn't bust very many" and "loved press coverage more than anything on earth."

During the 1904 campaign, Truman had run down several Kansas City blocks to hear "Teddy" speak, but mainly to see the President "grin and show his teeth, which he did." He disliked T.R.'s high-flown eldest child and warned his own daughter, Margaret, "Don't ever be an Alice Roosevelt . . . whatever you do."

As for T.R.'s fifth cousin, Truman considered Franklin Roosevelt "one of the greatest politicians that ever lived," but he had been poisoned forever by Roosevelt's treachery in helping Lloyd Stark against him. In his diary years later, Truman acidly called Roosevelt "the man who thought Stark was tops."

As President, he still resented FDR for looking down on him as a Pendergast stooge. Truman noted that it had never occurred to Roosevelt that the "rotten, moneygrabbing machines," whose support he was happy to exploit, usually found "honest men for public office"—like himself.

Damning with faint praise, Truman privately called Roosevelt "a great conversationalist, with marvelous flashes of humor," but complained that with his "swollen ego," he never shared credit with "anyone else."

In 1948, three of FDR's sons tried to draft General Dwight Eisenhower for the Democratic Presidential nomination because they doubted Truman could win.

Furious, Truman wished the three "amateurs" would realize that "any shithead behind this desk can get renominated." He told Jimmy Roosevelt he ought to have his "head punched."

Truman wondered "whether a President ought to have any descendants at all." He told his diary, "All Roosevelts want the personal aggrandizement. . . . I don't believe the U.S.A. wants any more fakirs—Teddy and Franklin are enough."

*   *   *

From his reading of history, Truman concluded that any American President should be married, to avoid "the distraction of attempting to live a celibate life."

He felt the "first victory" great leaders had to win was over "their carnal urges." Chatting with male guests after a White House dinner, Truman joked that perhaps instead of being President, he should have played piano in a whorehouse.

One Cabinet member replied he was glad Truman hadn't done so, because "we never would have known you."

Truman replied, "Why be so high and mighty, as though you had never been in a whorehouse?"

In October 1947, Eddie Jacobson implored the President to back the U.N. committee's proposal for Jewish and Arab states in Palestine. He wrote, "Harry, my people need help and I am appealing on you to help them."

The "future of one and one-half million Jews in Europe" was at stake: "How they will be able to survive another winter in concentration camps and the Hell holes in which they live, is beyond my imagination. . . . There is only one place where they can go—and that is Palestine."

The President endorsed Palestine's partition, but warned that the U.S. would not give money to a Jewish state, and that it lacked deployable forces to defend it from the Arab armies.

Furious that Truman had overruled him, Loy Henderson tried to whittle down the territory allotted for the Jews. He argued that the town of Jaffa was "essentially Arab" and that Arab herdsmen required the Negev desert for "seasonal grazing."

But after making it into the Oval Office, Chaim Weizmann, chief of the World Zionist Organization, unfolded maps and persuaded Truman that losing the Negev would undermine a Jewish state by blocking vital access to the Red Sea.

In late November 1947, at the U.N.'s temporary quarters in a converted skating rink at Flushing Meadows, Queens, Palestine's partition came up for a vote by the General Assembly.

Truman had ordered his U.N. envoys not to anger the Arabs by using

"improper pressures" to win support for partition. Thus in the initial bal-
loting, partition fell one vote short of the necessary two thirds.

Arguing that U.S. prestige would suffer if allies like the Philippines
and Haiti were seen voting against it, Clark Clifford persuaded Truman
to let his aides lobby for partition. As Clifford recalled, "I kept the ramrod up the State Department's butt."

Truman's aide Dave Niles, inherited from FDR, called a U.S. envoy
in Flushing Meadows and threatened "hell if the voting went the
wrong way."

When the final vote was taken, partition of Palestine passed over-
whelmingly. Complaining of pressure from Washington, Arab delegates
walked out.

At the White House, Niles reminded the President that during World
War II, many of those same Arabs had been "allies of Hitler."

A. J. Granoff and Eddie Jacobson "dug into our bank accounts" and flew
from Kansas City to Washington. In the Oval Office, they told Truman,
"We came here once in our lives not asking you for something. Just to say,
'Thank you and God bless you.' "

The President's friends knew that George Marshall was staunchly opposed to a Jewish state. As Granoff recalled, when they encountered the
Secretary of State outside Truman's office, Marshall refused to greet
them: "Just looked at us—stony. We despised him."

Truman was anxious that people might think he had backed partition
because of Zionist threats. Instead, he insisted he had "kept the faith . . .
in spite of some of the Jews."

After the U.N. vote, he warned a pro-Zionist New York Congressman
that "the pressure boys almost beat themselves. . . . I don't do business
that way."

In January 1948, he infuriated the *New York Post* publisher Ted Thackrey by saying that he wished "the Goddamn New York Jews would just
shut their mouths."

Married to FDR's old friend Dorothy Schiff, Thackrey replied, "I've
got to assume that by 'Goddamn New York Jews,' you must mean my wife,
who is also a Jew."

*   *   *

Unwilling to give up, Loy Henderson now tried to block a Jewish state by harping on Truman's aversion to using the U.S. Army to defend it.

At Henderson's behest, just after the U.N. vote for partition, the U.S. announced it would halt all military shipments to the Middle East. Since Britain was arming the Arabs, the chief target of the embargo would be the Jews of Palestine.*

Chaim Weizmann implored Truman to cancel the embargo: "The choice of our people, Mr. President, is between statehood and extermination." But Truman dug in his heels.

Instead, coming to the rescue of Palestine's Jews was none other than the FBI Director, J. Edgar Hoover. Jewish friends asked him not to have the Bureau enforce the arms embargo too strenuously, and Hoover agreed.

When the FBI impounded a shipment of military equipment (labeled "textile machinery") bound for Jewish Palestine, Hoover's friend Robert Nathan, a New Deal economist, assured him that the arsenal would never be used against the United States.

By Hoover's order, the equipment sailed from New York Harbor untrammeled.

In January 1948, Truman's Secretary of Defense, James Forrestal, told him that enforcing partition might require as many as 160,000 American ground troops. These would have to be diverted from Europe, where the President suspected that the U.S. might soon have to fight the Soviet army.

Loy Henderson proposed that since partition could not be imposed without a military commitment that Truman would not make, the U.N. should govern Palestine as a trustee when Britain withdrew in May.

From the other side, Clark Clifford warned Truman that the State Department was clearly "determined to sabotage" partition. Why should the U.S. be in the "ridiculous" position of "trembling before threats of a few nomadic desert tribes"?

---

* The State Department's order also revoked passports held by any Americans who wished to join "armed forces not under the United States government," which was intended to stop the growing number of American Jews who wished to fight alongside Jewish underground armies in Palestine like Haganah.

Horrified that Truman seemed to be wavering on a Jewish state, Chaim Weizmann rushed to New York, hoping to see the President.

But Truman told his aides he had seen enough Zionists: "The Jews are so emotional, and the Arabs are so difficult to talk with that it is almost impossible to get anything done."

B'nai B'rith's Frank Goldman called Eddie Jacobson in Kansas City. The President was "washing his hands" of Palestine: "You must help us, Eddie."

Jacobson wired Truman, "I have asked very little in the way of favors during all our years of friendship, but I am begging you to see Dr. Weizmann as soon as possible."

Tired of Zionist "badgering," the President wired Eddie that the Palestine problem was probably "not solvable."

Refusing to give up, Jacobson flew to Washington in hopes of changing his mind.

When Matt Connelly let Jacobson into the Oval Office, he warned him not to mention Palestine.

Truman told his friend, "Eddie, I know what you are here for, and the answer is no."

Surprised at his own "nerve," Jacobson asked the President to reconsider, which touched off an explosion. Truman bellowed that the "Eastern Jews" had "slandered and libeled" him since the moment he became President. He didn't want to discuss "Palestine or the Jews or the Arabs or the British." Let the United Nations handle it.

Tears rolled down Eddie's face. He felt "shocked" and "crushed" that his "dear friend" was "as close to being an anti-Semite as a man could possibly be."

Jacobson's eye caught a replica of the courthouse statue in Jackson County, Missouri, that Truman had worked so hard to build.

Improvising, he said, "Harry, all your life, you have had a hero. You are probably the best-read man in America on the life of Andrew Jackson." He recalled Truman sitting in a corner of their failed store, "reading books and papers and pamphlets" on Old Hickory.

"Well, Harry, I too have a hero—a man I never met, but who is, I think, the greatest Jew who ever lived. . . . Chaim Weizmann. He is a very sick man . . . but he traveled thousands of miles just to see you. . . .

"Now you refuse to see him just because you are insulted by some of our American Jewish leaders—even though you know that Weizmann had absolutely nothing to do with these insults. . . . It doesn't sound like you, Harry. . . . I thought you could take this stuff they have been handing out." *

Deep in thought, Truman drummed his desktop, then swiveled in his chair to gaze at the South Grounds, turning green with spring. For what seemed "like centuries," Eddie held his breath.

Then the President spun back around and uttered the most "endearing" words Jacobson had ever heard him speak: "You win, you bald-headed son-of-a-bitch! I will see him."

Trembling from his ordeal, "excited and very nervous," Jacobson rushed to the Statler Hotel bar "and drank *two double* Bourbons alone, something I never did before in my life."

After trying to walk off the liquor, he went upstairs in the hotel and gave the good news to Frank Goldman, who kissed him.

The next day, at the Waldorf-Astoria in New York, Eddie met Chaim Weizmann for the first time. He found that the "dear" old man, lying sick in bed, looked like his late immigrant father.

On hearing the good news, Weizmann broke out into what Jacobson called "the sweetest smile I have ever seen." He asked the President's friend to go with him to the White House, but Eddie declined: he should be "saved" for another run at Truman, in case, "God forbid," their conversation went sour.

On Thursday, March 18, after dark, the old man was slipped into the Oval Office. The President could never pronounce Weizmann's first name, so he called him "Cham."

Truman pledged to "press forward with partition." Worried about

---

* A. J. Granoff later admired Eddie's reference to his "hero" Weizmann as "quick thinking." He later good-naturedly needled Jacobson: "Here's a man you hardly ever thought of, and he became your hero, all of a sudden. . . . How could you talk about Weizmann . . . as your greatest hero, in front of the man who should have been your greatest hero—Harry Truman?" Years later, despite overwhelming documentary evidence, Margaret Truman argued that Jacobson's White House visits and his influence on her father were a "myth." She wrote, "I don't believe they ever discussed politics, except in the most offhand fashion."

leaks, he did not even tell his Secretary of State about Weizmann's visit.

The next day, Truman's U.N. Ambassador, Warren Austin, publicly told the Security Council that since peaceful partition into Jewish and Arab states seemed impossible, the United States now believed that the U.N. should rule Palestine as the world's trustee.

Informed that Austin had just trampled the President's private promise to Weizmann, Eddie Jacobson couldn't believe it: "I was as dazed as a man could be." Feeling "physically sick," he collapsed into bed for two days.

Unfolding his Saturday morning newspapers, Truman was incensed to read about his administration's "badly bungled" reversal on partition. Charlie Ross, his press secretary and boyhood friend, thought it was the "most embarrassing" moment of Truman's Presidency.

"This morning I find that the State Dept. has reversed my Palestine policy," Truman told his diary. "The first I know about it is what I see in the papers! Isn't that hell? I'm now in the position of a liar and a double-crosser. I've never felt so in my life."

Truman inveighed against the "people on the 3rd and 4th levels of the State Dept. who have always wanted to cut my throat." Now they had "succeeded in doing it. Marshall's in California and Lovett's in Florida."

The President called in Clark Clifford: "How could this have happened? I assured Chaim Weizmann I would stick to it. He must think I am a shit-ass. . . . My God, how can I ever face Weizmann again?"

Truman would not accept that George Marshall had known about Austin's turnabout in advance: the Secretary of State would "never do that to me."

Clifford disagreed: "The State Department all knew." At the very least, they had violated their "obligation" to warn the President that the speech was coming so that he could have "protected himself" politically.*

---

* The best explanation of what happened is that the officials at State thought Truman wanted trusteeship if early partition proved impossible. The President had actually approved a contingency draft of Austin's statement a month earlier. But with Henderson and his allies eager to shove the President away from a Jewish state, they made little effort to alert Truman to the importance of Austin's statement before it was too late.

Unsettled by Truman's naïveté, Clifford told an aide in strictest confidence that he wondered whether their chief was even "deserving of four years more" in the White House. Why couldn't he understand that Marshall "didn't know his ass from a hole in the ground?"

As profane in private as he was priggish in public, Clifford felt "enraged by the terrible fucking the Boss had gotten" from the State Department: thanks to Marshall and his officials, "every Jew thought that Truman was a no-good son-of-a-bitch."

CHAPTER TWENTY-EIGHT

I AM CYRUS!

Clark Clifford leapt to exploit Truman's fury at the State Department. He and Dave Niles had warned the President that Loy Henderson was so "unsympathetic" to the Jews that he would never "carry out your policy." Now they pushed hard for partition.

Truman was ready to listen. He had concluded that "striped-pants" boys who put the Jews "in the same category as Chinamen and Negroes" were trying to "put it over on me about Palestine." He wrote his brother Vivian that the "proper thing" for him now was "to do what I think is right and let them all go to hell."

Marshall and Henderson were summoned to the White House. This time, when Henderson smugly argued that partition should be "buried," Truman cut him off.

He was no longer impressed by Henderson's claim that the Arabs would retaliate against partition by cutting off oil to America. "I don't know what they'd do for a market," Truman later said. "We're using a large part of their oil. . . . What would they do with it? . . . Plug the wells and let them stand?"

As "an amateur Bible student," Clifford pulled out his Old Testament and showed Truman passages that promised the Jews "that someday they would have their own homeland."

Truman was not a regular churchgoer and disdained politicians who attended "for show." A grandfather had warned him that when someone prayed too loud, "you better go home and lock up your smokehouse."

But as Clifford well understood, Truman tried to be a serious Christian. He knew much of the Scriptures by heart and thought "every problem in the world would be solved if only men would follow the Beatitudes."

Truman was happy to be a Baptist because he thought that it gave a common man the shortest route to God. He knew that many fellow Baptists hoped the Jews would one day return to their homeland Zion.

Truman's favorite Psalm was Number 137: "By the rivers of Babylon, there we sat down, yea, we wept, when we remembered Zion."

Recovering in Kansas City from what he called "Black Friday," Eddie Jacobson took a call from Chaim Weizmann, who told him not to "feel badly."

Weizmann had been reassured by Truman's friend and former counsel, Sam Rosenman, that the President hadn't known of Ambassador Austin's speech in advance and that his commitment to partition still stood.

Weizmann told Eddie he was now "the most important single man in the world. You have a job to do, so keep the White House doors open."

Jacobson felt "encouraged" to "go on with the work which Fate put on my shoulders."

On Thursday, March 25, 1948, Truman told reporters that a U.N. trusteeship might have to "fill the vacuum" in Palestine when the British departed in May, but he was still for partition.

Three weeks later, Eddie Jacobson eluded reporters by entering the White House through the East Gate, "something I had never done before."

Briefed in advance by Weizmann, he informed Truman that a Jewish state would be declared as soon as the British were gone from Palestine. It was "vital" for the U.S. to recognize it.

As Eddie recalled, Truman "agreed with a whole heart," saying that "Henderson or a thousand Hendersons won't stop me." But he asked his friend not to mention this private pledge to anyone else.

Truman asked Sam Rosenman to take a secret message to "the little doctor" in New York. Weizmann was on his "conscience." If the Jews declared a state, the President would recognize it "immediately."

*   *   *

Ignorant of Truman's private commitments, the foes of a Jewish state went in for the kill.

Meeting with Nahum Goldmann of the Jewish Agency for Palestine, Marshall's Under Secretary, Robert Lovett, warned that if the Zionists didn't relent, the State Department would show the world what they had done to force Truman's hand.

"You see those files?" Lovett asked, waving an arm at his desk. "That is all evidence of the violent, ruthless pressures exerted on the American government—mostly by American Jews. I wonder to whom they feel they owe their primary loyalty!"

Quaking with outrage, Goldmann called Clark Clifford to report Lovett's threat.

Knowing that his knowledge of foreign policy did not match his skills as a political operator, Clifford had quietly asked for help on Palestine from Max Lowenthal, a Harvard-trained lawyer and passionate champion of a Jewish state.

He knew that Truman respected Lowenthal, who had helped him investigate the railroads and Wall Street while in the Senate. In 1937, Lowenthal had brought the bashful Missouri Senator to a tea party hosted by Justice Louis Brandeis, an early, fervent Zionist.

"It was a rather exclusive and brainy party," Truman had written Bess. "I didn't exactly belong, but they made me think I did."

Now Lowenthal kept Clifford supplied with written, unsigned arguments for a Jewish state. Knowing that Truman might be politically injured if a Zionist operative were seen working in the West Wing, Lowenthal stayed in the shadows.

Atop one of his memos, he wrote Clifford, "Clark, please do not let anyone else read this dynamite."

In May 1948, using Lowenthal's confidential memos, Clifford informed Truman that the Jews in Palestine were showing "unexpected military strength."

If the U.S. were to block a Jewish state, he asked, "how much further do we intend to go?" Would the President "send troops to unseat" a Jewish government in Palestine?

The "Arctic" eyes of Secretary of State George Marshall

Clifford warned that the Soviets would recognize a Jewish state as soon as it was declared. Should the U.S. follow, it would "seem begrudging." The President must not wait to "climb on the bandwagon" just to appease the "amour propre" of a few professional diplomats who were "frantically" trying to halt Jewish statehood.

Eleanor Roosevelt wrote Truman, "It would be a mistake to lag behind Russia."

While seeing Clifford on Friday, May 7, Truman placed a call to George Marshall, swiveling his chair so that Clifford could not see his face. Hanging up, he told Clifford that the Secretary of State "does not want to recognize at all—at least not now."

He asked Clifford to sit with Marshall and himself the following week and "make the case" for recognition:

"You know how I feel. . . . Present it just as though you were making an argument before the Supreme Court. . . . Be as persuasive as you can possibly be."

*   *   *

Now it was late Wednesday afternoon, May 12. The angry Marshall had just stalked out of the President's office, warning him not to recognize a Jewish state.

"Well, that was rough as a cob," Truman told Clifford.

"Boss, this isn't the first case I've lost."

"Suppose we let the dust settle a little," Truman said. "Then you can . . . see if we can get this thing turned around. I still want to do it. But be careful."

That evening, Bob Lovett had Clifford in for a drink at his Washington home: "The General's wrought up over the issue. Perhaps he responded with too much agitation."

"The President is not going to give an inch," replied Clifford.

Moving toward rapprochement the next day, Lovett proposed that as a concession to Marshall, Truman agree to recognize the Jewish state not legally but in fact. Clifford listened.

On Friday, May 14, in Tel Aviv, the Jews were poised to declare their new nation at 6:00 P.M., Washington time. Truman and Clifford expected the new state to be called "Judea."

That morning, Clifford told Lovett that Truman "doesn't care" whether Marshall endorsed recognition: "If you can get him simply to say that he will not oppose this, that's all the President would need."

Lovett warned him over lunch that Truman was about to throw away "many years of hard work with the Arabs."

Clifford replied, "Speed is essential to preempt the Russians."

At four o'clock, Lovett informed Clifford that Marshall would not publicly oppose recognition. The Secretary of State had decided that he should not quit "when the man who has the Constitutional authority to make a decision makes one."

Clifford told Lovett, "God, that's good news!" He wished Marshall would tell the President personally but suspected that for the proud General, it might be "too painful."

At 5:45 P.M., Clifford asked Assistant Secretary of State Dean Rusk to inform Warren Austin at the U.N. that Truman would recognize the Jewish state just after six. Rusk was aghast. Clifford told him it was the President's "order."

Truman and Clifford brushed off the outrage of the men at State. As Clifford later recalled, they had "fought us . . . all the way" and "if some of them didn't like the result . . . we could not care less."

There was "pandemonium" at Flushing Meadows. Warren Austin stormed out of the General Assembly hall.

General Marshall told Rusk, "Get up there to New York on the next plane and keep our delegation from resigning en masse."

At midnight in a heavily guarded art museum in Tel Aviv, David Ben-Gurion declared that after twenty centuries of wandering, there was now "a Jewish state in Palestine, to be called Israel."

As the nation's new Prime Minister, Ben-Gurion went on, "The land of Israel was the birthplace of the Jewish people. . . . Here they wrote and gave the Bible to the world. . . . The Nazi Holocaust, which engulfed millions of Jews, proved anew the urgency of . . . lifting the Jewish people to equality in the family of nations."

At 6:11 P.M. in the White House, Truman signed a document recognizing the Jewish state's "de facto authority," and scrawled the word, "Approved." Thinking of Weizmann, he said, "The old doctor will believe me now!"

George Marshall kept his promised public silence about Truman's decision, but from that day on, he never spoke to Clark Clifford again.

Eddie Jacobson wrote the President that through him, God had answered the prayers of his people, who had so long yearned for their own homeland.

Chosen as first President of Israel, Chaim Weizmann invited Jacobson to New York, where the good doctor asked him to be "temporary spokesman for the baby state." Eddie wrote, "What a thrill that was! The Lord is sure good to me when He gives me these honors."

The columnist Drew Pearson told readers that Truman's World War I buddy had lobbied him to recognize Israel. Eddie Jacobson feared the President might suspect he had leaked the information.

On Monday afternoon, May 17, when Eddie went to the Oval Office, Matt Connelly joked, "Mr. President, here's Drew Pearson!" Jacobson's "heart sank into my shoes." He was vastly relieved when Truman grinned and said, "This is not Drew Pearson. This is the ambassador from Israel."

As Weizmann's emissary, he told his old friend, "To the President of the greatest nation in the world, I bring you greetings from the President-to-be of the newest nation in the world."

Eddie found that Truman "got as big a thrill out of the incident as I." The President was less beguiled by Weizmann's request to halt the U.S. arms embargo and lend his new nation $133 million.

Eddie flew to New York. When his airport limousine approached the Waldorf, he saw a huge crowd staring up at the new blue and white Star of David flag, flying "beside the stars and stripes of my own country." He wrote, "That was the payoff!"

As Jacobson later recalled, "I stood on the sidewalk like a fool, and cried and cried and cried."

In late May, President Weizmann came to Washington, feeling like a "happy man" with a "light heart." He slept in Frank Blair's old mansion, Blair House, now the President's official guest quarters.

Clark Clifford noted that the State Department boys were "all a-dither" and "badly upset," saying Weizmann did not deserve such honored lodgings, given his country's mere de facto recognition by the United States.

Crowds sang the Israeli anthem "Hatikvah." In the White House Rose Garden, Weizmann gave the President a Torah.

"Thanks," said Truman. "I've always wanted one of these!"

Anyone who thought Truman, having recognized Israel, would give the new state substantial help was surprised. As the tiny country fought off Arab armies, he refused to lift the arms embargo, lend it money or grant formal recognition.

The new Israeli minister in Washington, Eliahu Epstein, complained that the President was giving his nation the "run-around."

This was just what Truman wanted to hear. He had promised George Marshall to let the Jewish state take care of its own problems, at least for a while.

Truman also wished to convince himself he had not recognized Israel merely to win Jewish voters that fall. In language that John Adams might almost have used, Truman had once asked his diary, "Am I a fool or an ethical giant? . . . Am I just a crook to compromise in order to get the job done?"

By refusing Israel's demands, Truman knew he would infuriate many Jewish voters who had been grateful to him for recognition, but he covered his ears.

"Those Goddamned Jews are never satisfied!" he barked at his aides. "They're always grabbing for more. We don't need them in November. To hell with them! I'm not going to give them another thing!"

In September 1948, President Weizmann was chagrined when George Marshall endorsed a U.N. plan to cut Israel's territory in half. He cabled Eddie Jacobson that "only the intervention of your friend, who has done so much for us, can avert the worst dangers."

Amid a Jewish outcry against the President, Jacobson boarded Truman's whistlestop train in Oklahoma City and told the President that Marshall's diplomats should use "their brains instead of their mouths."

Truman protected himself politically by announcing that the U.N. plan was merely a "basis" for peace efforts in Palestine.

Trying to help, Eddie took out a full-page advertisement in the *Kansas City Jewish Chronicle*, swearing that his "lifetime friend" would "NEVER break" his "PLEDGED WORD" to Israel.

Polls showed Truman running well behind Thomas Dewey, with Henry Wallace and Strom Thurmond siphoning normally Democratic votes from the left and the right.

Although Truman claimed to forget it, the previous year he had been so gloomy about his Presidential prospects that he privately told the popular General Dwight Eisenhower ("Ike won't quote me and I won't quote him") that he'd "be glad to run in second place" with him on the Democratic ticket in 1948.

"I like the Senate anyway," Truman had told his diary. "Ike and I could be elected and my family and myself would be happy outside this great white jail known as the White House." *

---

* When Ike later revealed Truman's offer in his memoirs, Truman denied it. However a passage of Truman's diary, discovered in 2003, confirms that Truman indeed asked to be Eisenhower's running mate.

But now that he was in the fight, Truman was one of the few Americans who thought he would win. By Clifford's account, Bess Truman asked her husband's counsel, "Do you really believe that he thinks that? Has the poor S.O.B. lost his mind?"

Clifford had expected that if the President recognized Israel, Jewish donors would pony up for his campaign. But Truman had warned him that by fall, the Jews would say "we've done nothing for them recently." They would be "off and on" him "sixteen times by then."

With his campaign treasury running dry, the President took a group of demoralized, wealthy supporters onto the Mansion's Truman Balcony (built by his own controversial order the previous year) and said, "Boys, if I can have the money to see the people, I'm going to win this election."

Abe Feinberg, a New York hosiery man, pledged to raise a hundred thousand dollars. Feinberg felt that "without Truman, Israel would have had very difficult days."

As Eddie Jacobson's daughter Elinor recalled, "Daddy rounded up some rich Jews in Kansas City."

Truman's donors were scarcely all Jewish, but such fund-raising made fodder for charges that Harry Truman had only recognized Israel because wealthy Zionists paid him to.

John Kennedy allegedly later insisted to the novelist-playwright Gore Vidal that Truman's "recognition of Israel was rushed through so fast" because a Zionist bagman handed the President "two million dollars in cash in a suitcase." *

Truman's Interior Secretary, Oscar Chapman, later told an even more outlandish tale.

By Chapman's account, sitting in a government office with Truman operatives, Abe Feinberg opened an umbrella, letting fat rolls of cash fall out—a hint of what the President could count on if he would "do something about Israel." Chapman's fable had Truman as its hero, ordering that "bastard" Feinberg to "go to hell."

---

* Kennedy's claims about Truman reflected his own resentment of some donors who wanted him to help Israel. In 1960, after a group of Jewish Democrats pledged him an initial contribution, Kennedy complained to a friend that "they wanted control" of his Middle East policy. He vowed that if elected, he would "do something" about a system that allowed such "outrageous" demands to be made on him.

*   *   *

When Truman won his surprise election victory in November 1948, he lost New York, New Jersey, Pennsylvania and Michigan, all abundant with Jewish voters. Much of the blame went to Henry Wallace, who complained that Truman wasn't sufficiently pro-Israel. From FDR's ninety percent of the Jewish vote in 1944, Truman's share dropped to seventy-five percent.

Clifford later claimed that Truman had not recognized Israel with the Electoral College in mind: if the President won the Democratic South and those states west of the Mississippi, "we could afford to write off the electoral votes of New York, New Jersey, Illinois and Ohio, with their large Jewish urban constituencies."

In their private strategy memorandum of 1947, Clifford and his friend Jim Rowe had advised Truman that the key to Jewish support would be his "liberalism": thus handle the "Palestine problem" on its "intrinsic merit."

After his victory, Truman wrote Chaim Weizmann that his "elation" on being reelected must resemble Weizmann's when the Jews had proclaimed their state.

The man who had once scored Jewish "underdogs" for being "intolerant" and "cruel" now told Weizmann that he and Israel were clearly both underdogs:

"We had both been abandoned by the so-called realistic experts on our supposedly forlorn lost causes. Yet we both kept pressing for what we were sure was right—and we were both proven to be right."

Truman claimed years later that he had "consistently favored . . . an independent state for the Jews in the Middle East," but in fact, he had followed a tortuously winding road toward recognition.

Although anxious to help the displaced Jews of Europe, Truman had been willing to rubber-stamp a 1946 British proposal that might have foreclosed a Jewish state. His commitment to Palestine's partition was shallow enough that, by early 1948, George Marshall and Loy Henderson came close to reversing it.

In the end, he recognized Israel for many different reasons. He was determined to show Marshall's underlings they couldn't push him around. The Jews' display of military strength in Palestine had convinced him that U.S. troops would not be needed to defend them. He feared that letting the Russians recognize Israel first would give them a foothold in Palestine.

Truman was also motivated by sheer politics. With a tough campaign ahead, he knew that if he did not recognize Israel, the backers of a Jewish state would make his life a living hell.

But he had to take the risk that immediate recognition might cause General Marshall and his lieutenants to quit in protest, warning the voters that Truman was bending foreign policy to his own selfish political needs.

Through all of Truman's vacillations, the one abiding influence on him that few outsiders glimpsed was his historical understanding of what it signified to give the Jews a homeland after two thousand years.

For the hard-bitten Marshall, who operated from cold facts on the ground, Israel was chiefly a potential burden for an overstressed U.S. military. But Truman realized helping to found a Jewish state was a historic act that might qualify him for some future edition of *Great Men and Famous Women.*

From the time he fought in France, Truman had admired Woodrow Wilson's passion for human rights and self-determination. By the spring of 1948, he realized that by helping the Jews to achieve a national home, America could put Wilson's ideas into action and help to heal the wounds left by Hitler's unrivaled crimes against humanity.

Truman understood that had the world's most powerful nation failed to recognize the new Jewish state, Israel's foes would have been emboldened to brand it an illegitimate fiction that did not deserve to survive.

By recognizing Israel, Truman knew he would be forever damned by people who did not want the Jews to have their own state—or who did not want it in Palestine.

But as Truman always told himself, the ultimate test of any Presidential decision was "not whether it's popular at the time, but whether it's right. . . . If it's right, make it, and let the popular part take care of itself."

The precocious Harry had written at age fifteen, "A true heart, a strong mind and a great deal of courage and I think a man will get through the world."*

Heir to the pioneers of Independence, Missouri gateway to the American West, Truman believed that great leaders must be optimists.

From his lifetime reading about the "land of milk and honey," he was sure that the Jews could make the Palestine desert bloom: they and those Arabs were "first cousins anyway," so why couldn't they get along?

After recognizing Israel, Truman tried to have Loy Henderson fired, complaining that the diplomat "lied to me" by claiming that the Jews could not defend their state without American help.

Reminded by Marshall that a Foreign Service Officer could not easily be sacked, the President got Henderson out of Washington by naming him Ambassador to India.†

Henderson's later account of his record on Palestine was hardly the same as Truman's. As he told the story in retirement, the President had been "looking for someone to tell him what he wanted to hear" about a Jewish state: "I simply was unable to do it. I and all the men in the field felt it was a tragic mistake."

Henderson complained to Dean Rusk, who by then had been Secretary of State under Presidents Kennedy and Johnson, "I have become the most detested villain in the drama of 'The Birth of Israel.' "

The life of Clark Clifford, who had bested Henderson in the battle for Truman's mind, careened toward a more dramatic finale.

Disappointed that Truman would not make him Attorney General, Clifford quit government to become an elegant Washington lobbyist, the first to earn a million dollars a year. As Secretary of Defense in 1968, he maneuvered Lyndon Johnson toward deescalation in Vietnam, just as he had moved Truman toward recognizing Israel.

Late in life, Clifford grabbed the chance to chair a Washington bank that turned out to be secretly owned by renegade Arab financiers. Indicted by the Manhattan District Attorney, Robert Morgenthau, for

---

* This comment appears in one of the Truman essays discovered in 2000.

† Truman's first notion had been Turkey, until he was reminded that Turkey's proximity to Israel might let Henderson make more trouble for the Jewish state.

fraud, bribery and money laundering, the man celebrated for his mastery of detail pleaded ignorance.

Slouching in his darkened office, with a glint of silver beard, the once fastidious Clifford lamented in 1993 to the author of this book that people who once admired him were now saying, "Who the hell is Clark Clifford? He's just . . . a guy who crawled up the greasy pole and . . . my God . . . has fallen clear to the bottom."

Clifford wondered aloud whether Morgenthau was motivated by lingering resentment that, after taking office, President Truman had abruptly fired his father from the Treasury.*

Clifford's cardiovascular disease spared him a trial, but he died in eclipse. Symbolizing how his luck had fled, Clifford's memorial service at the National Cathedral was held on the morning the House started impeachment hearings against President Bill Clinton, which cut down the attendance.

Eddie Jacobson's later life was much happier. In 1949, wearing a lucky hat inscribed by Truman, he made a pilgrimage to Israel, where he was feted in gratitude by President Weizmann and Prime Minister Ben-Gurion. While riding in a Tel Aviv motorcade, he was touched when a little boy cried out, "There's Eddie!"

A Kansas City rabbi told reporters that Jacobson should be president of Israel. Truman wrote his old friend that Israel "couldn't nominate a better man, but I sincerely hope you won't take it."

Jacobson explained that it was just "a silly dream of a very emotional rabbi." He was "too proud of my American citizenship to trade it for any office in the world."

When Truman retired in 1953, Eddie wanted to be escort for the ex-President's first visit to the nation whose birth they had both midwived: "I sincerely hope my dream comes true."

But in 1955, Eddie died of a massive heart attack. As a daughter remembered, when Truman called on the mourning family, he "put his head in his hands and started to sob," exclaiming, "I've lost my brother!"

---

* This was unlikely: Truman fired the elder Morgenthau before Clifford even joined the White House staff.

In 1965, an Eddie Jacobson Auditorium was built in Tel Aviv. Truman hoped "at long last" to "make my journey" to Israel, but a bruising fall in the shower had made him old almost overnight.

Instead he wrote a tribute to "my great and irreplaceable friend." Truman insisted that his "sympathies" for a Jewish state had been "always active and present," but that Eddie's "contribution was of decisive importance. . . . His name should be forever enshrined in the history of the Jewish people."

Interviewed by an Israeli reporter in Independence, Truman said, "Now remind me, how did Eddie use to say 'congratulations' in Hebrew—*Mazel* something? . . . Yeah, *tov. Mazel tov!*"

Nearing the end of his life, Harry Truman retained enough of his old private prejudices that as late as 1957, he derided New York City in a letter to Bess as "the U.S. Capital of Israel."

Truman once said that "a weeping man is an abomination." But with his reverence for the Bible and ancient history, Truman was profoundly moved to know he had helped regather the Jews in the Holy Land.

Told that an Israeli village had been renamed "Kfar Truman," the stricken President had to cover his face with a handkerchief.

When the chief rabbi of Israel came to the White House in 1949, he told Truman, "God put you in your mother's womb so you would be the instrument to bring about Israel's rebirth after two thousand years."

Even Dave Niles, who had fought for a Jewish homeland, thought the rabbi was "overdoing" it. But with "tears glistening in his eyes," Truman asked the rabbi if "the hand of the Almighty" had really guided him for "the sake of the Jewish people."

Soon the President was proudly comparing himself to the ancient Persian king who had enabled the Jews to return to Zion.

During a visit to the Jewish Theological Seminary in New York just after Truman left office, Eddie Jacobson introduced his old friend by saying, "This is the man who helped to create the state of Israel."

The ex-President brought Eddie up short: "What do you mean 'helped create'? I am Cyrus! I am Cyrus!"

CHAPTER TWENTY-NINE

THEY NEVER SHOW
THEIR PASSION

On Monday afternoon, June 10, 1963, a gleaming, jet-black Cadillac with Space Age tail fins drew up near the sunny White House Rose Garden.

With birds twittering, Attorney General Robert Kennedy stepped out of the car and walked up the path to his brother's Oval Office.

There John Kennedy was rocking on the chair prescribed for his injured back. With eyes dark-welled from lack of sleep, he jabbed a knuckle under his left cheekbone and nervously tapped his right foot.

JFK was worried that a dozen or more American cities were about to go up in flame over civil rights.

In 1960, he had promised to use a President's "immense moral authority" to give Negroes full equality. But after his narrow election (with ninety percent black support), he stepped back from that pledge.

With the House and Senate dominated by white Southerners and conservatives, he did not want civil rights to sink his whole program. He feared that when he ran for reelection, offending the white South would cost him the very states that had made him President.

But by 1963, African-Americans would not wait. "We've got to stop begging the Kennedys," cried one black leader. "We've got to start *demanding* our rights!"

*   *   *

That May, angry black men in Birmingham, Alabama—the "most segregated city in the United States"—smashed cars and torched buildings, shouting, "Let the whole fucking city burn!"

In the Oval Office, with the President's hidden tape recorder running, Bobby warned Jack that the rioting would provoke a white backlash: "You're going to have rallies all over the country, calling upon the President to take some forceful action—and 'Why aren't you protecting the rights of the [white] people in Birmingham?' "*

As for the Negroes, "the success they had in Birmingham" could "trigger off a good deal of violence"—and "not just in the South." Blacks were threatening that if the federal government wouldn't listen, "they're going to have to start following the ideas of the Black Muslims."

Bobby said that if the Negroes felt the government was "their friend," the President "could head some of that off." But if not, the civil rights problem would be "uncontrollable."

"Uncontrollable," repeated his anxious brother.

Now Alabama Governor George Wallace was poised to "stand in the schoolhouse door" to stop two Negroes from enrolling at his state university.

Waving his arm, Bobby told Jack that he had to give Americans—both black and white—the confidence that the civil rights revolution was safely "in the hands of the President."

The black man John Kennedy knew best throughout his life was his valet, George Thomas.

A small-town Virginian, Thomas had been commended to the new young Massachusetts Congressman by his father's Kentucky friend, the *New York Times* columnist Arthur Krock, who called him "a fat, good-natured Negro of high competence as a domestic."

JFK's only complaint was "Why can't he learn to tie a white tie?"

Upstairs at the White House, it was George who tickled Kennedy's feet to wake him without disturbing Jackie, and who parceled out the many pills the President took each day.

Since JFK changed his clothes, down to the flesh, at least four times

---

* Many of the conversations quoted in this and the two chapters that follow come from the secret recordings made by JFK in the Oval Office and Cabinet Room.

daily, it was Thomas who pressed the Presidential wardrobe in an over-heated room ("I ain't complaining!") and hung a fresh hand-sewn suit, matching shirt and tie, clean socks and boxer shorts in the little bathroom off the Oval Office.

In November 1963, just before Kennedy emerged from *Air Force One* in Dallas, he buoyantly told his valet, "George, I think this is a bigger town than you came from!"

Arthur Krock later declared that he "never saw a Negro on level social terms with the Kennedys" and "never heard the subject mentioned."

But it was not unusual for a well-heeled white New Englander of the time to grow up without close black friends. Of the four Negroes in his Harvard class, Jack had genial relations with Paul Davis, a fellow resident of Winthrop House, who felt that Kennedy treated him decently.

Like Joe Kennedy, whose indignation about bigotry was unfortunately limited to that against Irish Catholics, the young JFK sometimes used racial epithets. During his first House campaign in 1946, he joked to a friend that his *PT-109* heroism attracted more votes when he included "a Jew and a nigger in the story."

JFK's first valet was a black man named George Taylor, who had managed a Harvard Square laundry. Jack ribbed George about his whiskey. George ribbed Jack about his women.

During Kennedy's first campaign, Taylor served as cook, chauffeur and body man: "If you wanted to see Jack" and "I didn't like you, you couldn't see him."

But Taylor discovered that some black women he had recruited for the campaign had been excluded from a volunteers' luncheon hosted by JFK's sisters. He said, "Jack, I think that's bullshit. They're all giving their time. They're all human beings."

Kennedy replied, "George, you're thin-skinned."

Taylor soon decided that "I'd better leave Jack, and I did."

John Kennedy's aide and friend Ted Sorensen later conceded that during his early years as Congressman and Senator, his hero "simply did not give much thought" to civil rights.

While trying to become Adlai Stevenson's running mate in 1956, JFK courted white Southern support by avoiding the issue.

[237]

His chief rival, Senator Estes Kefauver of Tennessee, had inflamed white Southern delegates by refusing to sign the "Southern Manifesto" against integration.

Hoping to win their endorsement, JFK publicly refused to embrace the Supreme Court's landmark order of 1954 to desegregate American public schools. Asked about *Brown v. Board of Education*, Kennedy merely replied that it was "the law" and that as a Senator, he had had "nothing to do with that decision."

When Stevenson let the convention choose his running mate, Kennedy narrowly lost to Kefauver but took almost the entire white South. He assured a friend, "I'll be singing 'Dixie' for the rest of my life."

Kennedy hoped to keep his new Southern allies when the Senate in 1957 considered its first civil rights bill in eighty-two years. He refused liberals' appeals to help them pry the bill away from the segregationist Judiciary Committee chairman, James Eastland of Mississippi.

Delighted, a segregationist columnist in Birmingham wrote that Kennedy was becoming the "living antithesis" of Chief Justice Earl Warren, architect of the *Brown* decision. Kennedy thanked the columnist, writing that he felt "a common bond with many Southerners."

As the 1957 bill moved toward Senate passage, opponents proposed a crippling amendment requiring a jury trial for anyone accused of keeping Negroes from voting. They knew that all-white Southern juries would be unlikely to convict.

Georgia Governor Marvin Griffin vowed that blood would flow before any "nigger" entered Atlanta's white public schools. He wrote Kennedy, "Your many friends in Georgia are depending on you."

Planning by now to seek the Presidency in 1960, Kennedy backed the jury-trial amendment, moving the furious civil rights leader Roy Wilkins to renounce him: "No pal of Griffin can possibly be a pal of mine. Griffin thinks I'm an animal!"

Black leaders were outraged anew on discovering that JFK had served breakfast at his Georgetown home to the segregationist Governor of Alabama, John Patterson: what secret "price" had been paid by the "shameless" Kennedy to win Patterson's Presidential endorsement?

At a New York banquet, the baseball hero Jackie Robinson, the most

popular African-American of the day, refused to allow himself to be photographed with Kennedy.

By 1959, however, the Massachusetts Senator was changing his tune on civil rights.

Midterm Congressional victories had shifted the Democratic party's center of gravity toward Northern big cities. And with his recovery from a massive heart attack, Senate Majority Leader Lyndon Johnson was planning to base his own Presidential candidacy on the very white Southerners whom Kennedy had been wooing.

In the new political universe, JFK's private pollster Lou Harris warned him that his friendships in the Old South might be the "kiss of death."

Dropping his Southern strategy, Kennedy wrote Martin Luther King, Jr., to ask for a meeting. But the civil rights crusader had been appalled by Kennedy's courtship of the segregationists. He did not respond.

Campaigning for President in the spring of 1960, Kennedy sounded like a thoroughgoing liberal, demanding "equal opportunity at the polls, in the classroom, in the five-and-ten-cent stores, and at the lunch counter."

His opponent Senator Hubert Humphrey, who had implored Democrats in 1948 to enter the "sunshine of human rights," dismissed Jack's new rhetoric as just "politics."

Kennedy's aide Marge Lawson warned him that her fellow Negroes felt he had "little experience" and "no real understanding" of them.

By June, JFK was on the verge of sewing up the nomination. But his campaign manager, Bobby Kennedy, worried that liberal Democrats might stop his brother by drafting their sentimental favorite, Adlai Stevenson. In his effort to head off Stevenson, Bobby told aides to do "everything you need" to get Negro support.

Skeptical black delegates from Michigan were flown to Washington on the Kennedy plane, the *Caroline*, and entertained in the same Georgetown dining room where JFK had given breakfast to Governor Patterson.

"There was chicken and some fancy kind of eggs, and there were whites and Negroes waiting on us," recalled one Michigan guest. "After-

ward that man must have given away a hundred dollars worth of cigars from some foreign country. . . . We were all impressed."

JFK also trekked to Harry Belafonte's Manhattan apartment for advice on how to appeal to black holdouts like Jackie Robinson. The singer advised him, "Forget Jackie Robinson." Winning over Martin Luther King, Jr., would really "make a difference."

Under prodding from Belafonte, King consented to meet the Senator at Joe Kennedy's hideaway apartment on Central Park South.

Using his forthright charm, JFK confessed he had been slow to understand the moral importance of the civil rights movement. After their meeting, King said he had "no doubt" that as President, Kennedy would "do the right thing."

JFK had worse luck during a private session with Jackie Robinson. When he tried to explain his misalliance with Patterson, Robinson rejected it and asked why Kennedy would not look him in the eye.

Finally Kennedy asked him what it would take to win his support. Robinson bristled: "Look, Senator, I don't want any of your money!"

To foreclose any last-minute liberal rebellion, JFK approved a Democratic platform that promised the moon on civil rights and publicly vowed not to seek delegates from the white South.*

"I want to be nominated by the liberals," JFK told his liberal historian backer Arthur Schlesinger, Jr. "I don't want to go screwing around with all those Southern bastards."

But after he was nominated, Kennedy's first act was to choose Lyndon Johnson, the party's most famous white Southerner, for Vice President.

Bobby Kennedy advised inflamed blacks and liberals to "trust" his brother: "What do you think we're running a campaign for—Negroes alone?"

*　　*　　*

---

* Bobby warned JFK that the latter pledge would seem "a gratuitous insult to the Southern political leaders who have been interested in you." The candidate responded by having his most prominent Jewish supporter, Connecticut Governor Abe Ribicoff, announce that Kennedy would be "happy and proud" to claim support from "any part of the United States."

Jackie Robinson campaigning for Richard Nixon, October 1960

In the fall of 1960, JFK hoped to attract more black voters than Stevenson's sixty percent in 1956—but without alienating the white South.

To reassure Negroes, he asked Martin Luther King, Jr., to appear with him before the American Legion in Miami. King felt that Kennedy's opponent, Vice President Richard Nixon, had been more reliable on civil rights, but he agreed.

Then, when King learned that Nixon would be at the convention, he proposed that the Vice President join them too.

"The hell with that!" fumed Kennedy. "I'm taking a much greater risk in the South than Nixon. . . . Tell him it's off." *

That October, King strode into the segregated restaurant of an Atlanta department store. Jailed for trespassing, as well as earlier driving with an out-of-state license, he was severely oversentenced to six months of hard labor, in handcuffs and chains, at the Georgia state penitentiary.

---

* By "risk" Kennedy meant that his civil rights rhetoric was jeopardizing his party's traditional grip on the white "Solid South."

Fearing offense to the white South, Kennedy did not denounce King's sentence in public. But he quietly informed Georgia Governor Ernest Vandiver that King's release would be "of tremendous benefit to me."

Kennedy's civil rights aide Harris Wofford was distraught over the Senator's caution. He told JFK's brother-in-law, Sargent Shriver, who shared his convictions about human equality, "The trouble with your beautiful, passionate Kennedys is that they never show their passion."

At the O'Hare Inn outside Chicago, Shriver waited for other, more hard-boiled advisers to leave the room and then urged JFK to call King's scared, pregnant wife, Coretta: black voters wanted to know "whether you care."

Kennedy called Mrs. King and pledged to do what he could.

When Bobby discovered Shriver's caprice, he tore into him with a ferocity that damaged their relationship for years. He told his brother-in-law that three Southern governors had warned him that if Jack supported King, they would switch to Nixon: "Do you know that the election may be razor close, and you have probably lost it for us?"

As Robert feared, his brother's call to King's wife made the newspapers. Chastened by Bobby for his risky freelancing, JFK complained that some "traitor" must have leaked the news.

But Kennedy's call paid unexpected dividends. Upon his son's release from jail, Martin Luther King, Sr., a Nixon Republican, said he would hand his "suitcase full of votes" to the man who had "dried the tears" in his daughter-in-law's eyes.

Capitalizing on Daddy King's endorsement, Shriver sent a huge mass mailing to black households—a pale blue pamphlet called, " 'No Comment' Nixon versus a Candidate with a Heart, Senator Kennedy."

On Election Day 1960, African-Americans helped to put the "Candidate with a Heart" in the White House.

But Kennedy was nervous about his hairbreadth victory and the coalition of conservative Republicans and white Southern Democrats that now faced him on Capitol Hill.

He felt that if he proposed a major civil rights bill, only to be defeated, the blood would be on the water and he could be finished in Con-

gress as soon as he began—a peril to the nation at an "hour of maximum danger" from the Soviet Union.

Better to aim for a landslide reelection in 1964, hoping for a more liberal House and Senate that would follow his lead on civil rights. In the meantime, Attorney General Robert Kennedy could work under the radar with civil rights reforms by executive order.

Soon after JFK took office, Roy Wilkins came to the Oval Office and asked him to honor his campaign commitments. Wilkins was shocked when Kennedy airily replied, "Why don't you call Ted Sorensen? Write him a memo. We'll see what comes of it."

Father Theodore Hesburgh, president of Notre Dame and a friend of Joe Kennedy's, asked the President to keep his pledge to fully integrate the armed forces.

"Look, I have serious problems in West Berlin," replied JFK, "and I do not think this is the proper time to start monkeying around with the Army. I can't have them in the midst of a social revolution."

At that moment, Kennedy's chief concern about civil rights was that Soviet propaganda organs were crowing about the African diplomats who drove on Route 40 between Washington and New York and were shunned by restaurants and motels.

The President responded by sending someone up the highway to ask proprietors to open their doors for the sake of the Free World.

"The hell with your colored diplomats," one exploded. "Go back to Washington and tell Kennedy *he* can feed 'em!"

Frustrated, JFK told his protocol chief, "Can't you tell these African ambassadors not to drive on Route 40? It's a hell of a road.... I wouldn't think of driving from New York to Washington. Tell them to fly!"

CHAPTER THIRTY

GO GET HIM, JOHNNY BOY!

Among John Kennedy's close relatives and friends was almost no one who would press him on civil rights.

The President did not relax among ideologues. Pals like his Republican *PT-109* comrade Red Fay and the conservative Florida Senator George Smathers were the opposite of what JFK privately derided as "attitudinizing liberals."

Jacqueline Kennedy, though a serious woman in other areas of life, did not hector him about politics. Bobby explained that one source of Jackie's charm was that she never asked Jack what was "new in Laos." Mrs. Kennedy was so disengaged from domestic affairs that the first time she traveled west of Virginia as First Lady was in November 1963, when she and JFK flew to Texas.

The one member of Kennedy's immediate circle who kept reminding him about civil rights was Sargent Shriver, and he was there by marriage.

Shriver was a devout Catholic who considered racism a "sin." As Chicago school board president and head of the city's Catholic Interracial Council, Shriver had fought hard to get black children the education they deserved.

On civil rights, Kennedy was unaffected by his more casual faith. In fact, as the first Catholic President, he was determined to show Americans that his religion would not rule his politics. Thus he ignored crusading liberal Catholics like Shriver, who argued that "the heart of the race question is religious and moral."

*   *   *

Disheartened by Kennedy's foot-dragging, James Farmer and other civil rights leaders declared "Project Freedom Ride 1961."

That spring, thirteen "Freedom Riders," white and black, boarded buses for the South. Ostensibly they were testing a recent Supreme Court ruling integrating the bus terminals. But as Farmer later conceded, they actually hoped to "create a crisis" that would budge the President on civil rights.

Soon the crisis began. In Anniston, Alabama, a white mob beat Freedom Riders with crowbars and burned their Greyhound bus. In Birmingham, the notorious public safety chief Eugene "Bull" Connor held back his police force so that Ku Klux Klansmen could brutalize the outsiders without interference.

The President was about to meet Nikita Khrushchev in Vienna. Although appalled by the savagery in the South, he was focused on the danger that the Soviet leader would use the racial incidents to "embarrass" him. Bobby's deputy Nicholas Katzenbach was startled to learn that JFK considered the Freedom Riders "a pain in the ass."

Hoping to remove the distraction, Kennedy called Harris Wofford: "Tell them to call it off. Stop them. Get your friends off those buses!"

Robert Kennedy feared that offering the Freedom Riders federal protection would inflame the white South, while encouraging the riders to escalate their protest.

To keep the federal government out of the South, Bobby persuaded his brother's erstwhile ally Governor Patterson to have Alabama state troopers escort the riders to Mississippi. But when white Alabamans accused Patterson of abetting the "rabble-rousers," the Governor reneged.

Upon investigation, Bobby learned that without armed escort, no driver would drive any bus bearing Freedom Riders.

Angrily he called the Greyhound superintendent in Birmingham: "Better be getting in touch with Mr. Greyhound, or whoever Mr. Greyhound is, and somebody better give us an answer. . . . I am—the government is going to be very much upset if this group does not get to continue their trip."

To fix the problem, Bobby demanded that Greyhound assign a "colored driver." He was unaware that in the Alabama of 1961 such a request was in vain.

Finally the Freedom Riders were flown to New Orleans. Then ten more arrived in Birmingham. Bull Connor jailed them for "their own protection."

Desperate to cauterize the crisis, Bobby accepted Connor's offer to have the new riders driven to the Tennessee border. He did not stop to realize how dangerous it was to entrust the riders' safety to the wily old segregationist.

But Connor had them delivered safely. Then ten more Freedom Riders appeared in Birmingham, bound for the state capital of Montgomery.

Patterson told Bobby he wouldn't "guarantee the safety of fools." Kennedy replied, "You're making political speeches at me, John."

Under pressure from the Attorney General, Patterson sent Alabama troopers, but they abandoned the riders while in transit. When the Freedom Riders reached Montgomery, whites holding bricks, bottles and baseball bats cried, "Get them niggers!"

Bobby's aide and chum John Seigenthaler, whom he had sent from Washington to monitor the situation, was smashed in the skull while trying to stop the beating of a young white woman.

Raging about Seigenthaler's attack, Robert called Patterson, but was told that the Governor couldn't be found.

On Sunday, May 21, Martin Luther King, Jr., flew to Montgomery, demanding federal protection as an "interstate traveler."

Chagrined by JFK's lassitude on civil rights, King had sought a meeting with the President but got only a five-minute audience in the West Wing office of a Kennedy aide, during which JFK tried to impress King with his foreign policy troubles.

Robert Kennedy feared that King, the most famous symbol of his movement, might be murdered in Montgomery. To prevent such a tragedy, Kennedy ordered fifty U.S. Marshals ("like he was the President of the United States," sputtered Patterson) to escort King to a speech at the First Baptist Church.*

---

* A little-known means of federal enforcement, the U.S. Marshals Service of the early 1960s consisted of about a hundred Marshals and about three hundred deputies. John Adams had used Marshals to enforce the Sedition Act, Abraham Lincoln to find Confederate spies.

Despite the protective federal cordon, thousands of whites threw rocks and Molotov cocktails, shouting, "Nigger King!" The civil rights leader complained to Bobby by telephone that the Kennedy Administration wasn't doing enough to help.

"Now, Reverend, don't tell me that," said Kennedy. "You know just as well as I do that if it hadn't been for the United States Marshals, you'd be as dead as Kelsey's nuts right now."

Unfamiliar with the term, King later asked his aides, "Who's Kelsey? Anyone know Kelsey?" *

The next day at the White House, a Yale Law School visitor incensed the President by telling him it was time to propose a major civil rights bill to Congress.

Showing his inner frustration, JFK bloviated to an aide, "Doesn't he know I've done more for civil rights than any President in American history?"

Jailed in the Mississippi capital of Jackson, some of the Freedom Riders were forced to wear scratchy prison garb. One of them cried, "Gandhi wrapped a rag around his balls and brought the whole British Empire to its knees!"

Informed that the jailed riders were threatening a hunger strike, Robert Kennedy told Harris Wofford, "I wonder whether they have the best interest of their country at heart. . . . One of them is against the atom bomb—yes, he even picketed against it in jail!"

Trying to stop more Freedom Riders from going south, Bobby warned Martin Luther King that their protest would not have "the slightest effect" on his brother.

"Perhaps it would help if students came down by the hundreds of thousands," retorted King.

"Don't make statements that sound like a threat," said Bobby. "That's not the way to deal with us."

---

* King was understandably puzzled by Kennedy's comment. In the 1920s, referring to the bolts on wheels produced by the Kelsey Wheel Company, Americans would say that a miser was as "tight as Kelsey's nuts." In the early 1960s, referring to the gelded champion racehorse Kelso, they would call a dead man "deader than Kelso's nuts." In the tradition of American slang, both expressions merged.

Unfazed, King insisted that only nonviolent demonstrations could "save the soul of America." His father's generation had been too patient. He felt "the need of being free now!"

In July 1961, a reporter asked JFK what he thought of the Freedom Rides. The reply was intentionally bland: "Anyone who travels" should "be able to move freely in interstate commerce."

The *New York Times* acidly remarked that Kennedy's response "did not sound like a profile in political courage."

Being called gutless hit the President where he lived. As a Senator, he had hugely enhanced his reputation by writing a bestseller extolling American leaders of the past who had taken big political risks for a moral cause.

Written during his recovery from a near-fatal back operation, *Profiles in Courage* described eight U.S. Senators who had stared into their own political graves.*

In his notes for the book, Kennedy scrawled, "Politics is a jungle— torn between doing right thing & staying in office . . . between the private good of the politician and the general good."

Kennedy's curiosity about political courage had no doubt been stimulated by watching his father's political career. As Henry Luce once noted, Joe Kennedy had been forever torn between "earthy selfishness" and "higher loyalties."

In his book, JFK wrote, "Where else . . . but in the political profession is the individual expected to sacrifice all—including his own career—for the national good? . . . To decide at which point and on what issue he will risk his career is a difficult and soul-searching decision."

Some critics complained that *Profiles* was an attempt to deflect attention from Kennedy's failure to endorse the Senate's censure of the anti-Communist demagogue Joe McCarthy, who was popular in Massachusetts.

But members of the Pulitzer Prize board found it an inspirational lesson, coming from someone who had actually felt the scorching cross-

---

* They were John Quincy Adams and Daniel Webster of Massachusetts, Thomas Hart Benton of Missouri, Sam Houston of Texas, Edmund Ross of Kansas, Lucius Lamar of Mississippi, George Norris of Nebraska and Robert Taft of Ohio.

pressures on a politician. Overriding their academic jury, which had suggested more substantial works, the board gave *Profiles* their 1957 prize for biography.*

Kennedy gave his five-hundred-dollar prize money to the United Negro College Fund.

History had always been a large part of Kennedy's life. With the exception of John Quincy Adams, no other future President had seen more of it being made at high levels while growing up.

From his insatiable reading, JFK adorned his speeches and private conversation with references to the past. Before the 1960 election, for example, when he went to Hyde Park to make peace with Eleanor Roosevelt, who detested his father, he said it was like "the raft at Tilsit."†

But the cool, skeptical Kennedy had no Presidential heroes in the sense that T.R. adored Lincoln and Truman revered Andrew Jackson.

He was unsentimental enough about George Washington to hold a lavish dinner at Mount Vernon for Pakistan's Mohammed Ayub Khan, who had seized power by military coup.

At home in Gettysburg, ex-President Dwight Eisenhower exploded at how the "Goddamned" Kennedys had used his hero's sacred ground to celebrate a dictator: "What a desecration!"

The Kennedys invited friends for occasional evenings discussing history and other topics with well-known scholars. Alice Roosevelt Longworth, by now in her seventies, presumed the evenings would be "precious" but found them "all sorts of fun."

The "Hickory Hill Seminars" were named for their most frequent venue—the Potomac River house passed down over time from General George McClellan to Robert Kennedy and his wife, Ethel.

During one seminar in the Yellow Oval Room, upstairs at the White House, in February 1962, the Lincoln historian David Herbert Donald

---

* Joe Kennedy and Arthur Krock lobbied Pulitzer trustees to choose JFK's book, but such efforts may have hurt as much as they helped. After winning the prize, *Profiles* was shadowed by charges that in writing it, Kennedy had undue help from Sorensen. Here the public's understanding that politicians do not write everything they publish collided with the expectation that winners of important literary prizes should.

† Where the mutually hostile Napoleon and Czar Alexander I had met mid-river in 1807.

was disappointed to conclude that JFK's interest in history was largely utilitarian. Bluntly Kennedy asked him, "How do you go down in history books as a great President?"

One reason the question was on JFK's mind that winter was the rising liberal criticism for his failure to etch for himself a more courageous profile on civil rights.

"It will take some time, but I want you to know that we are going to do all these things," he assured Harris Wofford. "You will see. With time, I'm going to do them all." *

In the summer of 1962, the Supreme Court ordered the University of Mississippi to admit its first black student, an Air Force veteran called James Meredith.

The tightly wound Meredith had launched his legal battle to enter Ole Miss after listening to Kennedy's inaugural address and realizing that the new President had scarcely mentioned civil rights.

Meredith embodied the complexity of African-American history. He was the grandson of a slave—but also (few realized it) the illegitimate great-grandson of a white Mississippi Supreme Court Justice who had fought for white supremacy.

On Thursday, September 20, when Meredith tried to register at Ole Miss, Governor Ross Barnett stood in his way while crowds cried, "Go home, nigger!"

By telephone with the Attorney General, Barnett complained that his state was getting "kicked around": "Kennedy, you ought to rescind this order."

Bobby reminded the Governor that Mississippi was "part of the United States."

"I don't know whether we are or not," said Barnett.

"Are you getting out of the Union?"

"This thing is serious," said Barnett. "We're hearing you've ordered an Army here."

Kennedy said, "Oh no, Governor, I wouldn't do that."

*   *   *

---

* Tired of waiting, Wofford quit the White House to join Shriver at the Peace Corps.

After a failed effort to enroll him more quietly in Jackson, Robert told Barnett that Meredith would arrive in Oxford the next day for classes: "Why don't you try it for six months and see how it goes?"

Barnett said, "It's best for him not to go to Ole Miss." Kennedy retorted, "But he likes Ole Miss!"

On Wednesday morning, September 26, the Attorney General had Meredith accompanied by Chief U.S. Marshal Jim McShane, an ex-boxer who had been JFK's campaign bodyguard. But Barnett's state troopers blocked their way.

Bobby promised the Governor that if he let Meredith register that evening, the President would stage a show of federal intervention that would give Barnett the alibi that he had been forced to give in and preserve the public peace.

Intrigued, Barnett asked if a U.S. Marshal could dramatically point a revolver at his head. Kennedy replied, "Isn't it sufficient if I have one man draw his gun and the others keep their hands on their holsters?"

Kennedy and Barnett agreed to mount their theater of the absurd. But that night, as Meredith and his U.S. Marshals were driving toward Ole Miss, Barnett panicked and called off the deal.

Cursing the Governor, Kennedy ordered McShane and his men to turn back.

Recoiling from the national controversy when Eisenhower used the Army to integrate Little Rock Central High School in 1957, the Kennedys did not want to use U.S. soldiers to get Meredith into Ole Miss.

Feeling checkmated, however, Bobby told an aide, "We'd better get going with the military. . . . I wouldn't have believed it could have happened in this country, but maybe now we can understand how Hitler took over Germany."

That weekend, the President stayed at the White House to oversee the crisis. Before finally resorting to the Army, he wanted to bargain with Barnett himself.

As the call was being placed to Jackson, JFK imitated a boxing referee: "And now, Governor Ross Barnett!" With the same mordant sense of humor, Bobby said, "Go get him, Johnny boy!"

Before Barnett came on the line, JFK joked, "Governor, this is the

President of the United States—not Bobby, not Teddy, not Princess Radziwill." *

Anticipating the conversation, the President had turned on his new secret recording system, installed to protect him against people who might lie to others about what he told them in private—and to help him later write his memoirs.

"Well, now, here's my problem, Governor," Kennedy said. "I don't know Mr. Meredith, and I didn't put him in the University. But . . . under the Constitution, I have to carry out the order." He wanted an "amicable" solution without "a lot of people down there getting hurt."

Barnett said, "You know what I am up against," but promised to try. Before ringing off, he thanked the President for his help on "the poultry program."

Chuckling, JFK told his brother, "You've been fighting a sofa pillow all week." Reminded of the pols they knew in Boston, Robert exhaled, "What a rogue!"

Back on the telephone with the Attorney General, Barnett revisited the subject of a prearranged public melodrama: Meredith could be hastily registered in Jackson, after which the Governor could claim the Kennedys had tricked him.

Bobby refused. Then the President called Barnett and said he was willing to consider such a ruse, so long as the Governor ensured that "the state police will maintain law and order."

"Oh, we'll do that." Barnett pledged to guard Meredith with 220 state highway patrolmen.

But at an Ole Miss football game that evening, men with Rebel flags cried, "We want Ross!" His juices flowing from the acclaim, the Governor once again called Robert to say that their deal was off.

The President exclaimed, "Why, that Goddamn son-of-a-bitch!"

By midnight, his patience exhausted, JFK prepared to federalize the Mississippi National Guard.

Studying the authorizing documents, he sat at General Ulysses

* Jackie's sister Lee was married to a descendant of Polish royalty.

Grant's old desk in the upstairs Treaty Room, which Jackie had created with Victorian splendor. The forest green wallpaper, bordered with red diamonds, copied that of the boarding house room where Lincoln died.

While signing the orders, Kennedy mentioned to Assistant Attorney General Norbert Schlei, "You know, that's General Grant's table."

As Schlei started downstairs to brief the few reporters still there at that hour, JFK realized that white Southerners might presume he had deliberately chosen the Union commander's desk to sharpen his insult to the South.

Thus he called down to Schlei, "Wait, don't tell them about General Grant's table!"

Once the Kennedys federalized the Guard, Barnett knew they meant business. He called Bobby and tried to reopen bargaining over a new version of their street theater.

But the Attorney General was fed up. He told Barnett, "I think it is silly going through this whole facade of . . . our people drawing guns, your stepping aside. To me it is dangerous and it has gone beyond the stage of politics."

Barnett did not realize that the fun and games were really over. Like a movie star haggling over a script, he said, "I can't just walk back. I have to be confronted with your troops."

Robert told him the President was upset: "You broke your word to him." That evening, JFK would address the nation on television. If Barnett did not cooperate now, his brother would be compelled to reveal that the Governor had privately begged for a fake confrontation with federal troops at Ole Miss.

Knowing such a revelation would ruin him politically, Barnett gasped, "You don't mean the President is going to say that tonight? . . . Don't say that. Please don't mention it."

Thrusting another shiv into Barnett's belly, the Attorney General revealed that he and his brother had secretly recorded their conversations: "We have it all down."

Taking command, Bobby said that whether Barnett liked it or not, Meredith was going to sleep in an Ole Miss dormitory that night—and tomorrow the university would have its first black student.

Even when they had the upper hand, however, the Kennedys tried not to corner treacherous and unpredictable enemies.*

Bobby thus told Barnett that if he wished to save face, he could claim to Mississippians that the federal government had rushed Meredith into the dorm without warning. He gave the Governor until 7:30 P.M. Washington time to make such a speech.

Still terrified that the Kennedys would publicize his private conversations, Barnett pleaded, "Please let us treat what we say as confidential! I am sorry about the misunderstanding last night. I am extremely hurt over it. Really! I didn't know I was violating my agreement."

That evening, as Robert had warned, James Meredith was swept through a storm of rocks into Ole Miss by Nick Katzenbach and two dozen U.S. Marshals.

Despite his patrician manner, Katzenbach was the tough survivor of a World War II Nazi prisoner-of-war camp. Robert Kennedy had joked, "Hey, Nick, don't worry if you get shot because the President needs a moral issue!"

In the Cabinet Room, the President waited for Barnett to give his television speech in Mississippi. Told that the Governor was stalling, Kennedy gave him extra time, saying, "We can't take a chance with Meredith's life, or let that bastard make the federal government look foolish."†

Finally, at 9:30 P.M. Washington time, Barnett told Mississippians that he had "just been informed" of Meredith's installation at Ole Miss: "My heart still says 'never,' but my calm judgment abhors the bloodshed that would follow."

Then after his speech, Barnett pulled a fast one on the Kennedys by removing the state troopers protecting Meredith. Furious, Robert Kennedy called him and threatened to expose their secret bargaining to the public unless Barnett sent the troopers back.

The Oxford crisis had made the President feel so anxious and

---

* As they showed three weeks later against Nikita Khrushchev during the Cuban Missile Crisis.

† JFK showed similar restraint during the Missile Crisis, when he infuriated his generals by granting the Soviets extra time to meet his demands.

drained that he summoned his well-concealed amphetamine doctor, Max Jacobson, known to select Manhattan circles as "Doctor Feelgood," who arrived by private plane.

As Jacobson administered an invigorating shot, Kennedy told him that Ole Miss was a "ball-breaker."

Keeping abreast of the conflict, the President was patched in to Katzenbach, who had to shout into his telephone over the angry nighttime cries in Oxford. Kennedy asked, "What are they chanting?"

Since the President wanted to know, Katzenbach told him: "Go/ to/hell, J/F/K!"

Just before 10:00 P.M., Robert Kennedy walked into the Oval Office to report that Oxford was now engulfed by rioting, but the President was about to start his speech.

Looking into the camera, he declared that the "orders of the court" were being "carried out" at Ole Miss. He crisply noted that "few laws are universally loved," but Americans could not "disobey" them.

It was Kennedy's first major civil rights speech as President. When Martin Luther King heard it, he was angry that JFK had said nothing about the moral reasons why Meredith was being enrolled.

After the lights cooled, Kennedy called Barnett about the tumult in Oxford.* The Governor told him it had grown too dangerous. Meredith must leave the campus.

Irritated, JFK said, "How can I remove him, Governor, when there's a riot in the street, and he may step out of that building and something happen to him? . . . I don't think anybody, either in Mississippi or anyplace else, wants a lot of people killed."

Soon the Oxford resistance approached the level of armed insurrection. Not since the Civil War had there been such a violent showdown between the federal government and one of the American states.

As Robert recalled, he and the President "could just visualize" a "great disaster," with "a lot of marshals being killed or James Meredith being strung up. How would we explain that?"

---

* Which ultimately included the killing of a French reporter and a local jukebox repairman.

Convinced that he had no other choice, JFK deployed the U.S. Army. Although told that troops would reach Ole Miss in an hour, he waited endlessly for word that they had arrived.

By telephone he berated Army Secretary Cyrus Vance: "Where's the Army? Where are they? Why aren't they moving?"

Remembering his CIA's failed invasion of Cuba, Kennedy muttered, "I haven't had such an interesting time since the Bay of Pigs!"

"I would think they'd be on that fucking plane in about five minutes," carped the President's aide Ken O'Donnell. "Khrushchev would get those troops in faster."

By radio link to Memphis, JFK tore into the Army's operations chief, General Creighton Abrams: "People are dying in Oxford. This is the worst thing I've seen in forty-five years!"

Later the President told Bobby, "They always give you their bullshit about their instant reaction and their split-second timing, but it never works out. No wonder it's so hard to win a war."

Whipping up rebellion against Meredith's enrollment was Major General Edwin Walker.

A West Point Texan, Walker had fought in Italy, France and Korea. Against the General's will, President Eisenhower had ordered him to lead Army units taking the first black students into Little Rock High School.

Disgusted by his own complicity in Little Rock, Walker gave out radical right-wing handbills to the troops he commanded in Germany. JFK's Secretary of Defense, Robert McNamara, pushed him out of the Army and canceled his pension.

Hoping to banish his memories of Little Rock, Walker donned his old uniform and drove to Ole Miss, calling by radio for fresh volunteers.

At the White House, where he was still waiting for the Army to reach Oxford, Bobby told his brother, "General Walker's been out there, downtown, getting people stirred up."

The President said, "Imagine that son-of-a-bitch having been commander of a division up until last year. And the Army promoting him!"

* * *

At 2:30 A.M. on Monday, Washington time, the first hundred U.S. soldiers finally landed by helicopter in Oxford, flanked by the Mississippi National Guard.*

Soon the city would be guarded by thirty thousand troops, four times its civilian population. The President thought it "important" that "we got so Goddamn many in there."

JFK did not go to bed until 5:30 A.M. As Robert recalled, his brother was "furious at the Army, furious at Cy Vance, furious at the Army general." It was "the worst night I ever spent."

That morning, as the sun rose in Oxford, James Meredith was formally registered amid the lingering scent of tear gas and shouts of "Black bastard!" and "The blood is on your hands!" Governor Barnett had the state flag lowered to half-mast.

Later, when the Oxford crisis receded, JFK and the Attorney General insisted they had merely enforced the law. Writing the wife of the segregationist Mississippi Senator John Stennis, Bobby even claimed that "what we did at the University of Mississippi had nothing to do with integration or segregation."

Two weeks after Oxford, the Central Intelligence Agency unveiled a vastly more threatening problem—Soviet missiles in Cuba.

Still seething, Bobby quipped, "Can they hit Oxford, Mississippi?"

Mopping up after Ole Miss, Robert Kennedy had General Walker arrested for conspiracy and insurrection, then humiliated by psychiatric testing.

As McNamara's aide Joe Califano recalled, the Attorney General had decided "that Walker was not getting back out on the street, whatever it took." But the General was released on his promise to go home to Dallas. When he did, he resumed his angry struggle, flying the American flag upside down.

One night in April 1963, somebody fired a rifle through Walker's living room window, just missing his head.

---

* Whose troops included Ross Barnett, Jr.

At the time, no one knew who had tried to kill General Walker, except the sniper himself.

He turned out to be a twenty-three-year-old Marxist who had defected to the Soviet Union and returned—Lee Harvey Oswald, whose Russian wife, Marina, acerbically called him "Hunter for the Fascists." *

---

* In *Seven Days in May*, the director John Frankenheimer immortalized Walker as General James Mattoon Scott, who wages a military coup against an American President. Hoping the film would warn Americans against such a danger, JFK allowed Frankenheimer to shoot exterior scenes at the White House. In the mid-1970s, Walker's hopes of glory were finally dashed when he was twice arrested for trying to fondle plainclothes policemen in a Dallas public bathroom.

CHAPTER THIRTY-ONE

IT'S GOING TO BE A CIVIL WAR

As 1963 approached, Martin Luther King wanted President Kennedy to make a dramatic midnight gesture on New Year's Eve, the hundredth anniversary of Lincoln's Emancipation Proclamation.

During a visit to the White House, when JFK showed him the Lincoln Bedroom, where Lincoln had signed the momentous document, King asked him to issue a "second Emancipation . . . outlawing segregation."

King hoped the President would unveil such an order with a midnight speech at the Lincoln Memorial. But Kennedy was not interested. Instead he spent New Year's with his family in Palm Beach.

To mollify black leaders demanding a show of Kennedy's commitment, eight hundred African-Americans were invited to the White House on February 12, 1963, for a Lincoln's Birthday reception. More blacks would be present in one night than in all the years since John and Abigail Adams took up residence in 1800.

Some of the invited guests joked that it was "Collud Folks Night at the White House."

Perhaps recalling that Kennedy had spent New Year's in Palm Beach, Martin Luther King did not interrupt his Jamaica vacation to attend.

At JFK's behest, his press secretary, Pierre Salinger, quietly ensured that the Lincoln's Birthday event got extravagant coverage by African-American journals like *Ebony* and *Jet*, after persuading white reporters that the event was not worth covering.

Kennedy was "absolutely feathered" to see Sammy Davis, Jr., and his blond Swedish wife, Mai Britt, standing near the shrimp Creole buffet. He told an aide, "Get them out of here!"

Like other members of the Las Vegas "Rat Pack," Sammy had worked hard for the President's victory in 1960, but JFK had deeply hurt the black singer-dancer who had married a white woman by banning him from the inaugural to avoid disturbing the white South.

When Kennedy saw the Davises' names on the Lincoln Birthday list, he had crossed them off, but a brave African-American aide, Louis Martin, defied the Boss by quietly restoring them.

After spending precisely a half-hour with the black guests on the public floor of the Mansion, the President and Jackie went upstairs for a private dinner with Ben Bradlee of *Newsweek*, the diplomat Harry Labouisse and the *Making of the President* author Theodore White and their wives.

Kennedy made no effort to inform his friends that history was being made downstairs by the presence of so many black guests. White later wrote in his diary that during dinner with the President, he heard "noise and babble coming from somewhere."

The White House state rooms looked very different that evening from the day the Kennedys had arrived.

With the structure of the White House sagging, Harry and Bess Truman had moved out so that the Presidents' home could be saved. The Mansion was gutted, new subbasements dug and a steel superstructure built within the old shell.

Truman had hoped to restore the original paneling and plaster embellishments, but the Korean War inflated prices for steel and other materials. Running out of money, his architects cut corners. To refurnish the house, Truman made a bulk-purchase deal with the New York department store B. Altman and Company.

When Jackie arrived at the White House, she was aghast at what she called the "early Statler" hotel ambience. With hidden aid from a fabled Paris designer, she transformed the state floor into a living museum of American history.

Told the old brick houses around Lafayette Square and the Executive Office Building of 1888 were to be torn down, she rolled into action and saved them.

Disheartened by the tawdry souvenir shops she had seen while riding in the 1961 inaugural parade, Jackie also started the cleanup of Pennsylvania Avenue. At one moment of self-doubt, JFK told her that it might prove to be his only legacy to the country.

Jacqueline furnished Jack's Oval Office as "a New England sitting room," with antique tables and naval prints. At her behest, the old desk made from HMS *Resolute*'s timbers was brought over from the Mansion.

The First Lady's enthusiasm for painting, sculpture, furniture and architecture, however, sometimes diverted her from the larger historic currents of the period.

During Martin Luther King's visit to the Mansion, Jackie stepped into the tiny elevator, soot-faced, wearing jeans, and said, "Oh, Dr. King, you would be so thrilled if you could just have been with me in the basement this morning. I found a chair right out of the Andrew Jackson period—a beautiful chair."

King, whose interests were moral, not aesthetic, replied, "Yes, yes—is that so?"

Mrs. Kennedy said, "I've just got to tell Jack about that chair. But you have other things to talk to him about, don't you?"

The largely African-American household staff admired the First Lady's manners and her restoration of the Mansion they revered.

If the truth be told, they were less comfortable with her husband. This was not because they found the President laggard on civil rights. Most of the Southern blacks who had served the White House for years were anything but firebrands.

They were disconcerted by his complex private life, which was foreign to them and made them feel like accomplices against the First Lady they respected.

Kennedy's attitude was that a President's private relationships should be off limits, even to historians. When an Oxford friend once nattered about the mistress of some past leader, JFK cut him off: "Not at all a way to treat a great man."

By the spring of 1963, Martin Luther King feared that violent radicals like Malcolm X and his Black Muslims would hijack the civil rights movement.

Ratcheting up the pressure on JFK and other politicians, King singled out Birmingham, Alabama, which he considered "by far the worst big city in the United States." He warned protesters that they might not "come back alive."

That April, when King arrived in Birmingham for a march, Bull Connor's men ordered him and his fifty demonstrators to halt. Kneeling in prayer, King and his deputy, Ralph Abernathy, were hauled off to jail.

Robert Kennedy could not intervene because Connor had broken no federal laws. When a frightened Coretta King called the President, he told her the next day that the FBI had checked up on her husband and found him "all right."

Allowed to call his wife from jail, King said he had gotten a mattress and pillow. She told him of JFK's intercession. He said, "So that's why everybody is suddenly being so polite."

During his eight days in solitary, King used newsprint scraps and toilet paper to write his famous essay "Letter from Birmingham Jail": "For years now I have heard the word 'Wait!' . . . This 'Wait' has almost always meant 'Never.' "

Freed on bail, King launched a Birmingham "children's crusade." Hundreds of boys and girls marched and sang, "Ain't Gonna Let Nobody Turn Me Around." Connor's policemen took them off to jail.

When adolescents marched the next day, Connor turned on his fire hoses. Some protesters threw rocks. At Connor's order, German shepherds lunged at the marchers, tearing trousers and biting flesh.

Americans opened their morning newspapers to see a sickening front-page photograph of a dog baring its fangs against a young black man's abdomen.

Before Birmingham, only four percent of Americans had considered civil rights to be the country's number-one national problem. After Bull Connor's dogs, the figure had skyrocketed to fifty-two percent.

On the Saturday morning, May 4, that the Birmingham picture was published, John Kennedy welcomed leaders of the liberal Americans for Democratic Action to the Cabinet Room.

He warned them that the Russians would exploit the "terrible" new photograph: "I'm the President of this country, and that's a disastrous picture this morning."

The "sickening" front-page photograph of Bull Connor's dogs
on the attack in Birmingham

He and Bobby had "worked as hard as we possibly could, given the laws we had." But "what law can you pass" to restrain a Bull Connor?

He was exerting himself on voting rights.* He knew the "voting thing" wasn't the "whole answer," but "if we get enough Negroes registered," then the South would elect moderate governors and Senators.

One ADA leader told Kennedy that with the national disgust over Birmingham, he should go on television to educate the country, just as FDR had done with his radio fireside chats.

"Everybody has to do what they do best," replied Kennedy, adding that "Franklin Roosevelt didn't have that many fireside chats." Turning to Schlesinger, now a White House aide, he asked, "What's the total number, Arthur?"

---

* Kennedy had quietly and halfheartedly sent a minor voting rights bill to Congress in February.

"He never had more than three a year," said the historian.

"We do more, really, when you think of television," said JFK. "Quite a lot more. I haven't done it particularly well. . . . I don't have Franklin Roosevelt's voice. . . . I've always felt that a half-hour speech on television is pretty disastrous."

Dissatisfied by Kennedy's self-defense, Samuel Zitter of New Jersey told him to his face that the heart of the matter was the President's failure to use "moral suasion" on civil rights.

"Now, wait a minute!" Kennedy replied heatedly. "We have done—not enough because the situation's so desperate—but we have shoved and pushed. And the Department of Justice has. There's nothing that my brother's given more time to. I quite agree that if I were a Negro, I'd be sore."

Venting his spleen, the President related that a newspaper friend had carped to him about his caution on civil rights: "I said, 'Why are you eating over at the Metropolitan Club? They won't even let a Negro *ambassador* in!' "

JFK went on, "I think we *have* worked hard on civil rights. I think it's a national crisis. . . . I think it's very dangerous."

He claimed no "political reluctance" about the issue: "I doubt if the Democratic party carries any more than perhaps two—maybe three Southern states in 1964."

Kennedy could be almost rude when a critic struck a nerve. He thus told Zitter, "Everybody up in New Jersey may be upset by one thing or another that we haven't done. . . .

"What we're trying to do is fight it out with this Congress, given the balance which is there. . . . You, if I may say so, are really saying what Rockefeller and Keating are saying about Cuba. You don't know what it is you *want*, but you want *something*!" *

In an effort to stop the Birmingham demonstrations, Bobby's aide Burke Marshall tried to hammer out an agreement between Martin Luther King and the city's white businessmen.

King's bottom line was integrated lunchrooms, bathrooms and

---

* Governor Nelson Rockefeller and Senator Kenneth Keating had denounced Kennedy's failure to depose Fidel Castro.

drinking fountains, more black jobs, a biracial committee on desegregation and the dropping of all charges against the protesters.

Encouraged that Marshall was making progress, JFK called the black comedian-activist Dick Gregory: "Please don't go down to Birmingham. We've got it all solved."

But Gregory said he had promised Dr. King: "Man, I will be down in the morning."

From Birmingham, Marshall informed the President that they had a deal. JFK told him, "Now if it will only hold, we're over the worst."

But in Marshall's presence, the maverick Birmingham minister Fred Shuttlesworth warned King that "a snake half-dead is as bad as a snake all alive. It'll still bite you. You've been Mr. Big, Martin, but you'll be Mr. Shit if you pull out now. . . . You call it off, but I'm marching!"

Marshall pleaded that the President wanted to announce a settlement at his news conference that afternoon.

"Well, I'm going to go get in bed and wait till I see you and the President on TV calling off the demonstrations," said Shuttlesworth. "And then with the little strength I've got left, I'm going to lead three thousand students."

King explained, "Burke, we've got to have unity. People have suffered."

Then the Birmingham authorities retroactively increased the release bond for each of the hundreds of protesters to $2,500. King's brother A.D., who lived there, threatened "the biggest demonstrations this city has ever seen."

Seeking a quarter-million dollars to solve the problem, Robert Kennedy called union bosses. Harry Belafonte called rich New York liberals. New York Governor Nelson Rockefeller had a suitcase full of cash brought out of his brother David's Chase Manhattan Bank.

With the bail money paid, on Friday, May 10, Martin Luther King and his local allies ratified Burke Marshall's settlement. King told reporters that Birmingham now had the chance to be a "great, enlightened symbol" for the "entire nation."

But the following evening, A. D. King's house was torn open by a bomb blast. Another bomb was thrown at the outside wall of the motel room where Martin had just been sitting.

In a harbinger of the "long hot summers" of the later 1960s, young black men showed their rage. Birmingham's mayor blamed Bobby Kennedy for the violence: "I hope that every drop of blood that's spilled he tastes in his throat, and I hope that he chokes to death!"

On Sunday afternoon, May 12, at the White House, Robert told the President that Birmingham was nearing "complete chaos."

One of the city's black ministers had warned that Negroes would go "headhunting" for policemen that evening. They were "tough and mean" and would "shoot to kill."

Bobby warned his brother that they were seeing something new. In Birmingham, "the group that has gotten out of hand has not been the white people. It's been the Negroes, by and large."

He told Jack that from "the reports that we get from other cities—not just in the South," Birmingham was the menacing wave of their political future: the Negroes were "saying they've been abused for all these years" and "based on the success that they had in Birmingham . . . this could trigger off a good deal of violence around the country now."

Burke Marshall noted that segregationists like Alabama's Governor, George Wallace, were hoping that his brokered peace between King and local businessmen would "blow up." If that happened, black anger would erupt—"and I think not only in Birmingham."

Marshall predicted that when summer came, the "Negro mass in the North," aroused by Bull Connor's "dogs and hoses," would turn their fury on the "white cops" in America's cities.

That evening, Martin Luther King asked Birmingham's young black men to "stay off the streets."

Bull Connor was not impressed: "That son of a bitch! He's the only one that's caused any violence."

From the Oval Office, JFK told the nation on television that he was sending U.S. troops "trained in riot control" to two military bases near Birmingham. Fortunately he did not mention that one was Fort McClellan, named for the Union Army commander.

Robert Kennedy was disappointed by his brother's terse statement. He had asked Jack to declare that equality was "one of the great moral issues of our time"—and that "all of us have a moral obligation" to correct it. But the President had told him not yet.

*   *   *

Troubled by Birmingham and the violence looming elsewhere, the Kennedy brothers privately asked a group of Alabama newspaper editors not to be so critical of Martin Luther King.

Bobby said, "Remember, it was King who went around the pool halls and door to door, collecting knives, telling people . . . to be nonviolent." If King failed, "worse leaders are going to take his place"—like Malcolm X and the Black Muslims.*

During a helicopter flight to the NASA space center in Huntsville, Alabama, the President tried the same argument on Governor Wallace.

But Wallace would not hear of it. He told Kennedy that King was a "faker," competing with Fred Shuttlesworth over "who could go to bed with the most nigger women—and white and red women too!"

Robert Kennedy tapped his own independent sources on the fast-growing black revolution.

By telephone from Chicago, Dick Gregory warned him that after Birmingham, blacks were ready "to fight with white people"—especially in the Northern cities. They were "mad at the white liberals because . . . they just sit around."

Gregory told Kennedy of a bar "where the Negro underworld of Chicago hangs out. Ordinarily, if they hear a police car come down the street, they all run." But lately, when a white police captain walked in, the blacks told him to "get the hell out."

Chicago's Mayor Richard Daley, who had cinched JFK's victory on Election Night 1960, reported that he was expecting "a lot of trouble."

One of Bobby's friends, a well-to-do white woman, told him that even the "Negro maids and servants" had changed: "You don't know how they're sassing me back in my house."

At the White House, Bobby warned his brother that Negroes' patience was gone: "They're antagonistic and they're mad." If the President did not act, "you're going to have difficulty" in the urban North.

Robert thought the best way to prevent a conflagration was for JFK to

---

* Malcolm was still sufficiently unknown that Vice President Johnson called him "Muslim X."

propose the major civil rights bill he had postponed for more than two years. Legislation would be "damn helpful." It would be "good for the Negroes—relax this thing—and everybody thinks we've been doing something."

The President agreed that "people who object to mob actions" must be told there had to be a "remedy in law."

Jumping the gun, Burke Marshall advised the President that any civil rights bill must ensure free access to hotels and restaurants: being prevented from "eating at a lunch counter" made "all Negroes, regardless of age," the "maddest."

But Bobby's thinking was not so grandiose—at least not yet. He told Marshall such a demand would sink any legislation: "They can *stand* at the lunch counters. They don't have to eat there. They can pee *before* they come to the store!"

Feeling his way toward a civil rights bill, Robert invited a group of prominent African-Americans to his father's hideaway on Central Park South. To his shock, the guests pelted him not with rose petals but tomatoes.

An ex–Freedom Rider named Jerome Smith told the Attorney General, "I want to vomit, being in the same room with you." Smith said he would "never, never, never" take up arms for his country.

Kennedy asked, "How can you say something like that?" Irish-Americans had experienced discrimination too.

"Your family has been here for three generations and your brother's on top," barked the writer James Baldwin. "My family has been here a lot longer than that, and we're on the bottom!"

After three hours of a "violent, emotional assault," Kennedy was furious. Later he told JFK that some of his male guests must have been assuaging their guilt for having married white women.

Nevertheless such outrage from some of the most successful American blacks showed the Attorney General that it was far too late for caution on civil rights.

JFK began warning white Southern Democrats that the only way to avert dreaded black violence might be a civil rights bill.

Calling up Louisiana Governor Jimmie Davis, an ex–country music star ("You Are My Sunshine"), he forecast "a battle in the streets of

America. . . . It isn't just Jackson. It's Philadelphia—and it's going to be Washington, D.C., this summer."

"It's going to be the bloodiest thing," agreed Davis. "It's going to be a civil war."

"We're trying to figure out what we can do to put this stuff in the courts and get it off the streets," Kennedy said, "because somebody's going to get killed."

Bobby told his brother that before sending a civil rights bill to Capitol Hill, he should consult Martin Luther King.

JFK disagreed. Better to wait until his proposals were in Congress: "King is so hot these days that . . . I'd like to have some Southern governors or mayors or businessmen in first."

Kennedy added, "The trouble with King is that everybody thinks he's our boy anyway. . . . Everybody thinks we stuck him in there." If "Martin's coming to the White House," have him "well surrounded" by other black leaders.

JFK's chief lobbyist, Larry O'Brien, warned that a civil rights bill would make all hell break loose, rewarding the "extremes on both sides."

Ken O'Donnell acidly predicted that after the Boss committed his prestige for civil rights, "nothing is going to happen."

O'Brien advised that if the President's mind was made up, he must get Lyndon Johnson "married to this package." Otherwise the old Senate wizard would be "cutting" them behind their backs.

Following O'Brien's advice, JFK consulted his Vice President about civil rights. Seemingly more depressed than ever by his powerlessness and isolation, LBJ churlishly replied, "I haven't read the bill. Haven't seen it. . . . I'm not competent to counsel you."

Out of the President's earshot, however, Johnson told cronies that the Kennedys didn't know "any more about Capitol Hill than an old maid does about fucking."

As the Kennedys moved toward a civil rights bill, the courts ordered the University of Alabama to admit two black students.

Bobby wanted to prevent "another Oxford." But Governor Wallace wished to block the students' entry and exploit the dramatic scene for his own political ambitions, which included the Presidency.

On Monday morning, June 10, Bobby called Katzenbach, who was standing at a pay telephone in Tuscaloosa: "The President says it's important to make [Wallace] look silly."

Katzenbach agreed. He felt that from their ordeal at Ole Miss, they now "knew what the hell we were doing."

Before television cameras, in the hundred-degree heat, Katzenbach asked the Governor to step aside. Refusing to buckle, Wallace replied with a seven-minute diatribe against the "unwarranted action by the central government."

The President federalized the Alabama National Guard. A brigadier general told the Governor it was his "sad duty to ask you to step aside." Before he complied, Wallace denounced Kennedy's "military dictatorship."

The Wallace showdown had unfolded so smoothly that Kennedy's relieved aides told him he need not address the nation.

But JFK felt the televised images of Wallace blocking the door in Tuscaloosa gave him a splendid opportunity to educate Americans about civil rights. He personally asked network officials for broadcast time that evening.

With only six hours to write a speech, Bobby reached for some of the language that his brother had been too timid to use in his TV speech on Birmingham: this time Jack must speak "in moral terms."

Sorensen did the major drafting. Nervously the President popped into his aide's office—not his normal habitat—and asked, "How's it coming?"

With only five minutes to airtime, Sorensen gave him an unfinished script, leaving his boss to improvise at the end.

Kennedy's civil rights speech was by far the boldest of his Presidency. No longer did he offer a muzzled apology for enforcing the law.

Instead he told Americans, "We are confronted primarily with a moral issue . . . as old as the Scriptures and . . . as clear as the American Constitution. . . .

"If an American, because his skin is dark, cannot eat lunch in a restaurant . . . if he cannot vote . . . if he cannot send his children to the best public school . . . then who among us would be content to have the color of his skin changed and stand in his place?"

Congress must change all that: "One hundred years of delay have passed since President Lincoln freed the slaves, yet their heirs, their grandsons are not fully free."

Kennedy warned, "The fires of frustration and discord are burning in every city—North and South. . . . A great change is at hand, and our task—our obligation—is to make that revolution—that change—peaceful and constructive for all."

Black Americans realized that JFK had changed. The singer Nat "King" Cole's wife, Maria, wrote him to praise his "noticeable lack of 'tongue-biting.' "

The gospel singer Mahalia Jackson wired Kennedy that his speech "made me proud all over again that I am an American and that you are my President." The actor Tony Randall cabled the President three words: "I LOVE YOU."

Kennedy also got a thank-you telegram from his black college classmate Paul Davis, who wrote him from Ghana, "I have known personally your views since our Harvard days."

After watching Kennedy's speech at home in Atlanta, Martin Luther King wired the President that it was "eloquent, passionate and unequivocal . . . a hallmark in the annals of American history."

As King later recalled, he felt exhilarated to see "a new Kennedy, who had come to see the moral issues involved" and "was willing to stand up in a courageous manner for them."

King was proud that Kennedy's "soul-searching" had been provoked by his own Birmingham demonstrations. At long last, the President seemed to fully understand "that segregation was morally wrong."

King believed that JFK had experienced the same "agonizing moments" as Lincoln, who had "vacillated" over the Emancipation, but finally reached "the moral conclusion that he had to do it—no matter what it meant."

The President's civil rights address enchanted even his political foe Jackie Robinson. The baseball star declared that if the 1964 election were held tomorrow, he'd vote for Kennedy.

———•◆•———

CHAPTER THIRTY-TWO

A MAN HAS TO TAKE A STAND

In Jackson, Mississippi, before dawn after Kennedy's address, Medgar Evers, the state's chief civil rights organizer, was approaching his front door when he heard the crack of a deer rifle.

Shot in the back, Evers fell to the ground. Inside the house, his wife, Myrlie, and their three children heard the rifle shot and dropped to the floor. When silence came, they opened the door and saw the lifeless body. The children cried, "Please, Daddy, please get up!"

Informed of Medgar Evers's murder, JFK told Arthur Schlesinger he could understand why the Radical Republicans of Lincoln's time had wanted to punish the South: "When I see this sort of thing, I begin to wonder how else you can treat them."

Kennedy had written in *Profiles in Courage* about leaders who "sailed with the wind until the decisive moment when their conscience, and events, propelled them into the center of the storm."

Now he observed to a friend, "Sometimes you look at what you've done and the only thing you ask yourself is, 'What took you so long to do it?' "

Using language worthy of one of his *Profile* heroes, the President said, "There comes a time when a man has to take a stand."

Kennedy did not regret postponing his championship of civil rights. To him, acting in 1961 would have been a fool's errand, championed by liberals "in love with death."

But postponement had many costs. He had been forced to appease the Senate Judiciary Chairman, James Eastland of Mississippi, by naming five segregationist judges, including Eastland's Ole Miss roommate, who inveighed from his bench against "niggers" and "chimpanzees."

Kennedy had tried to hold off black leaders with the contrived argument that civil rights was really an economic issue: help pass his tax cut, and a rising tide would lift all boats, including theirs.

He had tried to sell impatient liberals on the notion that the big problems of the 1960s were not ideological, as in Franklin Roosevelt's day, but technical. With the nation roiled over civil rights and the Cold War, Kennedy made the astounding claim at Yale's commencement in 1962 that the "real" issues of his era were "rarely as dramatic" as those earlier in American history.

With greater historical imagination, Kennedy would have realized that his excuses for avoiding civil rights had the tinny echo of his father's old insistence that the danger from Adolf Hitler should be viewed chiefly in terms of military strength and global economics.

No one knew better than JFK that it was Churchill and Roosevelt whom history exalted for showing that Nazism was preeminently a test of basic human morality.

For two-and-a-half years, the President had let Martin Luther King and Bull Connor do much of his work for him. Thanks to them and their followers, by the summer of 1963, Americans no longer found the Negro's plight very abstract.*

By framing the issues and leading the protest, King helped the President see his moral duty—and that if he did not act, the cities might roast.

It was also crucial that his Attorney General was Robert Kennedy. No longer the nerveless campaign manager of 1960, Bobby had learned from the Freedom Riders, Oxford, Birmingham and his own painful self-education why blacks must no longer be asked to wait.

On Wednesday, June 12, 1963, the day after JFK's civil rights speech, Southern Democrats killed a routine Administration public works bill.

---

* This paralleled Kennedy's decision in 1963 to press the Soviets for a test ban treaty and some kind of détente. By showing Americans the danger of a continued Cold War, the near-miss of the Missile Crisis had changed the political climate. Kennedy gave what he called his "peace speech" at American University one day before his Oval Office address on civil rights.

The *New York Times* called it the President's "sharpest defeat" in Congress that year.

"I suppose that civil rights thing has just got 'em all excited," Kennedy told his House leader, Carl Albert.

"That's what did it," said Albert. "We lost some of the Southern boys that we would otherwise have had. I'm awfully sorry. . . . It's overwhelming the whole program."

Noting Medgar Evers's murder, the President told Albert, "Christ, you know, it's like they shoot this guy in Mississippi, and . . . this has become everything."

Kennedy feared that the sky was falling. He told Bobby, "Look at the trouble it has got us into!" Civil rights might prove his "political swan song."

Not only did he face Southern and border-state rebellion in Congress. His pollster Lou Harris warned that Irish-, Polish-, and Italian-Americans of the North, fearing the integration of their neighborhoods and black political power, might soon turn Republican.

Harris wrote the President that if the Democrats lost the old South in 1964, disgruntled Northern ethnics could make the election "close."

Robert Kennedy told his brother that nevertheless the racial issue "really had to be faced up to." If the riots got "worse during the summer," the President would have been vilified for his failure to act.

JFK agreed: "If we're going to go down, let's go down on a matter of principle."

The week after his civil rights speech, three dozen American cities erupted. Kennedy told Congress that "the predictions of increased violence have been tragically borne out."*

In the Cabinet Room, he met Martin Luther King and two dozen other civil rights leaders: "I may lose the next election because of this. I don't care."

Pulling a note from his pocket, he said one survey showed that his

---

* The bill would forbid hotels, restaurants, schools and other public institutions from discrimination, help African-Americans to vote and encourage federal lawsuits to desegregate schools and the workplace.

popularity had dropped from sixty to forty-seven percent: "You've got to remember that I'm in this too, right up to my neck now."

Recalling the Birmingham violence, he told the leaders not to be "too hard" on Bull Connor: "After all, Bull has probably done more for civil rights than anyone else!" They should call his legislation "Bull Connor's bill."

The leaders had been planning a "March on Washington" for civil rights.* Now they proposed to use the march to support Kennedy's bill.

JFK asked them to cancel it: "We want success in the Congress, not a big show on the Capitol. Some of these people are just looking for an excuse to oppose us. I don't want to give them the chance to say, 'Yes, I'm for the bill—but not at the point of a gun.' "

"Frankly I have never engaged in a direct-action movement that did not seem ill-timed," replied Martin Luther King. "Some people thought Birmingham was ill-timed."

"Including the Attorney General!" said Kennedy.

Philip Randolph reminded the President that "the Negroes are already in the streets."

Unable to stop the March, Kennedy feared that demonstrators would "piss on the Washington Monument," harming his civil rights bill. He ordered the protest moved from the Capitol grounds to the front of the Lincoln Memorial, where it would be easier to contain.

When the great pageant unfolded on Wednesday, August 28, the President stayed away. The orators might get out of control, and he did not want to imply that he endorsed them.

As an extra precaution, Bobby assigned one of his aides, John Reilly, to stay in front of the Memorial. If some speaker threatened to embarrass the President, Reilly would have him drowned out by an LP of Mahalia Jackson singing "He's Got the Whole World in His Hands."

JFK heard some of the speeches and chants through an open window of the third-floor White House Solarium. Gripping the windowsill, he

---

* The march was based on a 1941 plan by A. Philip Randolph, chief of the Brotherhood of Sleeping Car Porters, to push FDR for Negro jobs in the defense industry. After Roosevelt met his demands, Randolph called it off.

told the Mansion's courtly black doorman, Preston Bruce, "Oh, Bruce, I wish I were out there with them!"

When Martin Luther King cried out, "I have a dream!" with Lincoln's brooding statue behind him, Kennedy saw it on television. He had never heard a whole King speech before, and he was justifiably impressed.

Delighted to realize that the peaceful demonstration would only help his bill, he invited King and other speakers to the West Wing for sandwiches and coffee. Roy Wilkins found their host "bubbling over."

Grinning, Kennedy shook King's hand and said, "I have a dream!"

Still the brutality in Birmingham was not over. That September, a bomb tore through the Sixteenth Street Baptist Church, killing four black girls.*

At the White House, King warned the President that unless he gave blacks a "sense of protection," there would be "the worst race rioting we've ever seen in this country."

Kennedy replied that if Negroes decided to "shoot at whites, we lose." Congress would only endorse civil rights with "the support of the white community. . . . Once that goes, we're down to a racial struggle." He didn't want to use federal troops, "but it may come to that."

The President privately told a group of white Birmingham leaders that civil rights had become "our most difficult" problem—"and I never would have guessed that, even in February.

"We thought we were doing pretty well. . . . But suddenly this has exploded somehow, and I don't know whether we can get the genie back in the bottle again."

Southern Bell Telephone's Frank Newton demanded that Kennedy force "outside agitators" like Martin Luther King out of their city.

The President replied "flatly" that he lacked the power to "move these people in and out" of Birmingham: "King has got a terrific investment in nonviolence."

If extremist "sons of bitches" took command of the Negroes, "and you have ten percent of the population under the most radical leadership," it would be "very dangerous."

---

* One of the doomed girls, Denise McNair, was a friend of a future Secretary of State, nine-year-old Condoleezza Rice.

Newton told Kennedy that "a lot of people" thought his civil rights bill was "giving those people encouragement."

JFK replied, "My God, it's whether you can go into a store or a hotel!" He reminded Newton that most Negroes could not afford a fine hotel: "They don't go into [the] Statler, and they won't be coming into the hotel in Birmingham."

Kennedy's nightmare of losing the Southern states that had narrowly elected him in 1960 seemed to be coming true.

Segregationists in Florida and Louisiana were threatening to form unpledged slates of Presidential electors for 1964, joining Alabama, Mississippi and Georgia.* They hoped to compel JFK and his Republican foe to bargain for their support by pledging to halt civil rights reforms.

They recalled that in the contested election of 1876, Rutherford Hayes won the Presidency by pledging to end Reconstruction and take federal troops out of the South.

Louisiana Senator Russell Long told JFK that the segregationists hoped to make "some kind of a deal," like the one that elected Hayes.

"But this isn't 1876," replied Kennedy. Such seamy brokerage would be publicized: "And pretty soon, you've got the Goddamnedest mayhem."

He warned Long that if the "screwy" plot went forward, he and his opponent would simply have to say, "Christ, the South is so uncertain that I'd better just try to get my votes from the North." That meant courting the Negroes. "I think it's crazy for the South."

Despairing of most Southern states, JFK told friends, "We've got to carry Texas in '64."

But the President was unpopular in the Lone Star State. Democratic Governor John Connally, who opposed Kennedy's civil rights bill, had tried to keep him from touring Texas.

A Democratic banquet feting the President was planned for Austin on the evening of Friday, November 22, but tickets sold so slowly that Lyndon Johnson had to call in chits so that JFK would not be embarrassed in his home state.

---

* In 1960, fourteen unpledged Democratic electors in Alabama and Mississippi had cast their votes for the segregationist Virginia Senator Harry Byrd, Sr.

As the President and Jackie arrived in San Antonio, the civil rights bill had not yet reached the floor of the House of Representatives. To Kennedy's chagrin, the struggle would grind on into the campaign year of 1964, which would make it harder to pass.

When the Kennedys reached Houston, the crowds outside the Rice Hotel included Barbara Bush, whose husband was running for U.S. Senator, and her eldest son, George W., a senior at Andover, who was home for Thanksgiving.

JFK knew that Dallas was hostile terrain. In late October, protesters spurred by General Edwin Walker had spat on U.N. Ambassador Adlai Stevenson. When a woman struck Stevenson with a placard, he asked if she was "animal or human."

Stevenson told Arthur Schlesinger it was "ugly and frightening."

As a chauvinistic Texan, Lyndon Johnson thought it best to make light of the rumors of Dallas violence. He planned to introduce JFK at the Austin dinner with a joke: "Mr. President, we're glad you made it out of Dallas alive!"

The city had troubled Kennedy for years.

In November 1962, using his secret taping system, he had called to congratulate Connally on his election.

In this overlooked recording, the Governor-elect reports that a Republican "hate campaign" in Dallas generated "a hell of a protest vote" against "you and the Vice President and me."

JFK asks, "What did we lose Dallas by—do you remember—in '60?"

"Yes, sir, you lost by over sixty thousand votes."

"Sixty thousand votes!" cries Kennedy. "You know, they're up here talking to me—you remember—about having that federal building down there."

Then JFK speaks to the Governor in language chilling to hear in the afterknowledge of their doomed limousine ride into the city:

"I don't know why we do anything for Dallas. I'm telling you—they just *murdered* all of us!"

The week after John Kennedy's assassination, his widow asked their friend Teddy White to drive through near-monsoons to Hyannis Port.

As the night rains pounded the roof of her cottage, Jackie recounted the Dallas ordeal: "Jack turned back. . . . He had his hand out. I could see a piece of his skull coming off. . . . Then he slumped in my lap. . . . I saw them put him in the coffin. . . . He was naked. . . . Dr. Burkley was clutching me, shaking me."*

The widow vowed, "I'm not going to go around accepting plaques. I don't want medals to Jack. I'm not Mrs. Medgar Evers."

Deriding the "bitter old men" who wrote history, she wanted her husband to have his rightful place in American memory.

"History made Jack what he was," she told White. "This little boy, sick so much of the time, reading in bed." Jack believed "history was full of heroes," so his life must be studied by "other little boys."

After John Kennedy's murder, his successor persuaded Congress to pass his civil rights proposals as the late President's most fitting memorial. Thus, by dying at the moment he did, Kennedy had ensured the success of the bill that would so change the nation.

But in the hours after Dallas, Jacqueline Kennedy couldn't know that.

When Robert Kennedy told her that the suspected assassin was a Marxist, Jackie was outraged that "some silly little Communist" could have slain her husband: "He didn't even have the satisfaction of being killed for civil rights!"

---

* Admiral George Burkley was JFK's White House physician. The result of Mrs. Kennedy's interview with White was a *Life* article that fulfilled her wish to link her husband's White House years with the romantic legend of Camelot.

CHAPTER THIRTY-THREE

WE WIN AND THEY LOSE!

Now it was October 1980, and the autumn sun fell on Wexford, the Virginia hunt country estate created by Jackie Kennedy for weekends with Jack and their children.

Inside Jackie's old library, before a snapping fire, sat Nancy Reagan. For the duration of her husband's campaign against President Jimmy Carter, she and her husband had leased the estate to spare themselves long flights home to California.*

Carter was gaining that fall by charging that Reagan would "lead our country toward war." Reagan's pollster Richard Wirthlin warned his boss that Carter's attacks were persuading Americans—especially women—that Reagan would "push the nuclear button."

The previous summer, with soaring inflation and unemployment, Reagan had been running thirty points ahead. Now he and Carter were almost even.

At Wexford, Nancy told a reporter that Carter's assaults were "vicious." In a commercial, she insisted her husband was "*not* a warmonger."

Ronald Reagan's loathing of "godless Communism" was a cornerstone of his political identity. He complained that Presidents Kennedy and Johnson had "frittered away" America's nuclear superiority, leaving their successors with a stark choice: "Surrender or die."

---

* Finding that it evoked painful memories, Jackie had sold the estate in 1964. The Reagans leased it on the advice of Nancy's onetime MGM colleague Elizabeth Taylor, who lived nearby with her then-husband, Senator John Warner of Virginia.

Although they were all Republicans, Reagan thought that Presidents Richard Nixon and Gerald Ford—and their Secretary of State, Henry Kissinger—were too soft on the Soviets.

Campaigning against Ford for the Republican nomination in 1976, Reagan had denounced the Nixon-Ford-Kissinger "détente" for making Americans "second to the Soviets." He wrote a friend that détente "scares me to death."

In December 1979, the Soviets invaded Afghanistan. Reagan was appalled when President Carter, whom he found "a real phony," said the invasion had brought "a more dramatic change" in his opinion of the Russians "than anything they've done."

Reagan told a friend that Carter's confession would be "laughable . . . if it were not so tragic."

For most of the fall of 1980, Carter had ducked a debate with Reagan by insisting on the exclusion of a third-party candidate, John Anderson.

But in October, Anderson's poll numbers dropped below the fifteen percent required for his presence. Overruling advisers who knew that his television skills were no match for the movie and television actor's, Carter agreed to debate.

In their single encounter in Cleveland one week before the election, Carter declared that Reagan's "radical" "intention to escalate the arms race would violate the foreign policy of every President since Truman.

When Carter revealed that his thirteen-year-old daughter, Amy, thought the campaign's most important issue was "nuclear weaponry," some in the audience howled with laughter.*

Reagan looked into the cameras and vowed that he was no bomb-thrower: "I have seen four wars in my lifetime. I'm a father of sons."

Reassured by the challenger's debate performance and rankled by Carter's continuing failure to free fifty-two U.S. hostages held by Iran, the undecided vote stampeded to Reagan.

After his election victory, Reagan scrawled in his diary, "Finally an in-

---

* Carter may have subconsciously recalled Lyndon Johnson's once-aired 1964 "Daisy Girl" commercial, in which scenes of exploding H-bombs supplanted the image of a little girl who looked remarkably like Amy Carter.

terview with Teddy White. Yes, now I'll be in a book called 'The Making of the President.' "

Although glad to have a Republican President, Richard Nixon was unsettled by Reagan's election. During the 1976 primaries, he had quietly assured President Ford's chief of staff, Dick Cheney, that Reagan was a "lightweight" who shouldn't be "taken seriously."

During Nixon's presidency, Reagan would call up with suggestions that Nixon found ridiculous. In 1971, when the U.N. expelled Taiwan in favor of Communist China, the California Governor was so angry that he implored Nixon to "get the hell out of that kangaroo court." That would send a message to "these bums." *

Nixon replied, "It sure would!" But such proposals merely confirmed his opinion that Reagan was a right-wing yahoo. Annoyed by Reagan's relentlessness, Nixon told an aide that the ex-actor "just isn't pleasant to be around."

Now that Reagan was President-elect, however, Nixon kept such views to himself. Six years after his disgrace over the Watergate scandal, he hoped to use Reagan as his vehicle back to respectability.

Two days after Reagan's victory, Nixon made a rare public appearance at the Soviet Embassy in Washington, where the Russians were celebrating the sixty-third anniversary of their revolution.

Nixon took the Soviet Ambassador, Anatoly Dobrynin, aside and boasted of his intimacy with the new President. Like himself, Nixon said, Reagan was an anti-Communist, but a "pragmatic" one who, in time, would see the need to reach out to the Kremlin.

Nixon told Dobrynin he was trying to give Reagan a "better idea" of Soviet aims, implying that if the Russians wanted to play ball with the new President, they had better deal through Nixon.

Having nominated himself as Reagan's middleman with the Soviets, Nixon pushed the President-elect to appoint a Secretary of State who would cut him in on the foreign policy action.

Nixon's choice was Alexander Haig, his chief of staff during Watergate. "Al Haig is the meanest, toughest, most ambitious son of a bitch I ever knew," he told friends. "He'll make a great Secretary of State."

* Without Reagan's knowledge, Nixon taped their conversation.

After lobbying wealthy Los Angeles supporters who were helping Reagan choose his Cabinet, Nixon was delighted when Haig got the job. Having bagged this victory, Nixon savored his future as Reagan's éminence grise, helping a neophyte, no doubt grateful new President drop his campaign bromides and seek a "hardheaded détente."

There was only one problem: Reagan did not consider himself a lightweight and he really believed what he had been saying for years. As he told his aides, his theory of the Cold War was "We win and they lose!"

In January 1981, during his first Presidential news conference, Reagan was asked whether "détente is possible."

He replied, "Well, so far, détente's been a one-way street that the Soviet Union has used to pursue its own aims." He was ready to negotiate, but the Soviets sought a "one-world Communist state," reserving for themselves "the right to commit any crime, to lie, to cheat." *

After the President spoke, there was "an audible gasp" in the room. Standing by a wall, Al Haig rolled his eyes at Reagan's undiplomatic language. No President since at least Kennedy had talked so tough about the Kremlin in public.

Walking back to the Oval Office, the President asked his National Security Adviser, Richard Allen, whether the Russians really did "lie, cheat and steal." Allen assured him they did.

"I thought so!" said Reagan.

Haig thought it gauche for a President to start his diplomacy with name-calling. But he agreed that the Soviets must be shown that they were no longer dealing with Jerry Ford or Jimmy Carter.

Since the palmy days of détente, Anatoly Dobrynin had been the only foreign diplomat whose car could whoosh into the State Department's garage. Without consulting Reagan, Haig revoked the special privilege. When the Soviet car was stopped by U.S. guards, Dobrynin climbed out, looking befuddled.

The CBS anchor Walter Cronkite asked the President, "Don't you

---

* Reagan may have unwittingly borrowed his language from hearing the comedian Bob Hope joke at his inaugural gala that Reagan "doesn't know how to lie, exaggerate or cheat. He's always had an agent for that!"

think the Russians kind of think we're childish when we pull something like that?"

Reagan said, "Maybe they got a message!"

Seventy days into his Presidency, Reagan was shot in the chest by a demented young man outside the Washington Hilton.

Haig and Secretary of Defense Caspar Weinberger suspected the gunman was acting for the Soviets, who would have much preferred to deal with Reagan's more moderate Vice President, George Bush. Weinberger ordered a "standby alert" after learning that Soviet submarines were "closer than normal" to the American East Coast.*

In despair, Nancy Reagan wrote in her diary, "Nothing can happen to my Ronnie. My life would be over." That evening at the White House, she slept with one of his shirts to be comforted by the scent.

When Reagan opened his eyes at the hospital, he beheld the beetle-browed face of Senator Strom Thurmond, who had bluffed his way past the Secret Service detail, claiming he was the President's "close friend." Nancy Reagan had Thurmond thrown out of the room.

"These guys are crazy!" said her husband's chief of staff, James Baker. "They come over here trying to get a picture in front of the hospital and trying to talk to the President when he may be on his deathbed."

A doctor told White House aides that Reagan was exhausted because he felt he should "entertain his nurses all night with jokes."

When the President was well enough to receive political visitors in the hospital, his staff invited the Democratic Speaker of the House, Tip O'Neill.

The two Irish-Americans had already formed a surprisingly good relationship, but Reagan did not deceive himself about O'Neill. He told his diary that Tip could "like you personally" while "trying to beat your head in."

O'Neill was shocked to see Reagan so gaunt and frail. With tears in his eyes, he knelt and kissed the President's face, and the two men recited the Twenty-third Psalm.

*   *   *

* The subs' unusual proximity was soon explained by the fact that the Soviets changed their sea battalions once a month.

Throughout Reagan's presidency, many people scoffed when he insisted that he could not go to Sunday church because of the security risk.

But after his near-assassination, as he told his diary, he was indeed "a hazard to others." When he went to George Washington's old church near Mount Vernon, where FDR and Churchill had once worshipped, he did so in a bulletproof vest.

Reagan was in fact a determined Christian, which he owed to his late mother, Nelle, a lay Disciples of Christ preacher, who taught her son that everything was part of God's "Divine plan." As Reagan's daughter Maureen recalled, Nelle "had the gift for making you believe that you could change the world."

Reagan's Los Angeles pastor, Donn Moomaw, recalled that he and the President "spent many hours together on our knees," with Reagan part of "the total experience—the sadness, the rejoicing, the singing."

The President took the Bible literally. Of Jesus, he wrote a friend, "Either he was what he said or he was the world's greatest liar." * He felt that but for his belief in God, he would be "scared to death" and was chagrined that neither his daughter Patti Davis nor son Ron would "accept Christ."

Reagan also believed that the Messiah's second coming would be preceded by Armageddon, the end of the world.

In the Oval Office, he terrified a South Korean leader by jovially warning that the Apocalypse was near. After that, aides convinced the President to keep such views to himself—at least in the presence of foreigners.

But in private, Reagan insisted that recent "signs and events" showed the imminence of Armageddon, such as "wars fought to no conclusion" and "earthquakes, storms, volcanic eruptions." When the Apocalypse came, there would be "armies invading the Holy Land" and a plague in which "the eyes are burned from the head."

Reagan's longtime political consultant Stuart Spencer told him, "That's kind of scary to be talking about." The President replied, "Yeah, but it's going to happen."

Democrats used sporadic reports of Reagan's Armageddon beliefs to

---

* This argument reflected Reagan's reading of C. S. Lewis's small classic *Mere Christianity*.

claim the President was determined to incinerate much of humankind so that Jesus could come back.

After his shooting, Reagan told New York's Terence Cardinal Cooke that he had survived because God was "sitting on my shoulder." In his diary, he pledged, "Whatever happens I now owe my life to God and will serve him in any way I can."

Reagan had long had an almost primal ambition to reduce what he considered the world's "immoral" nuclear arsenal. He now believed the Almighty had spared him to "lessen the risk of nuclear war."

His mother had always told him that Soviet Communism would be swept away by religion. The President wrote a friend in 1981 that "religion might very well turn out to be the Soviets' Achilles heel."

Recovering from his shooting that spring, Reagan wore his bathrobe and slippers in the White House Solarium—the same rooftop eyrie from which John Kennedy had watched the March on Washington.

He worried that his defense buildup was overshadowing his wish to bargain with the Soviets. Especially after his brush with death, he wanted the Soviet leader, Leonid Brezhnev, to know how deeply he yearned for "a world without nuclear weapons."

He scrawled out a letter to Brezhnev, hoping to reach the Soviet leader "as a human being." In his draft, he asked the Soviet leader whether their two countries had let "ideology" keep them from considering people's "very real, everyday problems."

He told his diary, "Don't know whether I'll send it, but enjoyed putting some thoughts down on paper."

When Haig saw Reagan's letter, he had it rewritten. The disappointed President found that the "striped pants set" had changed his words almost beyond recognition. He said, "Well, I guess you guys are the experts."

"Wait a minute!" interjected his veteran aide Michael Deaver. "Nobody elected anybody in the State Department. . . . These guys have been screwing up for twenty-five years!"

The President told Haig, "I agree with that."

With some of his language restored, Reagan copied the final version by hand to show Brezhnev he was writing what was in his heart. He told

Deaver that since the shooting, he had decided "I'm going to follow my own instincts."

Brezhnev responded to Reagan's handwritten letter, and others that followed, with blistering indictments clearly produced by the Kremlin's propaganda mill. On one of Brezhnev's letters, Reagan scrawled, "He has to be kidding."

After a distraught appeal from the wife of Anatoly Sharansky, the Jewish human rights activist jailed in the Soviet gulag, Reagan told his diary, "D-m these inhumane monsters."

Still trying to reach Brezhnev's soul, Reagan asked the Soviet leader to "find it in your heart" to release Sharansky. If Brezhnev agreed, his gesture would stay "strictly between us."

But the Soviet leader refused. He insisted to Reagan that Sharansky was guilty of "grave anti-Soviet crimes."

While dismissing his claims that he was willing to negotiate, the Soviets were starting to comprehend that in their worldwide contest, Reagan would go the limit, if necessary.

During an air traffic controllers' strike in the summer of 1981, the President showed he was not all talk. From the Rose Garden, he warned the strikers that if they didn't halt their "illegal" strike "against the people," he would have them fired and their union abolished.

Predicting that no President would risk shutting down the nation's air lanes, union leaders advised members to stay off work. When Reagan made good on his threat, some of the leaders were put in handcuffs.

In December 1981, Reagan sought to ensure that Brezhnev would not use tanks to stop an incipient revolution in Poland.

All year, the President had been inspired by the maverick Polish shipyard worker Lech Walesa and his Solidarity movement, which was defying Poland's Soviet masters.

Shamed by earlier Presidents' failure to help anti-Soviet rebels in Hungary and Czechoslovakia, Reagan told his diary, "We can't let this revolution against Communism fail without our offering a hand. We may never have an opportunity like this in our lifetime."

When Poland's leaders declared martial law and jailed Walesa, Reagan warned Brezhnev over the "hot line" established by Kennedy and Khrushchev that further attempts to "suppress the Polish people" would "unleash a process which neither you nor we could fully control."

Reagan explained to his Senate leader, Howard Baker, that he was trying to bring the Soviets "to their knees. . . . We have them on the ropes economically. They are selling rat meat in the markets in Russia today."

CHAPTER THIRTY-FOUR

IT LEFT ME GREATLY DEPRESSED

But by the summer of 1982, Reagan was feeling a domestic backlash against his efforts to bolster the nation's defense and challenge the Soviet empire. Polls found that more than two thirds of Americans backed a movement to freeze the Soviet and U.S. nuclear arsenals at existing levels.

The President wrote in his diary that "the argument about a nuclear freeze is heating up." He preferred to "negotiate a substantial, verifiable reduction—then freeze."

Touring Western Europe in June, he faced crowds shouting, "No nukes!" That same month in Manhattan, almost a million people staged what the *New York Times* called the "largest political demonstration" in American history.

Privately Reagan scoffed, "You can get as many people as that to a rock concert!"

Still in November 1982, with Americans suffering from a severe recession, Reagan's party lost twenty-six seats in the House. Eight states endorsed a nuclear freeze. His approval rating dropped to forty-one percent.*

His daughter Patti Davis asked him to meet with Helen Caldicott, an Australian doctor who had quit her children's practice to campaign for a

---

* Stu Spencer insisted years later that the President did not use Wirthlin's extensive polling to influence his policies. Spencer said that Reagan "never took survey research very seriously. He liked all the good numbers, didn't like the bad numbers.... Dick Wirthlin dies when I say this, but Reagan really didn't care.... All he really wanted to know was, 'Am I ahead or behind?'"

freeze. After Caldicott gave one of her stemwinders at Hugh Hefner's "Playboy Mansion," Patti had told her she was the "only one" who might change her father's mind.

The President could not abide Patti's admiration for Jane Fonda and other antiwar liberal "traitors," but he loved his daughter and pledged to see the doctor.

During an off-the-record encounter in the little-noticed White House Library, he told Caldicott, "I don't want nuclear war either, but our ways of preventing it differ." Pulling out handwritten notes, he charged that the freeze movement was backed by the Soviets and "KGB dupes." She might not know she was being "manipulated."

"That's from *Reader's Digest*," she said.

"No, it's not. It's from my intelligence files." He showed her a map depicting a potential nuclear blast on Oregon: "These are handed out to grade-school students. . . . I don't think children should be frightened like that."

As Caldicott recalled, by the end of their long meeting, she "staggered out of the White House literally hardly able to walk, it was so frightening."*

Reagan told his diary that Caldicott "seems like a nice, caring person but is all steamed up and knows an awful lot of things that aren't true. . . . I'm afraid our daughter has been taken over by that whole d-m gang."

Although the meeting had been branded off the record, Caldicott later claimed to a Boston audience that Reagan believed that nuclear war was winnable. She said, "I wonder if we can make it for the next year and a half!"

Furious that Caldicott had violated the terms of their meeting and also misrepresented his views, the President carefully wrote Patti, "It isn't easy to learn we've misplaced our faith and trust in someone.

"I know. I've had that experience once with someone I thought was my closest friend. . . . I'm afraid the Dr. is so carried away by her cause she subscribes to the belief that the end justifies the means."

---

* On an Australian talk show in 2003, Caldicott insisted that when she explained the nuclear danger, Reagan got red-faced and "really upset . . . so I had to pat his hand and reassure him and I'd correct him." Pronouncing herself "a clinician able to assess his IQ," she declared it "about a hundred—average." She felt that Reagan "would have been a nice chicken farmer" but was "totally inappropriate to be President."

*   *   *

On Thursday, November 11, 1982, Reagan was awoken with the news that Brezhnev was dead.

He took a call from his new Secretary of State, George Shultz, who had assumed the job after Reagan concluded that Haig was "paranoid" and "power-hungry" and fired him.*

Shultz recommended that the President lead a large delegation to Brezhnev's funeral in hopes of starting a conversation with the new Soviet leader, Yuri Andropov.

Reagan thought the delegation Shultz had in mind was more suitable for the funeral of a British monarch. It would be "hypocritical" to honor the hostile Brezhnev: "Let Bush go."

Instead the President and Nancy went to the Soviet Embassy to sign the "grief book." Reagan wrote in his diary, "There is a strange feeling in that place—no one smiled. Well, that is, except Ambassador Dobrynin."

Like a naughty boy, Reagan murmured to his wife about Brezhnev, "Think they would mind if we just said a little prayer for the man?"

Two years into his Presidency, the President had not held a formal meeting with a major Soviet official.

On a Saturday night in February 1983, during one of the blizzards of the century, Reagan and Nancy invited Shultz and his wife, O'Bie, for a family White House dinner.

Shultz reported that he would be seeing Dobrynin on Tuesday afternoon: why not bring him to the White House for a "private chat"?

Reagan agreed, but said, "We have to keep this secret." He did not want to give the most anti-Soviet members of his administration a chance to thwart the meeting in advance.

He told his diary that some members of his National Security Council staff were "too hard line and don't think any approach should be made to the Soviets. I think I'm hard line and will never appease. But I do want to try to let them see there is a better world if they'll show *by deed* they want to get along with the Free World."

As the President described it in his journal, he "sneaked" Dobrynin into the Mansion, where in the upstairs Yellow Oval Room, "we got

---

* Haig would tell aides that Reagan "isn't a mean man—he's just stupid."

Jane Fonda and Patti Davis at the Hollywood Bowl, opposing Ronald Reagan's escalation of the Cold War

pretty nose to nose." Reagan conceded that many Soviets thought him a "crazy warmonger," but Andropov should know he was ready to "do business."

Seven Pentecostal Christians, punished for practicing their faith, had taken refuge in the U.S. Embassy in Moscow. Reagan asked Dobrynin, as a sign of good faith, to let the Pentecostals leave the Soviet Union.

He predicted that if the Kremlin let them go, Americans would "cheer" more than for any nuclear agreement: "It may sound paradoxical, but that's America." He pledged not to embarrass the Kremlin by "crowing" or taking credit for their release.

Andropov quietly freed the Pentecostals, but found it "odd, even suspicious" that the President should launch their relationship on what he considered such a trivial matter as religious freedom.

Three weeks after seeing Dobrynin, in March, Reagan proved he had not gone soft. Discarding more diplomatic language, he told evangelicals in Orlando, Florida, that the Soviet Union was an "evil empire."

In the Siberian gulag, when Anatoly Sharansky heard about Reagan's words, he called them down the toilet pipes of his cell to other dissidents, who were "ecstatic" that a U.S. President had "finally" spoken the "truth."*

From the White House, Reagan wrote a friend he was "wondering" about Armageddon: "Things that are news today seem an awful lot like what was predicted would take place prior to 'A' Day. Don't quote me."

That same month, without consulting his Secretaries of State or Defense, the President decided to smash his country's existing doctrine for a nuclear war against the Soviet Union.

He was disgusted by Nixon's Anti-Ballistic Missile (ABM) Treaty, which kept the peace by letting each side defend only one of its cities against nuclear attack: if either side pressed the button, there would be "mutual assured destruction."

Reagan thought it "immoral" for a President not to protect Americans from the nuclear danger. If scientists could create an anti-missile "shield," it could make the nuclear weapons that Reagan loathed obsolete and guard Americans from some nuclear-armed foreign madman.

The President was so eager to preempt opposition and surprise the world that he did not tell Shultz and Weinberger until the last moment. Shultz frankly told him his idea was "lunacy."

Nevertheless, after changing some language, Reagan unveiled his vision in a television speech from the Oval Office—a $17 billion "Strategic Defense Initiative" to discover technology that would "intercept and destroy" Soviet missiles before they struck the United States.

Reagan's critics derided SDI as "Star Wars"—a harebrained scheme that would cost too much and would never work.†

After his speech, the President took coffee in the Mansion with scientists and ex–foreign policy officials. "I guess it was okay," he told his diary.

---

* Reagan was still trying to free Sharansky, who, in 1986, was finally allowed to emigrate to Israel.
† Dick Wirthlin felt that, although intended to be derisive, the term "Star Wars" helped Americans "visualize the concept in a way that SDI just couldn't."

"They all praised it to the sky. . . . I made no optimistic forecasts—said it might take 20 years or more but we had to do it."*

To Yuri Andropov, the only explanation for SDI was that Reagan was pushing to win the Cold War and dictate terms of surrender to the Soviet Union. Why else would the President open a new, unsettling competition on a battlefield he was sure to dominate?

From his long service as chief of the KGB, Andropov feared American technology. He knew that U.S. high school students owned computers more advanced than some of the Soviet military's. His country was so backward that top military scientists sometimes had to leave their posts to help farmers with the fall harvest.

For Andropov, the SDI surprise was merely Reagan's latest, biggest affront. Since Reagan's inauguration, the U.S. had flown provocative missions along the edge of the Soviet Union, testing radar, keeping the Soviet military off balance.

Anxious about what he considered the growing menace of a U.S. surprise attack, Andropov had created a worldwide early-warning system called Operation RYAN.

By the spring of 1983, KGB stations around the world were warned that the American danger was "urgent."

The Kremlin was not only nervous about the border flights and SDI. The U.S. had escalated covert action against Soviet power on every continent, and was planning the biggest military exercise ever staged in the northwest Pacific. When Pershing missiles were installed in Western Europe, the Soviets would lose warning time against a surprise assault.

Andropov warned that Reagan was "putting the entire world in jeopardy."

George Shultz told the President it was more necessary than ever to meet with the top Soviet leader.

Reagan agreed to invite Andropov to Washington. Dropping a fat hint, he told the Soviet leader in a handwritten letter that their prede-

* Although Reagan's SDI proposal seemed to have sprung out of nowhere, the Republican platform of 1980, at his behest, had included a little-noticed pledge to develop strategic defense. Worried that Reagan already sounded too unorthodox on the Cold War, his advisers had persuaded him to avoid the issue that fall.

cessors had done better "when communicating has been private and candid."

But then on Thursday, September 1, 1983, near Japan, the Soviets shot down Korean Air Lines Flight 007, killing 269 people.

Reagan was riding at Rancho del Cielo, his beloved ranch atop California's Santa Ynez Mountains.

After taking the call in a White House Chevy Suburban, he remounted his horse and beat his fist on the saddle: "Those damned Russians, they knew that was a civilian aircraft! My God, have they gone mad?"

The President flew back to Washington and told the nation that the "Korean Air Line massacre" was "the Soviet Union against the world."

Insisting that the downed aircraft had been an American spy plane, Andropov retorted that Reagan had shown why dealing with him was "impossible."

In the wake of KAL 007, the U.S. and its Western allies were planning a vast military game for November 1983 called "Able Archer," which would include a simulated nuclear missile launch.

Some in the KGB suspected that the West might use Able Archer, coming just before Pershings went into Europe, as camouflage for a surprise attack on the Soviet Union.

The KGB chief in London, Oleg Gordievsky, was certain that nuclear war was closer than at any time since the Cuban Missile Crisis. Gordievsky sent out a flash warning that U.S. forces in Europe had gone on sudden alert.

That fall at Camp David, Reagan screened an advance print of ABC Television's two-hour movie *The Day After*, starring Jason Robards and John Lithgow.

Afterward he told his diary that the film showed "Lawrence, Kansas, wiped out in a nuclear war with Russia." He found it "powerfully done, all $7 million worth."

In a rare confession for a President who claimed he was "always in a good mood," he told his diary that *The Day After* had "left me greatly depressed."

*   *   *

Armed with reports from Gordievsky, who was about to defect to the West, the CIA Director, William Casey, warned Reagan that the Kremlin feared an American surprise attack.

Incredulous, the President asked Casey, "Do you suppose they really believe that?"

He told his diary, "Maybe they are scared of us and think we are a threat." Perhaps "without being in any way soft" on the Russians, "we ought to tell them no one here has any intention of doing anything like that. What the h-l have they got that anyone would want?"

Nancy Reagan told her husband that the confrontation with the Soviets had grown "ridiculous."

No Presidential couple had ever had a closer marriage. Reagan asked his diary, "What if she'd never been born? I don't want to think about it."

After World War II, when his first wife, Jane Wyman, left him, Reagan, by his own account, woke up with women he scarcely knew: "Then along came Nancy Davis, and saved my soul."

Growing up an alcoholic's son, the ever-shifting alliances of Hollywood, his postwar box office decline and Wyman's sudden walkout—such life experiences did not move Reagan to confide in others.

The President's son Ron observed that his father was "one of the warmest, most amiable, gentlemanly, kindest people you'd ever want to meet," but that he had "no close friends." Reagan's longtime press aide Lyn Nofziger felt that the President liked people: "He just didn't need people."

Even Nancy felt she could not quite leap the "barrier" around Ronnie. Her perpetual state of anxiety and her acute sensitivity to hidden dangers complemented his fatalism and willingness to take people at face value, which "sometimes . . . infuriates me," she wrote. "I did the worrying for both of us."

Although Reagan's poll numbers had rebounded by the end of 1983, the First Lady asked political aides what issue might defeat him for reelection. Their reply: the growing fear of war with the Soviet Union.

Prodded by Nancy and Mike Deaver, her closest ally on the staff, the President agreed to make a television speech heralding a "turning point" in American-Soviet relations. The address was scheduled before Christmas, but Mrs. Reagan's hidden astrologer advised that the following month would be more propitious.

The President's adviser on Soviet affairs, Jack Matlock, insisted the address include a quote from John Kennedy's "peace speech" of 1963, well remembered in Moscow, asking Khrushchev for a détente.

But Reagan was no Kennedy fan. He suspected, without proof, that JFK and his brother Bobby had retaliated for his orations against their policies by quietly persuading General Electric to fire him as its spokesman and host of *General Electric Theater,* which was cancelled.

When Matlock pressed him on the Kennedy reference, Reagan said, "Well, all right. But make the quote as short as possible."

Speaking from the East Room on Monday, January 16, 1984, Reagan declared that Americans had "come a long way" from their years of "self-doubt."

Since the Soviets had "counted on us to keep weakening ourselves," they now charged that America had increased the "danger" of nuclear war. But actually, he said, the world was now "safer" because the Kremlin could not "underestimate our strength or question our resolve."

No longer lacerating an "evil empire," Reagan asked the Soviets for "a constructive working relationship" that would let both sides "greatly reduce" their nuclear arsenals.

Imagining an "Ivan and Anya" meeting a "Jim and Sally," he insisted that "people don't make wars."

The Kremlin was unmoved. *Pravda* gibed that as an average American, "Jim" was probably unemployed, so he and "Sally" would have to invite their new Soviet friends to a soup kitchen for the destitute.

Andropov wrote Reagan, "Let us be frank, Mr. President. There is no way of making things look as if nothing has happened. The tension has grown dangerously."

In her effort to change her husband, the First Lady ensured that Ronnie heard new and different voices about the Soviet Union.

The day after the "Ivan and Anya" speech, Suzanne Massie, author

Reagan greets Suzanne Massie in the Oval Office

of a popular history of czarist Russian culture, *Land of the Firebird*, came to the Oval Office. Massie was startled to find Reagan "a bit nervous—maybe because someone had told him that I was an 'expert.' "

She described how, during a recent trip to Moscow, she had been summoned by a KGB general "with flashing black eyes" who pounded a table and warned, "You don't know how close war is!"

Reagan asked her, "How much do they believe in Communism over there?"

"I can only tell you what the Russians say about their leaders," she replied. "They call them 'the Big Bottoms' and say, 'They love only their chairs.' "

Massie found the President "very worried" that "if there was no religious or spiritual ethic" in Russia, "this could cause Armageddon."

Unaware that she was echoing Reagan's cherished late mother, she told him Christianity would one day sweep away the Soviet autocracy.

Emotive and theatrical, Massie made a hit. Reagan extended their scheduled five-minute meeting to nearly an hour. After she left, he told his diary that Massie had "no truck with the government types" in Moscow and was "most complimentary about my speech."

Yuri Andropov died in February 1984. When George Shultz suggested that Reagan attend his funeral, the President refused: "I don't want to honor that prick!"

Instead he asked Vice President Bush to assure the new Soviet leader, Konstantin Chernenko, that "a fatal confrontation" between their peoples was "by no means certain."

Reagan was eager to bargain with Chernenko himself. He told his diary, "I have a gut feeling I'd like to talk to him about our problems man-to-man."

From his years facing Hollywood studio bosses as president of the Screen Actors Guild, Reagan was certain of his skills. He was sure the Russians couldn't be "any tougher than Y. Frank Freeman and Harry Cohn."*

But the Soviets hoped Americans would elect a new, more docile President. Reagan told his diary, "They're utterly stonewalling us."

After visiting Moscow, French President François Mitterrand told Reagan there was no chance of a summit anyway: Chernenko was so clearly sick he could barely speak a spontaneous word.†

Reagan's Democratic opponent, Walter Mondale, who had been Carter's Vice President, ran commercials warning that the President's "Star Wars scheme" would extend the Cold War "into the heavens."

Dick Wirthlin assured Reagan that Mondale's "Star Wars" broadsides actually increased the President's support.

Reagan told his diary, "The press is after me because of a little band of clerics who charge that I'm basing my policies on the expectation of Armageddon." But the "desperate" Mondale "keeps dropping in the polls, so I guess the high road is best."

---

* Of Paramount and Columbia Pictures, respectively.

† One Soviet official later acidly wrote in his diary, "A worldwide sensation: Chernenko's voting on TV. Turns out, his hospital ward was 'transformed' into an election center. A man half-dead. A mummy. . . . Meanwhile he 'appears' every day with addresses, replies, forewords and memoranda!"

Reagan's managers pushed him to counter Mondale's complaint that he was the first President since Herbert Hoover who had not met his Soviet counterpart.

With Chernenko unavailable, the President asked the Soviet Foreign Minister, Andrei Gromyko, to the White House. By autumn, the Kremlin had concluded that Reagan was likely to win the election: why not buy some goodwill by doing him this favor?

On Friday, September 28, Reagan told his diary, "The big day—Andrei Gromyko."

Although it was Indian summer, the President was photographed talking with his Soviet guest in the Oval Office in front of a photogenic fire.

Gromyko had come well briefed on Nancy Reagan's influence. George Shultz noted that when the Foreign Minister met her before a "working luncheon" in the State Dining Room, he "didn't pay attention to anybody else."

Raising a glass of cranberry juice, Gromyko asked her to whisper "Peace" into the President's ear every night. She said, "I will, but now I'll whisper it into your ear too—Peace!"

The following month, when the seventy-three-year-old Reagan debated Walter Mondale, his faltering performance aroused fears that he was too old to be President.

"I have to say I lost," Reagan confided to his diary. "I'd crammed so hard on facts and figures in view of the absolutely dishonest things he'd been saying in the campaign, I guess I flattened out. Anyway, I didn't feel good about myself."

During their rematch, the President climbed off the mat by joking that he would not exploit "for political purposes" his opponent's "youth and inexperience."

Years later Mondale recalled, "You'll see that I was smiling. But I think if you come in close, you'll see some tears coming down because I knew he had gotten me."

On Election Day, Reagan won every state but Mondale's Minnesota. In his diary, he wrote that despite the "beautiful day," the press was "trying to prove it wasn't a landslide or, should I say, a mandate."

*   *   *

In a secret session after Reagan's reelection, the Joint Chiefs of Staff praised his military buildup.

"What a meeting," Reagan told his diary. "Apparently the U.S. has never had in peacetime such readiness, quality of manpower, weaponry and reserves. I came out of the Cabinet Room feeling ten feet tall."

Reagan told Shultz it was time "to lean on the Soviets, but to do so one on one, not in the papers."

The Secretary of State said he was tired of fighting Cap Weinberger and Bill Casey to improve relations. "It's so out of hand George sounds like he wants out," Reagan informed his diary. "I can't let that happen. . . . I'm going to meet with Cap and Bill and lay it out to them. Won't be fun but has to be done."*

That December, the Reagans went to the annual honors performance at the John F. Kennedy Center for the Performing Arts. At the end, Roberta Peters led the cast in singing "Let There Be Peace," which they dedicated to the man at the front of the Presidential box.

As Reagan told his diary, "I made it a point to be the first to stand and applaud when the last note was sung."

---

* As Shultz expected, Reagan's aversion to personal confrontation kept him from laying down the law. Casey remained at the CIA until he suffered a stroke in 1986. Weinberger stayed at the Pentagon until his wife's grave illness compelled him to leave in 1987.

CHAPTER THIRTY-FIVE

DON'T WORRY THAT I'VE
LOST MY BEARINGS

By March 1985, Chernenko was dead. The new Soviet leader was the fifty-four-year-old Mikhail Gorbachev, whom Western observors had dubbed the Kremlin's "crown prince."

After meeting Gorbachev at Chernenko's funeral, Vice President Bush warned Reagan that he would package the Kremlin's line "much more effectively than any (I repeat any) of his predecessors." Before the President could "figure out who this man really is," members of Congress would be "eating out of his hand."*

Reagan complained that a sycophantic press was already doing its "psycho job" on Gorbachev: "I wonder what I'd have to do to get such treatment from *Time* and several other magazines." He was "too cynical to believe" that "Gorby" was "a different type than past Soviet leaders."

Nevertheless Reagan wanted a summit. He told Shultz, "If they insist on a neutral locale, make it Geneva."

When the Soviets agreed, Reagan started private tutorials that his staff called "Soviet Union 101." Knowing how to reach their President, the CIA made him a motion picture called "Gorbachev the Man."

Reagan's friend Barney Oldfield, who did business in Moscow, sent

---

* In the spirit of their private schoolboy camaraderie, Bush wrote Reagan, "This Gucci Comrade brings the General Secretariat a quantum leap forward in overall appearance. His tailor does not rival Deaver's man at Adler's [a Washington haberdashery] but he beats the hell out of the Penney's basement look that some of his predecessors projected."

him some new anti-Soviet jokes, like the one about the Russian who ordered his secretary to strip naked. She told him if they were going to make love, they had better close the door.

Noting Gorbachev's campaign against alcohol, her boss replied, "No, they would think we're drinking!"

Oldfield reported a rumor that Gorbachev was planning to admonish Reagan in Geneva for insisting that Lenin had said Communism must rule the world.

"Thanks for the tip on the Lenin quote," Reagan replied. "Of course they are not telling the truth. They have about 55 volumes on their messiah, Mr. Lenin, but all have been carefully sanitized. That particular quote goes way back before [the Nazi propagandist] Herr Goebbels.

"I'll give you a Russian story I picked up. Two Soviet citizens are talking and one says . . . 'Have we really achieved full communism?' The other one says, 'Hell no, things are going to get a lot worse!' "

On the eve of his departure for Geneva, Reagan was interviewed by four Soviet journalists. He told his diary, "I wonder if they'll print my answers as I gave them." If not, he could use his tape of the interview to "expose" the Russians.

Nevertheless he was serious about bargaining with Gorbachev. Suzanne Massie advised him to use his acting skills because Russians "learn from stories, from feeling, from observation."

During one visit with Reagan, Massie "screwed up my courage" and asked, "What is it that you want from the Russians?"

"I want to get rid of those nuclear weapons," he replied. "Every one!"

On Sunday morning, November 16, 1985, Reagan awoke in the splendid house of the Aga Khan's son on Lake Geneva.

He walked around Maison Fleur d'Eau, where he would host the first day's talks. "I hope to get Gorbachev aside for a one on one," he told his diary. "There is a poolhouse down on the lake shore, complete with fireplace. I'll try to talk him into a walk."

Reagan knew that this was not normal custom, but he once told his friend Brian Mulroney, the Canadian Prime Minister, "Protocol is spelled bullshit."

Nervous about his talks with Gorbachev, Reagan remembered his flop in the first Mondale debate, telling his diary, "Lord, I hope I'm ready and not over trained."

To stoke his self-confidence, he rehearsed with Jack Matlock, who played a convincing Gorbachev. As he recorded, on Monday evening, "Nancy surprised me with a masseur. . . . I fell asleep about four times while he was massaging me."

Reagan pledged to his diary that he would never give up SDI. If Gorbachev tried, he would find "an irresistible force meeting an immovable object."

In his journal for Tuesday, November 19, the President wrote, "This was the big day. Mr. G and I met. We were scheduled for 15 minutes of private one on one. We did *an hour*, which excited the h-l out of the press."

When Gorbachev, bundled against the cold, arrived, the smiling Reagan greeted him hatless and coatless. One of Gorbachev's aides complained that his boss looked like "a KGB agent from a bad American film." *

Settled in stiff-backed chairs, Reagan told the Soviet leader that Americans detested his system because it wanted to conquer the world.

"You are not a prosecutor," said Gorbachev. "I am not the accused."

Staring into Gorbachev's eyes, Reagan issued a steely warning: they could either reduce their nuclear arsenals or start a new arms race. If the latter, there was "no way" he would ever let the Soviets win.

Shocked and offended by Reagan's threat, Gorbachev told his staff, "I have met a caveman! A dinosaur!"

After luncheon, Reagan suggested a trip to the poolhouse for "some fresh air." During their walk, he complained to Gorbachev that some Soviet official had dismissed him as a "B-movie actor."

The President did not let on how badly his feelings could be hurt by criticism of his acting. His personal aide Jim Kuhn recalled the time a lady told Reagan he was "the best President I've ever witnessed" but that she had "never liked you as an actor."

The "stunned" President later told Kuhn, "Nobody's ever told me they thought I was a bad actor."

---

* At the end of the day's meetings, Gorbachev joked to Reagan, "Coats on or coats off?"

President Theodore Roosevelt with his wife, Edith, and children, 1903. T.R. felt he had the "happiest home life" of anyone he knew.

Mark Hanna, the Republican boss who tried to tame the
accidental President he called a "damned cowboy."

J. P. Morgan, hailed as the "most powerful man in the world,"
whose mighty railroad trust was shattered by T.R.

21

T.R., romantically portrayed in 1903 as crusader against all forms of corruption.

22

Theodore at his 1905 inauguration, having defied angry
conservatives in his party and on Wall Street.

23

Franklin Roosevelt in the Oval Office, 1940,
as if sizing up a threatening visitor.

24

Eleanor Roosevelt defending her husband, 1940, although she privately lamented that
he had become a "stranger" to her.

25

Charles Lindbergh, 1940. The trans-Atlantic flier charged that FDR and the Jews were dragging the nation into war against Hitler. Roosevelt privately said he was "absolutely convinced" Lindbergh was a Nazi.

26

Joseph Kennedy, FDR's Ambassador to London, threatened to expose the President's secret relationship with British Prime Minister Winston Churchill and warn American voters that Roosevelt was plotting to take them to war.

27

Wendell Willkie and his secretly estranged wife, Billie, campaign against FDR.

28

Defying his terrified political aides, Roosevelt presides over the first draft lottery a week before the 1940 election. Secretary of War Henry Stimson is blindfolded to choose the first number.

President Harry Truman with his daughter, Margaret, and wife, Bess, 1947. After she complained that Harry was freezing her out, he consulted her every evening about his greatest dilemmas, including the prospect of a Jewish homeland, for which Bess showed no particular sympathy.

Truman visiting his old Kansas City haberdashery partner Eddie Jacobson, who overcame his reticence to implore Harry to help give the Jews their own state.

30

31

British troops halt Holocaust survivors arriving in Palestine aboard the *Exodus 1947*.

32

President John Kennedy and his wife, Jackie, 1962. She did not think it her role to push Jack on public matters like civil rights.

Martin Luther King, Jr., being kissed by his wife, Coretta, October 1960, after his release from a Georgia jail with JFK's help.

33

34

Robert Kennedy was furious when Jack intervened to have King freed. But as Attorney General, he prodded him do more for civil rights.

35

Freedom Riders as their bus is burned by an angry white mob, Alabama, May 1961.

Riots against JFK's use of the Army to integrate the University of Mississippi, October 1962.

36

37

To placate impatient African-American leaders, JFK hosts a Lincoln's Birthday reception, February 1963, with more black guests than ever before at the White House. Some deride it as "Collud Night at the Kennedys."

38

Martin Luther King arrested in Birmingham, Alabama, May 1963, before narrowly escaping a motel bombing.

39

Nancy Reagan congratulating Ronnie on his victory over Jimmy Carter, Election Night, Los Angeles, 1980.

40

Reagan meets in the Oval Office with Soviet defector Oleg Gordievsky, whose secret reports had warned that the Soviets feared Reagan would launch a first-strike nuclear attack on their country.

41

With Nancy's strong encouragement, Reagan tries to connect with the new Soviet leader, Mikhail Gorbachev, Geneva, 1985. Reagan mistakenly convinced himself that Gorbachev was a secret Christian.

42

Reagan angrily stalking out of his private meeting with Gorbachev, Reykjavik, Iceland, October 1986. Having neared a deal to abolish nuclear weapons, Reagan accuses Gorbachev of trying to "trap" him.

43

Shaken by illness and the Iran-Contra scandal, Reagan appeared so frail that Richard Nixon demanded that the President not be allowed to see Gorbachev alone. At left and right are Senators John Tower and Edmund Muskie, who were investigating the affair.

Ex-Presidents Reagan and Gorbachev at Rancho del Cielo, California, May 1992. Having collaborated with Gorbachev to end the Cold War, Reagan does not want to embarrass him in front of reporters by telling him his new Stetson is on backwards.

As they neared the poolhouse, Reagan insisted to Gorbachev that people thought some of his movies were "good."

Gorbachev replied that while preparing for their summit, he had enjoyed watching that film "where your legs were cut off. Which one was that?"

"*Kings Row,*" said Reagan.

"What is it like to see yourself so young on the screen?"

"You've set me up for a great one-liner," said Reagan. "It's like meeting a son you never knew you had!" *

Reagan was right to expect that Gorbachev would try to talk him out of SDI. He told the President, "Scientists say any shield can be pierced." The Soviet Union would "build up to smash your shield. . . . You haven't thought this through."

Reagan retorted that Americans demanded a shield so that Soviet missiles wouldn't "blow up everything in our country."

By the end of the day, the President told aides he had enjoyed arguing with Gorbachev. It was like dealing with Tip O'Neill. "You could almost get to like the guy. I keep telling myself I mustn't do it, because he could turn."

Nancy Reagan had no similar affection for her Leninist counterpart. "That Raisa Gorbachev is one cold cookie," she told Ronnie. "Who does that dame think she is?"

That evening, the Gorbachevs held a formal dinner. "And what a dinner," Reagan told his diary. "Course after course after course, and for half of them, I thought each one had to be the entrée."

In his toast, obviously advised that religious talk would ingratiate the President, Gorbachev cited the Bible's warning that there was a time to throw stones and a time to gather them.

Echoing the apostle Paul, Reagan responded, "We are all of one

---

* The following year, aides asked him to screen *Kings Row* at Camp David. Reagan told his diary, "I'd forgotten how really good that picture is." He generally shook his head at 1980s cinema. After seeing Jane Fonda, Dolly Parton and Lily Tomlin in *9 to 5,* he told his diary that "one scene made me mad. A truly funny scene if the three girls had played getting drunk, but no, they had to get stoned on pot." He found Candice Bergen's *Rich and Famous* "pornographic." Richard Gere's *An Officer and a Gentleman* was "spoiled by nudity, language and sex."

blood, regardless of where we live on the earth." He went on to observe that if hostile aliens ever arrived on Halley's Comet, such an attack "would unite all the peoples of the world." *

Impressed by Gorbachev's religious references and his confession that his grandmother had read him from the Bible, Reagan later said, "I'm *sure* this man believes in God. If I could only get him alone, I'm *sure* I could talk to him about these things!"

On Wednesday morning, Gorbachev took another run at SDI. He said one of his scientists had explained that the only reason Reagan would back such a farfetched scheme was that SDI would pump a trillion dollars into America's military-industrial leviathan.

Reagan dismissed Gorbachev's notion as uninformed "fantasy." He joked that perhaps the reason he felt so strongly about SDI was that "in a previous life" he had been "the inventor of the shield" before his reincarnation as President.

Reagan promised to share his anti-missile research, but Gorbachev carped, "You Americans won't even share your milk-processing technology with us!"

Dismissing Gorbachev's warning that SDI would violate their ABM Treaty, Reagan charged that the Soviets were doing their own secret anti-missile research.† Gorbachev asked him not to utter "banalities" more suited for press conferences.

Reagan proposed reducing both of their nuclear arsenals by fifty percent. Then he and Gorbachev could sit down and decide whether to deploy SDI. "Isn't that a fair deal?"

Gorbachev asked the President not to treat him like a "simpleton." As Reagan wrote in his diary, "The stuff really hit the fan. He was really belligerent and d-m it, I stood firm."

Before leaving Geneva, Reagan and Gorbachev agreed to meet one year hence in Washington, then a year later in Moscow. Reagan found that during their final handshake, Gorbachev's hand was "really crushing" his own.

---

* Reagan's aides, who often heard him make this argument, would say, "Here come the little green men again!"

† The ABM Treaty allowed each side to defend one site. The Americans charged that the Soviets were defending both Moscow and an installation at Krasnoyarsk.

After reporting to Congress, he told his diary, "I haven't got such a reception since I was shot. . . . The members wouldn't stop clapping and cheering." He felt that "the air of success in the meetings is widespread, but probably not with our cynical press."

The day after returning from Geneva, Reagan held a fateful meeting with his aides. "Subject was our hostages in Beirut," he informed his diary. "We have an undercover thing going by way of an Iranian which could get them sprung momentarily."

As George Shultz once observed, any American "held captive and mistreated overseas was a matter of personal agony" for this President.

"Was shown the photos recently taken by the bastards who are holding our kidnap victims in Lebanon," Reagan had told his diary. "Heartbreaking. There is no question but that they are being badly treated."

The President told Suzanne Massie he wouldn't "let myself get euphoric," but he had felt "something of a chemistry" with Gorbachev.

He wrote his old Hollywood friend former Senator George Murphy that it was "foolish to believe the leopard will change its spots." Gorbachev was "a firm believer in their system (so is she)" but knew that "his economy is a basket case."

He assured the hard-line Murphy, "Now don't worry that I've lost my bearings."

In April 1986, at Chernobyl, the Soviets suffered history's worst nuclear disaster. After a botched effort by Gorbachev to conceal the gravity of the accident, Reagan offered to send U.S. experts.

Gorbachev resented the offer as a ploy to show off America's technological mastery. George Shultz warned Reagan that "the Soviets are becoming increasingly defensive and withdrawn."

Suzanne Massie told the President that Chernobyl was the Ukrainian word for "wormwood." She noted that the Book of Revelation had related that "a star from heaven fell on water" and "men died of the water because it was bitter."

The President marveled to his aides that Chernobyl was "predicted in the Bible two thousand years ago." He wondered whether the accident was yet another sign of Armageddon.

*   *   *

That August, the Soviets jailed a *U.S. News & World Report* correspondent named Nicholas Daniloff on charges of espionage.

At his ranch, Reagan was told that Daniloff had clearly been nabbed as trading material for Gennadi Zakharov, a Soviet attaché arrested in New York for buying classified U.S. documents.

Reagan sent Gorbachev his "personal assurance" that Daniloff had "no connection whatever with the U.S. Government," but the Soviet leader would not believe it. Reagan told his diary, "Gorbachev's response to my letter was arrogant. I'm mad as hell."

He wrote a friend that his "number one duty" was Daniloff's rescue, "and I won't rest until he's safely back here in the United States."

Gorbachev had been stalling for months about the summit he had promised for Washington. Now he wrote Reagan suggesting "a quick one-on-one meeting—let us say in Iceland or in London, which may be just for one day—to engage in a strictly confidential, private and frank discussion."

"I opt for Iceland," Reagan told his diary. "But we made it plain we wanted Daniloff returned to us before anything took place."*

After intense bargaining, Shultz and Soviet Foreign Minister Eduard Shevardnadze agreed on a complex arrangement to let the two prisoners return home.

Reagan complained to his diary that the press was "laying into me," claiming he had traded Daniloff for Zakharov: "That's a lot of crap and they don't know what they were talking about."

On Thursday, October 9, 1986, Reagan flew to Reykjavik for a weekend "mini- summit" with Gorbachev.

He recorded, "It was dark and raining when we arrived, even though it was afternoon." Having devoured Tom Clancy's thriller *Red Storm Rising*, "I think I know every square foot of Iceland."

Told that wives were not invited, the President had left Nancy at home. He was irritated to find that Gorbachev had brought Raisa, who wondered aloud why Nancy wasn't there, saying, "Maybe she's ill."

---

* Shultz had recommended the Icelandic capital of Reykjavik, "an isolated city where the host government would not interfere"—unlike Margaret Thatcher's London.

On Saturday morning, Gorbachev walked into the white clapboard cottage called Hofdi House with an offer designed to "sweep Reagan off his feet."

He told the President he was accepting his long-standing offers to cut their strategic nuclear arsenals in half and remove all of their intermediate-range missiles from Europe.

As for SDI, both sides would agree to honor the ABM Treaty for at least ten years, with no research or testing "outside of laboratories." After that, both sides could decide on how to revise the treaty.

Using a Russian proverb Suzanne Massie had given him, Reagan told Gorbachev, "*Doveryai no proveryai.* Trust, but verify. How do we know that you'll get rid of your missiles, as you say you will?" *

Gorbachev offered to relax his country's eternal aversion to on-site inspections.

The President said Gorbachev's offer was "very encouraging," but that he was "refusing to see the point of SDI. . . . I'm older than you are. When I was a boy, women and children could not be killed indiscriminately from the air. Wouldn't it be great if we could make the world as safe today as it was then?"

Reagan pledged that if the U.S. perfected a shield, he would share it with the Soviets and deploy only after both sides destroyed their nuclear arsenals.

"Excuse me, Mr. President, but I cannot take your idea of sharing SDI seriously. . . . Sharing SDI would provoke a second American revolution! Let's be realistic and pragmatic." †

In private, an exhilarated George Shultz told Reagan that Gorbachev's astounding proposals were "the result of five years of pressure from us."

On Sunday morning, Gorbachev warned that this moment might never come again. A year from now, he might not be so generous. The President shouldn't cling to SDI.

---

* In this and later meetings, Reagan said, "Trust, but verify" so often that Gorbachev would cover his ears.

† Gorbachev was right to be skeptical. Reagan officials like Frank Carlucci and Jack Matlock later agreed that probably no President would ever share such hard-won technology with the Russians.

But Reagan said he had promised Americans a shield. While aides bargained in another room, he asked Gorbachev to disown the Marxist notion that socialism would be successful only if it ruled the world.

Recalling Reagan's well-known gibe while debating Jimmy Carter, Gorbachev said, "There you go again—talking about Marx and Lenin!" He complained that Reagan had called his country "an evil empire."

Suggesting that his own system would prevail, Reagan said he looked forward to the day he could welcome Gorbachev as "a new member of the Republican party."

The Reykjavik meeting was supposed to end with lunch, but Reagan and Gorbachev were on the verge of the biggest arms control deal in history. That afternoon, upping the ante, they ruminated about cutting half of their arsenals by 1992, the rest by 1997.

Reagan said they should come back to Iceland to destroy their two last missiles: "I'll be so old you won't recognize me. I'll say, 'Mikhail?' You'll say, 'Ron, is that you?' " After that, they'd throw "the biggest damn party for the whole world."

Gorbachev said he didn't expect to survive another decade. Reagan had made it through a man's "danger period," so he would live to be a hundred. As for himself, "I'll have the burden of having gone through all these meetings with a President who didn't like concessions."

"I can't live to a hundred worrying that you'll shoot one of those missiles at me," said Reagan. "I told my people I wouldn't give up SDI."

But Gorbachev kept demanding that Reagan confine his anti-missile research to the laboratory for ten years.

During a break, crowding with his team into their anti-eavesdropping "bubble," Reagan asked Shultz if he was right to insist on SDI.

"Absolutely!" said the Secretary of State.

Someone suggested that Reagan stay on through Monday in quest of a deal.

But the exhausted President said, "Oh, shit!" He wanted to fly home for Sunday dinner with Nancy. No one dared try to change his mind.

*   *   *

Rejoining Gorbachev, Reagan said they were close to "an agreement we can be very proud of." Why destroy it over one word? "What the hell difference does it make? . . . We may not build SDI in the end. It might be too expensive."

Gorbachev asked if this was the President's "final position." Reagan explained that if he gave up SDI, he would be "badly hurt." The "so-called right wing" was already kicking his brains out.

Gorbachev told Reagan he was now "three steps away from becoming a great President." But if he wouldn't keep SDI in the laboratory, he would have to "forget everything we have discussed."

"You would turn down a historic opportunity because of a single word?"

Gorbachev said if he gave up that word, the Soviet people would think him a "village idiot."

As a "favor," Reagan asked him to reconsider, so they could "go on and bring peace to the world."

"There are favors—and there are favors," said Gorbachev. "I did everything I could."

Reagan grimaced: "The meeting is over." Turning to Shultz, he said, "Let's go, George, we're leaving."

As the President donned his pale raincoat, Gorbachev pleaded, "Can't we do something about this?"

"It's too late," said Reagan. Later he wrote in his diary that Gorbachev "tried to act jovial," but "I was mad . . . and it showed."

When Gorbachev escorted him to his limousine, Reagan accused him: "You planned from the start to come here and put me into this situation!"

The Soviet leader asked what more he could have done.

Reagan said, "You could have said yes!"

Boarding *Air Force One*, the President stalked down the aisle, pinching thumb to forefinger: "We came *this close*!"

After takeoff, Reagan's old friend Charles Wick, Director of the U.S. Information Agency, came to his stateroom to cheer him up.

The President told Wick that he hadn't been "bluffing" about SDI. If the Soviets were forced to match the program, it would "break" them: "They couldn't possibly spend the kind of money we're spending to create this."

Wick told him in that case, "you just defeated the Soviet Union and won the Cold War."

Soon Reagan was smiling again. He told an aide, "I know I made the right decision back there. We couldn't give up SDI—not for America's future."

CHAPTER THIRTY-SIX

A MIRACLE HAS TAKEN PLACE

Three weeks after Reagan returned from Reykjavik, a Lebanese journal revealed that his ex–national security aide Robert McFarlane had secretaly journeyed to Tehran to barter for the release of U.S. hostages in Beirut. Soon the President faced a firestorm for breaking his own pox against such bargaining.

Incensed at the "irresponsible press bilge," Reagan said he had merely been trying to encourage Iranian moderates. He told his diary, "The media looks like it's trying to create another Watergate."

He complained to a friend that Republican Presidents were always persecuted by Congress—"Ike for the Sherman Adams affair, Dick [Nixon] for Watergate, Jerry [Ford] for CIA and now my own lynching."*

But in late November, the world learned that proceeds from secret arms sales to Iran had been used to finance the Nicaraguan "Contras," who were fighting their country's Marxist government.

Funding the Contras defied a recent act of Congress. If the evidence showed Reagan had approved it, he could be impeached and evicted from the Presidency.

Denying knowledge of the scheme, Reagan was indignant to learn that sixty percent of Americans "don't think I'm telling the truth." He felt "a bitter bile in my throat."

From his Hollywood days, Reagan had fed off the acclaim of the pub-

---

* Eisenhower's chief assistant, Sherman Adams, was accused of influence peddling. Gerald Ford was President when Congress investigated decades of CIA malfeasance.

lic. As a new President, he had raved into his diary about the cheering crowds in New York City, which was not exactly Reagan Country:

"I wore my arms out waving back to them. . . . I keep thinking this can't continue, and yet their warmth and affection seems so genuine I get a lump in my throat. I pray constantly that I won't let them down."

After a university speech in 1985: "What a morale booster that was— thousands of students telling me they loved me."

But now the audience was threatening to walk out of the theater. Amid the sudden political crisis, Reagan's new National Security Adviser, Frank Carlucci, found him "in a daze. He didn't know what hit him."

In February 1987, Reagan met in the Oval Office with members of the commission he had created to investigate the Iran-Contra affair. Recovering from prostate surgery, he unsettled his guests by mistakenly reading aloud from the stage directions given him by aides.

Doctors found no proof of the Alzheimer's disease that ultimately afflicted him, only the deterioration of a seventy-six-year-old man who had experienced a shooting, colon cancer and prostate surgeries, and, now, a scandal that might oust him from the White House.

Through memos, telephone calls and intermediaries, Richard Nixon's backstage influence had increased along with Reagan's eagerness to build a relationship with Mikhail Gorbachev.

Insisting that Nixon's Watergate punishment had been too severe, Reagan had long wished to host a White House dinner for the former President but never went through with it. Suspecting that the First Lady was the obstacle, Nixon privately carped that Nancy was a "bitch" and that she "runs Ronald Reagan."

In April 1987, Nixon was invited to the White House for his first non-ceremonial visit since his resignation. He could not have been happy when Reagan's aides sneaked him upstairs like a common thief. At the height of Iran-Contra, they did not wish to advertise a meeting with the architect of the Watergate cover-up.

Swallowing his pride, Nixon advised Reagan on how to deal with Gorbachev, and found him "somewhat fuzzy . . . far older, more tired and less vigorous than in public."

Nixon wrote to himself that Reagan was clearly not "on top of the issues. . . . There is no way he can ever be allowed to participate in a private meeting with Gorbachev."

In the summer of 1987, a Congressional investigation concluded that the President had indeed traded arms for hostages, but had not authorized the illegal diversion of arms sales money to the Contras.

Reagan wrote George Murphy that Congress hadn't "gotten the noose around my neck" because "I've been telling the truth for eight months."

With Nancy's strong encouragement, he sought to jump-start his Presidency by redoubling his efforts to wind down the Cold War.

George Shultz told a colleague, "Ronald Reagan has had the landing lights on and the flaps down for the last year. Now we're going to have to step up to the plate on foreign policy."

In the Oval Office, the President sought advice from Oleg Gordievsky, the KGB colonel who had defected to the West after warning in 1983 of possible imminent war. Reagan told his diary that Gordievsky had been forced to leave his "wife and two little girls behind" in Moscow: "We've been trying to get them out to join him."

During a scheduled visit to Berlin, Reagan planned to insist that Gorbachev open the ugly wall that divided the city. Most of his diplomats feared such a seemingly hopeless demand would only inflame the Soviet leader.

Reagan said, "I'm the President, aren't I?" Just as when he had used the epithet "evil empire," which the pros had also scorned, he hoped to inspire those behind the Iron Curtain with the knowledge that he was trying to liberate them.

Mounting a platform near the Brandenburg Gate, Reagan was furious when he peered through binoculars and saw East Berliners trying to hear him being pushed away by police.

Deciding with his actor's instinct to let his anger show, Reagan shouted, "Mr. Gorbachev, tear down this wall!" *

---

* Reagan's challenge is recalled even by people who have no idea what he was talking about. After his death in 2004, a woman waiting outside his Presidential library was asked for her favorite Reagan saying. Her reply: "Tear down these walls!"

*   *   *

In the Kremlin, Gorbachev was advised by his counselor Alexander Yakovlev that the American right wing had instigated the Iran-Contra scandal as "retribution to Reagan" for nearing a deal with the Russians at Reykjavik.

Yakovlev wrote his boss that by insisting on SDI, Reagan had "missed his best chance to go down in history as a statesman, not a clown." Nor was the President "intellectual enough" to "have an epiphany" now.

Gorbachev was exhorted to feel more sanguine about SDI. With America's "growing financial difficulties" and the recent Democratic takeover of the Senate, the anti-missile program would have rough sledding.

Thus reassured, Gorbachev pursued part of the offer he had made in Iceland—a treaty to ban U.S. and Soviet intermediate-range nuclear forces. After brisk bargaining, Reagan and Gorbachev planned to sign the pact at a December summit in Washington.

Even while dealing with matters of global importance, Reagan maintained his lack of pretense. Sending a top-secret report to his new Defense Secretary, Frank Carlucci, he used a cover slip adorned by a picture of a teddy bear atop a stack of papers, with the printed saying, "It's lonely at the top."

Just as in Hollywood, the President felt awkward posing for still photographs, asking his diary, "Why do I hate photo sessions so?"

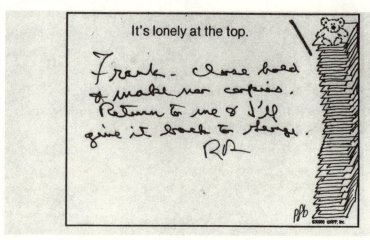

Reagan's notepaper reflected "his lack of pretense."

*   *   *

Earlier that year Reagan had heard an alarming report from Suzanne Massie: a Soviet official had warned her that Gorbachev "might be killed" if he came to the United States.

As Reagan told his diary, he did not find Massie's report "outlandish." So many Russians were angry at Gorbachev's reforms that "they could murder him and then pin the whole thing on us. . . . The KGB is capable of doing just that."

Washington remained the site of the summit, but for security and other reasons, Gorbachev declined the President's invitation to stay at his California ranch.

Reagan was disappointed. He had dreamt of taking the Soviet leader up in a helicopter over all those Los Angeles split-levels with their swimming pools and boasting, "Those are the workers' houses!" *

On the eve of the Washington summit, during an interview with TV network anchors, Reagan said that Gorbachev had convinced him that the Soviets had given up their old passion to rule the earth. He regretted that some Americans still believed that "that war is inevitable."

For some American conservatives, Reagan's comment broke the camel's back. "Apologist for Gorbachev," said the direct-mail king Richard Viguerie. "A very weak man with a strong wife," said the Conservative Caucus's Howard Phillips.†

Reagan's longtime backer Nackey Loeb, publisher of New Hampshire's *Union Leader*, wrote him sadly that she no longer recognized him. He insisted, "Nackey, I'm still the Ronald Reagan I was and the evil empire is just that."

Before the Gorbachevs arrived on Tuesday morning, December 8, 1987, Nancy Reagan kissed her husband and said, "Knock 'em dead!"

Nancy felt hurt that Raisa did not ask about her recent breast cancer

---

* Almost certainly Reagan's wish was borrowed from remembered news accounts of President Eisenhower in 1959 taking his Soviet counterpart, Nikita Khrushchev, by helicopter from the White House to Camp David, flying low so that Khrushchev could see all the middle-class houses and cars on the highways.

† The Intermediate Nuclear Forces (INF) Treaty was also opposed by less partisan conservatives like Nixon and Kissinger, who feared it would leave Western Europe too vulnerable to Soviet conventional forces.

surgery or the death of her mother. Instead Mrs. Gorbachev gibed, "We missed you in Reykjavik."

After a twenty-one-gun salute and colonial fife and drum parade on the South Grounds, the two leaders had what Reagan considered a "good rousing" debate about human rights: "He thinks we have fewer of those than they do."

To Gorbachev's initial discomfort, Reagan suggested that they start using first names: "Mine is Ron."* Although Gorbachev did not wear French cuffs, Reagan gave him a pair of gold cuff links depicting Isaiah's old dream of beating swords into plowshares.

In the East Room at exactly 1:45 P.M.—thanks to Nancy's astrologer— Reagan and Gorbachev signed the INF Treaty on the Ulysses Grant used by JFK during the Ole Miss riots.

Taking the microphone, Reagan recited his now favorite Russian maxim: "Trust, but verify." Showing his irritation, Gorbachev replied, "You repeat that at every meeting!"

Reagan said, "I like it!"

When the two leaders met that afternoon, so many aides wished to be present that Shultz ordered the meeting moved from the Oval Office to the Cabinet Room.

The President's newest National Security Adviser, General Colin Powell, knew this would be trouble because "sudden changes threw Ronald Reagan off his form."

As Gorbachev expostulated on nuclear weapons, the President displayed what Powell called "a fixed, pleasant expression."

Then Reagan told one of his most hackneyed Soviet jokes. An American asked a young Moscow cabdriver what he would do when he got out of school. The driver replied that the authorities hadn't told him yet. Triumphantly Reagan said, "That's the difference between our systems!"

Frowning and red-faced, Gorbachev asked him to please stop having his Moscow envoys send him such tales.

For the rest of the meeting, the deflated President let his Secretary of

* With his outsized sense of decorum, Gorbachev did not like such informality. Moreover, Reagan called him "Mikhail," rather than the more proper "Mikhail Sergeyevich."

State carry the ball. Afterward Shultz told Reagan, "Mr. President, that was a disaster! That man is tough, he's prepared and you can't just sit there telling jokes."

At a White House dinner that evening, featuring Joe DiMaggio, Billy Graham, Pearl Bailey and Jimmy Stewart, the pianist Van Cliburn brought tears to Gorbachev's eyes by playing "Moscow Nights."

The next morning, in his study next to the Oval Office, Reagan gave Gorbachev a baseball from DiMaggio, who wanted them both to sign it.*

The President told Gorbachev he wished they could have stayed at his ranch: "You haven't seen America until you've seen California."

As Reagan wrote in his diary, when they moved to his office, "things got a little heated." For the first time, Gorbachev confessed that matching the U.S. anti-missile research program would "wear out" his economy.

The Soviet leader claimed that if the Americans ever deployed SDI, the Soviets would match them with their own "less costly" version: "Go ahead. Build it! We can do the same, a hundred times cheaper."

Exploiting the opening, Reagan needled, "Oh, so you *are* working at strategic defense." †

"I didn't say that!" said Gorbachev.

On Thursday morning, Reagan paced the Oval Office carpet, glaring at his wristwatch. He was a stickler for punctuality, and Gorbachev was more than an hour late.

During luncheon in the Family Dining Room, while their aides bargained in the West Wing, Gorbachev explained that while riding over, he had stepped out of his car and chatted with Americans. Touched by their friendliness, he had not wished to break off the conversation.

No longer angry, Reagan told a story about American bureaucrats. During World War II, a government clerk had asked to destroy a ton of

---

* Feeling like "a witness to history," DiMaggio later said "they were the only two autographs I ever sought." After DiMaggio's death in 1999, the signed baseball was auctioned for $27,600.

† Reagan had told his diary in 1984 that the Soviets were secretly pushing "twice as hard as us" to gain "military superiority in outer space."

Gorbachev, Reagan and DiMaggio at the White House, December 1987

useless official documents. Permission was granted—so long as he made copies of all the records to be destroyed.

Gorbachev retorted by joking about the Soviet official who was accused of using his government car to go to a bathhouse. His defense was that he couldn't be guilty: he hadn't bathed in two years!

When the Gorbachevs departed in the rain, Reagan told his diary it was "the best summit we've ever had." He noted that Dick Wirthlin had found the meeting "a big plus," boosting his approval rating to sixty-seven percent.

Walking into the Cabinet Room to brief House and Senate leaders, Reagan got a rare standing ovation. With his Irish grin, he asked, "Did you just see one of my old movies?"

Reveling in the warm blast of restored public affection, the President and Nancy spent their usual New Year's Eve at Walter Annenberg's estate near Palm Springs: "Dolores Hope, Dinah Shore and Frances Bergen sang some songs of our time. Bob Hope told some jokes and it was midnight and 'Auld Lang Syne.' "

*   *   *

In May 1988, Ronald Reagan made his first trip to Moscow. "We couldn't believe the friendliness and warmth," he wrote a friend. "Wherever we went, they were massed on the curb, waving, smiling and cheering."

In Red Square, Gorbachev lifted a baby and said, "Shake hands with Grandfather Reagan!" Asked if it was still an "evil empire," Reagan said, "No, I was talking about another time, another era."

Meeting with Gorbachev in the Kremlin, Reagan found it was too late in his Presidency to close the deal he had hoped for, cutting nuclear arsenals by fifty percent.* Instead he used their private talks to advance his mother's old wish that the wellsprings of religious feeling be loosed to sweep away Soviet Communism.

Reagan told Gorbachev he had a "kind of personal dream." He had been reluctant to raise it, but now he and Mikhail were friends. If anyone leaked it, he'd deny they'd ever had this conversation.

He asked Gorbachev to "see his way" to let all Soviet citizens attend "the church of their choice." Americans had "endured a long sea voyage to a primitive land to worship as they pleased."

If Gorbachev granted religious freedom, he would be a "hero" and much of the world's anti-Soviet feeling would evaporate "like water in the hot sun."

Gorbachev replied that Soviet society had "evolved" beyond mass religion. Although he had been baptized, he did not believe in God. Turning the tables, he asked why Americans did not give nonbelievers their full rights.

Reagan said, "They do." In American public schools, "you can't even say a prayer." He noted that his son Ron was "an atheist, although he calls himself an agnostic."

Reagan told Gorbachev about a letter from a young World War II soldier to his faraway wife. Although a professed atheist, he wrote that he was praying God would accept him if he died in battle. The soldier belonged to the Soviet army. The letter was found on his corpse.

Trying to change the subject, Gorbachev proposed a U.S.-Soviet mission to Mars.

---

* In 1991, Gorbachev and President George H. W. Bush finally signed a Strategic Arms Reduction (START) Treaty, which drastically reduced the arsenals and delivery systems of both sides.

Smiling, Reagan retorted that Mars was "in the direction of heaven," but not as close as what they'd been discussing. He said he'd always yearned to serve his atheist son "a perfect gourmet dinner, have him enjoy the meal, then ask him if he believed there was a cook."

Tired of arguing, Gorbachev said, "The only possible answer is yes."

In January 1989, Reagan retired to Los Angeles. The raw space used for his new penthouse offices in Century City had been used to film *Die Hard*, with Bruce Willis as a New York cop preventing terrorists from blowing up a tall building.

During the Cold War's final throes, Reagan wrote his friend Barney Oldfield, "A miracle has taken place."

In November 1989, Mikhail Gorbachev allowed the Berlin Wall to be torn down. Told the news at his ranch, Reagan at first thought it must be some kind of joke, then was rushed down the mountain to Los Angeles to give television interviews, elated and beaming.

With the post–World War II division of Europe ended, the Cold War seemed to be truly over.

When people praised him for ending the long struggle, Reagan said, "No, this couldn't have happened were it not for Gorbachev." *

But in September 1990, he crossed the Atlantic for what his staff called his "victory lap." In Berlin, he chiseled at the Berlin Wall while ex-Communists cried out, "Thank you!"

Before he and Nancy flew on to Moscow, his chief of staff, Fred Ryan, proposed that he give Gorbachev a bear hug when they met.

The macho Reagan was not enthusiastic, but Nancy told Ryan it would be an expression of the world-important friendship the two men had built: "Remember to have Ronnie embrace Gorbachev!"

At the Kremlin, Reagan found the Soviet leader waiting in his office doorway. When he threw his arms around him, Gorbachev stepped back in mild horror.

Reagan felt baffled and embarrassed. He had not been warned that embracing a Russian in a doorway suggested that one wished to break off

* In defense of his own contribution, Gorbachev rightly claimed credit for shirking his predecessors' attitude of "I'll take my ten years as emperor and what comes after, the hell with it!"

friendship. He was much relieved when after reaching the center of the room, Gorbachev gave him a vigorous bear hug.

On Christmas Night 1991, Reagan grew emotional watching television as Gorbachev declared the Soviet Union dead and himself out of power, with the hammer and sickle lowered over the Kremlin for the last time.

Reagan told family and friends they had seen "the triumph of good over evil."

In May 1992, the old man finally got Gorbachev to Rancho del Cielo.

For years, Reagan had imagined taking the Soviet leader by chopper over Los Angeles to see the ranch houses and swimming pools of American workers.

Now, before Gorbachev arrived, Reagan sent him word to make sure to look down at the working-class neighborhoods.

When they embraced at the airport, Reagan asked, "Did you see the swimming pools?"

At Reagan's ranch, the tensions of their summit meetings were forgotten. The once-combative Nancy and Raisa held hands.

Gorbachev was startled by the modesty of Reagan's adobe house and grounds. Fred Ryan thought he had been expecting "something from the set of *Dallas*."

Reagan loaded his guest into his blue Jeep (license plate: "GIPPER"), showed him his horses and tack room and gave him a ten-gallon Stetson.

When they posed for photographers, Reagan did not want to embarrass Gorbachev by telling him that his new hat was on backward.

With sweeping arm, Nancy told their guest, "I want you to know that Ronnie built all of these fences."

Gorbachev quipped, "Trust, but verify!"

Unlike more ordinary politicians who followed the slightest downdraft in the political atmosphere, Ronald Reagan's strong beliefs and optimism moved him to do things from which others might have flinched.

In 1980, although Afghanistan had undeniably made Americans more militant toward Moscow, a more nervous and calculating Presidential candidate than Reagan would have taken a position on the Soviet Union that was closer to the political center of the time.

Although more than willing to adjust his rhetoric, Reagan felt that if his anti-Soviet belligerence scared people, they were welcome to vote against him. As promised, he used his landslide victory as a mandate to set about convincing the Russians that America had regained its political will.

The self-confidence that kept Reagan from worrying too much about falling poll numbers, however, also deafened him to how his escalation of the Cold War was terrifying many Americans. More dangerous was the Soviet fear that Reagan was plotting a first-strike attack that might lead to World War III.

Reagan had always told the public that if turning up the pressure on the Soviets made them bargain seriously, he would not only deal but try to abolish nuclear weapons. When they heard this, many of his conservative champions had winked, presuming that he didn't really mean it.

But when Gorbachev showed that he had similar ambitions, Reagan proved that he meant what he had said. At Reykjavik, he tried to end the nuclear arms race once and for all—even if it infuriated some of his earliest supporters. Like the most effective American Presidents, Reagan ultimately proved that he was not the captive of his political base but its leader.

The last time Ronald Reagan met Mikhail Gorbachev as the two most powerful leaders on earth was in December 1988.

The site was Governors Island, south of Manhattan in the Hudson River. In 1776, General George Washington had ordered the little island fortified against the advancing British fleet.

Gorbachev was in New York City to address the United Nations. For a farewell luncheon with Reagan, the Secret Service had chosen Governors Island because, just as in General Washington's time, it was easily secured.

Reagan would not have chosen this as the venue for his last formal session with the Soviet leader. When Gorbachev once asked him what was the best thing about New York City, Reagan replied, "California!"

Photographers swarmed in as the two leaders sat with President-elect George H. W. Bush in the Admiral's House. Chatting away, Reagan recalled from his television career that "the lights can make you look twelve years younger."

Speaking of the press, had he ever told Gorbachev the one about Lyndon Johnson saying that if he ever managed to walk on water, reporters would complain he couldn't swim?

Chuckling, Gorbachev said that yes, the President had told him that story before.

Reagan reported that eighty percent of Americans endorsed his peace efforts with the Soviet Union, though there would always be a "fringe." Some Americans even believed that "Hitler was a nice guy."

"Nobody I know!" chimed in George Shultz.

Bush said he realized that if he didn't follow Reagan's example in making peace, the ex-President would be on the phone from California, "getting on my case and telling me to get going."

Rising from the table, the three men were driven to the north side of Governors Island and ushered onto a platform.

While cameramen snapped away in the cold, Reagan gestured across the Hudson at the newly restored Statue of Liberty. Then, turning to his right, he showed off the tallest buildings in New York City, the gleaming World Trade Center.

Reagan would have been thunderstruck to learn that thirteen years

into the future, the twin towers would be destroyed in the opening fusillade of America's next major world struggle.

But he would not have been surprised by the cause. During one of
their private meetings, he had warned Gorbachev that their two countries, both "born of revolution," must watch out for the spreading "fun-
damentalist Islamic revolution . . . which teaches that the way to heaven
is to kill a nonbeliever."

During their visit to Governors Island, Reagan and Gorbachev
missed seeing a nearby landmark reaching two centuries into the American past.

A red-brick, star-shaped military fortress, it was named in 1798 for the
patrician New Yorker who had hammered out a bitterly disputed treaty
for President Washington, which kept Great Britain from halting the
march of American history almost before it began.

The old island fort was named for John Jay.*

---

* After taking power in 1801, Thomas Jefferson's party banished the name of the Federalist hero they reviled, and rechristened the installation Fort Columbus. But with his fine
sense of history, President Theodore Roosevelt had it renamed Fort Jay in 1904.

PRESIDENTIAL COURAGE

Before they are sworn in, modern Presidents are briefed on terrorist threats, U.S. covert activities and the nuclear "football"—the brief-case that will let them, if it should ever come to that, incinerate much of the earth.

New First Families are offered a tour of a little known warehouse outside the Capital, jammed with their predecessors' desks, chairs, tables, mirrors, paintings, busts and Oriental rugs. This was the ware-house that Jackie Kennedy combed for "treasures" that would help her transform the "early Statler" ambience she found at the White House.

Such rituals remind new Presidents and their families that earlier Americans experienced similar exhilarations and ordeals. So does read-ing about the past. Harry Truman said he could never have functioned as President had he not read his eyes out about the leadership qualities of his predecessors.

From his own reading of history, John Kennedy feared that the changing political environment was making it more difficult for Ameri-cans to practice the kind of leadership that had shaped our past.

In 1955, he complained that politics had become "so expensive, so mechanized and so dominated by professional politicians and public re-lations men." Thanks to "the tremendous power of mass communica-tions," he wrote, "any unpopular or unorthodox course arouses a storm of protests."

A half-century later, such trends had spiraled far beyond anything

Kennedy might have imagined. A leader without courage and wisdom can be broken by them.

The ancient Romans surrounded their young leaders with paintings and sculpture to encourage qualities of greatness.

Should Americans ever follow such a practice, one of the public rooms of the White House might be enhanced with artifacts reminding Presidents that since George Washington, courage has been a requirement of the Presidency.

First might be the baseball that Joe DiMaggio asked Ronald Reagan and Mikhail Gorbachev to sign. Then, moving backward through time, the dented helmet worn by one of the U.S. Marshals sent by JFK to integrate Ole Miss.

Next might be the Torah that moved Harry Truman to tears after he helped ensure the Jewish people a home—and the black cathedral radio that told FDR on Election Night 1940 that he might be defeated by the isolationists.

After that would be a miner's torch given to Theodore Roosevelt by grateful anthracite coal workers, and T.R.'s relic of his own hero—the gold ring containing hair snipped from Abraham Lincoln's head after his murder for liberating a race.

Beside the Lincoln ring would be the cameo that Andrew Jackson wore around his neck: the sad, soulful face of his wife, Rachel—victim, he was certain, of his plutocratic enemies.

Then, propped upright, a serving plate from the beloved family home that John Adams called Peacefield—a reminder that if halting war with France cost him reelection, he could return to a rich life with Abigail, surviving comrades from the American Revolution and, in the end, when he was almost alone, his books.

Looming on a shelf above all these objects would be the quill pen and inkwell used by President Washington on those storm-swept nights in August 1795 to write all of those letters defending John Jay's peace treaty with the British.

But not all Presidents are affected by historical artifacts. In that case, they might be taken to Mount Vernon, and up the stairs to the bedroom where George Washington died.

Standing there, to this day, is the wooden four-poster deathbed where the Father of His Country looked up into his doctor's kindly, worried eyes and croaked his near-to-last words.

General Washington was referring to his medical prognosis, but his words conveyed what he hoped his example would say to future Presidents of the United States.

What Washington told the doctor was, *"Don't be afraid!"*

NOTES

Chapter One: A SPEEDY DEATH TO GENERAL WASHINGTON!

Washington at Mount Vernon, Aug. 1795: Jackson and Twohig, vol. 6, pp. 669–72, Ferling, *First of Men*, p. 458, Freeman, pp. 204–8, Richard Norton Smith, *Patriarch*, pp. 236–39, Flexner, *Washington*, pp. 216–20. "Violent Rain": Washington Diaries, Aug. 2, 1795, in Jackson and Twohig, vol. 6, p. 206. "Serious anxiety" and "trouble and perplexities": George Washington to John Jay, May 6, 1796. All George Washington correspondence is in George Washington Papers, unless otherwise indicated. Previous acclaim for Washington: Ellis, *His Excellency*, pp. 183, 221, 147–51, Henriques, p. 50. "That damned treaty": Elkins and McKitrick, p. 432, Henriques, pp. 59–60.

"Electric velocity": James Madison to James Monroe, Dec. 20, 1795, James Monroe Papers. Guillotine cartoons: Burns and Dunn, *Washington*, p. 111. "A speedy Death": DeConde, *Entangling*, p. 133. Forgeries and alleged bribery: Flexner, *Washington*, p. 246. "With what justice": *Aurora*, Oct. 6, 1795. "Infamous scribblers": George Washington to Alexander Hamilton, June 26, 1796. "Washington has been classed": *Federal Gazette*, Jan. 21, 1796, in DeConde, *Entangling*, p. 119. British troubles of 1794, suggested responses, and "within a year": Flexner, *Washington*, p. 203, Bemis, *Jay's Treaty*, pp. 10–13, Elkins and McKitrick, pp. 375–96, Freeman, pp. 614, 662, Ellis, *His Excellency*, pp. 226–27. Martha Washington on Hamilton: Chernow, *Hamilton*, p. 126, Jean Edward Smith, p. 68.

Hamilton–Jefferson clashes: Reardon, p. 211, Freeman, pp. 636–37. "Tearing our vitals": George Washington to Thomas Jefferson, Aug. 23, 1792. Hamilton urges envoy and choice of Jay: Chernow, *Hamilton*, pp. 461–62, Stahr, pp. 108–12, 172–77, 311–19. Jay to wife and crowds on departure: John Jay to Sarah Jay, Apr. 9, 1794, Jay Papers, and Stahr, pp. 319–20. "The most open" and "family quarrel": George Washington to John Jay, Aug. 20, Nov. 1, and Dec. 18, 1794, and John Jay to George Washington, Sept. 13, Oct. 29, and Nov. 19, 1794, Feb. 25 and Mar. 6, 1795. Signing of treaty in London and delivery to Washington: Stahr, pp. 329–35, Flexner, *Washington*, pp. 237–39, Ellis, *His Excellency*, pp. 227–28.

George Washington and the Morris house: *Transactions of the American Philosophical Society*, vol. 43, 1953, "The President's House in Philadelphia," Independence Hall Association, 2006, "Picturing the President's House," White House Historical Association, 2004, *Philadelphia Inquirer*, Feb. 22, 1952, Seale, p. 4. "The best *Single*": George Washington to Tobias Lear, Sept. 5, 1790. "I will have no woman": Charles Biddle, p. 285. Washington and slaves: Wiencek, pp. 315–16, Wood, pp. 40–41, Helen Bryan, pp. 315–18. "I wish to have it": George Washington to Tobias Lear, Apr. 12, 1791. Washington reaction to Jay's Treaty: George Washington to Edmund Randolph, July 22, 1795. "Rigidly" secret: Randolph, p. 28. "A Battle Royal": John Adams to Abigail Adams, Feb. 9, Feb. 10, June 9, June 19, Aug. 9, 1795, Adams Papers.

Description of Senate and Senators: *Congress Hall.* "The *secrecy*": *Aurora*, June 22, 1795. "Daily outrages" and subscription canceled: Ellis, *His Excellency*, p. 222. Senate action on treaty: Freeman, pp. 664–65. Bache obtains and publishes copy of treaty: Freeman, p. 666. "Illegitimately begotten": Donald Stewart, p. 198. "Made its public entry": George Washington to Alexander Hamilton, July 3, 1795. Demonstrations against treaty: Timothy Pickering to George Washington, George Washington to Edmund Randolph, Edmund Randolph to George Washington, all July 27, 1795, Oliver Wolcott to George Washington, Sept. 26, 1795, Richard Norton Smith, *Patriarch*, pp. 236–37, Ellis, *His Excellency*, pp. 420–21, Flexner, *Washington*, p. 217, Elkins and McKitrick, pp. 420–21.

Jay on effigies: Stahr, p. 337, Freeman, p. 667. "May it please": Donald Stewart, pp. 214–18, Stahr, pp. 336–37. "Execrable . . . infamous" and "acquiescence": Thomas Jefferson to Edward Rutledge, Nov. 30, 1795, and Thomas Jefferson to Henry Tazewell, Sept. 13, 1795, Thomas Jefferson Papers. "Simple and plain": Alexander Hamilton–George Washington correspondence, July 1795. Provision Order and Washington's reaction: Randolph, p. 29. Randolph's advice and talk with George Hammond: Edmund Randolph to George Washington, July 31, 1795, Reardon, pp. 302–3, Flexner, *Washington*, pp. 213–14, Randolph, pp. 31–32. "Never" sign: George Washington to Edmund Randolph, July 29, 1795, Randolph, p. 32.

Protest against Hamilton: Chernow, *Hamilton*, pp. 489–90, Brookhiser, *Hamilton*, p. 125, Elkins and McKitrick, p. 835, Freeman, p. 670. "Kick this damned": Elkins and McKitrick, p. 473. "Public pulse": Thomas Jefferson to James Monroe, Mar. 2, 1796. "The country rising": Oliver Wolcott to Alexander Hamilton, July 30, 1795. "Extremely embarrassing": George Washington to Edmund Randolph, July 29, 1795. "Pre-concerted plan": George Washington to John Adams, Aug. 20, 1795. "To follow Washington": *Gazette of the United States*, July 13 and Aug. 4, 1795.

Chapter Two: KICK THIS TREATY TO HELL!

"Suffocating": Freeman, p. 668. "Relaxation": George Washington to Alexander Hamilton, July 14, 1795. "Well-informed": George Washington to Boston Citizens, July 28, 1795. "Have Veal," meeting with chiefs and departure: George Washington to William Pearce, June 28, 1795, Jacob Cox Parsons, p. 215. "Hot and disagreeable": George Washington to Alexander Hamilton, July 29, 1795. "No doubt": George Washington to Edmund Randolph, July 18, 1795. "Small Westerly": Washington Diaries, Aug. 2, 1795, in Jackson and Twohig, vol. 6, p. 206. Washington at

Mount Vernon: Dalzell and Dalzell, pp. 5–223, Bellamy, p. 140, Fitzpatrick, *George Washington Himself*, p. 440.

"Nothing pleases me": George Washington to William Pearce, Oct. 6, 1793. Jefferson carp about Washington leisure: Thomas Jefferson to Dr. Walter Jones, Jan. 2, 1814, Thomas Jefferson Papers. "Like a state prisoner": Martha Washington to Fanny Bassett Washington, Oct. 23, 1789, Fields, p. 220. Martha's finances and "Lady Washington": Caroli, pp. xv, 340, Bryan, p. 299. "Modest and unassuming": Mitchell, p. 19. Martha Washington on "Infirmities of Age": John Adams to Abigail Adams, Feb. 10, 1796, Adams Papers. "The cry against" and "the most abominable" and "working like bees": George Washington to Alexander Hamilton, July 29, 1795. "Victory more": George Washington to Timothy Pickering, July 27, 1795.

"Too rude to merit": George Washington handwritten note on "Letter Book" copy of Resolutions of the Citizens of Bordentown, Crosswicks, Black Horse, and Reckless Town, N.J., July 28, 1795. "Tenor indecent": George Washington handwritten note on "Letter Book" copy of Resolution of the Citizens of Petersburg, Virginia, Aug. 1, 1795. "Solomon": George Washington to Edmund Randolph, July 22, 1795. "In every act": George Washington to Boston Selectmen, July 28, 1795. "What it was": George Washington to Edmund Randolph, July 22, 1795. "Obnoxious" and "better to ratify": George Washington to Edmund Randolph, July 13 and 22, 1795, George Washington to Alexander Hamilton, July 13, 1795.

"Violent paroxysm" and "crisis is approaching" and "anarchy": George Washington to Charles Cotesworth Pinckney, Aug. 24, 1795, George Washington to Patrick Henry, Oct. 9, 1795. "Run down": Edmund Randolph to George Washington, July 20, 1795. "Such vast magnitude" and "to leave home": George Washington to Edmund Randolph, July 29, 1795. "Preparing my mind": George Washington to Edmund Randolph, July 29, 1795. "Quit the ground" and "but one straight course": George Washington to Edmund Randolph, July 31, 1795. "Return with all convenient": Timothy Pickering to George Washington, July 31, 1795. "The suddenness" and "miserably torn": Fitzpatrick, *Writings*, vol. 34, pp. 270–71.

Randolph background and Randolph affair: Mary Bonsteel Tachau, "George Washington and the Reputation of Edmund Randolph," *Journal of American History*, vol. 73 (1986), Combs, pp. 165–70, 192–96, DeConde, *Entangling*, pp. 120–27, Elkins and McKitrick, pp. 422–30, Ferling, *First of Men*, pp. 456–62, Flexner, *Washington*, pp. 213–42, 672–85, Richard Norton Smith, *Patriarch*, pp. 24–249, Reardon, pp. 4–334. Pickering explains charge against Randolph: Flexner, *Washington*, pp. 224–26, Freeman, pp. 672–73, Ferling, *First of Men*, pp. 458–59, Tachau, pp. 25–28, Elkins and McKitrick, pp. 424–25. "First characters": George Washington to George Fairfax, June 25, 1786. "My friends . . . seem": George Washington to Edmund Randolph, Mar. 28, 1787.

"Would confer pre-eminence": George Washington to Edmund Randolph, Sept. 28, 1789. Washington deliberates alone: Flexner, *Washington*, pp. 224–29, Richard Norton Smith, *Patriarch*, pp. 244–45, Freeman, pp. 673–74, Ferling, *First of Men*,

p. 459, Tachau, p. 28, Elkins and McKitrick, pp. 426–29. Washington and Benedict Arnold: Flexner, *Washington*, p. 386, Flexner, *Young Hamilton*, pp. 307–8, Chernow, *Hamilton*, pp. 140–42. Randolph complaint of poverty: Flexner, *Washington*, p. 226.

Chapter Three: THE DAMNEDEST LIAR

Cabinet meeting, Aug. 12, 1795: Flexner, *Washington*, pp. 231–32, Elkins and McKitrick, p. 425, Richard Norton Smith, *Patriarch*, p. 245, Reardon, pp. 308–9. "I will ratify": Freeman, p. 674. "Unutterable": Randolph, p. 54. Washington and Randolph before treaty sent: Flexner, *Washington*, pp. 232–34, Richard Norton Smith, *Patriarch*, pp. 245–46, Freeman, pp. 675–77, Reardon, pp. 309–10. Washington confronts Randolph: Flexner, *Washington*, 234–36, Randolph, pp. 1–7, Freeman, pp. 676–78, Richard Norton Smith, *Patriarch*, pp. 246–47, Reardon, pp. 210–12. "Your confidence in me": Edmund Randolph to George Washington, Aug. 19, 1795. "I feel happy": Edmund Randolph to James Madison, Nov. 1, 1795, James Madison Papers.

Randolph goes to Newport and "appeal to the people": Tachau, p. 31, Reardon, pp. 313–15, Richard Norton Smith, *Patriarch*, p. 248, Freeman, pp. 682–83, Randolph, pp. 9–17, Edmund Randolph to George Washington, Sept. 15, 1795. Randolph request for letter and "publish, without reserve" and "exhibit to public view": Edmund Randolph to George Washington, Aug. 19, Sept. 15, and Oct. 8, 1795, and George Washington to Edmund Randolph, Aug. 20 and Oct. 21, 1795. "See what relation": George Washington to Edmund Randolph, unsent, Oct. 25, 1795. "Full of innuendoes": George Washington to Edmund Randolph, Oct. 25, 1795. Randolph's book: Reardon, pp. 331–34. "A Piece of Revenge": John Adams to Abigail Adams, Dec. 21, 1795, Adams Papers.

"My *final* decision": Syrett, vol. 19, p. 356. "By the eternal God": Richard Norton Smith, *Patriarch*, p. 248. "He was written and published": Elkins and McKitrick, p. 431, Pickering and Upham, vol. 3, pp. 226–27, Brookhiser, *Founding Father*, pp. 117–18. Wolcott announcement, Randolph's loss in courts and later life: Reardon, pp. 337–65. "The great body of Yeomanry" and "abominable misrepresentations": George Washington to Henry Knox, Sept. 20, 1795. "Voice of malignancy": George Washington to John Stone, Dec. 6, 1795. "To wound": George Washington to Timothy Pickering, Mar. 3, 1797. "As the head of a British": John Beckley to James Madison, Sept. 10, 1795, James Madison Papers.

Forgeries and Washington's suspicion about source of personal facts: Flexner, *Washington*, p. 246, Richard Norton Smith, *Patriarch*, p. 253. Expense account charges and Wolcott's explanation: Freeman, pp. 686–87, Flexner, *Washington*, p. 246. Washington exonerating letter: George Washington to Timothy Pickering, Mar. 3, 1797. "(For the present time)": George Washington to John Stone, Dec. 6, 1795. "Dominating spirit": George Washington to John Jay, Aug. 13, 1795, George Washington to Alexander Hamilton, Aug. 31, 1795. British vice consul pursues sailors: Flexner, *Washington*, pp. 246–47. "Sour the minds": George Washington to

John Jay, Aug. 31, 1795. "Without a full": Flexner, *Washington*, pp. 251–56, Richard Norton Smith, *Patriarch*, p. 255. Washington's 1795 annual message: Dec. 8, 1795, Flexner, *Washington*, pp. 251–54.

Federalist counterattack: Combs, p. 179, Freeman, p. 694, DeConde, *Entangling*, pp. 137–38, Todd Estes, "Shaping the Politics of Public Opinion: Federalists and the Jay Treaty Debate," *Journal of the Early Republic* (2000). "It is time": James McHenry to Robert Oliver, Apr. 12, 1796, James McHenry Papers. "Like a High-wayman": James Madison to Thomas Jefferson, Apr. 18, 1796, Thomas Jefferson Papers. Hamilton's broadsides: Chernow, *Hamilton*, pp. 494–96. "Pleasure": George Washington to Alexander Hamilton, July 29, 1795. "Middling performances": Thomas Jefferson to James Madison, Sept. 21, 1795, Thomas Jefferson to Tench Coxe, Sept. 10, 1795, Thomas Jefferson to James Monroe, Sept. 5, 1795, Thomas Jefferson Papers.

Chapter Four: HE MAY RETIRE WITH UNDIMINISH'D GLORY

Washington senses tide turning and Treaty of San Lorenzo: Freeman, pp. 690–91, DeConde, *Entangling*, p. 133, Bemis, *Pinckney's Treaty*, 249–81, Richard Norton Smith, *Patriarch*, pp. 258–59, George Washington to John Stone, Dec. 6, 1796, Maryland Legislature to George Washington, Nov. 25, 1795. "Difficult to see": John Adams to Abigail Adams, Apr. 19, 1796, Adams Papers. House protest against Washington's Birthday and "with all the insolence": Freeman, p. 690. "Era of strange" and "In these wild times": George Washington to Alexander Hamilton, May 8, 1796, and Alexander Hamilton to George Washington, May 5, 1796. House debate on Jay's Treaty: Todd Estes, "The Art of Presidential Leadership: George Washington and the Jay Treaty," *Virginia Magazine of History*, Spring 2001, pp. 148–54, Combs, pp. 171–87, Flexner, *Washington*, pp. 259–76, Freeman, pp. 691–97, DeConde, *Entangling*, pp. 134–40.

"A crude mass" and "These are unpleasant": George Washington to Henry Knox, Apr. 4, 1796, Alexander Hamilton to George Washington, Mar. 7, Mar. 24, Mar. 28, Mar. 29, Mar. 31, and Apr. 2, 1796, George Washington to Alexander Hamilton, Mar. 31, 1796, George Washington to Edward Carrington, May 1, 1796, George Washington to Charles Carroll, May 1, 1796, Flexner, *Washington*, p. 267fn. "Set a host of Scribblers": George Washington to John Jay, Mar. 31, 1796, George Washington to Henry Knox, Apr. 4, 1796. "Anxiety is on": Freeman, p. 692. "Bite like savages": John Adams to Abigail Adams, Mar. 11, 1796. Washington Mar. 30, 1796, message: Fitzpatrick, *Writings of George Washington*, vol. 35, pp. 2–5.

"A few outlandish": John Adams to Abigail Adams, Apr. 16, 1796, Adams Papers. Gallatin-Tracy argument: Freeman, p. 695. Republican reversals on treaty: Elkins and McKitrick, p. 447. "It would give you": Thomas Jefferson to Philip Mazzei, Apr. 24, 1796, Thomas Jefferson Papers. Fisher Ames illness and speech and "threw a spell": Bernhard, pp. 263–75, John Adams to Abigail Adams, Apr. 21, 1796, Adams Papers, Flexner, *Washington*, pp. 275–76. "My God, how great": Bernhard, p. 272,

DeConde, *Entangling*, p. 139. "Jack Asses": John Adams to Abigail Adams, Apr. 30, 1796, Adams Papers. "An occasion so glorious": Bernhard, p. 272. Muhlenberg's vote and "If you do not give": Timothy Pickering to George Washington, July 27, 1795, Charles Lee to John Marshall, May 5, 1796, John Marshall Papers, Richard Norton Smith, *Patriarch*, p. 265, Wallace, pp. 284–86, Combs, p. 184.

Washington gratitude to Ames and "a respectable member": George Washington to William Pearce, May 29, 1796, George Washington to Fisher Ames, May 31, 1796. Ames's later life: Bernhard, pp. 275, 348. "Mortifying": John Adams to Abigail Adams, Apr. 19, May 3, and May 5, 1796, Adams Papers. "Worried and growing old" and "may retire": John Adams to Abigail Adams, Feb. 10, Mar. 3, 1796, Adams Papers. Ridden "out the Storm" and "pernicious" and "disseminating the poison" and "worn away" and "dishonorable": George Washington to John Jay, May 8, 1796. "Certain Jackasses": Alexander White to George Washington, Sept. 17, 1795. "Buffitted": George Washington to Alexander Hamilton, July 26, 1796, in Syrett, vol. 20, p. 237.

Drafting of Farewell Address: George Washington to Alexander Hamilton, May 8 and May 15, 1796, Alexander Hamilton to George Washington, July 5 and July 30, 1796, Chernow, *Hamilton*, pp. 505–8, Flexner, *Washington*, pp. 294–300, Ellis, *His Excellency*, pp. 232–40. Farewell Address: Sept. 17, 1796, in Fitzpatrick, *Writings of George Washington*, vol. 35, p. 237. "Cruelly inflicted": Daniel Jones to George Washington, Nov. 23, 1796, and George Washington to Daniel Jones, Nov. 24, 1796. "Every heart": *Aurora*, Sept. 19, 1796. Party anger of 1796: Freeman, p. 712. Jackson vote against Washington and "the insulting Cringing": Remini I, pp. 179–80.

Hostile Republican toast to Washington: Ferling, *First of Men*, p. 484. "Prematurely embarrass" and "twenty years' peace": George Washington to Charles Carroll, May 1, 1796. "Command of its own fortunes": Farewell Address, Sept. 17, 1796. "Scarcely any part": George Washington to Catherine Macauley Graham, Jan. 9, 1790. "I am *sure*": George Washington to John Jay, May 8, 1796. "I have a consolation": George Washington to Henry Lee, July 21, 1793. "The shade of my Vine": George Washington to George Washington Parke Custis, Feb. 27, 1797, and George Washington to George Clinton, Feb. 28, 1797.

"Closing scenes" and "I have not a wish": George Washington to Henry Knox, Mar. 2, 1797. "A few years" and "seclude myself": George Washington to Sir John Sinclair, Dec. 10, 1796, and George Washington to Henry Knox, Mar. 2, 1797. "My Successor to the Chair": George Washington to Henry Knox, Mar. 2, 1797. "Streaming eyes": John Adams to Abigail Adams, Mar. 9, 1797, Adams Papers. "Farmer Washington": Flexner, *Washington*, p. 339. Washington appearance at hotel and departure: Flexner, *Washington*, pp. 333, 339, Ferling, *First of Men*, p. 485, Bellamy, pp. 375–76, Bryan, pp. 248–49, *New York Herald*, Mar. 11, 1797.

Chapter Five: RIVALRIES IRRITATED TO MADNESS

"Popularity was never": John Adams to James Warren, Jan. 9, 1787, Adams Papers. All John and Abigail Adams correspondence is in John and Abigail Adams Papers, unless otherwise indicated. "Talents of a very Superior": John Adams to Abigail Adams, Dec. 27, 1796. Washington treatment of Adams as Vice President: McCullough, *Adams*, pp. 408, 415. "I loved and revered the man": John Adams to Benjamin Rush, July 24, 1805, Page Smith, p. 1084. "Very superficially": Chernow, *Hamilton*, p. 520, Wood, p. 33. "Old Muttonhead": Chernow, *Hamilton*, p. 520. "Turn the World upside down": John Adams to Benjamin Rush, Apr. 22, 1812, Schultz and Adair, p. 214, Ferling, *Adams*, p. 333.

"Puffed like an air balloon": John Adams to Benjamin Rush, Aug. 23, 1805, Schultz and Adair, p. 35, Ferling, *Adams*, p. 424. A "viceroy": John Adams to Benjamin Rush, Sept. 30, 1805, Schultz and Adair, p. 42, Ferling, *Adams*, p. 424. Hamilton and 1796 electors: McCullough, *Adams*, pp. 393–94. Abigail Adams on Hamilton: Abigail Adams to John Adams, Jan. 28, 1797. "Inconveniences": George Washington, Dec. 7, 1796, in Fitzpatrick, *Writings of George Washington*, vol. 35, p. 318. French danger in 1797: DeConde, *Quasi-War*, pp. 1–35, McCullough, *Adams*, p. 474. "Those Treaty breaking": Abigail Adams to John Adams, Feb. 7, 1797. "Neither John Bull": John Adams to John Quincy Adams, Mar. 17, 1797.

"Insults": *Porcupine's Gazette*, Mar. 3, 1797. "Many bellied Monster": Ferling, *Adams*, p. 340. "An excellent assurance": Chernow, *Hamilton*, p. 552. "Reconcile" the "misunderstanding": John Adams to John Quincy Adams, Mar. 31, 1797, in *Works of John Adams*, vol. 8, p. 537. Adams's effort to recruit Jefferson for France: DeConde, *Quasi-War*, pp. 15–16, Elkins and McKitrick, pp. 541–44, Ferling, *Adams*, p. 341. "I am of no party": John Adams to Dr. Walsh, Mar. 10, 1797. "Sick of residing": Elkins and McKitrick, p. 542. "Just as the bubble": Ellis, *Passionate Sage*, p. 27. Adams consults Cabinet on France, spring 1797: Ferling, *Adams*, p. 341, DeConde, *Quasi-War*, pp. 21–24. "Exhaust the expedients": Alexander Hamilton to Oliver Wolcott, Mar. 30, 1797, Chernow, *Hamilton*, pp. 546–47, Lodge, vol. 10, pp. 249, 268.

"Half-war": DeConde, *Quasi-War*, p. 328. "Wound in the American": John Adams message to Congress, May 16, 1797, in *Works of John Adams*, vol. 10, p. 111. Adams lisp and tremor: Chernow, *Hamilton*, p. 520, McCullough, *Adams*, p. 459. Congress response to Adams message: Page Smith, p. 967, DeConde, *Quasi-War*, pp. 90–91. Timid imbeciles: Abigail Adams to John Adams, Dec. 9, 1796, Page Smith, p. 940. "Horrible tyrants": Syrett, vol. 20, p. 559. "English faction": Oberg, vol. 30, p. 468. "Eaten to a honeycomb": John Adams to Uriah Forrest, June 20, 1797, in *Works of John Adams*, vol. 8, pp. 546–47. "However wise": John Adams to John Quincy Adams, Nov. 3, 1797. "Rivalries have been irritated": John Adams to Abigail Adams, Feb. 22, 1799, in *Works of John Adams*, vol. 1, p. 544.

"The two most impartial": John Adams to Dr. Walsh, Mar. 10, 1797. "An honest and firm man": Billias, p. 262. "Constancy and fidelity": John Adams to Abigail Adams, Jan. 9 and 11, 1797. Elbridge Gerry's background: Ellis, *Passionate Sage*, p. 80. Adams not Cabinet's "slave": Billias, p. 259. Pickering effort to stop Gerry appointment: McCullough, *Adams*, p. 486. "It is ten to one": Elkins and McKitrick, p. 556, and Billias, p. 262. Jefferson talks with French consul: McCullough, *Adams*, p. 489, Elkins and McKitrick, pp. 565–66, Chernow, *Hamilton*, pp. 547–48.

Chapter Six: OH, THAT I WAS A SOLDIER!

"Guillotined": George Washington to James McHenry, Mar. 4, 1798, in Fitzpatrick, *Writings of George Washington*, vol. 36, p. 179. Adams receives and reads dispatch from Paris: DeConde, *Quasi-War,* pp. 66–68, Ferling, *Adams,* pp. 352–53. Contents of dispatch from Paris: DeConde, *Quasi-War,* pp. 46–52, Elkins and McKitrick, pp. 569–79. Talleyrand on nation of "debaters": Page Smith, p. 931. "No, no, not a sixpence" and "Millions for defense": DeConde, *Quasi-War,* pp. 93, 178. Adams to Cabinet on "arrogance": John Adams to Heads of Department, Mar. 13, 1798, in *Works of John Adams*, vol. 8, p. 568. "*Real Americans*" and "national ruin": Ferling, *Adams,* pp. 352, 353. "Bulwark": John Quincy Adams to William Vans Murray, Jan. 27, 1798, Murray Papers.

Abigail orders coffee and sugar: Page Smith, p. 941. Adams draft of request for war declaration: John Adams Notes, March 1798, Adams Papers. Adams reconsiders: DeConde, *Quasi-War,* p. 68. Adams actual message to Congress: Mar. 19, 1798, in *Works of John Adams*, vol. 9, p. 156. "Bald, blind" and Abigail's reaction: Abigail Adams to Mary Cranch, Apr. 28, 1798, and Page Smith, p. 961. House demands and Adams provides correspondence: Ferling, *Adams,* p. 354. "Proof as strong": Page Smith, p. 959. "Abominable corruption": Alexander Hamilton to Timothy Pickering, Mar. 25, 1798, in Syrett, vol. 21, p. 371, Chernow, *Hamilton,* p. 550. House and Senate treatment of XYZ file: DeConde, *Quasi-War,* p. 70.

Americans respond to XYZ Affair: McCullough, *Adams,* pp. 499–500. "Very fast": DeConde, *Quasi-War,* p. 75. "Most magical effects": Chernow, *Hamilton,* p. 550. "Like windfalls": Page Smith, p. 959. Jefferson reaction to XYZ report: Thomas Jefferson to James Madison, Apr. 6, 19, and 26, 1798, in Oberg, vol. 30, pp. 250, 279, and 299, and Elkins and McKitrick, p. 588. "Most noted ill fame" and "great obstacle": Ferling, *Adams,* p. 354, Chernow, *Hamilton,* p. 551. "War party": Dunn, p. 100. "War hawks": Thomas Jefferson to James Madison, June 21, 1798, in Oberg, vol. 30, p. 417. "Men who have been intimate": Thomas Jefferson to Edward Rutledge, June 24, 1797, in Oberg, vol. 29, pp. 456–57, McCullough, *Adams,* p. 493. "Wives and daughters": DeConde, *Quasi-War,* p. 88.

Rumors of Adams murder and slave liberation and Adams orders muskets: DeConde, *Quasi-War,* pp. 84–85. "Treachery" and "reign of terror": John Adams to Abigail Adams, June 19, 1795, DeConde, *Quasi-War,* p. 81. "Terrorism": Diggins, *Portable John Adams,* p. 483. "Warlike character" and "humiliation, fasting": Ferling, *Adams,* p. 357, and Page Smith, p. 965. "True *martial* qualities" and "true manliness" and "ardently to be a soldier": Ferling, *Adams,* pp. 21–22. "Run away" and "too brittle": Ferling, *Adams,* p. 180. "Oh, that I was": Ferling, *Adams,* p. 133. Adams in dress uniform: McCullough, *Adams,* p. 501. "Greater luster": Ferling, *Adams,* p. 356. "The President Shines": Riccards, p. 194.

"Like *Samson*": Abigail Adams to William Smith, Mar. 30, 1798, Ellis, *Founding Brothers,* p. 190. "TYRANTS of France" and Titus Manlius: Chernow, *Hamilton,* pp. 551–52, and Syrett, vol. 21, pp. 408, 418, and vol. 24, p. 584. "I have always cried": DeConde, *Quasi-War*, p. 112. Congress creates Provisional Army and other measures: DeConde, *Adams*, p. 102. Alien and Sedition Acts: Elkins and McKitrick, pp. 590–95, Ferling, *Adams*, pp. 365–68, McCullough, *Adams*, p. 505. Adams "consented": Elkins and McKitrick, p. 590, McCullough, *Adams*, p. 505. "Wicked and base": Abigail Adams to William Smith, July 7, 1798. Pickering and Sedition Act: McCullough, *Adams*, p. 506.

"Desperadoes": *Gazette of the United States*, July 3, 1798. Bache indictment and death: *Gazette of the United States*, June 27, 1798, Ferling, *Adams*, p. 367. "Spitting Lyon" jailed: Ferling, *Adams*, p. 367. "Reign of witches": Chernow, *Hamilton*, p. 577. Adams ambivalence about choosing Washington: Ferling, *Adams*, pp. 357–58. "No qualifications": John Adams to George Washington, June 22, 1798, Washington Papers. "In case of *actual* invasion": George Washington to John Adams, July 4, 1798, Adams Papers, Fitzpatrick, *Writings of George Washington*, vol. 36, p. 313. "Much surprised" and "prepossessions": Alexander Hamilton to George Washington, July 8, 1798, in Lodge, *Writings of Alexander Hamilton*, vol. 10, pp. 295–96. "All the world": John Adams to James McHenry, July 6, 1798, in *Works of John Adams*, vol. 8, p. 573.

"In a crisis so awful": James McHenry to George Washington, June 26, 1798, in Twohig, vol. 2, p. 360. "Finally determined": George Washington to John Adams, July 13, 1798, in Fitzpatrick, *Writings of George Washington*, vol. 36, p. 329. "Make observations": George Washington to James McHenry, July 4, 1798, in Fitzpatrick, *Writings of George Washington*, vol. 36, p. 306. "Extremely desirable": John Adams to James McHenry, July 6, 1798, in *Works of John Adams*, vol. 8, p. 573. "Will gladly be *Your Second*": Timothy Pickering to George Washington, July 6, 1798, in Twohig, vol. 2, p. 386. "At *almost* any price": George Washington to Timothy Pickering, July 11, 1798, in Fitzpatrick, *Writings of George Washington*, vol. 36, pp. 323–24. See also George Washington to John Adams, Sept. 25, 1798, in Fitzpatrick, *Writings of George Washington*, vol. 36, p. 327.

Adams suggestion based on seniority: Ferling, *Adams*, p. 359, Chernow, *Hamilton*, pp. 554–57. "Reasonable wishes": Syrett, vol. 22, p. 13. Adams on Abigail's illness: John Adams to George Washington, Oct. 9, 1798, in *Works of John Adams*, vol. 8, p. 600, Page Smith, p. 982. "There has been too much intrigue": John Adams to James McHenry, Aug. 29, 1798, in *Works of John Adams*, vol. 8, pp. 587–89. "If I should consent": John Adams to Oliver Wolcott, unsent, Sept. 24, 1798, Adams Papers. "Delicate situation": George Washington to John Adams, Sept. 25, 1798, in Fitzpatrick, *Writings of George Washington*, vol. 36, p. 454.

"Violation of the terms": George Washington to James McHenry, Sept. 26 and Oct. 1, 1798, in Fitzpatrick, *Writings of George Washington*, vol. 36, p. 464, Twohig, vol. 3, p. 45. "No more at liberty": Ferling, *Adams*, p. 362. "The most restless, impatient": Parton, *Aaron Burr*, p. 235.

Chapter Seven: ROCKS AND QUICKSANDS ON ALL SIDES

Adams remorse at supporting war program and "monstrous fortunes": Ferling, *Adams*, pp. 372–74. "Simplemen": *Works of John Adams*, vol. 5, p. 473. "Electioneering purposes": John Adams to George Washington, Feb. 19, 1799, in *Works of John Adams*, vol. 8, p. 626. "Proclaim a Regal Government": Elbridge Gerry Notes of Meeting with John Adams, Mar. 26, 1799, Gerry Papers, Billias, pp. 297–98. Adams on Hamilton's "mad" dream: McCullough, *Adams*, p. 518. "There is no more prospect": John Adams to James McHenry, Oct. 22, 1798, in *Works of John Adams*, vol. 8, p. 613. *"Duplicity* and *treachery"*: Billias, pp. 292–94. Protests against Gerry: Billias, p. 290. Adams–Gerry visit at Peacefield, Oct. 1798: DeConde, *Quasi-War*, pp. 51–59, 142–47, 160–61, McCullough, *Adams*, pp. 511–12, Ferling, *Adams*, pp. 373–74, Billias, pp. 283–86, 293–96.

Adams journey back from Quincy, 1798: Ferling, *Adams*, p. 370. "Act of humiliation": Ferling, *Adams*, p. 370. Logan visits with Adams and Pickering: DeConde, *Quasi-War*, pp. 154–57, 163–66, 172, Ferling, *Adams*, pp. 374–75. Logan Act: DeConde, *Quasi-War*, p. 172. William Vans Murray dispatches: DeConde, *Quasi-War*, pp. 147–62, Hill, pp. 102–31. Adams sees report on shipping: DeConde, *Quasi-War*, p. 199. Adams 1798 annual message: Dec. 8, 1798, in *Works of John Adams*, vol. 9, pp. 128, 134–35. "Talleyrand is like a cat": *Gazette of the United States*, Nov. 8, 1798. Adams sees Thomas: McCullough, *Adams*, p. 522. Murray sends Talleyrand letter: DeConde, *Quasi-War*, p. 174.

Washington sends Barlow letter and "with pleasure and alacrity": George Washington to John Adams, Feb. 1, 1799, Joel Barlow to George Washington, in Fitzpatrick, *Writings of George Washington*, vol. 37, p. 120. "Wretch": John Adams to George Washington, Feb. 17, 1799, in *Works of John Adams*, vol. 8, p. 625, DeConde, *Quasi-War*, pp. 173–76. Adams message to Congress: Feb. 18, 1799, in *Works of John Adams*, vol. 9, p. 161. Federalist reaction: Page Smith, p. 1000, DeConde, *Quasi-War*, p. 183, McCullough, *Adams*, p. 524. "A statesman must act": *Porcupine's Gazette*, Feb. 21, 1799. "A ruined merchant": DeConde, *Quasi-War*, p. 182. "Every real *patriot*": Timothy Pickering to George Washington, Feb. 21, 1799, Washington Papers. "I beg you": Timothy Pickering to Alexander Hamilton, Feb. 25, 1799, in Syrett, vol. 12, p. 500.

"Confidence in the President": Timothy Pickering to George Washington, Feb. 21, 1799, in Twohig, vol. 3, p. 389. "Babyish and womanly blubbering": John Adams to George Washington, Feb. 19, 1799, in *Works of John Adams*, vol. 8, p. 624. "I was surprised at the *measure*": Syrett, vol. 23, p. 574. "A very intelligent Gentmn": George Washington to Timothy Pickering, Mar. 3, 1799, in Fitzpatrick, *Writings of George Washington*, vol. 37, p. 142. Sedgwick meeting with Adams: McCullough, *Adams*, p. 524, DeConde, *Quasi-War*, p. 182, Hill, pp. 137–38, *Works of John Adams*, vol. 8, pp. 248–50. Pickering drafts instructions: DeConde, *Quasi-War*, p. 186. "Great Colds": Stuart Mitchell, p. 75. "Talkative Wife" and "A peck of Troubles": John Adams to Abigail Adams, Dec. 13, 1798, and Jan. 1, 1799.

"Be chosen President a second time": John Adams to Abigail Adams, Feb. 22, 1799. "Old woman" and "This was pretty saucy": Abigail Adams to John Adams, Feb. 27 and 28, 1799, McCullough, *Adams*, p. 525. Federalist anger and plots against Adams: Jonathan Trumbull to George Washington, in Twohig, vol. 4, pp. 143–44. "Thoroughly convinced": Flexner, *Washington*, p. 429. Adams's depression at Peacefield: Page Smith, p. 1006, Ferling, *Adams*, p. 391, Ferling, *Adams vs. Jefferson*, p. 122. Washington on Adams's absence: Fitzpatrick, *Writings of George Washington*, vol. 37, p. 314. "Most open, unsuspicious": Shaw, p. 265. "I was uneasy": John Adams to William Cunningham, Nov. 7, 1808, in *Correspondence of John Adams and William Cunningham*, p. 46.

"Artful designing men" and "read over and over": Benjamin Stoddert to John Adams, Aug. 29 and Sept. 13, 1799, in *Works of John Adams*, pp. 18–19, 25–29, and John Adams to Benjamin Stoddert, Sept. 9 and 21, 1799, in *Works of John Adams*, pp. 19–20 and 33–34. Adams journey to Trenton, accommodations, home remedy: John Adams to Abigail Adams, Oct. 24, 1799, Page Smith, p. 1015. *"Made up his mind"*: Timothy Pickering to George Washington, Oct. 24, 1799, in Twohig, vol. 4, pp. 362–63. "The fruits of their past": James McHenry to George Washington, Nov. 10, 1799, in Twohig, vol. 4, p. 399. "Stricken dumb": George Washington to James McHenry, Nov. 17, 1799, in Fitzpatrick, *Writings of George Washington*, vol. 37, p. 428.

Adams–Hamilton confrontation and order for envoys to sail: John Adams to William Cunningham, Nov. 7, 1808, in *Correspondence of John Adams and William Cunningham*, pp. 46–48, Chernow, *Hamilton*, pp. 597–600, Ferling, *Adams*, pp. 385–86. "This business seems": George Washington to Alexander Hamilton, Oct. 27, 1799, in Fitzpatrick, *Writings of George Washington*, vol. 37, pp. 409–10. "Anxious and painful": George Washington to James McHenry, Nov. 17, 1799, in Fitzpatrick, *Writings of George Washington*, vol. 37, p. 428. Hamilton accosts Ellsworth: DeConde, *Quasi-War*, p. 221. "Washington was the painted wooden head": Rogow, p. 177. Funeral dinner and Abigail's astonishment: Ferling, *Adams*, p. 390.

Chapter Eight: THE MOST SPLENDID DIAMOND IN MY CROWN

Eighteen hundred backlash against Federalists: Ferling, *Adams vs. Jefferson*, pp. 148–49, McCullough, *Adams*, p. 533. "The wise, the rich": Schlesinger, *History of U.S. Political Parties*, vol. 1, p. 17. "Between the Rich": Alexander Hamilton to King, May 4, 1796, in Syrett, vol. 20, p. 158. "Rage and despair" and Adams's new strategy: Ferling, *Adams vs. Jefferson*, pp. 127, 132–33. "Sovereign Pontiff": Shaw, p. 304. Adams–McHenry confrontation: James McHenry to Alexander Hamilton, June 2, 1800, in Syrett, vol. 24, pp. 552–65, James McHenry to John McHenry, May 29, 1800, and James McHenry to Oliver Wolcott, Aug. 30, 1800, in Gibbs, vol. 2, pp. 346–48 and 413–14, Page Smith, pp. 1027–28, McCullough, *Adams*, p. 538, Chernow, *Hamilton*, p. 613.

Adams fires Pickering: John Adams to Timothy Pickering and Timothy Pickering to John Adams, May 12, 1800, in *Works of John Adams*, vol. 9, pp. 54–55, John Adams to William Cunningham, Oct. 15, 1808, in *Correspondence of John Adams and William Cunningham*, pp. 39–40, and Chernow, *Hamilton*, p. 614. "Wildest extravagances": *Works of John Adams*, vol. 9, p. 290. "Mad" and "wicked": Chernow, *Hamilton*, p. 615. "Aegis": DeConde, *Quasi-War*, p. 264. "Violent and vindictive": Oliver Wolcott to Fisher Ames, Aug. 10, 1800, in Gibbs, vol. 2, pp. 401–2. Hamilton's pamphlet: Syrett, vol. 25, pp. 186–234. "A super-abundance of secretions": Flexner, *Young Hamilton*, p. 62.

Marshall on France stalling and Adams response: John Marshall to John Adams, Aug. 25, 1800, in Cullen, vol. 4, pp. 240–41, DeConde, *Quasi-War*, pp. 280–81. Paris negotiations: DeConde, *Quasi-War*, pp. 225–56, 279–83, Elkins and McKitrick, pp. 571–90, Hill, pp. 145–201. "Exceedingly rude": William Vans Murray Diary, Mar. 24, 1801, Murray Papers. "But events have been very much against": William Vans Murray to John Quincy Adams, Aug. 19, 1800, in DeConde, *Quasi-War*, p. 280. Negotiations conclude: William Vans Murray to John Quincy Adams, Sept. 27 and Dec. 22, 1800, in DeConde, *Quasi-War*, pp. 255–56.

Signing at Mortefontaine: DeConde, *Quasi-War*, pp. 256–58, Hill, pp. 194–96. "Toasts to perpetual peace": William Vans Murray to John Quincy Adams, Oct. 5, 1800, in *Letters of William Vans Murray*, pp. 654–55. "Glorious News": *Baltimore Telegraph*, Nov. 7, 1800, DeConde, *Quasi-War*, p. 283. Adams learns about South Carolina: McCullough, *Adams*, p. 556. "The insolent triumph": Thomas Boylston Adams to William Smith Shaw, Dec. 14, 1800, Adams Papers. "Always regret": William Vans Murray to John Quincy Adams, Nov. 7, 1800, in *Letters of William Vans Murray*, pp. 660–61. "In my memory and hopes": Hill, p. 219. Adams in Washington and describes his own mood: John Adams to William Tudor, Jan. 20, 1801, John Adams to Elias Boudinot, Jan. 26, 1801, in *Works of John Adams*, vol. 9, pp. 93–94.

"Another chapter in the book": DeConde, *Quasi-War*, pp. 288–93, Ferling, *Adams*, pp. 408–9. Adams's departure from Washington and "sufficient notice": McCullough, *Adams*, p. 564, Ferling, *Adams*, p. 413. "Polluted water": *Aurora*, Mar. 3, 1801. "Condemned" and "with hard service": Ferling, *Adams*, p. 427, Shaw, p. 282. "I am buried": Ferling, *Adams*, p. 418. "All my life": John Adams to William Tudor, Jan. 20, 1801. "I am not, never was": John Adams to Benjamin Rush, Feb. 27, 1805. "Little faith": John Adams to Jedediah Morse, Mar. 4, 1815, in *Works of John Adams*, vol. 10, p. 133. "Keep my Eyes off it": John Adams to Louisa Adams, May 3, 1821. "Some characters now obscured": John Adams to William Bentley, Aug. 18, 1819.

"If ever an Historian": John Adams to William Cunningham, Feb. 22, 1809, in Pickering, *A Review of the Correspondence Between John Adams and William Cunningham*, p. 49. "The most splendid diamond": John Adams to James Lloyd, Feb. 16, 1813, in *Works of John Adams*, vol. 10, p. 113. "Great is the guilt": McCullough, *Adams*, p. 474. "You speak of the fortunate issue": John Adams to William Cunningham, Mar. 20, 1809, in *Correspondence of John Adams and William Cunningham*, pp. 100–102.

"Must run the risk": John Adams to James Warren, Jan. 9, 1787. "Preserve my independence": John Adams to Abigail Adams, Dec. 3, 1778. "Scheming for

Power": Butterfield, *Diary of John Adams*, vol. 1, p. 337. "Clear as a crystal glass": Ferling, *Adams*, p. 411. "Into a peaceable and safe port": John Adams to Thomas Boylston Adams, Jan. 24, 1801, and DeConde, *Quasi-War*, p. 259. "Defend my missions to France": John Adams to James Lloyd, Jan. 1815, in *Works of John Adams*, vol. 10, p. 113. Adams reaction to son's election as President: Page Smith, p. 1135. "Independence Forever!": Ellis, *Passionate Sage*, p. 277. "Hand in hand": Ellis, *Passionate Sage*, p. 210. "A clap of thunder": Nagel, p. 312. "Here lies John Adams": John Adams to James Lloyd, Jan. 1815, in *Works of John Adams*, vol. 10, p. 113.

Chapter Nine: I WILL KILL IT!

Jackson bedtime ritual: Remini II, p. 332, James, pp. 591–92. Jackson blames Rachel's death on enemies: Remini II, pp. 148–55, James, p. 482, Brands, *Jackson*, pp. 406–7. Derivation of "Old Hickory": Brands, *Jackson*, p. 86, James, p. 150. Jackson killed a man for slandering wife: Remini (Abridged), pp. 2, 52–54, Remini II, pp. 1–2, Parton III, p. 636. Jackson–Van Buren conversation, July 8, 1832: Van Buren, p. 625, Parton III, p. 602, James, p. 601, Remini (Abridged), p. 325, Wilentz, *Jackson*, p. 81. "A spectre in physical": Van Buren, p. 625. "Hydra-headed monster": Remini II, p. 366. "By the Dozzen": Andrew Jackson to William Lewis, Apr. 29, 1833, in Remini, *Bank War*, p. 15. "Moneyed aristocracy": Remini II, p. 33. "The Bank, Mr. Van Buren": Van Buren, p. 625.

Jackson's early life: Brands, *Jackson*, pp. 15–18, Remini I, pp. 1–56. "By God, if one of you": Parton I, p. 64, Remini I, p. 9. "Law of my life": Remini I, p. 11. "Removed Erased and obliterated": Remini I, pp. 79–80. "The best republican": James, p. 116. "Before I get too old" and "fight England again": Buell, p. 171. "Corrupt bargain": Brands, *Jackson*, pp. 348–66, Remini II, pp. 74–99, James, pp. 381–445. "The *Judas* of the West": Andrew Jackson to William Lewis, Feb. 14, 1825, Jackson Papers, also Moser and Clifft, vol. 6, pp. 29–30. "Bare-faced corruption" and "military chieftain": James, pp. 442, 445. "To the Judgment of an enlightened": James, p. 448. "Triumph" over "intrigues": Remini II, p. 147. "My heart is nearly broke": Remini II, p. 156. "Midnight assassins": Brands, *Jackson*, p. 401.

"Golden favors": William Lewis to Nicholas Biddle, Oct. 16, 1829, Biddle Papers, also in McGrane, p. 80. "Lords, Dukes and Ladies": Andrew Jackson to Thomas Hart Benton, June 1832, in McGrane, p. 446. "I weep for the liberty": Remini II, p. 30. "Ragg money": Remini II, pp. 14–18, 25–31. "Always been opposed": Schlesinger, *Age*, p. 77. "Country afloat": Govan, p. 114. Biddle's background: James, pp. 553–56, Brands, *Jackson*, pp. 429–32, Remini, *Bank War*, pp. 32–35, Govan, pp. 1–111, Wilentz, *Jackson*, pp. 76–77. History of Second Bank: Schlesinger, *Age*, pp. 74–75, Bray Hammond, pp. 243–46, Catterall, pp. 1–185, Wilentz, *Jackson*, pp. 75–76. "The Bank is neither Jackson man": Nicholas Biddle to Samuel Smith, Dec. 29, 1828, Biddle Papers. William Lewis and Jackson: Govan, p. 118.

"There is one glory": Nicholas Biddle to William Lewis, Nov. 15, 1829, Biddle Papers. Andalusia: "Andalusia on the Delaware," The Andalusia Foundation (http://andalusiahousemuseum.org), *New York Times*, Mar. 11, 2005. White House under Jackson: Remini III, pp. 389, 391–92, Remini (Abridged), pp. 317–22, Seale, pp. 172–209. Spittoons: Remini II, p. 181. Buchanan's reprimand and Jackson's response: Parton III, p. 604, Remini III, p. 397. Jackson–Biddle 1829 conversation: Undated Biddle Memorandum in Biddle Papers, Nicholas Biddle to J. Potter, Dec. 14, 1829, Biddle Papers, Govan, pp. 120–21.

Chapter Ten: NOT A MAN TO BE FORCED

"The Little Magician": Bowers, p. 449, James, p. 496, Remini II, pp. 114, 213, 324. Van Buren sends James Hamilton: Cole, *Jackson Man*, p. 138. "Your father was not in favor": Hamilton, pp. 67–71, Bowers, pp. 200–202. "In a loose, newspaper" and "what have you said": Hamilton, pp. 149–50, Remini II, pp. 222–23. Jackson's message: Dec. 9, 1829, Jackson Papers. Jackson explanation to Hamilton: Andrew Jackson to James Hamilton, Dec. 19, 1829, Jackson Papers. Bank and *McCulloch v. Maryland*: Brands, *Jackson*, pp. 469–70, Wilentz, *Jackson*, p. 82. "Exceedingly hurt and pained": Nicholas Biddle to William Lewis, May 8, 1830, in McGrane, p. 100. "Honest though erroneous": Nicholas Biddle to Alexander Hamilton, Jr., Dec. 12, 1829, in McGrane, p. 91.

"Personal . . . opinion": Nicholas Biddle to Samuel Smith, Jan. 2, 1830, in McGrane, p. 94. "The die is now cast": Alexander Hamilton, Jr., to Nicholas Biddle, Dec. 10, 1829, in McGrane, p. 88. Biddle and Congressional rebuttal: Nicholas Biddle to Hoffman, Dec. 15, 1829, Biddle Papers. Never "abused" the Bank's power: Nicholas Biddle to William Lewis, May 8, 1830, Biddle Papers. "Hydra of corruption": Andrew Jackson to James Hamilton, May 3, 1830, in Hamilton, pp. 164, 167. Jackson frustration with Duff Green and *Telegraph*: Remini, *Bank War*, p. 68. Biddle loan to Green: McGrane, p. 124, Bowers, p. 207. Blair and founding of the *Globe*: Bowers, pp. 161–68. "Send it to Blahr" and "patronize the *Globe*": Schlesinger, *Age*, p. 72, James, p. 629. Blair House and Blair's milk deliveries: James, p. 626.

"Damned head off": Benjamin Crowninshield to Nicholas Biddle, Dec. 17, 1830, Biddle Papers. "Hopes" and "fears": Andrew Jackson Annual Message to Congress, Dec. 6, 1830. "The destruction of the Bank": Nicholas Biddle to Jonathan Roberts, Jan. 15, 1831, and Nicholas Biddle to Gallatin, Dec. 28, 1830, Biddle Papers. "Whole influence" and "If a grocer": Nicholas Biddle to James Hunter, May 4, 1831, Biddle Papers. "Retirement to the peaceful shades": Bassett, vol. 4, p. 351. "Magic power" and "monster": Andrew Jackson to John Randolph, Nov. 11, 1831, in Bassett, vol. 4, p. 372, Bowers, p. 317. "Known friend": Remini, *Bank War*, p. 72. McLane–Biddle talk: Nicholas Biddle Memorandum, Oct. 19, 1831, in McGrane, pp. 128–35, Govan, pp. 169–70, Remini, *Bank War*, pp. 72–74, Remini II, pp. 337–38, Wilentz, *Jackson*, p. 79.

Taney warning: Remini II, pp. 338–39. Jackson on Cabinet challenges: Andrew Jackson to John Randolph, Dec. 22, 1831, in Bassett, vol. 4, p. 387. "Pain and mortification": Van Buren, p. 581. John Randolph's advice: John Randolph to Andrew Jackson, Dec. 19, 1831, Jan. 3 and Mar. 1, 1832, in Bassett, vol. 4, pp. 386, 395, 413. "Ruined himself": Remini II, pp. 341–42. Jackson suspicions about McLane: Remini II, pp. 341–42. "By education and character": Remini II, p. 342, Schlesinger and Israel, vol. 2, pp. 505–7, 540–66. "No connexion" and Biddle loan to Clay: Remini, *Clay*, pp. 68–71, 149, 206–7, 227, 240, 274, 467, 516. Clay advice to Biddle on charter and Biddle's response: Henry Clay to Nicholas Biddle, Sept. 11, 1830, Dec. 15, 1831, Daniel Webster to Nicholas Biddle, Dec. 18, 1831, in McGrane, pp. 110–14, 433, Wiltse, vol. 3, p. 139.

"Not a man to be forced" and "into a Corner": N. D. Merth to Nicholas Biddle, Dec. 14, 1831, in Remini II, p. 343. Cadwalader's advice: Thomas Cadwalader to Nicholas Biddle, Dec. 21–23, 25–26, 29, 31, 1831, Biddle Papers. "Ten times more disposed": Nicholas Biddle to Samuel Smith, Jan. 4, 1832, in McGrane, p. 164. "War upon the Bank": Nicholas Biddle to Charles Ingersoll, Feb. 11, 1832, in McGrane, pp. 180–81.

Chapter Eleven: I WAS BORN FOR THE STORM

"I will prove to them": Hamilton, p. 243. "I was born for the storm": Whitcomb and Whitcomb, p. 67. "Need not fear": Andrew Jackson to John Coffee, Feb. 19, 1832, Coffee Papers, Remini, *Webster*, p. 357. "Corrupting monster" and "my veto": Remini II, p. 345. "No child in the United States": Nicholas Biddle to Charles Ingersoll, Feb. 11, 1832, Biddle Papers. "Beware of our power!": Roger Taney to Ellicott, Jan. 25, 1832, Taney Papers. "A trial of strength": Willie Mangum to Gaston, Jan. 19, 1832, Biddle Papers. "Few men": Martin Van Buren to Andrew Jackson, Jan. 13, 1832, Jackson Papers. "Sisyphean labor to perform": John Randolph to Andrew Jackson, Jan. 3, 1832, Jackson Papers. "There is a time" and "his duplicity": Andrew Jackson to John Coffee, Jan. 21, 1832, in Bassett, vol. 4, p. 40.

Eighteen thirteen Benton–Jackson struggle and fate of bullet: Remini II, p. 346 and James, p. 591. "Display the evil" and "attack incessantly": Benton, vol. 1, pp. 220–24, 235–36, Govan, p. 178. "Bane-ton and the people": Schlesinger, *Age*, p. 60. Capitol and Senate chamber of 1832: Allen, pp. 169, 176, 182. "Duke of Cincinnati!": Brands, *Jackson*, pp. 466–67. "With so much kindness": Govan, pp. 187–88, Brands, *Jackson*, p. 440, Schlesinger, *Age*, p. 87n. "Shedding a tear": Andrew Jackson to Sarah Jackson, May 6, 1832, in Remini II, p. 364. "Our life depends": Thomas Cadwalader to Nicholas Biddle, May 31, 1832, Biddle Papers. "Let him write the whole charter": Nicholas Biddle to C. J. Ingersoll, Feb. 13, 1832, in McGrane, *Correspondence*, p. 182.

"We may as well give up the rule": John Watmough to Nicholas Biddle, July 10, 1832, Biddle Papers. "I will veto him!": Remini, *Clay*, p. 398, Wilentz, *Jackson*, p. 84. Worry about Pennsylvania: Parton III, p. 394. "Knowing that we have to die": Andrew Jackson to Sarah Jackson, June 21, 1832, in Remini II, p. 387. "Preserve the Republic": Andrew Jackson to Amos Kendall, July 23, 1832, in Bassett, vol. 4, p. 465. Jackson's religion: Brands, *Jackson*, pp. 449–51, Remini (Abridged), pp. 339–41, Remini II, pp. 10–11. Jackson's unhappiness after Rachel: Remini II, p. 156. Kendall's background: Cole, *Jackson Man*, pp. 9–17, 19–30, Bowers, pp. 144–51, James, pp. 579–80. Origin of "Kitchen Cabinet": Safire, p. 389. Biddle on "Kitchen Cabinet": Nicholas Biddle to R. M. Gibbes, Dec. 13, 1831, Biddle Papers.

Kendall's work on veto message: Remini II, pp. 365–66, Cole, *Jackson Man*, pp. 164–70, Schlesinger, *Age*, p. 89, James, p. 579. "Gratuity of many millions": Jackson Message to Congress, July 10, 1832. Importance of veto: Remini, *Bank War*, pp. 82–84, Remini II, pp. 366–71, Schlesinger, *Age*, pp. 90–94, James, pp. 600–604, Brands, *Jackson*, pp. 468–71. "With one voice": *Manufacturer* (Pittsburgh), 1832. "Its death-blow": *Globe*, July 12 and 20, 1832, Remini II, p. 371. FDR on "government by organized money": Oct. 31, 1936, Address. "Manifesto of anarchy" and "a chained panther" and "the dominion": Nicholas Biddle to Henry Clay, Aug. 1, 1832, in McGrane, p. 196. Biddle prints veto message: Remini II, p. 376.

Webster and Ames address: Remini, *Webster*, p. 62. Webster on Jackson's veto: Daniel Webster to Nicholas Biddle, July 10, 1832, in Wiltse, vol. 3, p. 186, Daniel Webster Address, July 11, 1832, in Wiltse, vol. 1, pp. 501–29, Remini, *Webster*, p. 370. Biddle loan to Webster: Remini, *Webster*, pp. 369–70. "As an organ fills": Remini II, pp. 371–73, Remini, *Clay*, p. 21. "Perversion of the veto," Benton rebuttal and succeeding exchange: *Register of Debates*, U.S. Senate, 22nd Congress, 1st session, July 13, 1832, pp. 1293–96, Remini, *Clay*, pp. 399–401, Poore, vol. 1, pp. 144–45.

"Tyrant" and "redemption" and "heal the wounds": Remini, *Clay*, p. 408. "In everybody's mouth": Remini, *Clay*, p. 407. "Suits, judgments and executions": Benton, U.S. Senate, July 13, 1832.

"Constitution is gone!": *National Intelligencer*, Washington, D.C., Sept. 6, 1832. "Jacksonism" meant "ANARCHY": *Boston Advertiser*, Oct. 22, 1832. Biddle spending: Bowers, pp. 238–39. "Shower of gold": Bowers, p. 248. "Two-legged, strutting, mouthing": *Globe*, Aug. 29 and Sept. 8, 1832. "Leader of the aristocratic" and "Down with bribery": Schlesinger, *Age*, p. 94, *Globe*, Oct. 1832. "A lie!": Bowers, pp. 248–49. "The virtue of the people": Andrew Jackson to John Coffee, Oct. 1832, in Remini II, p. 374. "The *Globe* revolves": Andrew Jackson to William Lewis, Aug. 9, 1832, in Remini II, p. 376. "Spends his days at the gaming": James, p. 606. Kendall's organization: Amos Kendall to William Lewis, Aug. 18, 1832, in Remini II, pp. 375, 391. Jackson rallies: Bowers, p. 246, Remini II, p. 384, *Globe*, Oct. 20, 1832.

"No more paper money": Parton III, p. 420, Remini II, p. 379. Lexington throng and "Never have I seen": Andrew Jackson to Andrew Donelson, Oct. 5 and 10, 1832, Donelson Papers. "Works well" and "that the veto would destroy": Andrew Jackson to Amos Kendall, July 23, 1832, Andrew Jackson to William Lewis, Aug. 13, 1832, Jackson Papers, and Andrew Jackson to Andrew Donelson, Aug. 16, 1832,

Donelson Papers. "Will not get one electoral vote": Andrew Jackson to Martin Van Buren, Aug. 16, 1832, Van Buren Papers, Gammon, p. 152. "If our fellows didn't raise": Bowers, pp. 250–51, James, p. 606. "Ignorant, passionate, hypocritical": Henry Clay to Francis T. Brooke, Aug. 2, 1833, Clay Papers, Remini, *Clay*, pp. 410, 438.

Chapter Twelve: WHO WOULD HAVE HAD THE COURAGE?

"Counts on" and "The serpent is scotched": James Hamilton to Andrew Jackson, Feb. 28, 1833, in Bassett, vol. 5, pp. 22–23. "Buy up all Congress" and Jackson decision to remove deposits: Remini III, p. 85, Govan, pp. 223–35, James, pp. 629–30, 649, Bowers, pp. 290–95, Cole, *Jackson Man*, pp. 177–84. "Better to fail": Amos Kendall to Andrew Jackson, Mar. 20, 1833, Jackson Papers. "Why, I would veto": Parton III, pp. 505–6. Kendall's explorations: James, p. 646, Cole, *Jackson Man*, pp. 183–88. "A chip of the old block": Parton III, p. 507, Bowers, pp. 287–88. Duane's refusal to withdraw federal deposits: Duane, pp. 88–112, Remini III, pp. 94–103, James, pp. 648–51. "Bankruptcy and distress": Andrew Jackson to William Duane, June 26, 1833, Jackson Papers. "My object, sir": Duane, p. 57. "How shall we answer": Govan, p. 241.

"My conscience told me": Andrew Jackson to Andrew Jackson, Jr., Oct. 11, 1833, in Bassett, vol. 5, p. 217. Effect of Duane's firing: Duane, pp. 100–102, Remini III, pp. 97–103. "Golden vaults": *Globe*, Oct. 17, 1832. Duane complaints and Donelson response: William Duane to Andrew Donelson, Sept. 27 and Oct. 5, 1833, and Andrew Donelson to William Duane, Sept. 29, 1833, in Duane, pp. 114–24. "As tho Mr. Duane": Remini III, p. 103. "Ready with the screws": Andrew Jackson to Martin Van Buren, Oct. 5, 1833, Van Buren Papers. "BIDDLED, DIDDLED": *Boston Post*, Oct. 18, 1833, Schlesinger, *Age*, p. 102. "Because he has scalped": Nicholas Biddle to Joseph Hopkinson, Feb. 31, 1834, in McGrane, p. 222. "In half an hour": Nicholas Biddle to J. Barbour, Apr. 16, 1833, in McGrane, p. 207. Biddle and "suffering": Nicholas Biddle to William Appleton, Jan. 27, 1834, in McGrane, p. 219.

Hamilton report on New York merchants: James Hamilton to Martin Van Buren, Dec. 30, 1833, Van Buren Papers. Virginia Senator on bankruptcy: John Tyler to Lucretia Tyler, Feb. 17, 1834, in Remini, *Bank War*, p. 128. Clay on Jackson's "experiment" and Van Buren reaction: Stanton, pp. 205–6, Remini, *Bank War*, pp. 139–40. "Put your finger there": Parton III, p. 554, Remini (Abridged), p. 8. God would "punish": Parton III, p. 553, Remini III, p. 162. "Sign a charter for any bank": Andrew Jackson to Martin Van Buren, Feb. 3, 1834, Van Buren Papers, Parton III, p. 551. "Go to the monster!" and "Didn't I manage": Parton III, pp. 549–50, Catterall, pp. 351–52. Biddle fled: Parton III, p. 550. "King Andrew the First": Remini III, pp. 142–62. "A cover for bald Federalism": Remini, *Clay*, p. 461. Clay's censure demand and Clay–Biddle talk: Remini, *Clay*, pp. 455, 458.

Whigs on Jackson possible aversion of censure: Bowers, p. 330. "Reckless and as full of fury": Parton III, p. 542, and Andrew Jackson to Andrew Jackson, Jr., Feb. 16,

1834, Jackson Papers. Benton warns against censure: Remini II, pp. 372–73. Jackson's "Protest" message: Apr. 15, 1834, Bowers, p. 338. JFK to United Auto Workers: May 8, 1962, Address. "Driven into the coffin": Remini, *Clay*, pp. 455, 467. "Nicholas Biddle now rules": Remini III, pp. 170–72, 175, 266. Jackson and pensions: Remini III, pp. 130–31. Anger at Whigs: Bowers, p. 363. "Despondency": Seager, vol. 2, p. 751. "After staggering": Weed, p. 431. "Gang of banditti": Nicholas Biddle to H. Cope, Aug. 11, 1835, in Govan, pp. 292–93. Biddle establishes new bank: Govan, pp. 277–90. "Chrysalis": Nicholas Biddle to John Quincy Adams, Feb. 10, 1836, Biddle Papers.

Senate votes to expunge: Poore, p. 142, Bowers, pp. 457–71, Remini III, pp. 377–81, Remini, *Bank War*, p. 174. Jackson's response: Parton III, p. 620, Bowers, p. 457, Remini III, pp. 380–81. Democrats on censure for President Clinton: *New York Times*, Sept. 3 and 27, 1998. "The tyrant to the last" and "no longer a place": Remini, *Clay*, p. 496. Jackson's Farewell Address: Mar. 4, 1837, Jackson Papers, Remini III, pp. 351–52, 414–19. Jackson to Blair: James, pp. 723–24. "Ready to serve" and "I could have stood": Parton III, p. 630. "For the sake of the country": Nicholas Biddle to Joel Poinsett, May 8, 1837, in McGrane, p. 274. "I stand ready": Nicholas Biddle to T. Cooper, May 8, 1837, in Govan, pp. 352–55.

"Got out of the scrape": *Pennsylvania Magazine of History* (1877), p. 78. "A handsome building": Bray Hammond, p. 526. "Elegant retirement": Hone, vol. 2, p. 206. Economic effects of Bank's abolition: Latner, pp. 187–92. "Awful *will* stood alone": Schlesinger, *Age*, p. 448. "I care nothing about clamors": Parton III, p. 605. "Who but General Jackson": George Blair to Willie Mangum, Dec. 8, 1832, in Remini II, p. 391. "All would be well": Parton III, p. 675. Jackson on "slave question" and "southern confederacy": Andrew Jackson to John Coffee, Apr. 9, 1833, in Remini III, p. 42.

Chapter Thirteen: I AM GOING TO BE BEATEN

"You think I don't know": Butler, vol. 5, p. 35, Waugh, p. 267. "If the dumb cattle are not worthy": John Hay to John Nicolay, Aug. 25, 1864, in Dennett, *Lincoln and the Civil War*, pp. 211–12. "Very beautiful place" and "as secluded as we please": Mary Lincoln to Hannah Shearer, July 11, 1861, in Turner and Levitt, p. 94. Soldiers' Home generally: Pinsker, pp. 1–17, and Brownstein, pp. 1–232. Mary Lincoln customary Soldiers' Home farewell and 1864 vacation: Pinsker, p. 8, Baker, pp. 326–27. Lincoln's office: Seale, p. 91. "They are buzzing": John Nicolay to Therena Bates, July 20, 1864, Nicolay Papers, Waugh, p. 258. "Ten thousand drowned cats": Donald, *Lincoln Men*, 210.

"This morning, as for some days past": Abraham Lincoln Memorandum, Aug. 23, 1864, in Basler, vol. 7, p. 514. "Down on my knees to ask votes": Burlingame, *Inner World*, p. 312. "There is more at stake" and "the people scrutinize": Keckley, pp. 129–30. Use of "First Lady": Safire, pp. 252–53, Donald *Lincoln*, p. 311. Mary worries about assassination: Baker, p. 241. Near-shooting of Lincoln, Aug. 1864:

Lamon, pp. 265–70, Pinsker, p. 163, Donald, *Lincoln*, pp. 277–79. "Doesn't it strike you as queer": Warren, p. 225. "Eating my life out": Carpenter, p. 17. "Presentiment" and "never live to see the end": Carpenter, pp. 263–64. Lincoln's arrival in Washington in disguise: Donald, *Lincoln*, p. 278. "I never injured anybody" and cousin's fear of "dangerous" inauguration: Thayer, vol. 1, p. 279.

"Felt it" and "something would befall Abe": Wilson and Davis, pp. 106–9. "Rather be assassinated": Feb. 22, 1861, in Basler, vol. 4, p. 240. "Deep earnestness" and "outstrip and override": Wilson and Davis, p. 127. "Be President of the United States!": Wilson and Davis, pp. 126–27. "Read all the books": Wilson and Davis, pp. 21, 107, 146–47. Lincoln's reading of Weems: Speech in Trenton, N.J., Feb. 21, 1861, in Basler, vol. 4, pp. 235–36, Wilson and Davis, pp. 41, 125. Weems quotations: Onuf edition, p. 172.

Lincoln to Herndon on biographies: Wilson and Davis, p. 519, and Silas Bent, p. x. "Greater than that which rested": Speech in Springfield, Ill., Feb. 11, 1861, in Basler, vol. 4, p. 190. "Immortal Farewell Address": Abraham Lincoln Memorandum, Feb. 19, 1862, in Basler, vol. 5, p. 136. "We were all Jackson boys": Wilson and Davis, p. 114. "Turned Whig": Wilson and Davis, p. 103. "Burning appetites": Speech in Springfield, Ill., Feb. 22, 1842, in Basler, vol. 1, p. 275. Lincoln's admiration of Clay: Abraham Lincoln Eulogy for Henry Clay, Springfield, Ill., July 6, 1852, in Basler, vol. 2, pp. 125–32, Donald, *Lincoln*, pp. 76–77, Wilson and Davis, p. 499.

Clay's son sends snuff box: John Clay to Abraham Lincoln, Aug. 4, 1862, and Abraham Lincoln to John Clay, Aug. 9, 1862, in Basler, vol. 5, p. 363. "Marriage in the Aristocracy" and Lincoln's response: Basler, vol. 1, p. 320. "The tail of the Hermitage lion": Abraham Lincoln to U.S. House of Representatives, July 24, 1848, in Basler, vol. 1, p. 508. Blair father and son in 1861: Elbert Smith, vol. 1, pp. 502–3, 516, Laas, p. 3, Cooling, pp. 115–16, Baker, p. 228. "The voice of the people": Wilson and Davis, p. 182. Admirer sends Jackson letter: William Burt to Abraham Lincoln, Mar. 5, 1864, Andrew Jackson to Andrew Crawford, May 1, 1833, Lincoln Papers. "None of us—no man or woman": Wilson and Davis, p. 360. John Hay on Lincoln's "superiority": Wilson and Davis, p. 332.

"Chief gem of my character": Donald, *Lincoln Men*, p. 44. "Yielded to the views of others": Wolf, p. 156, Chittenden, p. 448. "There is no Washington in that": Abraham Lincoln to Baltimore Committee, Apr. 22, 1861, in Basler, vol. 4, p. 341, Donald, *Lincoln*, p. 298.

Chapter Fourteen: TOO ANGELIC FOR THIS
DEVILISH REBELLION

Union setbacks, summer 1864: McPherson, pp. 689–773, Weigley, pp. 317–57. "In blood and agony": Charles F. Adams, Jr., in Long, *Civil War Day by Day*, June 4, 1864, p. 515. "I cannot bear it!": Benjamin Thomas, p. 423. Early's raid: Cooling, pp. 102–12, 249–52. "Let us be vigilant": Basler, vol. 7, pp. 437–38. "Almost crushed": Donald, *Lincoln*, p. 518. Lincoln's irritation at Stanton's precautions: Thomas and

Hyman, pp. 319–20. Early's troops at Blair farms: Elizabeth Blair Lee to Samuel Preston Blair, July 31, 1864, in Laas, pp. 412–14, Goodwin, *Team of Rivals*, pp. 640–42, Cooling, pp. 115–17, Elbert Smith, *Francis Preston Blair*, pp. 358–60, Waugh, pp. 238–40. Blair mansions fall in late 1950s: *Silver Spring Voice*, Sept. and Oct. 2003.

Lincoln at Fort Stevens: Cooling, pp. 125–55, Waugh, pp. 240–42, Pinsker, 134–43, Goodwin, *Team of Rivals*, p. 643. "We haven't taken Washington": Weigley, p. 347. Might "actually catch some of them": John Hay, July 14, 1864, in Burlingame, *Inner World*, p. 223. "Hordes of Secesh-sympathizers": "Lizzie W.S." to Abraham Lincoln, July 1864, Lincoln Papers. "Abe's contract is nearly up": Kimmel, p. 188. Greeley peace mission: Kirkland, pp. 66–86, Hale, pp. 280–84, David Long, pp. 116–22, Waugh, pp. 246–54. "Our bleeding, bankrupt": Horace Greeley to Abraham Lincoln, July 7, 1864, Lincoln Papers. "While Mr. Greeley means right": Waugh, p. 249. "Any person anywhere": Abraham Lincoln to Horace Greeley, July 9, 1864, in Basler, vol. 7, p. 435.

"*Somehow* . . . seek a peaceful solution": Horace Greeley to Abraham Lincoln, July 10, 1864, Lincoln Papers. "Disappointed": Abraham Lincoln to Horace Greeley, July 15, 1864, in Basler, vol. 7, p. 440. Hay and Lincoln: Donald, *Lincoln Men*, pp. 177–211, Nicolay, pp. 75–88, 114, Thayer, vol. 1, pp. 74–220, Burlingame and Ettlinger, pp. xi–254. "Backwoods Jupiter": Donald, *Lincoln*, p. 429. Hay and Nicolay White House quarters: Author's conversation with William Allman, 2007. "Uproarious peal": Donald, *Lincoln Men*, p. 194. "The Hellcat": Randall, p. 294. Mary's resentment at Hay and Nicolay: Donald, *Lincoln*, p. 429. "The greatest character since Christ": Wilson and Davis, p. 332. Hay's and Nicolay's names for Lincoln: Donald, *Lincoln*, pp. 310, 429, Waugh, p. 18. "To Whom It May Concern": Abraham Lincoln Letter, July 18, 1864, in Basler, vol. 7, p. 451. "A false-looking man": Thayer, vol. 1, p. 180.

"Bungling" and "cuddling": Thayer, vol. 1, p. 181. "No truce! No mediation!": Horace Greeley to Abraham Lincoln, Aug. 9, 1864, Lincoln Papers. "A very good ambassador" and "rotten": Tarbell, vol. 2, p. 198, Waugh, p. 254. Welles, vol. 2, p. 112. Jaquess-Gilmore peace mission: Basler, vol. 7, p. 429, Waugh, pp. 254–57, Long, pp. 125–29, Kirkland, pp. 89–96, Gilmore, pp. 259, 272, Grimsley and Simpson, p. 2. "The stupid tyrant who now disgraces": Basler, vol. 7, pp. 459–60. "Born of poor white trash": Guelzo, *Emancipation*, p. 51. "Murdering your country": Trefousse, *Andrew Johnson*, p. 149. Lincoln proposal to pay Southern states: Donald, *Lincoln*, pp. 348, 355. Lincoln reads draft of Emancipation and Cabinet dialogue: Carpenter, Guelzo, *Emancipation*, p. 137, Pinsker, p. 41.

"The social and political equality": McPherson, p. 186. Lincoln August 1862 meeting with African-American leaders: Basler, vol. 5, pp. 370–75, Guelzo, *Emancipation*, pp. 139–41, Donald, *Lincoln*, pp. 343–45, 367–68. Frederick Douglass's reaction: Guelzo, *Emancipation*, pp. 143–46, John David Smith, *Black Soldiers*, p. 15, Blight, p. 139. "If God gave us": McPherson, p. 139. "Am I doing anything wrong?": Fehrenbacher, p. 41, the Lincoln Institute, www.mrlincolnandfriends.org. "Never . . . felt more certain that I was doing right": Guelzo, *Emancipation*, pp. 182–83. "Could save the Union without freeing": Abraham Lincoln to Horace Greeley, Aug. 22, 1862, in Basler, vol. 5, p. 388. Lincoln and *The Song of Hiawatha*: Cuomo and Holzer, p. 373. "Too angelic": Randall, p. 118. "After all, their faces": Dennett, *Lincoln and the Civil War*, p. 108. "Laid waste and made a desert": Trefousse, *Thaddeus Stevens*, p. 112. Lincoln and Wade-Davis Bill: Donald, *Lincoln*, pp. 509–11, Waugh, pp. 222–29, Dennett, *Lincoln and the Civil War*, pp. 205–6. "Rash" and "dictatorial": *New York Daily Tribune*, Aug. 5, 1864, Waugh, p. 259.

"The most grievous affliction": Brooks, p. 264. "The obscene ape of Illinois": *New York World*, Aug. 16, 1864, Waugh, p. 262. "Commands the confidence": Catton, p. 348. "They can't compel me": *McClure's*, May-Oct. 1899, pp. xiii, 277. Lincoln's 1864 draft call: Donald, *Lincoln*, p. 539. Sherman on reducing draft call: Lloyd Lewis, p. 442. Theodore Roosevelt, Sr., relationship with Lincolns: McCullough, *Mornings*, pp. 58–60, Edmund Morris, *Rise*, p. 9. "He had done a very wrong" and son's eagerness for combat: Nathan Miller, p. 33, Edmund Morris, *Rise*, pp. 9–10, Brands, *Last Romantic*, p. 18. "Drag you from your home": David Long, p. 137. "Deader than dead": p. 122. "I am quite willing" and "even if I am defeated" and "What is the Presidency worth": *McClure's*, May-Oct. 1899, p. 276, Nicolay and Hay, *Abraham Lincoln*, vol. 9, p. 364.

Chapter Fifteen: A WELL-MEANING BABOON

"McClellan is dear to them": Francis Blair to Abraham Lincoln, Dec. 18, 1862, Lincoln Papers, Sears, *Young Napoleon*, p. 351. McClellan's background: Sears, *Young Napoleon*, pp. 1–27. "By some strange operation": George McClellan to Ellen McClellan, July 27, 1861, McClellan Papers, McPherson, p. 359. "Save the country" and "much under my influence" and "not a man": McClellan, pp. 85, 160. "A well-meaning baboon": McPherson, p. 364. McClellan snubs Lincoln at home: Thayer, vol. 1, p. 125. "Slows" and personal "bodyguard": Williams, p. 103. "A ruined man" and "what the horses": Sears, *Young Napoleon*, pp. 330, 334. "Did not want to hurt": John Hay Diary, Sept. 25, 1862, Hay Papers, Burlingame, *Inner World*, p. 186.

"A great mistake": Sears, *Young Napoleon*, p. 341. "How much they loved me": George McClellan to Ellen McClellan, Nov. 10, 1862, Sears, *Civil War Papers*, p. 522. "Fight with the South to free": Sears, *Young Napoleon*, p. 117. "Prejudice in favor of my own race": Sears, *Young Napoleon*, p. 116. "Best people" and wealthy Democrats' support of McClellan and "the people's eyes": George McClellan to William Aspinwall, July 19, 1862, in Sears, *Civil War Papers*, pp. 365–66, Sears, *Young Napoleon*, pp. 344–45, 358, 359. Stanton efforts against McClellan: George McClellan to Samuel Barlow, Sept. 21, 1864, McClellan Papers, Sears, *Civil War Papers*, pp. 600–601, Sears, *Young Napoleon*, pp. 347, 363–64, Thomas and Hyman, pp. 328–32. McClellan's response: George McClellan to Elizabeth McClellan, July 3, 1864, in Sears, *Civil War Papers*, pp. 581–82.

Blairs' efforts to tame McClellan: Montgomery Blair to Samuel Barlow, May 1, 1864, and George McClellan to Samuel Barlow, May 3, 1864, in Sears, *Civil War Pa-*

pers, 364, 574–75, Elbert Smith, *Francis Preston Blair,* p. 344, Waugh, pp. 274–75, Sears, *Young Napoleon,* pp. 365–66. "Monster" McClellan rally: *New York Times,* Aug. 11 and 12, 1864, *New York World,* Aug. 11, 1864, *New York Herald,* Aug. 12, 1864, *New York Tribune,* Aug. 11, 1864, Waugh, p. 273. Greeley publishes letter: Horace Greeley to John Hay, Aug. 4, 1864, Hay Papers, Abraham Lincoln to Horace Greeley, Aug. 6, 1864, in Basler, vol. 7, p. 482. "In the interest of the black race": Huntzicker, p. 122. "Takes us War Democrats clear off": Charles Robinson to Abraham Lincoln, Aug. 7, 1864, Lincoln Papers.

"Saying re-union and abandonment": Abraham Lincoln Notes, Aug. 1864, Lincoln Papers. Lincoln talk with Randall: Interview with Alexander T. Randall, Aug. 19, 1864, in Basler, vol. 7, pp. 506–8, Pinsker, pp. 159–61, Goodwin, *Team of Rivals,* pp. 651–52. "A complete surrender of your anti-slavery": Quarles, pp. 258–59, Pinsker, p. 159, Goodwin, *Team of Rivals,* p. 650. "Obvious depression and panic": Nicolay and Hay, vol. 9, p. 219. "The country's gone": J. K. Herbert to Benjamin Butler, Aug. 6, 1864, and Colonel Shaffer to Benjamin Butler, Aug. 17, 1864, in Butler, vol. 5, pp. 9–10, 67–68. "Weak-kneed d—d fools": John Nicolay to John Hay, Feb. 25, 1864, Nicolay Papers. Swett friendship and visit with Lincoln: Leonard Swett to Mrs. Swett, Aug. 1864 and Sept. 8, 1864, *McClure's,* May-Oct. 1899, pp. 277–78, Colonel Shaffer to Benjamin Butler, Aug. 17, 1864, in Butler, vol. 5, pp. 67–68, Wilson and Davis, pp. 629, 772.

Raymond proposal to Lincoln and Lincoln's response: Henry Raymond to Abraham Lincoln, Aug. 22, 1864, Abraham Lincoln Draft Letter to Henry Raymond, Aug. 24, 1864, Lincoln Papers, Nicolay and Hay, *Abraham Lincoln,* vol. 9, pp. 218–21, Basler, vol. 7, p. 518, McPherson, p. 770, Burlingame, *With Lincoln in the White House,* p. 152, Burlingame, *At Lincoln's Side,* pp. 92, 106. Lincoln downs tumbler of water: *Harper's Monthly,* 1894. "To desert me": Weik, p. 3. Lincoln sees Schurz: Schurz, vol. 2, pp. 395–96, Pinsker, pp. 156–57.

Chapter Sixteen: THE COUNTRY WILL BE SAVED

"Play hermit for a fortnight": Nicolay and Hay, *Complete Works,* vol. 2, pp. 561–62, Carpenter, p. 305. "You've got no equal": Burlingame, *Inner World,* p. 312, Helm, p. 144. "Child-wife" and "control your grief" and "All imagination!": Keckley, pp. 212, 88, 103. "Need to be taught a lesson": Burlingame, *Inner World,* p. 281, MacKaye, vol. 1, pp. 105–6. "That was the worst speech": Burlingame, *Inner World,* p. 281, Sandburg and Angle, pp. 110–12. "Wounded" "in unguarded moments": Keckley, p. 128. "Notwithstanding our opposite natures": Baker, p. 228, and Turner and Levitt, p. 200. "Sacred Concert of profane music": Donald, *Lincoln Men,* p. 206.

Lincoln's early religious beliefs: Guelzo, *Redeemer,* pp. 152, 156, 261, 312–15, 318, 323–24, 373, 441–43, 445–46, Wolf, pp. 33–114, Wilson, pp. 76–85, 186–87, 309–12, 334–35, Wilson and Davis, pp. 107, 156, 215, 233, Donald, *Lincoln,* pp. 48–49. "An open scoffer": Wolf, pp. 44–48, 73–74, Wilson and Davis, pp. 432, 472,

Donald, *Lincoln*, p. 49. "Crystallization": Wolf, p. 143, Carpenter, p. 189, Carwardine, pp. 32–44. "I have been all my life a fatalist": Newton, p. 38. "An humble instrument": Speech to New Jersey Senate, Trenton, Feb. 21, 1861, in Basler, vol. 4, p. 234. "He finds a way of letting me know it": Chittenden, p. 448. "The will of God prevails": Dated Sept. 2, 1862, in Basler, vol. 5, p. 403. Douglas Wilson and other scholars, including the current author, believe the date might be inaccurate (Wilson, *Lincoln's Sword*, pp. 254–56, also Douglas Wilson to author, December 10, 2006, and Allen Guelzo to author, December 12, 2006).

"The best gift God has given": Sept. 7, 1864, in Basler, vol. 7, p. 542, Wolf, p. 135. Lincoln's visit with Speed: Donald, *Lincoln*, p. 514. "Peace Snakes": Dennett, *Lincoln and the Civil War*, p. 211, Waugh, p. 276. "Concocted to destroy" and "for a thousand" and "look in the face": Sears, *Young Napoleon*, pp. 374–75. "Goodbye, 'little Mac' ": Waugh, p. 342, Sears, *Young Napoleon*, p. 379. Sherman's Atlanta victory: Carter, pp. 315–16, Sherman, p. 819. "The dark days are over": *Chicago Tribune*, Sept. 15, 1864. "The people wanted me": Donald, *Lincoln*, p. 544. "The September victories have changed all": Norman Judd to Abraham Lincoln, Oct. 5, 1864, Lincoln Papers. Tad and father on Election Day 1864: Waugh, p. 347.

"Worth more to the country": Grant, vol. 12, p. 398, Waugh, pp. 36–361. "If I know my heart": Basler, vol. 8, p. 96. Lamon protects Lincoln: John Hay Diary, Nov. 9, 1864, Hay Papers, Burlingame and Ettlinger, p. 246. "Seldom in history": Cabot, p. 609. "The country will be saved": Donald, *Lincoln*, p. 542. "A wonderful gift": Calhoun, p. 195, Dodge, pp. 15–16. Lincoln and "The Building of a Ship": Peterson, *Lincoln*, pp. 112–13. "A momentous thing to be the instrument": Wolf, p. 167. Illinois's "DeWitt Clinton": Wilson and Davis, p. 476. "The central act of my administration": Carpenter, p. 90. Cabinet meeting, Nov. 11, 1864: John Hay Diary, Nov. 11, 1864, Hay Papers, Burlingame and Ettlinger, pp. 247–49, Monaghan, pp. 323–24.

Chapter Seventeen: I SEE DYNAMITE

John Hay's life since Lincoln: Thayer, vol. 2, pp. 1–331, Dennett, *John Hay*, pp. 57–337, O'Toole, pp. 39–47, 53–54, 141–46, 217–20, 288–355. "So little ability": John Hay Diary, June 14, 1905, Hay Papers. T.R. sees Hay at home and receives Lincoln letter: John Hay to Theodore Roosevelt, Oct. 23, 1904, John Hay Diary, Oct. 23, 1904, Hay Papers, Theodore Roosevelt to Lyman Abbott, July 3, 1905, in Morison, vol. 4, pp. 1258–59, Thayer, vol. 2, p. 256, Dennett, *John Hay*, p. 345, Edmund Morris, *Theodore Rex*, p. 240. "Fatal elevation" and "The President will": John Hay Diary, Oct. 23 and Nov. 3, 1904, Hay Papers. "Wouldn't have gotten away": Edmund Morris, *Theodore Rex*, p. 4. "My husband is so young!": Sylvia Jukes Morris, *Edith Kermit Roosevelt*, p. 220. "My old-time love": John Hay to Theodore Roosevelt, Sept. 15, 1901, Theodore Roosevelt Papers.

"Political prime minister": Croly, p. 302. "Selfishness": Croly, p. 364. Hanna at McKinley's death: *Washington Post*, Sept. 14, 1901, Croly, p. 359, Russell, pp. 40–41.

"Cried like a child" and Hanna chooses casket: Elmer Dover Statement, Sept. 1905, Hanna-McCormick Papers. "Madman": Leech, p. 537. "That damn cowboy": Burns and Dunn, *Three Roosevelts*, p. 61. Hanna's cigars: Elmer Dover Statement, Sept. 1905, Hanna-McCormick Papers. T.R. talks with Hanna after McKinley death: Theodore Roosevelt to Lincoln Steffens, June 24, 1903, in Morison, vol. 4, pp. 1254–55, Mark Hanna to Theodore Roosevelt, Oct. 12, 1901, in Joseph Bishop, vol. 1, p. 154, Pringle, pp. 238–39, Edmund Morris, *Theodore Rex*, pp. 16–17, 30, 36, 38–39.

"Me big Injun!": Croly, p. 207. "Patent medicine": Nathan Miller, p. 245. Hanna role in 1896 campaign: Beer, pp. 135–66, Russell, pp. 1–41, Croly, pp. 209–27, and Leech, pp. 82–92. "Selling the White House kitchen": Beer, p. 175. McKinley clears vacancy: Croly, p. 233. "Crazy": Charles W. Bailey, "The Odd Couple," *Cosmos* (1997). "Your *duty*": Leech, p. 542. "Hanna treats me": Pringle, p. 239. "Startling" rise: Annual Message to Congress, Dec. 3, 1901, Theodore Roosevelt Papers, Edmund Morris, *Theodore Rex*, pp. 68, 70–77. "I see dynamite": Mark Hanna to Theodore Roosevelt, Nov. 10, 1901, Theodore Roosevelt Papers. Creation of Northern Securities: Albro Martin, pp. 508–12, Klein, pp. 238–39, Strouse, pp. 431–34, Edmund Morris, *Theodore Rex*, pp. 59–62, Brands, *Last Romantic*, pp. 434–36.

"You can now ride": *Collier's Weekly*, Nov. 30, 1901, Edmund Morris, *Theodore Rex*, p. 65. Hanna on Northern Securities and asks for stock: Edmund Morris, *Theodore Rex*, p. 64. James J. Hill and Hanna: James J. Hill Statement, Oct. 31, 1905, Hanna-McCormick Papers. T.R. opposition to business corruption: Theodore Roosevelt to Henry Cabot Lodge, Aug. 10, 1899, in Morison, vol. 2, p. 1048. "Sullenly grumbling": Hibben, p. 224. "Great law-defying corps": Theodore Roosevelt to Douglas Robinson, Oct. 4, 1901, in Morison, vol. 3, p. 160. "Swinish indifference": Brands, *Last Romantic*, p. 545. "Soul" did not "rise up": Theodore Roosevelt to Nicholas Murray Butler, Feb. 6, 1908, Theodore Roosevelt Papers. T.R. and Morgan before Presidency: Theodore Roosevelt to Elihu Root, Dec. 5, 1900, in Morison, vol. 2, p. 1450, Theodore Roosevelt, *Autobiography*, p. 470, Strouse, p. 242, Chernow, *House of Morgan*, p. 430.

"Violent fluctuations": Theodore Roosevelt to Herschel Jones, Feb. 26, 1903, in Morison, vol. 3, p. 236. T.R.–Hanna breakfast, Feb. 1902: Pringle, pp. 253–57, Albro Martin, p. 514. Edmund Morris, *Theodore Rex*, p. 89. Hanna learns of lawsuit on train: Edmund Morris, *Theodore Rex*, p. 89, and Albro Martin, p. 515. "Stormy petrel" and "hit Pierpont": Henry Adams to Elizabeth Cameron, Feb. 23, 1902, *Letters of Henry Adams*, vol. 5, pp. 344–46. Jack Morgan's reaction: Strouse, p. 440. "The gentlemanly thing": Chernow, *House of Morgan*, p. 106. "Look out for us": Beer, pp. 275–76. Hanna confesses blindsiding: Albro Martin, p. 515.

"Whole party" and "Pierpont refused": Henry Adams to Elizabeth Cameron, Feb. 24, 1902, *Letters of Henry Adams*, vol. 5, p. 346. Chauncey Depew: Depew, Strouse, pp. 197, 248–49, 257. T.R.–Morgan meeting on Northern Securities and T.R.–Knox conversation: Pringle, pp. 256–57, Joseph Bishop, vol. 1, pp. 184–85,

Brands, *Last Romantic*, pp. 437–39, Strouse, pp. 440–42, Edmund Morris, *Theodore Rex*, pp. 91–92. Morgan's fury: Joseph Bishop, vol. 1, p. 185. Morgan accedes to dinner: Edmund Morris, *Theodore Rex*, p. 90. Morgan partners' request to remove name and Knox response: Edmund Morris, *Theodore Rex*, p. 90. "Theodore's vanity": *Letters of Henry Adams*, vol. 5, p. 376. "Blind-drunk" and "naughty boy": Strouse, p. 443.

"Theodore absorbed" and "scuttle gracefully": Henry Adams to Elizabeth Cameron, Jan. 12, 1902, *Letters of Henry Adams*, vol. 5, p. 365. "Cross themselves": Theodore Roosevelt to Philander Knox, May 6, 1902, Theodore Roosevelt Papers, Brands, *Last Romantic*, p. 442. "Enemy of Property": Theodore Roosevelt, *Autobiography*, p. 385. Hanna complaint about customers: Strouse, p. 443. "A raid on Canfield's": Brands, *Last Romantic*, p. 620. "Chief fight" and "typical American multimillionaire": Theodore Roosevelt to George Otto Trevelyan, Jan. 1, 1908, in Morison, vol. 6, p. 883. "Incorruptible foe": Theodore Roosevelt to Frederic Harrison, Dec. 18, 1907, in Morison, vol. 6, p. 866. "Enormous sums of money": Theodore Roosevelt, *Autobiography*, p. 346. "Fit to live": Nathan Miller, p. 562. "Parts of the same Great Adventure": Brands, *Last Romantic*, p. 815.

T.R. and early frailties: Joseph Bishop, vol. 1, pp. 3–4, McCullough, *Mornings*, pp. 36, 90–108, Dalton, pp. 37–39. "Rather absurd": Theodore Roosevelt to Pierre de Coubertin, June 15, 1903, in Morison, vol. 3, p. 497. T.R. and boxers: Thayer, *Theodore Roosevelt*, p. 271. "The horror of it hangs" and T.R. on assassin trading life: Brands, *Last Romantic*, pp. 432–33. "They would have to be mighty quick": Brands, *Last Romantic*, pp. 432–35.

Chapter Eighteen: BLACK STORM

"Mere dream": Brands, *Last Romantic*, p. 215. "Perfect torrent of wrath": Theodore Roosevelt, *Winning of the West*, vol. 4, pp. 194–95. "The woods were green": Theodore Roosevelt to Kermit Roosevelt, June 1, 1907, in Morison, vol. 5, p. 675. T.R. on Biddle and Jackson: Theodore Roosevelt, *Thomas Hart Benton*, pp. 116, 73. "A great admirer": T.R. to William Dodd, Feb. 13, 1902, in Morison, vol. 7, p. 501. T.R. sees Lincoln coffin: Lorant, p. 43, Sylvia Morris, *Edith Kermit Roosevelt*, pp. 514–15, Dalton, p. 34. T.R. and "Lincoln bed": Joseph Bishop, vol. 1, pp. 350–52. "Think of Lincoln": Theodore Roosevelt to Henry Pritchett, Dec. 14, 1904, Theodore Roosevelt Papers.

"Irritated" and "so far as one who is not": Joseph Bishop, vol. 1, p. 352. "Plain people" and "commercial conservatism": Theodore Roosevelt to Benjamin Wheeler, June 17, 1908, in Morison, vol. 6, p. 1082. "Farmers, mechanics": Theodore Roosevelt to George Otto Trevelyan, June 19, 1908, in Morison, vol. 6, p. 1087. "The tyranny of the mob": Watts, p. 63. T.R. preference for well-born leaders: Theodore Roosevelt to Cecil Spring-Rice, Dec. 27, 1904, in Morison, vol. 4, p. 1083. "The voice of God": Brands, *Last Romantic*, p. 170. "Lincoln-Jackson school" and "do anything": Brands, *Last Romantic*, p. 420. "No more use for the Constitution": Whitcomb and Whitcomb, p. 226.

T.R.'s transformation of White House: Sylvia Morris, *Edith Kermit Roosevelt*, pp. 238–50, Edmund Morris, *Theodore Rex*, pp. 174–76, Seale, pp. 654–739, Whitcomb and Whitcomb, p. 235. T.R. reminded of New York ballrooms: Sylvia Morris, *Edith Kermit Roosevelt*, p. 257. T.R. and townhouse: Seale, vol. 2, p. 669. Anthracite coal strike, general: Harbaugh, pp. 166–81, Strouse, pp. 448–52, Edmund Morris, *Theodore Rex*, pp. 132–69, Brands, *Last Romantic*, pp. 450–62. "Black storm": Theodore Roosevelt to Winthrop Crane, Oct. 22, 1902, in Morison, vol. 3, p. 366. "Wits' end": Theodore Roosevelt to Henry Cabot Lodge, Aug. 7, 1902, in Morison, vol. 3, p. 332. Danger of "revolution": McGerr, p. 125.

"Big moneyed men" and "grant favors": Theodore Roosevelt to Henry Cabot Lodge, Aug. 7, 1902, in Morison, vol. 3, p. 332. "Striving to find some Constitutional": Theodore Roosevelt to Winthrop Crane, Oct. 22, 1902, in Morison, vol. 3, p. 360. T.R. trolley accident: Edmund Morris, *Theodore Rex*, pp. 140–43, 148–49, Brands, *Last Romantic*, pp. 449–50. T.R. meeting with barons and Mitchell: Harbaugh, pp. 172–74, Edmund Morris, *Theodore Rex*, pp. 155–61, Brands, *Last Romantic*, pp. 454–56. "Arrogance" and "gross blindness": Theodore Roosevelt to Joseph Bucklin Bishop, Oct. 13, 1903, Theodore Roosevelt Papers. Mitchell as gentleman: Harbaugh, p. 173. "Instigators": Brands, *Last Romantic*, p. 455.

"Are you asking us": Sullivan, p. 433. "High office": Brands, *Last Romantic*, pp. 455–56. "Putting a very heavy burden": McGerr, p. 124. "Radical experiment": Theodore Roosevelt to Mark Hanna, Oct. 3, 1902, in Morison, vol. 3, p. 337, Theodore Roosevelt to Philander Knox, Aug. 21, 1902, in Morison, vol. 3, p. 323, Theodore Roosevelt to Henry Cabot Lodge, Sept. 27, 1902, in Morison, vol. 3, p. 331. "The most terrible riots": Theodore Roosevelt to Lyman Abbott, Sept. 5, 1903, in Morison, vol. 3, p. 592. T.R. sees Schofield: Joseph Bishop, vol. 1, pp. 211–12, Edmund Morris, *Theodore Rex*, p. 165, Theodore Roosevelt, *Autobiography*, pp. 489–90, Harbaugh, p. 178, Brands, *Last Romantic*, pp. 458–59.

Butler in New Orleans: Theodore Roosevelt to Winthrop Crane, Oct. 22, 1902, in Morison, vol. 3, p. 363. "Would have raised his voice": Theodore Roosevelt, *Autobiography*, p. 364. "What about seizing property": Sullivan, vol. 2, pp. 437–38, Harbaugh, p. 177, Edmund Morris, *Theodore Rex*, p. 165. Truman and steel strike: Harbaugh, p. 178. For the "sake" of "our nation": Theodore Roosevelt to J. P. Morgan, Oct. 15, 1902, in Morison, vol. 3, p. 352. "By the throat": Theodore Roosevelt to Robert Bacon, Oct. 5 and 7, 1902, in Morison, vol. 3, pp. 339–41, 343–44, Theodore Roosevelt to William Allen White, Oct. 6, 1902, in Morison, vol. 3, p. 343. Root and Morgan on *Corsair*: Edmund Morris, *Theodore Rex*, pp. 165–66.

Morgan agrees: Theodore Roosevelt to J. P. Morgan, Oct. 16, 1902, in Morison, vol. 3, p. 353, Edmund Morris, *Theodore Rex*, pp. 165–67. "Began talking at the oysters": Edmund Morris, *Theodore Rex*, p. 168. "Screaming comedy" and "nearly wild" and "woodenheaded": Theodore Roosevelt to Winthrop Crane, in Morison, vol. 3, pp. 365–66, Joseph Bishop, vol. 2, p. 216, Edmund Morris, *Theodore Rex*, pp. 167–69. "Going to the circus": Theodore Roosevelt to Theodore Roosevelt, Jr., Oct. 31, 1902, in Morison, vol. 3, p. 372. "A nightmare" and "being for the moment": Theodore Roosevelt to Lyman Abbott, Sept. 5, 1903, in Morison, vol. 3, p. 592. "Heavens and earth": Edmund Morris, *Theodore Rex*, p. 169.

Chapter Nineteen: A ROUGH-AND-TUMBLE MAN

"Overpraised by everybody": Brands, *Last Romantic*, p. 462. "Made a serious mistake": Franklin Roosevelt to Sara Delano Roosevelt, Oct. 26, 1902, Franklin Roosevelt Papers. "I gave mortal offense" and "fight it out" and "much rather": Theodore Roosevelt to George Otto Trevelyan, May 28, 1904, in Morison, vol. 4, p. 807. "Rather be a one-term President": Richard Nixon Speech, Apr. 30, 1970, *New York Times*, May 1, 1970. "I love all of these children": Renehan, p. 11. "Mother and I took a walk": Theodore Roosevelt to Kermit Roosevelt, Nov. 16, 1902, in Morrison, vol. 3, p. 374. "The happiest home life": Theodore Roosevelt to Bamie Roosevelt, Aug. 30, 1904, Sylvia Jukes Morris, *Edith Kermit Roosevelt*, p. 279.

"Highest of all joys": Theodore Roosevelt to Bessie Van Voorst, Oct. 18, 1902, in Morison, vol. 3, p. 355. "The morals of a green-grocer" and "loose living": Reisner, pp. 286, 288. "Barnyard" and T.R. turns back: Reisner, pp. 289–90. Katy Mann episode: Ted Morgan, pp. 90–91. "Flagrant man-swine": Cook, vol. 1, p. 62. "Of course, they paid her off": Author's interview with Richard Nixon, 1992. "The ideal house": Theodore Roosevelt to Maria Longworth Storer, Dec. 8, 1902, in Morison, vol. 3, p. 392. "Unchanged and unmarred": Theodore Roosevelt to Cass Gilbert, Dec. 19, 1908, Theodore Roosevelt Papers. "Yahoo": Theodore Roosevelt to Lawrence Abbott, Mar. 14, 1904, in Morison, vol. 4, p. 753. "Awful open mouths": Edmund Morris, *Theodore Rex*, pp. 175–76.

T.R.'s new office and heliotrope: Sylvia Jukes Morris, *Edith Kermit Roosevelt*, pp. 246–47, 210–11, 296–98, Seale, vol. 2, pp. 681, 690–91. "I look up to that picture": Seale, vol. 2, p. 678, Peterson, *Lincoln in American Memory*, p. 164. "Opportunity": Edmund Morris, *Theodore Rex*, p. 281. T.R. wins Commerce Department: Theodore Roosevelt to Mark Hanna, Jan. 23, 1903, in Morison, vol. 3, p. 410, Pringle, pp. 341–42, Chernow, *Titan*, pp. 434–35, Edmund Morris, *Theodore Rex*, pp. 205–7. "Been to see me": Theodore Roosevelt to George Lorimer, May 12, 1906, in Morison, vol. 5, p. 267. "Swing open as easily": Theodore Roosevelt to Edward Packard, Nov. 26, 1903, in Morison, vol. 3, p. 658. "Good jolt": Edmund Morris, *Theodore Rex*, pp. 271–72. "Not one man jack": Theodore Roosevelt to James Clarkson, July 16, 1903, in Morison, vol. 3, p. 519.

"Decidedly blue": Theodore Roosevelt to John Hay, Aug. 12, 1902, in Pringle, p. 258. Robert Lincoln's attitude: *New York Times*, Apr. 29, 1912. "Anything tangible": Pringle, p. 339. "The big New York" and "knockdown and dragout": Theodore Roosevelt to Henry Cabot Lodge, May 27, 1903, Theodore Roosevelt Papers, Brands, *Last Romantic*, p. 494. "Rough-and-tumble man": Theodore Roosevelt to Charles Smith, June 22, 1903, in Morison, vol. 3, p. 499. "Stop shilly-shallying" and "suppliant": Theodore Roosevelt to Henry Cabot Lodge, May 27, 1903, in Joseph Bishop, vol. 1, pp. 244–45. "Better to have a fight": Joseph Bishop, vol. 1, p. 245. T.R. corners Hanna: Joseph Bishop, vol. 1, pp. 243–46, Croly, pp. 422–28, Brands, *Last Romantic*, pp. 492–95, Edmund Morris, *Theodore Rex*, pp. 231–33. "Sufficiently equivocal": Theodore Roosevelt to Nicholas Murray Butler, Nov. 28, 1903, in Morison, vol. 3, p. 661.

"Tired of going to the White House": George Cortelyou Statement, Apr. 18, 1906, Hanna-McCormick Papers. "Half" convinced: Theodore Roosevelt to Lyman Abbott, Nov. 5, 1903, in Morison, vol. 3, p. 647, Theodore Roosevelt to Theodore Roosevelt, Jr., Jan. 29, 1904, in Morison, vol. 4, p. 713. "Hanna would have been nominated": Cornelius Bliss Statement, Oct. 20, 1905, Hanna-McCormick Papers. Hanna's ailments: Cornelius Bliss Statement, Oct. 30, 1905, James Dempsey Statement, May 22, 1905, Charlotte Rhodes Hanna Statement, May 18 and Nov. 1, 1905, Hanna-McCormick Papers. "Get on a steamer": James Dempsey Statement, May 22, 1905, Hanna-McCormick Papers. "Big Wall Street men who resent": Theodore Roosevelt to Lyman Abbott, Nov. 5, 1903, in Morison, vol. 3, pp. 647–48. "Most formidable Democrat" and "Morgan and other Wall Street": Theodore Roosevelt to Henry Cabot Lodge, May 23, 1903, in Joseph Bishop, vol. 1, p. 241. "The wealthy capitalists": Theodore Roosevelt to Nicholas Murray Butler, Nov. 4, 1903, in Morison, vol. 3, p. 641. Morgan and Hanna at Thanksgiving 1903: Edmund Morris, *Theodore Rex*, pp. 299–300. "If we renominate": N. B. Scott to Mark Hanna, Dec. 23, 1903, in Croly, p. 439. "I cannot tell you": Theodore Roosevelt to Joseph Bishop, in Morison, vol. 3, p. 700. "With colors flying": Joseph Bishop, vol. 1, p. 313. Hanna's collapse and death: Croly, pp. 452–57, Edmund Morris, *Theodore Rex*, pp. 310–11.

"You touched" and "Indeed it is your letter": Joseph Bishop, vol. 1, p. 315 and Croly, p. 454. "I am very, very sorry": Brands, *Last Romantic*, p. 501. "Did I tell you": Theodore Roosevelt to Elihu Root, Feb. 15, 1904, in Morison, vol. 4, p. 730. Alice Roosevelt: Felsenthal, Teague, Dalton, pp. 250–52. "Much more of a poseur": Felsenthal, p. 263. "So slightly": Felsenthal, p. 73. "Eyes swam with tears" and "I shall not give" and "He was a fine": George Cortelyou Statement, Apr. 18, 1905, Hanna-McCormick Papers. "Burly strength": Theodore Roosevelt to Theodore Roosevelt, Jr., Feb. 13, 1904, Theodore Roosevelt Papers. "He stood by them": Theodore Roosevelt to Elihu Root, Feb. 15, 1904, and Theodore Roosevelt to Henry White, Feb. 17, 1904, in Morison, vol. 4, pp. 731–32. "A blow to your father": Strouse, p. 535.

Chapter Twenty: I UPSET THEM ALL

Northern Securities ruling: Strouse, pp. 533–35, Edmund Morris, *Theodore Rex*, pp. 313–16. "A judge with more backbone": John Hay Diary, May 15, 1904, Hay Papers. "Amuck": *New York Times*, May 16, 1904. Republican convention of 1904: Schlesinger and Israel, vol. 5, pp. 1968–72, Edmund Morris, *Theodore Rex*, pp. 331–37, 352–53. Democratic convention of 1904: Schlesinger and Israel, vol. 5, pp. 1972–84, Edmund Morris, *Theodore Rex*, pp. 339–42. Wall Street contributions to T.R.: Harbaugh, p. 227. Cortelyou as manager: Brands, *Last Romantic*, pp. 503–4. T.R. campaign finance allegations and response: Pringle, pp. 354–58, Brands, *Last Romantic*, pp. 509–12, Edmund Morris, *Theodore Rex*, pp. 354–63. *New York World* on T.R. money: Oct. 1, 1904.

"Lies . . . as foul": Theodore Roosevelt to Kermit Roosevelt, Apr. 9, 1904, in Morison, vol. 4, pp. 772–73. "Hit back as savagely" and "a single promise": Theodore Roosevelt to George Cortelyou, Oct. 1, 1904, in Morison, vol. 4, p. 963, Edmund Morris, *Theodore Rex*, p. 357. Standard Oil report and Parker response: Edmund Morris, *Theodore Rex*, pp. 510–11. "Past relations": Theodore Roosevelt to George Cortelyou, Oct. 26, 1904, in Morison, vol. 4, pp. 995–96. Bliss assurance and Standard Oil contribution: Edmund Morris, *Theodore Rex*, p. 511. "Monstrous" and "something foolish or wicked": Theodore Roosevelt Statement, Nov. 4, 1904, Theodore Roosevelt Papers, Theodore Roosevelt to Kermit Roosevelt, Nov. 3, 1904, in Morison, vol. 4, p. 1014, Theodore Roosevelt to Anna Lodge, Nov. 10, 1904, in Morison, vol. 4, pp. 1025–26, Edmund Morris, *Theodore Rex*, p. 363.

Personal "merit": Corinne Robinson, p. 217. "Something to do with depressing": Henry Cabot Lodge to Theodore Roosevelt, July 25, 1904, Theodore Roosevelt Papers. "In the last hours": Henry Cabot Lodge to Theodore Roosevelt, Nov. 3, 1904, Theodore Roosevelt Papers. "Everybody thinks you are": Henry Cabot Lodge to Theodore Roosevelt, Sept. 29, 1903, in Pringle, p. 350. "I am lying still": Corinne Robinson, p. 255. Edith "anxious": Sylvia Jukes Morris, *Edith Kermit Roosevelt*, p. 279. "Never permitted myself": Theodore Roosevelt to William Howard Taft, Aug. 24, 1908, in Morison, vol. 6, p. 1195.

"If beaten I shall be sorry": Theodore Roosevelt to Rudyard Kipling, Nov. 1, 1904, Joseph Bishop, in vol. 1, pp. 332–33. "It makes no difference": Sylvia Morris, *Edith Kermit Roosevelt*, p. 280. "I am no longer": Nathan Miller, p. 436. "No free discussion" and "day of greatest triumph": Theodore Roosevelt to Kermit Roosevelt, Nov. 11, 1904, in Morison, vol. 4, p. 1024. "Have swept the country": Theodore Roosevelt to Henry Cabot Lodge, Nov. 8, 1904, in Morison, vol. 4, p. 1018. "Personal ambition" to "perpetuate": Theodore Roosevelt to Henry Cabot Lodge, Oct. 10, 1904, in Morison, vol. 4, p. 1021, Theodore Roosevelt, *Autobiography*, p. 387, Edmund Morris, *Theodore Rex*, p. 364.

"Abraham Lincoln's 'plain people' " and "I upset them all": Wister, p. 211. T.R. "proudest of" lawsuit and strike settlement: Theodore Roosevelt to Lyman Abbott, Oct. 29, 1903, in Morison, vol. 3, p. 639. "I am on their side": Wister, p. 211. "Only for his own success": Joseph Bishop, vol. 2, p. 23. "Man in the arena": Address in Paris, Apr. 23, 1910, Theodore Roosevelt Papers. T.R. friends: Theodore Roosevelt to George Lorimer, May 12, 1906, in Morison, vol. 5, p. 263. Roughneck pal: Whitcomb and Whitcomb, p. 231. "It is a good and necessary thing": Reisner, p. 307. "Felt soured at not having more": Theodore Roosevelt to Kermit Roosevelt, June 21, 1904, in Irwin, pp. 66–67.

Hay's gift of Lincoln ring: Theodore Roosevelt to George Otto Trevelyan, May 6, 1905, in Morison, vol. 4, p. 1133, *Rail Splitter*, Spring 2002. "The hair in this ring": John Hay to Theodore Roosevelt, Mar. 3, 1905, Theodore Roosevelt Papers. "A gift for which he cared": Corinne Robinson, p. 223. "Put human rights": Theodore Roosevelt, *Autobiography*, p. 385. "Love and gratitude": Theodore Roosevelt to

John Hay, Mar. 3, 1905, in Morison, vol. 4, p. 1131. Hay's gift to McKinley: Leech, pp. 109–10. "Lie in the orchard": Dennett, *John Hay*, p. 440. Hay's Lincoln dream: John Hay Diary, June 13, 1905, Hay Papers.

Nineteen-five inauguration: Harbaugh, pp. 212–14, Edmund Morris, *Theodore Rex*, p. 277, Felsenthal, p. 191. "Old friends with whom I had lived": Theodore Roosevelt to George Otto Trevelyan, Mar. 9, 1905, in Morison, vol. 4, p. 1133. T.R. at wedding of Franklin and Eleanor: *New York Times*, Mar. 18, 1905, Lash, *Eleanor and Franklin*, pp. 136–41, Ward, *Before the Trumpet*, pp. 339–41, Ted Morgan, pp. 102–3, Burns and Dunn, *Three Roosevelts*, pp. 78–80, Edmund Morris, *Theodore Rex*, p. 378. "I'd be shot": Pottker, p. 86. "As fond of Eleanor": Theodore Roosevelt to Franklin Roosevelt, Nov. 29, 1904, Franklin Roosevelt Papers, Ward, *Before the Trumpet*, pp. 338–39.

"Sweetheart": Theodore Roosevelt to Eleanor Roosevelt, Nov. 29, 1904, Franklin Roosevelt Papers. "Well, Franklin": Brands, *Last Romantic*, p. 521. FDR's annoyance: Ward, *Before the Trumpet*, p. 308. FDR and pince-nez: Ward, *First-Class Temperament*, p. 38. "A good chance to be President": Schlesinger, *Crisis of the Old Order*, p. 330. "My father spent his whole life": Author's interview with Franklin Roosevelt, Jr., 1977.

Chapter Twenty-one: WE MUST PROTECT THE CHIEF!

Election Night 1940 at Hyde Park: Reilly, pp. 65–66, Burns, *Lion*, pp. 451–54, *Time*, Nov. 11, 1940. "Shudder" and FDR's fear of forces behind Willkie: Franklin Roosevelt to Samuel Rosenman, Nov. 13, 1940, Harold Ickes Diary, Aug. 8, Nov. 9, Dec. 21, 1940, Ickes Papers. "So many sinister stories": Eleanor Roosevelt to Anna Roosevelt Boettiger, Nov. 15, 1940, Eleanor Roosevelt Papers. "Really alarmed": Lash, *Love, Eleanor*, p. 322. "A greater menace": Eleanor Roosevelt to Lady Florence Willert, Nov. 16, 1940, Eleanor Roosevelt Papers.

"Anti-war psychology" and "within easy striking distance": *New York Times*, Oct. 27 and 30, 1940. "Merchants of death" and "the Morgans": Morison, Commager and Leuchtenburg, vol. 2, p. 530. "The victim of propaganda": *Gallup Poll*, vol. 1, pp. 192–93. Ludlow Amendment: Stimson and Bundy, p. 313. FDR–Churchill relationship and correspondence: Meacham, pp. 40–81, Kimball, vol. 1, pp. 3–20. Joseph Kennedy's background and worry about impending war: Whalen, pp. 335–56, Koskoff, p. 187, Beschloss, *Kennedy and Roosevelt*, p. 162. "Keeping the war away" and "blow up" and "conniving mind" and "complete lack of understanding": Joseph Kennedy Diary, Oct. 5 and 6, 1939, Joseph Kennedy Papers.

Kennedy lunch with King and Queen, Dec. 1939: Joseph Kennedy Diary, Nov. 28, 1939, Joseph Kennedy Papers. "Much better" than "that last horrible picture": Joseph Kennedy Diary, Mar. 11, 1940, Joseph Kennedy Papers. Kennedy meeting with FDR, Dec. 1939: Joseph Kennedy Diary, Dec. 10, 1939, Joseph Kennedy Papers. Kennedy Mar. 1940 meeting with Churchill: Joseph Kennedy Diary, Mar. 12,

14, 28, 1940, Joseph Kennedy unpublished diplomatic memoir, pp. xxxxi, 3–4, Joseph Kennedy Papers. Kennedy May 1940 meeting with Churchill and "within a month": Joseph Kennedy Diary, May 15 and 16, and Aug. 15, 1940, Joseph Kennedy Papers.

"Forty or fifty of your older": Winston Churchill to Franklin Roosevelt, May 15, 1940, Franklin Roosevelt Papers. "Been any meat on the bone": Joseph Kennedy Diary, June 11, 1940, Joseph Kennedy Papers. "My belly on the sheet": Joseph Kennedy Diary, May 14 and Sept. 24, 1940, Joseph Kennedy Papers. "Too depressed": Joseph Kennedy Diary, May 16, 1940, Joseph Kennedy Papers. FDR duplicity and "complete violation of the law": Joseph Kennedy Diary, May 16 and 17, 1940, Joseph Kennedy Papers.

Tyler Kent's background, criminal offenses and arrest: Tyler Kent to John Toland, Feb. 19, 1978, and John Toland interview with Tyler Kent, Apr. 1, 1978, Toland Papers, *Washington Post*, July 23, 1961, Beschloss, *Kennedy and Roosevelt*, pp. 206–7, Bearse and Read, pp. 8–10, Whalen, pp. 310–13. "Shocked" by "barefaced conspiracy" and "largely controlled": John Toland interview with Tyler Kent, Apr. 1, 1978, Toland Papers. Clare Boothe Luce and Kennedy: Sylvia Morris, *Rage*, pp. 364, 372, Bearse and Read, p. 139. Kennedy's reaction to Kent's arrest and confrontation with Kent: Joseph Kennedy unpublished diplomatic memoir, pp. xxxxiv, 14–18, Joseph Kennedy Papers, Bearse and Read, pp. 148–49, 251, *Washington Post*, July 23, 1961.

Kennedy approves British trial and "too close a connection": Joseph Kennedy Diary, Aug. 15, 1940, Joseph Kennedy Papers, Bearse and Read, pp. 204–5. Long on Kent's arrest: Breckinridge Long, p. 113. FDR approval of warrantless wiretapping: Franklin Roosevelt to Robert Jackson, May 21, 1940, Robert Jackson Papers, Henry Morgenthau, Jr., Diary, May 20, 1940, Henry Morgenthau, Jr., Papers, U.S. Senate, Final Report of the Select Committee to Study Governmental Operations with Respect to Intelligence Activities, Apr. 26, 1976, pp. 7–14, *San Francisco Chronicle*, Jan. 25, 2006, Robert Jackson, pp. 68–69, Francis Biddle, pp. 166–68, Gentry, pp. 231–32.

"Right and wrong": Robert Jackson, p. 74. "If you are a good Attorney General": Arthur Schlesinger, Jr., *Coming of the New Deal*, p. 538. Jackson's second thoughts and later Presidential use of Jackson's ruling: Gentry, p. 232. Hoover's response to Jackson's death: Gentry, pp. 232–33, Trohan, p. 406. Hickory Hill's lineage and later history: Hilty, p. 97.

Chapter Twenty-two: GLOOM PERSONIFIED

"Spies, saboteurs and traitors": May 26, 1940, radio address, in Roosevelt Library. FDR asks Hoover to investigate: Gentry, pp. 225–26. "Hysterical chatter": Moss, p. 125. Kennedy on Lindbergh and "Absolutely convinced": Joseph Kennedy Diary, Nov. 28, 1939, Joseph Kennedy Papers, Henry Morgenthau, Jr., Diary, May

20, 1940. "Gloom personified": Eleanor Roosevelt to Anna Roosevelt Boettiger, May 17, 1940, Eleanor Roosevelt Papers. "Terrible world" and "kick, scream": Lash, *Eleanor and Franklin*, p. 617. Lucy Mercer affair during World War I: Lash, *Eleanor and Franklin*, pp. 225–27, Ward, *First-Class Temperament*, pp. 362–66, 414–16.

"More and more that FDR": Eleanor Roosevelt to Lorena Hickok, Oct. 16, 1936, Eleanor Roosevelt Papers. "Now, Franklin" and "He blew": Asbell, p. 410. FDR and Suckley: Ward, *Closest Companion*, Chaps. 9–17. "The President is a MAN": Ward, *Closest Companion*, p. x. "Eros": Ward, *Closest Companion*, pp. 31–36. FDR and Lucy: Meacham, pp. 219–23, 275. FDR and Schiff: Author's interview with Dorothy Schiff, 1978, *Newsweek*, June 7, 1976, *New York Times*, July 27, 1976, and Aug. 31, 1989, Potter, pp. 143, 146. "Not until you get rid of": Collier and Horowitz, *The Roosevelts*, p. 291, and Beschloss, *Kennedy and Roosevelt*, p. 113.

"I found this the other day": Franklin Roosevelt to Margaret Suckley, Sept. 23, 1935, in Ward, *Closest Companion*, p. 37. Nixon's use of Lincoln quote: Nov. 3, 1969, address, in *New York Times*, Nov. 4, 1969. Generally on FDR and Lincoln: Pedersen and Williams, pp. 10–60. FDR tells of Lincoln and Lafayette Park tryst: Robert Jackson Notes, May 29, 1940, Robert Jackson Papers, Robert Jackson, pp. 149–50. Press secretary's relationship to General Jubal Early: Trohan, p. 128, *Dictionary of American Biography*, vol. 7, p. 235. "Repudiated" and "one of our own": Franklin Roosevelt to Claude Bowers, Apr. 23, 1929, Franklin Roosevelt Papers.

"Best light of democracy": Carl Sandburg to Franklin Roosevelt, Mar. 29, 1935, Franklin Roosevelt Papers, Niven, *Sandburg*, p. 49. "Expect me some day" and "fine sense": Carl Sandburg to Franklin Roosevelt, Mar. 8, 1938, Franklin Roosevelt Papers, and Mitgang, p. 360. "Young man, I think": June 5, 1940, transcript in Franklin Roosevelt Papers. "Superficial things": Franklin Roosevelt to Ray Stannard Baker, Mar. 20, 1935, Franklin Roosevelt Papers. Hyde Park–Oyster Bay antagonisms and "I'd rather vote": Collier and Horowitz, *The Roosevelts*, pp. 299, 388, 394. "Itching": Theodore Roosevelt, Jr., to Alice Roosevelt Longworth, Sept. 1, 1939, in Collier and Horowitz, *The Roosevelts*, p. 394. "Mischief and dislike": Felsenthal, p. 195. FDR and Kermit: Collier and Horowitz, *The Roosevelts*, pp. 397–98.

FDR appoints Stimson and Knox: Burns, *Soldier*, pp. 38–39, Goodwin, *No Ordinary Time*, p. 71. Willkie's background, candidacy and nomination: Neal, Chaps. 1–3, Peters, pp. 22–33, 93–97, 196–98, Shogan, p. 109. "What many a U.S. citizen": *Time*, June 10, 1940, Neal, p. 76. Willkie and Van Doren and "politics makes strange": Harold Ickes Diary, Sept. 8, 1940, Ickes Papers, Neal, pp. 38–44, Daniels, *Witness*, p. 119, Gentry, p. 227. Vidal use of Mrs. Willkie's quote in *The Best Man* and "is Gore": Vidal, p. 18.

Chapter Twenty-three: SALUTE YOUR CAESAR?

Willkie a "crook": Lash, *Love, Eleanor*, p. 304. "The sleight-of-hand fellow": Franklin Roosevelt to Edward Kelly, Aug. 28, 1940, Franklin Roosevelt Papers. Eel named "Wendell Willkie": Francis Biddle, pp. 135–36. "Corporate state": Harold Ickes

Diary, June 29, 1940, Ickes Papers. Hoover asked and refuses to investigate: Gentry, pp. 227–29. Hopkins in hotel room: Harold Ickes Diary, July 19, 1940, Ickes Papers, Kenneth Davis, *Into the Storm*, p. 593. "Cries of ecstasy": Gromyko, p. 5. Joe Kennedy, Jr., vote against FDR: Koskoff, p. 238.

FDR changes platform draft: Rosenman, pp. 211–12. Boiler room accident: Samuels and Samuels, p. 2. FDR speaks to delegates: Reilly, p. 76, July 19, 1940, radio address. "Undignified playacting": Harold Ickes Diary, July 12, 1940, Ickes Papers. "You can't say that everyone": Divine, p. 50. Hans Thomsen's activities: Higham, pp. 1–40, Wayne Cole, p. 471. "Will you find out": Wayne Cole, p. 486. "Eighty-five percent" opposition press: Schlesinger, *Politics of Upheaval*, p. 590. FDR and Senator's false claim: Kenneth Davis, *F.D.R.: Into the Storm*, p. 615. FDR's Oval Office recording system: *American Heritage*, Feb.–Mar. 1982, Kenneth Davis, *Into the Storm*, pp. 615–16, Doyle, *Inside*, pp. 6–44.

FDR morning routine: Reilly, pp. 15–25. Renovations of West Wing and Oval Office: Seale, vol. 2, pp. 921–25. "Now you'd be *amazed*": Franklin Roosevelt Recording, Aug. 22, 1940, Roosevelt Library, and Doyle, *Inside*, p. 20. Containment of potential Wallace scandal: Robert Jackson, pp. 43–45, Daniels, *Witness*, pp. 182–85. "It has now become most urgent": Winston Churchill to Franklin Roosevelt, July 31, 1940, Franklin Roosevelt Papers. "We will all go down the drain": Joseph Kennedy notes, 1940, Joseph Kennedy Papers. "Might very possibly depend": Moss, p. 267. Knox and destroyer exchange and FDR–Pittman conversation: Harold Ickes Diary, June 29 and Aug. 4, 1940, Ickes Papers, Franklin Roosevelt Memorandum, Aug. 2, 1940, Franklin Roosevelt Papers. "Sail for North America": Goodhart, p. 155.

"Inconsiderate": and "deceiving the U.S. people" and "wants to get us into war": Joseph Kennedy Diary, Aug. 16 and Sept. 2, 1940, Joseph Kennedy Papers. "I can't guarantee either of you": William Allen White to Franklin Roosevelt, Aug. 1, 1940, Franklin Roosevelt Papers, Harold Ickes Diary, Aug. 4 and 10, 1940, Ickes Papers, Goodhart, pp. 155–56. "No chance": Goodhart, p. 157. "They will get into a row": Robert Jackson, p. 99. "Congress is going to raise hell": Tully, p. 244, Moss, p. 198. "Probably the most important thing" and "any two thirds vote": Press Conference, Sept. 3, 1940. "The most dictatorial": Kenneth Davis, *Into the Storm*, p. 611. "Good trade" and "seven modern guns": Franklin Roosevelt to David Walsh, Aug. 22, 1940, Franklin Roosevelt Papers.

"Pa is thrilled": Eleanor Roosevelt to Anna Roosevelt Boettiger, Aug. 30, 1940, Eleanor Roosevelt Papers. "The turning point": Stimson and Bundy, p. 359. "Never before, since Jamestown": Sept. 29, 1940, address. "Trouble with Willkie": Franklin Roosevelt Recording, Oct. 4, 1940, Roosevelt Library, Harold Ickes Diary, Oct. 7, 1940, Ickes Papers. "Secret deals" and "Mr. Third-term" and "If his promise": Beschloss, *Kennedy and Roosevelt*, pp. 213, 15, and Burns, *Lion*, p. 443. Willkie October surge: *Time*, Nov. 4, 1940, *New York Times*, Oct. 30, 1940, Neal, pp. 160–61, Divine, pp. 71–73.

Lewis speech: *New York Times*, Oct. 26, 1940, Dubovsky and Van Tine, pp. 256–58. "Falsifications of fact": July 19, 1940, radio address. "Simply *must* make some speeches": Harold Ickes Diary, Jan. 19, 1941, Ickes Papers. "So much scurrilous": Lash, *Love, Eleanor*, pp. 317–18. "Within twelve hours" and flying "impossible": Franklin Roosevelt to Oscar Ewing, Oct. 22, 1940, Franklin Roosevelt Papers. "Must have realized": Reilly, p. 161. T.R. advice on possible assassination: Ted Morgan, p. 369, and Collier and Horowitz, *The Roosevelts*, p. 336. "Solemn assurance": Oct. 23, 1940, address.

"I am not doing a damn thing": Joseph Kennedy Diary, Aug. 1, 1940, Joseph Kennedy unpublished diplomatic memoir, pp. xxxxviii, 2–4, Joseph Kennedy Papers, Beschloss, *Kennedy and Roosevelt*, p. 211. "Damned fresh" and "would be quite embarrassing": Joseph Kennedy to Edward Moore, Aug. 2, 1940, Joseph Kennedy Papers. "That little pimp" and "inspiration" and "I suspect!": Joseph Kennedy Diary, Oct. 11 and Nov. 30, 1940, and Joseph Kennedy unpublished diplomatic memoir, Chap. 52, p. 4, Joseph Kennedy Papers. "Damned sick and disgusted" and "resign today": Joseph Kennedy Diary, Oct. 11 and Sept. 24, 1940, Joseph Kennedy Papers.

"Sensational" broadside: Lord Halifax to Lord Lothian, Oct. 10, 1940, Hutton to Graham, Nov. 18, 1940, British Foreign Office Archives (FO 371), Beschloss, *Kennedy and Roosevelt*, p. 213. "Put twenty-five million Catholic votes": Harold Ickes Diary, June 29, 1940, Ickes Papers, Joseph Kennedy unpublished diplomatic memoir, Chap. 52, pp. 1–2, Joseph Kennedy Papers, Beschloss, *Kennedy and Roosevelt*, p. 16. "I don't want a new man" and "having a row": Joseph Kennedy Diary, Oct. 17, 1940, and Joseph Kennedy unpublished diplomatic memoir, Chap. 50, p. 8, Joseph Kennedy Papers.

Chapter Twenty-four: WE HAVE AVOIDED A PUTSCH

"Terrifically spoiled": Franklin Roosevelt to John Boettiger, Mar. 3, 1941, Franklin Roosevelt Papers. "Give us a fascist form": Harold Ickes Diary, July 3 and Sept. 5, 1938, Ickes Papers. "Temperamental Irish boy": Franklin Roosevelt to John Boettiger, Mar. 3, 1941. "Immediately after your arrival" and "indignant": Franklin Roosevelt to Joseph Kennedy, Oct. 25, 1940, Joseph Kennedy Diary, Oct. 23 to Dec. 27, 1940, Joseph Kennedy Papers. FDR receives Kennedy call: Krock, p. 399. McCarthy on LBJ throat-slitting: Author's conversation with Eugene McCarthy, 1998. "Nothing to say": *New York Times*, Oct. 28, 1940. "More charm": Schlesinger, *Robert Kennedy*, p. 24. "You can't say you don't": Joseph Kennedy Notes, Oct. 1940, Joseph Kennedy Papers.

FDR–Kennedy Oct. 27, 1940, meeting: Joseph Kennedy Diary, Oct. 27 and Nov. 6, 1940, Joseph Kennedy unpublished diplomatic memoir, Chap. 51, pp. 2–6, Joseph Kennedy Papers, Arthur Krock Memorandum, Dec. 1, 1940, Arthur Krock Papers, Author's interviews with Franklin Roosevelt, Jr., James Roosevelt, Grace Tully, Thomas Corcoran, Clare Boothe Luce, Benjamin Cohen, 1977–1978, Beschloss, *Kennedy and Roosevelt*, pp. 216–19. *Resolute* desk: Seale, vol. 1, pp. 493–94. "Butter up Joe": Author's interview with Grace Tully, 1977. FDR offer to back Joe Jr.: Author's interview with Clare Boothe Luce, 1978. FDR speculation on threat: Beschloss, *Kennedy and Roosevelt*, p. 218. "The red meat on the floor": Bearse and Read, p. 222. "That deep down in his heart" and "firmly embedded": Joseph Kennedy Diary, Jan. 17, 1942, Joseph Kennedy Papers.

Cocktail party scene: Harold Ickes Diary, Nov. 9, 1940, Ickes Papers. Lucy at Madison Square Garden: Daniels, *Quadrille*, pp. 281–82. FDR at draft lottery: *New York Times*, Oct. 30, 1940, Address, Oct. 29, 1940. "Driving nails": *Time*, Aug. 12, 1940. "Fraught with political disaster" and "in all probability": Vic Donohey to Franklin Roosevelt, Aug. 1, 1940, and Franklin Roosevelt to Vic Donohey, Aug. 3, 1940, Franklin Roosevelt Papers. Norman Thomas's complaint and FDR reply: Norman Thomas to Franklin Roosevelt, July 24 and Aug. 5, 1940, and Franklin Roosevelt to Norman Thomas, July 31, 1940, Franklin Roosevelt Papers.

"When men are actually called": Harold Ickes Diary, Oct. 7, 1940, Ickes Papers. Passage of draft bill: Harold Ickes Diary, Aug. 4, 1940, Ickes Papers, Edward Michelson to Stephen Early, Sept. 29, 1940, Stephen Early Papers, *Time*, Aug. 12, 1940. "Cowardly": Black, p. 593. Mrs. Luce's letter: Clare Boothe Luce to Joseph Kennedy, Oct. 28, 1940, Joseph Kennedy Papers. Kennedy later explains to Luce: Author's interview with Clare Boothe Luce, 1978. "Trying to involve": *New York Times*, Oct. 30, 1940, Beschloss, *Kennedy and Roosevelt*, p. 219. "I have just listened": Franklin Roosevelt to Joseph Kennedy, Oct. 29, 1940, Franklin Roosevelt Papers. "Exactly the opportunist": Beschloss, *Kennedy and Roosevelt*, p. 229.

FDR implored to reassure mothers: Sherwood, p. 191. "I have said this before": Oct. 30, 1940, Address. "Lied us into a war" and "That hypocritical" and "Your President says": *New York Times*, Oct. 14, 1944, Beschloss, *Kennedy and Roosevelt*, p. 221, *New York Times*, Nov. 3, 1940. "We seem to have avoided": Lash, *Eleanor and Franklin*, p. 633, Lash, *Love, Eleanor*, p. 319. "Irreconcilable hostility": *New York Times*, July 23, 1997. Kent's jailing and later life: Bearse and Read, pp. 165–66, 258–74. "Keeping out of war": *Gallup Poll*, vol. 1, p. 193. "You have led public opinion": George VI to Franklin Roosevelt, June 3, 1941, Franklin Roosevelt Papers.

FDR and religion: Kenneth Davis, *New Deal Years*, pp. 34–35, 39, 148–49, Ward, *Before the Trumpet*, pp. 156–57. "Broad shoulders": Franklin Roosevelt to Margaret Suckley, Aug. 3, 1941, in Ward, *Closest Companion*, p. 139. "I am a tough guy!": Remarks to Congressional delegation, Apr. 13, 1934, Franklin Roosevelt Papers. "Thank God on their knees": *New York Times*, Apr. 13, 1945. "There is a great storm": *New York Times*, Nov. 3, 1940, Rosenman, pp. 252–53. "If there is a Chinese nigger" and "you will go down": Joseph Kennedy Diary, Nov. 6 and Dec. 1, 1940, Joseph Kennedy Papers. Kennedy–FDR January 1941 meeting: Joseph Kennedy Diary, Jan. 21, 1941, Joseph Kennedy unpublished diplomatic memoir, Chap. 52, p. 7, Joseph Kennedy Papers.

"Admitted" to Churchill: Joseph Kennedy Diary, Jan. 17, 1942, Joseph Kennedy Papers. Kennedy's Dec. 1942 visit with FDR: Joseph Kennedy Diary, Dec. 5, 1942, Jan.

17, 1943, Joseph Kennedy Papers. "For a guy who did his God-damnedest": Trohan, pp. 320–21. "That crippled son of a bitch": Merle Miller, p. 186. FDR–Kennedy October 1944 meeting: Joseph Kennedy, "Diary Notes on the 1944 Political Campaign," Joseph Kennedy Papers. "So sad for you": Joseph Kennedy Diary, Jan. 31, 1946, Joseph Kennedy Papers. "British propaganda" and "tear your reputation" and "if Howard wasn't": Felix Frankfurter Memorandum, Jan. 16, 1941, Franklin Roosevelt Papers.

FDR–Willkie visit of January 1941: Harold Ickes Diary, Jan. 19, 1941, Ickes Papers, *New York Times*, Jan. 19 and 20, 1941, Black, p. 610. "Sail on, Oh Ship": Franklin Roosevelt to Winston Churchill, Jan. 20, 1941, Franklin Roosevelt Papers. Willkie sees Queen and Churchill: Winston Churchill to Franklin Roosevelt, Jan. 28, 1941, Franklin Roosevelt Papers, and *New York Times*, Jan. 28, 1941. "Give us the tools": Winston Churchill Radio Address, Feb. 10, 1941, in *New York Times*, Feb. 11, 1941. "That made President Lincoln cry": Franklin Roosevelt to Carl Sandburg, Apr. 7, 1941, Franklin Roosevelt Papers, *Collier's*, June 14, 1941, Detzer, pp. 195–97, Golden, p. 165. "In these hours of ordeal": Carl Sandburg to Franklin Roosevelt, Dec. 7, 1940, Franklin Roosevelt Papers.

Chapter Twenty-five: NO PEOPLE EXCEPT THE HEBREWS

Truman's Oval Office: Harry S. Truman desk inventory, history of desk plaque, and 1947–1948 photographs, Truman Library. "The great one of the age": Harry Truman Diary, Feb. 18, 1941, Truman Papers. Truman's 1948 birthday dinner: *Time*, Jan. 3, 1949, Steinberg, p. 429, Benson, p. 183. Nineteen forty-six Democratic defeat: McCullough, *Truman*, pp. 523–24. Truman's spring 1948 approval ratings: *Gallup Poll*, vol. 1, pp. 724–27. Truman–Marshall meeting, May 12, 1948: Jonathan Daniels interview with Clark Clifford, 1950, Clark Clifford oral history, Richard Holbrooke interview with Clark Clifford, 1988, Truman Library, *American Heritage*, Apr. 1977, Clifford, pp. 9–13, Pogue, pp. 371–72, Benson, pp. 151–58, Cohen, pp. 212–14.

Jewish worry about Truman, 1945: "Note on the new President of the United States," Apr. 13, 1945, Eliahu Epstein memo, Nov. 20, 1945, Weizmann Papers. Truman and the Viners: Sarah Viner oral history, 1973, Jewish Community Center, Kansas City, Frank Adler to Benedict Zobrist, Aug. 29, 1977, Truman Papers. Truman's essay on Shylock: "Shylock," 1899, Truman Library, *Prologue*, Fall 2004. "Kike town" and "screamed like": Harry Truman to Bess Truman, Mar. 27, 1918, June 30, 1935, Truman Library. "Jew boys": Morgenthau, p. 435. "The Jews claim God Almighty": Truman Diary, June 1, 1945, Truman Papers. "Everyone else who's been dragged": *American Heritage*, April 1977.

Truman at Potsdam on Holocaust survivors: Cohen, p. 51. "He will never jeopardize": Merkley, p. 176. "Always anxious to have someone pull": Eleanor Roosevelt to Truman, Nov. 20, 1945, Truman Papers. Groucho letter to Truman: Groucho Marx to Harry Truman, Oct. 8, 1946, Truman Papers, *Prologue*, Spring 2001. "Because they do not want too many of them": *New York Times*, June 13, 1946, Acheson, p. 173. "Raw, ignominious": Benson, p. 69. "Today they are cheating": Elath, p. 55. Anglo-American committee report and Truman response and "the elimination": Cohen, pp. 127–28. American Jewish postwar self-criticism: Cohen, pp. 63–64. Truman and Rabbi Silver: Benson, p. 96. Truman meeting with McDonald and Senators: James McDonald, undated report to Jewish Agency on July 27, 1946, meeting, Weizmann Papers.

"This is all political": Benson, p. 93, Cohen, p. 134. "Jesus Christ couldn't please them": Henry Wallace Diary, July 30, 1946, Wallace Papers, Blum, *Price*, pp. 606–7. "Blind as a mole": McCullough, *Truman*, p. 41. "Just smiled his way along": Hamby, p. 15. Truman and snubs and "the representative of the devil": Harry Truman to Nellie Noland, May 9, 1940, Truman Papers, Beschloss, *Conquerors*, p. 218. Truman and FDR's tacit endorsement of Stark: Harry Truman to Mary Colgan, Aug. 12, 1940, Truman Papers, McCullough, *Truman*, pp. 241–42. Truman as Vice President and "Hate to bother you": Truman to FDR, Apr. 5, 1945, Truman Papers. "I certainly set him straight": Hamby, p. 286. "Jews are like all underdogs": Harry Truman to Eleanor Roosevelt, July 23, 1947, Truman Papers.

Chapter Twenty-six: THE RIGHT PLACE AT THE RIGHT TIME

On *Exodus 1947* episode, see Gruber. Morgenthau background: Beschloss, *Conquerors*, pp. 44–45. "Had no business whatever to call me": Harry Truman Diary, July 21, 1947, Truman Papers. Truman order not to see more Zionists: Benson, p. 98. "Do you know a man": A. J. Granoff oral history, Truman Library, *Kansas City Star*, May 13, 1965. Jacobson's background and history with Truman: Daniel Fellman interviews with Gloria and Elinor Jacobson, Loeb Granoff, Herb Jacobson, and Frank Adler, 2004, Truman Library, *Kansas City Star*, May 13, 1965, Adler, pp. 199–200, Ferrell, *Truman*, pp. 60–61, 72–90, McCullough, *Truman*, pp. 143–48. "Jew clerk": Harry Truman to Bess Truman, Mar. 10, 1918, Truman Papers. "Jewish ability" and "lucky Jew": Harry Truman to Bess Truman, Feb. 13, 1948, Truman Papers. "Trumanheimer" and "very pretty girl": Harry Truman to Bess Truman, Feb. 23, 1918, Truman Papers.

"Those were happy": Adler, p. 200. "I lost all I had": Richard Miller, p. 163. "Losing our asses": A. J. Granoff oral history, Truman Library. Truman and Goering's baton: *Kansas City Star*, June 18, 1945. "Pleased to death you are back": Harry Truman to Eddie Jacobson, Feb. 19, 1945, Truman Papers. "Gave me a lot of publicity": Eddie Jacobson to Truman, May 10, 1945, Truman Papers. "I thought you'd need this sale" and "some red hot bowties": *Joplin Globe* and *Chicago Tribune*, June 29, 1945, *Time* and *Newsweek*, June 8, 1949, Truman Papers. "Well, all you peons": Daniel Fellman interview with Gloria Jacobson, 2004, Truman Library. "We never discussed Jewish questions": A. J. Granoff oral history, Truman Library, Adler, p. 201.

"Always be glad" and "kindly heart": Eddie Jacobson to Josef Cohn, Mar. 27, 1952, Jacobson Papers, *Kansas City Jewish Chronicle*, Sept. 21, 1945, Adler, p. 203, Benson,

p. 122. "Harry Truman will do what's right": *Kansas City Star*, May 13, 1945. "You know that I am not the praying": Eddie Jacobson to Harry Truman, May 10, 1945, Truman Papers. "My Dad always said": Daniel Fellman interview with Gloria Jacobson, 2004, Truman Library. "What the hell are you doing": Cohen, p. 16. "Sit down, you bastards" and "You guys": A. J. Granoff oral history, Truman Library, *Kansas City Star*, May 13, 1965. *"Takhles"*: Daniel Fellman interview with Gloria Jacobson, 2004, *Kansas City Star*, Apr. 29, 1998. Henderson's background and warnings against Jewish state: Loy Henderson oral history, Truman Library, Brands, *Inside the Cold War*, pp. 166–92, Allen Podet, "Anti-Zionism and a Key U.S. Diplomat," *American Jewish Archives*, Nov. 1978, *New York Times*, Mar. 26, 1986. Tyler Kent and Henderson: Bearse and Read, pp. 18, 21–23.

"Zionist juggernaut" and "I was attacked": Loy Henderson oral history, Truman Library, Loy Henderson to Robert Stewart, Jan. 9, 1974, Henderson Papers. "Striped-pants boys": Benson, p. 87. Barkley's story: Harry Truman to David Morgan, Jan. 28, 1952, Truman Papers. "Highly complex" and "watch my step": Edward Stettinius to Harry Truman, Apr. 18, 1945, Truman Papers, Transcript of Truman dictation, 1953, Truman Library. "Nobody seemed to think": Benson, p. 77. Henderson called to White House: Loy Henderson oral history, Truman Library. "The unwarranted influence of the Zionists": Harry Truman to Claude Pepper, Oct. 20, 1947, Truman Papers.

"Everything that came up": Weber, p. 320. "Little blue-eyed" and "the most beautiful": Margaret Truman, *Harry S. Truman*, p. 10. "Dirt farmers": Whitcomb and Whitcomb, p. 327. "Very, very angry": Margaret Truman, *Bess W. Truman*, p. 271. "I guess you couldn't think": Margaret Truman, *Bess W. Truman*, pp. 280–81. "You can never appreciate": Harry Truman to Bess Truman, Dec. 28, 1945, Truman Papers. "Each night for a long": Margaret Truman, *Bess W. Truman*, p. 286. "The Wallaces were aristocracy": Merle Miller, p. 104. "We met and knew the President": Daniel Fellman interview with Gloria Jacobson, 2004, Truman Library. "You're a Jew, David": Humes, p. 35.

Chapter Twenty-seven: HOW COULD THIS HAVE HAPPENED?

"Almost smell the big hunk": J. B. West, p. 106. "Dolled up" and "Jefferson designed": *New Yorker*, Apr. 28, 1951. "Just imagine old Andy" and "damn place": Harry Truman to Bess Truman, June 12, 1945, Truman Papers. Truman reads on retiring: McCullough, *Truman*, p. 557. "Tried to increase my knowledge": Margaret Truman, *Where the Buck Stops*, p. 160. "There's nothing new": Merle Miller, pp. 25–26. "The truth is all I want": Harry Truman to George Elsey, undated 1950, in Elsey, p. 122. "Propagandists" and "Madison Avenue boys": Weber, pp. 95–96. Truman and *Great Men and Famous Women*: Author's conversation with Henry Graff, 2000, Margaret Truman, *Harry S. Truman*, p. 52.

Truman on George Washington: Weber, pp. 44, 292, Margaret Truman, *Where the Buck Stops*, pp. 50–51, 77–78, 157–67, 177–85. Truman and Andrew Jackson statue:

Merle Miller, p. 135. Truman on Andrew Jackson: Weber, pp. 49, 124–26, Margaret Truman, *Where the Buck Stops*, pp. 273–305, 372–73, Merle Miller, p. 135. Truman on Abraham Lincoln: Weber, p. 226, Margaret Truman, *Where the Buck Stops*, pp. 11–12, Merle Miller, pp. 407–8. Truman relatives thought Lincoln deserved assassination: Margaret Truman, *Where the Buck Stops*, p. 11. "Everything loose": Merle Miller, p. 33. "You tell Harry": Margaret Truman, *Harry S. Truman*, p. 244, McCullough, *Truman*, p. 385. "Didn't bust very many": Margaret Truman, *Where the Buck Stops*, pp. 14, 100. Truman sees T.R.: Merle Miller, p. 85, Margaret Truman, *Where the Buck Stops*, p. 14. "Don't ever be an Alice": Harry Truman to Margaret Truman, Apr. 22, 1950, Truman Papers.

"One of the greatest": Merle Miller, p. 187, Margaret Truman, *Where the Buck Stops*, pp. 361–66. "The man who thought": Harry Truman Diary, Oct. 22, 1949, Truman Papers. "Rotten, moneygrabbing": Harry Truman Diary, Dec. 22, 1952, Truman Papers. "A great conversationalist": Margaret Truman, *Where the Buck Stops*, pp. 362, 366. "Amateurs" and "any shithead" and "head punched": Janeway, p. 63, Weber, p. 205. "Whether a President": Weber, p. 276. "All Roosevelts want the personal": Margaret Truman, *Harry S. Truman*, p. 26. "The distraction of attempting to live": Margaret Truman, *Where the Buck Stops*, p. 24. "First victory" and "their carnal urges": Harry Truman Diary, May 14, 1934, Truman Papers. "We never would have known you": Blum, *Price of Vision*, p. 478. "Harry, my people": Eddie Jacobson to Harry Truman, Oct. 3, 1947, Truman Papers.

Truman and partition: Benson, pp. 104, 128. Henderson tries to whittle territory: Benson, pp. 103–4. Weizmann sees Truman: Benson, pp. 128, 135. "Improper pressures": Benson, p. 106. "I kept the ramrod": Jonathan Daniels interview with Clark Clifford, 1950, Truman Library. "Hell if the voting": Loy Henderson oral history, Truman Library. "Allies of Hitler": David Niles to Harry Truman, May 12, 1947, Truman Papers. Granoff and Jacobson thank Truman and "Just looked at us": A. J. Granoff oral history, Truman Library. "Kept the faith . . . in spite": McCullough, *Truman*, p. 603. "The pressure boys almost beat": Harry Truman to Emmanuel Celler, Dec. 14, 1947, Harry Truman to Joseph Proskauer, Dec. 1947, unsent, Truman Papers.

Truman to Thackrey on New York Jews: Potter, pp. 202–3. Arms embargo: Cohen, pp. 174–75. "The choice of our people": Jewish Telegraph Agency, May 21, 2004. Hoover and arms embargo: Grose, p. 280. Forrestal's advice: Benson, pp. 109–10. Henderson and trusteeship: Loy Henderson oral history, Truman Library, Clifford, pp. 9–10. "Determined to sabotage": Hahn, p. 47. "Ridiculous": Grose, p. 270. "The Jews are so emotional": Harry Truman to Eddie Jacobson, Feb. 27, 1948, Truman Papers. Goldman appeal to Jacobson: Eddie Jacobson to Josef Cohn, Mar. 27, 1952, Jacobson Papers. "I have asked very little": Eddie Jacobson to Harry Truman, Feb. 21, 1948, Truman Papers. "Badgering": Merkley, p. 173. "Not solvable": Harry Truman to Eddie Jacobson, Feb. 27, 1948, Truman Papers.

Jacobson meeting with Truman, Mar. 12, 1948: Eddie Jacobson to Josef Cohn, Mar. 27, 1952, Jacobson Papers, A. J. Granoff oral history, Daniel Fellman interviews with Gloria and Elinor Jacobson, 2004, Truman Library, *Kansas City Star*, May 13, 1965, and Apr. 28, 1998. Granoff on "quick thinking": A. J. Granoff oral history, Truman Library. Margaret Truman on Jacobson: Margaret Truman, *Harry S. Truman*, p. 387. Elinor Jacobson on Bess and Margaret Truman: Daniel Fellman interview with Gloria Jacobson, 2004, Truman Library. Jacobson sees Weizmann: Eddie Jacobson to Josef Cohn, Mar. 27, 1952, Jacobson Papers, Daniel Fellman interview with Elinor Jacobson, 2004, Truman Library. Truman sees Weizmann: Eddie Jacobson to Josef Cohn, Mar. 27, 1952, Jacobson Papers, Cohen, p. 187, Benson, pp. 128–35. Austin's statement: Loy Henderson to William Quandt, Apr. 11, 1969, Henderson Papers, Cohen, pp. 190–91, Benson, p. 136. "I was as dazed": Eddie Jacobson to Josef Cohn, Mar. 27, 1952, Jacobson Papers. "Badly bungled": *New York Times*, Mar. 26, 1948. "Most embarrassing": Benson, p. 138. "This morning I find": Harry Truman Diary, Mar. 20, 1948, Truman Papers.

"How could this have happened?": Cohen, p. 193. "Never do that to me" and Clifford's response: Clark Clifford oral history and Richard Holbrooke interviews with Clark Clifford, Truman Library. "Deserving of four years more": Elsey, p. 162. "Enraged by the terrible" and "every Jew thought": Jonathan Daniel interview with Clark Clifford, 1950, Truman Library.

Chapter Twenty-eight: I AM CYRUS!

"Unsympathetic": David Niles to Harry Truman, July 29, 1947, Truman Papers. "In the same category as Chinamen": Harry Truman dictation, Oct. 28, 1953, Truman Papers. "Put it over on me": *Jerusalem Post*, Aug. 3, 2004. "Proper thing": Harry Truman to Vivian Truman, Mar. 22, 1948, Truman Papers. Truman cuts off Henderson: Benson, p. 141. "I don't know what they'd do": Weber, p. 253. "An amateur Bible student": Richard Holbrooke interview with Clark Clifford, 1988, Truman Library. Truman and religion: McCullough, *Truman*, p. 597, Hamby, pp. 21, 474, Ferrell, *Truman*, p. 179, Cohen, pp. 4–7. "For show" and "you better go home": Weber, p. 123.

"Every problem in the world": Cohen, p. 6. "Black Friday" and "feel badly" and "the most important single": Eddie Jacobson to Josef Cohn, Mar. 27, 1952, Jacobson Papers, Grose, pp. 276–77. Rosenman talk with Weizmann: Benson, p. 143. "Fill the vacuum": Press conference, Mar. 25, 1948. Jacobson's Apr. 12, 1948, visit with Truman: Eddie Jacobson to Josef Cohn, Mar. 27, 1952, Jacobson Papers, *Kansas City Jewish Chronicle*, Apr. 30, 1965. Rosenman on Truman's "conscience": Grose, pp. 277–78. Lovett's warning to Goldmann: Grose, pp. 288–89, Kurzman, pp. 212–13. Lowenthal's background and role in spring 1948: Max Lowenthal to Clark Clifford, Mar. 26, 1948, George Elsey and Max Lowenthal oral histories, Truman Library, *Nation*, June 14, 1971.

"It was a rather exclusive": Harry Truman to Bess Truman, Dec. 23, 1937, Truman Papers. "Clark, please do not let": Max Lowenthal (unsigned) to Clark Clifford, May 11, 1948, Truman Papers. Clifford arguments: Max Lowenthal (unsigned) to

Clark Clifford, May 7, 9, and 11, 1948, Truman Papers. "It would be a mistake": Eleanor Roosevelt to Harry Truman, May 11, 1948, Truman Papers. "Does not want to recognize": Clifford, pp. 5–6. "Well, that was rough" and Clifford–Lovett negotiations: Clifford, pp. 15–21, Richard Holbrooke interview with Clark Clifford, 1988, Truman Library. Expectation of name "Judea": Richard Holbrooke interview with Clark Clifford, 1988, Truman Library, *New York Times Magazine*, Jan. 1, 1948. Clifford to Rusk: Richard Holbrooke interview with Clark Clifford, 1988, Truman Library, Rusk, p. 150, Clifford, pp. 21–23.

"Fought us . . . all the way": Richard Holbrooke interview with Clark Clifford, 1988, Truman Library. Austin storms out: McCullough, *Truman*, p. 618. "Get up there to New York": Richard Holbrooke interview with Dean Rusk, 1988, Truman Library. Ben-Gurion declares Jewish state: *New York Times* and *Washington Post*, May 15, 1948, Gilbert, pp. 180–90. Truman signs recognition: Eben Ayers Diary, May 14, 1945, Truman Library. Marshall's refusal to talk to Clifford: Clifford, p. 13. "Temporary spokesman" and "What a thrill" and Jacobson worry about Pearson and visit with Truman: Eddie Jacobson to A. J. Granoff, May 16, 1948, Eddie Jacobson to Josef Cohn, Mar. 27, 1952, Jacobson Papers. "Beside the stars and stripes" and "I stood": Eddie Jacobson to Josef Cohn, Mar. 27, 1952, Jacobson Papers, Daniel Fellman interview with Elinor Jacobson, 2004, Truman Library.

"Happy man" and "light heart": Eddie Jacobson to Josef Cohn, Mar. 27, 1952, Jacobson Papers. "All a-dither" and "badly upset": Eben Ayers Diary, May 25, 1948, Truman Library. "Thanks, I've always wanted": *New York Times*, May 26, 1948. Truman refuses substantial help to Israel and promise to Marshall: Benson, p. 110, Cohen, pp. 240–56. "Am I a fool": Hamby, p. 160. "Those Goddamned Jews": Elsey, p. 162. "Only the intervention": Chaim Weizmann to Eddie Jacobson, Sept. 27, 1948, Truman Papers. "Their brains instead of their mouths": Benson, p. 96. Truman protects himself: *New York Times*, Oct. 25, 1948. Jacobson's advertisement: *Kansas City Jewish Chronicle*, Oct. 29, 1948. Truman effort to be Ike's running mate: Harry Truman Diary, July 25, 1947, Truman Papers. Truman's refusal to admit offer to Eisenhower: Hamby, pp. 437–38, McCullough, *Truman*, p. 398, Harry Truman, vol. 2, pp. 186–87.

"Do you really believe": Richard Holbrooke interview with Clark Clifford, 1988, Truman Library. "We've done nothing for them": Eben Ayers Diary, Dec. 2, 1947, Truman Library. "Boys, if I can have the money" and "without Truman": Abe Feinberg oral history, Truman Library, Richard Holbrooke interview with Clark Clifford, 1988, Truman Library. "Daddy rounded up": Daniel Fellman interview with Elinor Jacobson, 2004, Truman Library. "Recognition of Israel was rushed": Shahak, pp. vii–viii, Cockburn and Cockburn, pp. 26–27. Kennedy complaints about Jewish Democrats: Schlesinger, *Thousand Days*, p. 31, Hersh, pp. 96–97, Warren Bass, p. 55. Chapman's version: McCullough, *Truman*, p. 598. Jews and 1948 election: Cohen, pp. 258–59.

"We could afford to write off" and Clifford and Rowe on Jewish support: *American Heritage*, Apr. 1977. "We had both been abandoned": Harry Truman to Chaim

Weizmann, Nov. 29, 1948, Truman Papers. "Consistently favored": Harry Truman to George Marshall, Sept. 11, 1948, Truman Papers, Richard Holbrooke interview with Clark Clifford, 1988, Truman Library. Truman's admiration for Woodrow Wilson's ideas: Hamby, p. 266, McCullough, *Truman*, p. 356. "Not whether it's popular": Weber, p. 100. "A true heart, a strong mind": Harry Truman, "Courage," Truman Papers, *Prologue*, Fall 2004. "First cousins": Weber, p. 317. Truman exiles Henderson: Matthew Connelly oral history, Truman Library, Cohen, p. 229. "Looking for someone": Allen Podet interview notes, 1976, Henderson Papers. "I have become the most detested": Loy Henderson to Dean Rusk, Nov. 20, 1977, Henderson Papers.

Clifford's later life: Frantz and McKean, pp. 104–400, *New Yorker*, Sept. 9, 1993. "Who the hell is Clark Clifford?": Author's interviews with Clark Clifford, 1992 and 1993. Jacobson in Israel, 1949: Daniel Fellman interview with Gloria Jacobson, 2004, Truman Library, *Newsweek*, Apr. 11, 1949, *New York Times*, Apr. 24, 1949. "Couldn't nominate a better man": Rabbi Tibor Stern to Eddie Jacobson, undated, and Harry Truman to Eddie Jacobson, Dec. 2, 1952, Jacobson Papers. "A silly dream": Eddie Jacobson to Harry Truman, Dec. 7, 1952, Truman Papers. "I sincerely hope my dream": Eddie Jacobson to Abba Eban, Aug. 17, 1955, Jacobson Papers.

"Put his head in his hands": Daniel Fellman interview with Elinor Jacobson, 2004, Truman Library. "At long last" and "my great and irreplaceable": Harry Truman to A. J. Granoff, May 7, 1965, Truman Papers, *Kansas City Star*, May 23, 1965. "Now remind me": *Jerusalem Post*, Aug. 3, 2004. "The U.S. Capital of Israel": Harry Truman to Bess Truman, Feb. 13, 1957, Truman Papers. "A weeping man": Harry Truman to Bess Truman, Aug. 14, 1914, Truman Papers. Kfar Truman: Eban, pp. 164–65. "God put you in your mother's" and Truman's response: McCullough, *Truman*, p. 620. "This is the man" and "I am Cyrus!": Warren Bass, p. 15, Benson, 240, Merkley, p. 191.

Chapter Twenty-nine: THEY NEVER SHOW THEIR PASSION

Scenes of RFK arriving and JFK in Oval Office, June 10, 1963: *Crisis: Behind a Presidential Commitment* (Television documentary produced by Robert Drew, aired on ABC, Oct. 21, 1963). "Immense moral authority": Wilkins, p. 276. Black vote for JFK in 1960: Bryant, pp. 187–88. "We've got to stop begging": Bryant, p. 363. "Most segregated city": Martin Luther King, *Testament of Hope*, p. 528. "Let the whole fucking city": David Levering Lewis, p. 202. "You're going to have rallies" and "uncontrollable": John F. Kennedy Recording, May 13, 1963, Kennedy Library. "Stand in the schoolhouse": Dan Carter, 133. "In the hands of the President": *Crisis*. George Thomas and JFK: Krock, p. 365, Bryant, p. 219, Blair and Blair, p. 515, Jim Bishop, *Confession*, p. 384. "George, I think": Manchester, *Death*, p. 129. "Never saw a Negro": Blair and Blair, p. 515, O'Brien, p. 364.

JFK and Paul Davis: 1940 Harvard College yearbook, Paul Davis to JFK, June 12, 1963, John F. Kennedy Papers. "A Jew and a nigger": Parmet, *Jack*, p. 111. George Taylor and JFK: George Taylor oral history, Kennedy Library. "Simply did not give": Sorensen, p. 471. Kennedy's Vice Presidential maneuvering: Bryant, pp. 50–60. "Nothing to do with that": CBS News transcript, July 1, 1956, Sorensen Papers. "I'll be singing 'Dixie' ": Krock, p. 359. JFK courts South: Bryant, pp. 61–97. "Living antithesis": Birmingham *Post-Herald*, June 27, 1957. "A common bond": John F. Kennedy to John Temple Graves, July 11, 1957, John F. Kennedy Papers. Marvin Griffin pledge on blood flowing: Bryant, p. 73. "Your many friends": Marvin Griffin to John F. Kennedy, July 26, 1957, John F. Kennedy Papers.

"No pal of Griffin": Bryant, p. 88, *Berkshire Eagle*, Apr. 28, 1958. Patterson breakfast and demand to know "price": Bryant, pp. 104–5. Jackie Robinson refuses picture: Bryant, p. 105, Jackie Robinson to JFK, May 25, 1959, John F. Kennedy Papers. JFK changes strategy after 1958 elections: Bryant, pp. 99–112. "Kiss of death": Lou Harris to John F. Kennedy, Dec. 29, 1959, John F. Kennedy Papers. King refuses meeting: Bryant, p. 111. "Sunshine of human rights": *New York Times*, July 14, 1948. JFK on "equal opportunity" and Humphrey response: Detroit speech, Mar. 26, 1960, John F. Kennedy Papers, Bryant, p. 118. Lawson warning to JFK: Marjorie Lawson to John F. Kennedy, June 6, 1960, John F. Kennedy Papers. "Everything you need": Harris Wofford oral history, Kennedy Library. JFK meets with Michigan delegates: *Time*, July 4, 1960, and Bryant, pp. 131–32. Belafonte meeting: Bryant, pp. 127–28, Branch, pp. 307–8.

King meeting: Bryant, p. 133. Robinson meeting: Rampersad, p. 345, Bryant, p. 135. JFK promises moon in platform: Bryant, pp. 142–44. JFK pledge not to seek Southern delegates: *New York Times*, June 28, 1960. "a gratuitous insult": Robert Kennedy to John F. Kennedy, June 24, 1960, John F. Kennedy Papers. Ribicoff "happy and proud": Bryant, p. 135. "I want to be nominated": John Bartlow Martin, p. 496. "What do you think we're running": Bryant, p. 149. JFK bid to appear with King: Bryant, pp. 179–80. "The hell with that": Branch, p. 349. JFK, King's liberation from jail and political aftermath: Wofford, pp. 11–28, Branch, pp. 351–70, Stossel, pp. 163–69, Bryant, pp. 180–86. "The trouble with your beautiful": Wofford, p. 18.

"Do you know that the election" and "traitor" and JFK worry about narrow margin: Bryant, pp. 185, 191–92. "Hour of maximum danger": Address to Congress, Jan. 30, 1961, John F. Kennedy Papers. "Why don't you call": Roy Wilkins oral history, Kennedy Library, Wilkins, p. 280, Bryant, p. 206. "Look, I have serious problems": Theodore Hesburgh oral history, Kennedy Library, Bryant, p. 226. JFK and Route 40: Wofford, p. 127, Bryant, pp. 220–21. "Can't you tell these": Harris Wofford oral history, Kennedy Library, Wofford, pp. 127–28.

Chapter Thirty: GO GET HIM, JOHNNY BOY!

"Attitudinizing liberals": Bryant, p. 30. "New in Laos": Schlesinger, *Thousand Days*, p. 666. Jacqueline first trip west of Virginia: Manchester, *Death*, p. 9. Shriver and race and "the heart": Stossel, pp. 125–29. "Freedom riders" and "rabble-rousers": Arsenault, pp. 1–526, Wofford, pp. 125–26, 150–60, Branch, pp. 171–72, 449–50, Bryant, pp. 261–82. "Create a crisis" and "a pain in the ass": Bryant, pp. 262, 264. "Tell them to call it off": Wofford, p. 153. "Better be getting": Transcript of telephone call, May 15, 1961, Robert Kennedy Papers. "Their own protection": Arsenault, p. 190. RFK–Patterson conversation: Schlesinger, *Robert Kennedy*, p. 296, John Seigenthaler oral history, Kennedy Library. "Get them niggers!": Bryant, p. 288. King–JFK meeting, Apr. 22, 1961: Martin Luther King oral history, Kennedy Library, Wofford, p. 216, Branch, pp. 404–6, Bryant, pp. 261–62. RFK provides escort to King and "Nigger King": Bryant, p. 271.

"Now, Reverend": Martin Luther King and Robert Kennedy oral histories, Kennedy Library, Guthman, pp. 177–78, Bryant, p. 273. Kelsey's nuts: Wofford, p. 154. Explanation of "Kelsey's nuts" is guided by Cassell's *Dictionary of Slang* (London: Weidenfeld & Nicolson, 2005), p. 340, and by the equestrian scholar Michael Korda. "Doesn't he know I've done more": Harris Wofford oral history, Kennedy Library. "Gandhi wrapped a rag": Arsenault, p. 376. U.S. Marshals Service: www.us marshals.gov/history. "I wonder whether they have" and RFK warns King: Wofford, pp. 155–56. JFK press conference on freedom riders: *New York Times*, July 20, 1961. "Did not sound like a profile": *New York Times*, July 23, 1961. Writing of *Profiles*: Dallek, p. 210, Parmet, *JFK*, pp. 320–33. "Politics is a jungle": Schlesinger, *Thousand Days*, p. 101. "Earthy selfishness": Beschloss, *Kennedy and Roosevelt*, p. 64. "Where else . . . but in the political profession": John F. Kennedy, *Profiles*, p. 7. Critics on JFK and McCarthy: Parmet, *Jack*, p. 323.

Pulitzer board selection of *Profiles*: Parmet, *Jack*, pp. 394–97, Dallek, p. 210. JFK dispensation of prize money: Parmet, *Jack*, p. 395. "Raft at Tilsit": Burns and Dunn, *The Three Roosevelts*, p. 560. JFK use of Mount Vernon for Ayub Khan: Sally Bedell Smith, pp. 217–19. "What a desecration!": Ewald, p. 315. "All sorts of fun" and "Hickory Hill Seminars": Sally Bedell Smith, pp. 244–45, Schlesinger, *Robert Kennedy*, pp. 592–93. "How do you go down": Reeves, *Kennedy*, p. 278. "It will take some time": Wofford, p. 125. Ole Miss crisis: Doyle, *Insurrection*, pp. 1–318, Bryant, pp. 331–56. Meredith's background: Doyle, *Insurrection*, pp. 16–21, Branch, p. 46, Dallek, p. 514. Barnett conversations, Sept. 25–26, 1962: Transcripts, Burke Marshall Papers, John F. Kennedy Recordings, Kennedy Library, Doyle, *Insurrection*, p. 84, Schlesinger, *Robert Kennedy*, pp. 317–21.

"We'd better get going": Guthman, p. 197. JFK–RFK–Barnett conversations, Sept. 29, 1962: Transcripts, Burke Marshall Papers, John F. Kennedy Recordings, Kennedy Library, Rosenberg and Karabell, pp. 36–46, Schlesinger, *Robert Kennedy*, pp. 320–21. JFK taping system: Doyle, *Inside*, pp. 102–5, Sally Bedell Smith, p. 283. Barnett at Ole Miss football game and reneges: Rosenberg and Karabell, p. 46, Doyle,

Insurrection, pp. 112–15, Bryant, pp. 342–43. "Why, that Goddamn": Bryant, p. 35. JFK federalizes National Guard: Norbert Schlei oral history, Kennedy Library, Doyle, *Insurrection*, pp. 114–15, Bryant, p. 345. RFK–Barnett conversation, Sept. 30, 1962: Transcript, Burke Marshall Papers, Rosenberg and Karabell, pp. 49–68. "Hey, Nick, don't worry": Branch, p. 661. "We can't take a chance": Bryant, p. 345. Barnett Speech, September 30, 1962: *New York Times*, Oct. 1, 1962, Doyle, *Insurrection*, p. 146.

JFK and RFK after Barnett speech and Max Jacobson: Reeves, *Kennedy*, p. 364, Bryant, pp. 245–46. JFK speech, Sept. 30, 1962: Doyle, *Insurrection*, pp. 152–53, Bryant, pp. 346–47. King anger at JFK speech: Bryant, p. 444. JFK–Barnett conversation, and West Wing conversations later that evening: John F. Kennedy Recordings, Sept. 20, 1962, Kennedy Library, Rosenberg and Karabell, pp. 49–68. Edwin Walker background: Doyle, *Insurrection*, pp. 13–15, McMillan, pp. 242–43. Walker at Oxford: Doyle, *Insurrection*, pp. 133–35, 167–72, 267–69. "General Walker's been out there": John F. Kennedy Recording, Sept. 29, 1962, Kennedy Library, Rosenberg and Karabell, pp. 63–64. "We got so Goddamn many": Rosenberg and Karabell, p. 104. "Furious at the Army": Robert Kennedy oral history, Kennedy Library. Meredith's registration: Doyle, *Insurrection*, pp. 116, 257–58.

"What we did at the University": Robert Kennedy to Coy Hines Stennis, Mar. 29, 1963, Robert Kennedy Papers. "Can they hit Oxford": Schlesinger, *Robert Kennedy*, p. 506. "That Walker was not getting back": Califano, pp. 103–4. Oswald firing at Walker and "Hunter for the Fascists": McMillan, pp. 259–300, Doyle, *Insurrection*, p. 308. JFK and *Seven Days in May*: Author's conversation with John Frankenheimer, 2002, *New York Times*, July 9, 1976, Mar. 18, 1977, Schlesinger, *Robert Kennedy*, p. 450, Doyle, *Insurrection*, p. 309.

Chapter Thirty-one: IT'S GOING TO BE A CIVIL WAR

"Second Emancipation": Bryant, pp. 294, 365–66. "Collud Folks Night": Sammy Davis, Jr., pp. 387–89, Branch, p. 698, Reeves, *Kennedy*, p. 464, Bryant, pp. 368–69. JFK dinner with Bradlee and White: Author's conversation with Ben Bradlee, 2006, Notes in Theodore White Papers, Kennedy Library, Bradlee, pp. 132–33. Truman restoration of White House: Seale, vol. 2, pp. 1002–51. Jacqueline's restoration of White House and rescue of Lafayette Square and Pennsylvania Avenue: Sally Bedell Smith, pp. 104, 304–5, 313.

"A New England sitting room": Sally Bedell Smith, p. 80. "Oh, Dr. King, you would be so thrilled": Wofford, p. 128. Mansion household staff and Kennedys: Author's conversation with Mary Lynn Kotz, literary collaborator with the Kennedy White House's Chief Usher, J. B. West, 2006. "Not at all a way to treat": Sally Bedell Smith, p. 330. General on Birmingham demonstrations, 1963: McWhorter, pp. 303–587, Branch, pp. 673–802, Bryant, pp. 391–95. "By far the worst big city": Martin Luther King to John F. Kennedy, Dec. 15, 1962, John F. Kennedy Papers. "Come back alive": Bryant, pp. 381–82. "So that's why everybody": Coretta Scott King, p. 227. "Letter from Birmingham Jail": *Autobiography of Martin Luther King*, pp. 187–204.

May 2 and 3, 1963, protests: Branch, pp. 756–63, McWhorter, pp. 366–76, Bryant, pp. 386–87. JFK talks to Americans for Democratic Action leaders: John F. Kennedy Recording, May 4, 1963, Kennedy Library. "Please don't go down" and "Now if it will only" and "a snake half-dead": McWhorter, pp. 392, 400, 412, 415. "The biggest demonstrations": McWhorter, p. 433. Bail money produced for King: McWhorter, pp. 418–22, Bryant, pp. 390–91. "Great, enlightened symbol": Bass, *Blessed*, p. 231. Birmingham bombing and riots: McWhorter, pp. 427–37, and Bryant, pp. 391–92. "I hope that every drop": McWhorter, p. 433. JFK–RFK White House conversation: John F. Kennedy Recording, May 12, 1963, Kennedy Library, Rosenberg and Karabell, 96–106, Bryant, pp. 392–94.

"That son of a bitch!": McWhorter, p. 441. JFK speech: May 12, 1963, John F. Kennedy Papers. JFK refuses Robert's language: May 12, 1963, notes, John F. Kennedy Papers, Bryant, p. 394. Meeting with Alabama editors: Navasky, p. 218, Bryant, p. 395. JFK–Wallace conversation: Pierre Salinger notes, May 18, 1963, Kennedy Library, Dan Carter, p. 128, Bryant, p. 399. Robert taps independent sources and "They're antagonistic" and exchange with Burke Marshall: John F. Kennedy Recording, May 20, 1963, Kennedy Library, Rosenberg and Karabell, pp. 116–20. RFK meeting with prominent blacks: Reeves, *Kennedy*, pp. 505–6, Evan Thomas, pp. 243–45, Bryant, pp. 402–3. JFK–Jimmie Davis conversation: John F. Kennedy Recording, June 3, 1963, Kennedy Library. "King is so hot these days" and "The trouble with King": John F. Kennedy Recording, May 29, 1963, Kennedy Library, Rosenberg and Karabell, p. 125. "Extremes on both sides" and "married to this package": Rosenberg and Karabell, pp. 121–22. "I haven't read": John F. Kennedy Recording, June 1, 1963. "Any more about Capitol Hill": Caro, p. 1036.

University of Alabama confrontation: Evan Thomas, pp. 246–48, McWhorter, pp. 96–104, 459–65, Bryant, pp. 417–18, Dallek, pp. 599–606. "Knew what the hell we were doing": Doyle, *Insurrection*, p. 297. JFK prepares civil rights speech: Evan Thomas, p. 248. "We are confronted primarily": Television address, June 11, 1963, John F. Kennedy Papers. Response to civil rights speech: Maria Cole to John F. Kennedy, June 17, 1963, Mahalia Jackson, Tony Randall, and Paul Davis to John F. Kennedy, June 12, 1963, John F. Kennedy Papers. "Eloquent, passionate": Martin Luther King to John F. Kennedy, June 11, 1963, John F. Kennedy Papers. "A new Kennedy": Martin Luther King oral history, Kennedy Library. Jackie Robinson would vote for Kennedy: Bryant, p. 424.

Chapter Thirty-two: A MAN HAS TO TAKE A STAND

Medgar Evers murder: Nossiter, pp. 61–62. "When I see this sort of thing": Schlesinger, *Thousand Days*, p. 326. "Sailed with the wind": John F. Kennedy, *Profiles*, p. 21. "Sometimes you look": White, p. 26. "There comes a time when a man": O'Brien, p. 839, Dallek, p. 605. "In love with death": Robert Kennedy oral history,

Kennedy Library. JFK judicial appointments: Bryant, pp. 287–88. JFK on civil rights as economic: Martin Luther King, Jr., oral history, Kennedy Library. "Rarely as dramatic": Yale Commencement address, June 11, 1962, John F. Kennedy Papers. "Sharpest defeat": *New York Times,* June 13, 1963. "I suppose that civil rights thing": John F. Kennedy Recording, June 12, 1963, Kennedy Library. "Look at the trouble" and "political swan song": Robert Kennedy oral history, Kennedy Library, Schlesinger, *Robert Kennedy,* p. 348. Lou Harris warning: Lou Harris to John F. Kennedy, Nov. 19, 1962, John F. Kennedy Papers.

"Really had to be faced" and "If we're going to go down": Robert Kennedy oral history, Kennedy Library, Guthman, p. 223. "The predictions of increased violence": John F. Kennedy Message to Congress, June 19, 1963, John F. Kennedy Papers. "I may lose the next election": Robert Kennedy oral history, John F. Kennedy Recording, June 22, 1963, Kennedy Library, Schlesinger, *Thousand Days,* p. 808. JFK and March on Washington and "piss on the Washington Monument": Author's conversation with John Reilly, 2006, Evan Thomas, pp. 250–51, Bryant, pp. 4–10. "Oh, Bruce, I wish": Bruce, p. 97, Author's conversation with Preston Bruce, 1985. JFK sees March leaders: John F. Kennedy Recording, Aug. 28, 1963, Kennedy Library, Rosenberg and Karabell, pp. 131–42, Bryant, p. 10.

Sixteenth Street Baptist bombing: Dallek, pp. 646–47. Condoleezza Rice and bombing: *Jet,* Nov. 7, 2005. "The worst race rioting": John F. Kennedy Recording, Sept. 19, 1963, Kennedy Library. JFK meeting with white Birmingham leaders: John F. Kennedy Recording, Sept. 23, 1963, Kennedy Library, Rosenberg and Karabell, pp. 149–73. Possibility of Louisiana and Florida segregationist slates in 1964: *New York Times,* July 14, 1961, and Jan. 5, May 3, June 4 and 14, and July 14, 1964, Doyle, *Insurrection,* p. 63. JFK–Russell Long conversation: John F. Kennedy Recording, May 27, 1963, Kennedy Library. "We've got to carry Texas": Bradlee, p. 218. Connally effort to stop Texas visit: Reston, p. 237. LBJ calls in chits: Manchester, *Death,* pp. 3, 7, 23. Bushes outside Rice Hotel: Author's conversation with Barbara Bush, 2003.

Stevenson in Dallas and warning to Schlesinger: John Bartlow Martin, p. 774, Manchester, *Death,* p. 38. "Mr. President, we're glad you made": Beschloss, *Crisis Years,* p. 665. JFK to Connally on Dallas: John F. Kennedy Recording, Nov. 7, 1962, Kennedy Library. Theodore White conversation with Jacqueline Kennedy: Notes, Nov. 29, 1963, and Theodore White to Jacqueline Kennedy, Apr. 27, 1964, White Papers, *Life,* Dec. 6, 1963, *Washington Post,* May 21, 1995. "Some silly little Communist" and "He didn't even have the satisfaction": Manchester, *Death,* p. 407.

Chapter Thirty-three: WE WIN AND THEY LOSE!

Kennedys and Wexford: Sally Bedell Smith, pp. 306–7. Reagans and Wexford: *Washington Post,* Aug. 29, 1980, Oct. 17, 1980, Associated Press, Oct. 13, 1980. "Lead our country toward war": *New York Times,* Oct. 7, 1980. Wirthlin's advice and "push the nuclear button": Richard Wirthlin to Ronald Reagan, Aug. 9 and Oct. 9,

1980, Reagan Papers, *Christian Science Monitor*, Oct. 21, 1980. Reagan and Carter poll ratings: *New York Times*, Oct. 23, 1980. "Vicious" and "*not* a warmonger": Associated Press, Oct. 22 and 26, 1980. Reagan early hatred of Communism: Kengor, *God and Ronald Reagan*, pp. 103–13, Kengor, *Crusader*, pp. 10–29, Cannon, pp. 293–98, Reeves, *Reagan*, pp. 109–10. "Frittered away": Ronald Reagan to Frances Cooke, Dec. 1971, Reagan Papers. "Scares me to death": Ronald Reagan to Edwin Gray, spring 1976, Reagan Papers.

"A real phony": Ronald Reagan to Lorraine Wagner, Oct. 26, 1976, Reagan Papers. Carter on "dramatic change" after Afghanistan: *Washington Post*, Jan. 1, 1980. "Laughable": Ronald Reagan to Professor Nikolaev, Jan. 1980, Reagan Papers. Reagan–Carter debate: Transcript, Oct. 28, 1980, Jordan, pp. 355–56. Movement of undecided vote: Mieczkowski, p. 132. "Finally an interview": Ronald Reagan Diary, May 18, 1981. Citations here and below to this handwritten diary refer to quotes from it transcribed by Robert Lindsey while collaborating on President Reagan's memoirs in 1989–1990, kindly shared with the author by Mr. Lindsey. "Lightweight": Jerry Jones to Don Rumsfeld and Dick Cheney, Sept. 26, 1975, Ford Papers.

"Get the hell out": Richard Nixon Recording, conversation with Ronald Reagan, Oct. 1971, National Archives. "Just isn't pleasant": Richard Nixon Recording, conversation with H. R. Haldeman, Aug. 1972, National Archives. Nixon at Soviet Embassy: Associated Press, *New York Times*, and *Washington Post*, Nov. 7, 1980, Dobrynin, pp. 465–66, Anson, pp. 238–39. Nixon lobbying for Haig: Richard Allen oral history, 2002, Miller Center, Anson, pp. 239–40. "Hardheaded détente": Richard Nixon to Ronald Reagan, Nov. 11, 1980, Reagan Papers, Aitken, pp. 554–55, United Press Intl., Aug. 18, 1982. "We win and they lose!": Richard Allen oral history, 2002, Miller Center. Reagan at first press conference: Transcript, Jan. 29, 1981, Reagan Papers. "Doesn't know how to lie": *Washington Post*, Jan. 20, 1981. "An audible gasp" and Haig reaction and "I thought so!": Richard Allen oral history, 2002, Miller Center.

Haig stops Dobrynin's car: *Washington Post*, Jan. 30, 1981, Haig, pp. 101–2. "Don't you think the Russians": CBS News transcript, Mar. 3, 1981. Haig-Weinberger response to shooting: Caspar Weinberger and Martin Anderson oral histories, 2002, Miller Center, *Atlantic*, Apr. 2001, *Today*, NBC News, Mar. 20, 2001, *Larry King Live*, CNN, Mar. 30, 2001. "Nothing can happen to my Ronnie": Nancy Reagan, p. 11. Sleeping with shirt: Patti Davis, p. 18. Thurmond intrusion and "These guys are crazy!": Max Friedersdorf oral history, 2002, Miller Center. "Entertain his nurses": Caspar Weinberger oral history, 2002, Miller Center. O'Neill visit to hospital: Max Friedersdorf oral history, 2002, Miller Center. "Like you personally": Ronald Reagan Diary, Mar. 17, 1983. "A hazard to others": Ronald Reagan Diary, Oct. 4, 1981, Ronald Reagan to Jerry Mueller, May 31, 1984, Reagan Papers. Reagan at Washington's church: Ronald Reagan Diary, Mar. 21, 1982. Reagan's religious beliefs: Ronald Reagan to Dorothy Conaghan, undated, c. 1976, Ronald Reagan to Jean Wright, Mar. 13, 1984, Reagan Papers, Kengor, *God*, pp. ix–334, Reeves, *Reagan*, p. 175.

Nelle Reagan and "had the gift": Ronald Reagan to Mrs. Van Voorhis, undated, c. 1976, Reagan Papers, Kengor, *God*, pp. 1–48, Cannon, pp. 177, 212, Kengor, *Crusader*, p. 53. "Spent many hours together": Kengor, *God*, pp. 119–20. "Either he was what he said": Ronald Reagan to Rev. Thomas Griffith, Mar. 1, 1978, Reagan Papers. "Scared to death" and "accept Christ": Kengor, *God*, pp. 152, 118. Reagan and Armageddon: Author's interview with Michael Deaver, 2003, Cannon, pp. 288–91. "Signs and events": Ronald Reagan to Lorraine Wagner, Feb. 16, 1991, in Skinner and Anderson, p. 821. "Armies invading the Holy Land": Cannon, p. 289. "That's kind of scary": Stuart Spencer oral history, 2001, Miller Center.

"Sitting on my shoulder": Nancy Reagan interview for PBS, *The American Experience*, 1998. "Whatever happens I now owe": Ronald Reagan Diary, Apr. 11, 1981, Ronald Reagan to Mrs. S. G. Harrod, June 15, 1981, Reagan Papers. "Lessen the risk of nuclear war": Ronald Reagan, p. 265. "Religion might very well turn out": Ronald Reagan to John Koehler, July 9, 1981, Reagan Papers. Reagan in Solarium: Ronald Reagan, pp. 265–68.

Reagan writes to Brezhnev and result: Ronald Reagan to Leonid Brezhnev, Apr. 24, 1981, Reagan Papers, Author's interview with Michael Deaver, 2003, Ronald Reagan, p. 270, Cannon, p. 301. "Don't know whether I'll send": Ronald Reagan Diary, Mar. 18, 1981. "Striped pants set": Ronald Reagan Diary, Apr. 21, 1981. "I'm going to follow my own": Deaver, *Different Drummer*, p. 152. "He has to be kidding": Margin of Leonid Brezhnev to Ronald Reagan, May 20, 1982, Reagan Papers.

"D-m these inhumane monsters": Ronald Reagan Diary, May 28, 1981. "Find it in your heart": Ronald Reagan to Leonid Brezhnev, June 16, 1981, Reagan Papers. "Grave anti-Soviet crimes": Leonid Brezhnev to Ronald Reagan, Oct. 30, 1982, Reagan Papers. Air traffic controllers' strike and Soviet reaction to it: *Washington Post*, Aug. 4 and 5, 1981, *New York Times*, Aug. 3, 1981, Cannon, p. 497, Reeves, *Reagan*, p. 104. Reagan and Poland: Haig, pp. 238–60, Cannon, pp. 314–16, Matlock, pp. 14–15, 25–33, Kengor, *Crusader*, pp. 84–115. "We can't let this revolution": Ronald Reagan, p. 304. "Suppress the Polish people": Ronald Reagan to Leonid Brezhnev, Dec. 25, 1981, James Nance to Ronald Reagan, Dec. 25, 1981, Reagan Papers. "To their knees": Farrell, *Tip O'Neill*, p. 607.

Chapter Thirty-four: IT LEFT ME GREATLY DEPRESSED

Nuclear freeze movement: Reeves, *Reagan*, pp. 106, 139–40. "The argument about a nuclear freeze": Ronald Reagan Diary, Apr. 3, 1982. Reagan protested in Europe: Reeves, *Reagan*, p. 106, *New York Times*, July 11, 1982. "You can get as many people as that to a rock concert!": Helen Caldicott address, Apr. 15, 2000, American University. Nineteen eighty-two election results and Reagan approval rating: Reeves, *Reagan*, p. 131. "Never took survey research": Stuart Spencer oral history, 2001, Miller Center. Patti Davis, Caldicott meeting, and aftermath: Caldicott interview for PBS, *The American Experience*, 1998, Pacifica Radio, June 7, 2004, Australian Broadcasting Corp., June 23, 2003, *Newsday*, May 21, 1996, *Washington Post*, Dec.

11, 1982, and Feb. 14, 1983, *Reader's Digest*, Oct. 1982, *Time*, Nov. 15, 1982, Patti Davis, pp. 248–66, Caldicott, pp. 256–66.

"Seems like a nice, caring person": Ronald Reagan Diary, Dec. 6, 1982. "I wonder if we can make it": United Press Intl., May 23, 1983. "It isn't easy to learn": Ronald Reagan to Patti Davis, May 23, 1983, Ronald Reagan Papers. Reagan told of Brezhnev death and response: Ronald Reagan Diary, Nov. 11–13, Dec. 11, 1982, Stuart Spencer oral history, 2001, Miller Center, Dobrynin, pp. 511–12, Shultz, pp. 124–27. "Paranoid" and "power-hungry": Ronald Reagan Diary, June 14, 1982, Nancy Reagan, p. 242. "Isn't a mean man": Reeves, *Reagan*, p. 111. "There is a strange feeling": Ronald Reagan Diary, Nov. 13, 1982. "Think they would mind": Kengor, *God*, p. 272. Reagan–Shultz dinner: Author's interview with George Shultz, 2003, George Shultz oral history, 2002, Miller Center, Shultz, pp. 163–64, 246, 270. "Too hard line and don't think any approach": Ronald Reagan Diary, Apr. 6, 1983. Reagan–Dobrynin meeting and Pentecostals release: Ronald Reagan Diary, Feb. 15, Apr. 6 and 12, 1983, Dobrynin, pp. 517–20, Shultz, pp. 165, 270.

"Evil empire": *New York Times*, Mar. 9, 1983. Sharansky reaction: *Time*, Mar. 31, 2003. "Things that are news": Ronald Reagan to Peter Hannaford, Feb. 10, 1983, Reagan Papers. Reagan and origins of SDI: Author's interview with Martin Anderson, 2003, FitzGerald, pp. 147–209, Reeves, *Reagan*, pp. 141–46, Martin Anderson, pp. 80–99, Cannon, pp. 325–33. Shultz initial reaction to SDI: Author's interview with George Shultz, Cannon, p. 331, Shultz, pp. 249–56. SDI speech: Reeves, *Reagan*, pp. 143–44. Criticism of "Star Wars": FitzGerald, pp. 210–12. Wirthlin on "Star Wars" term: Wirthlin, p. 117. "I guess it was okay": Ronald Reagan Diary, Mar. 23, 1983. Andropov reaction to SDI and Reagan challenges: Dobrynin, pp. 522–26, Wohlforth, pp. 71–72. Operation RYAN: Benjamin Fischer, "A Cold War Conundrum," Center for the Study of Intelligence, Central Intelligence Agency, Christopher Andrew, pp. 471–72, 476–77, 498. "Putting the entire world": *Washington Post*, Mar. 27, 1983.

Shultz advice to Reagan to meet: Shultz, p. 275, Reeves, *Reagan*, p. 138. "When communicating has been private": Ronald Reagan to Yuri Andropov, July 11, 1983, Reagan Papers, Ronald Reagan, p. 576. Korean Air Lines downing: Reeves, *Reagan*, pp. 167–70. "Those damned Russians": Barletta, pp. 51–52, Nancy Reagan, p. 260. "Korean Air Line massacre": Address, Sept. 9, 1983, Reagan Papers, Ronald Reagan Diary, Sept. 5 and 9, 1983. Dealing with Reagan "impossible": *Washington Post*, Nov. 25, 1983. Able Archer and Soviet reaction: Oleg Gordievsky interview for CNN, *Cold War*, 1998, Benjamin Fischer, "A Cold War Conundrum," *The Times*, London, Mar. 14, Oct. 21, 1990, *Washington Post*, Oct. 16, 1988, Dobrynin, pp. 527–39.

The Day After: *Time*, Jan. 2, 1984, *New York Times*, Nov. 27, 1983, *National Journal*, Nov. 26, 1983. "Lawrence, Kansas, wiped out" and "left me greatly depressed": Ronald Reagan Diary, Oct. 10, 1983. "Always in a good mood": Edmund Morris, *Dutch*, p. 631. Casey report on Soviet fear: Christopher Andrew, p. 477, Powaski, pp. 40–42. "Maybe they are": Ronald Reagan Diary, June 14, 1984. "Without being in any way soft": Ronald Reagan Diary, Nov. 18, 1983. "Ridiculous": Nancy Reagan, p. 64, Cannon, p. 508. "What if she'd never been born?": Ronald Reagan Diary, July 6, 1983. "Then along came Nancy": Edmund Morris, *Dutch*, p. xv. "One of the warmest": Ron Reagan interview for PBS, *The American Experience*, 1998. "He just didn't need people": Lyn Nofziger oral history, 2003, Miller Center. "Barrier" and "sometimes it infuriates" and "I did the worrying": Nancy Reagan, pp. 106–8.

Nancy asks political aides about reelection: Author's interview with Michael Deaver, 2003, Stuart Spencer oral history, 2001, Miller Center, Cannon, p. 508. Drafting of "turning point" speech and astrologer: Ronald Reagan Diary, Jan. 17, 1984, Matlock, pp. 80–83, Nancy Reagan, pp. 50–54, Cannon, pp. 583–85. Reagan no Kennedy fan and suspicions: Patti Davis, p. 67. "Well, all right": Matlock, p. 83. "Come a long way": Address, Jan. 16, 1984, Reagan Papers. *Pravda* on speech: *New York Times*, Jan. 25, 1984. "Let us be frank": Yuri Andropov to Ronald Reagan, Jan. 28, 1984, Reagan Papers. Reagan and Suzanne Massie: Ronald Reagan Diary, Jan. 17 and Mar. 1, 1984, May 20, June 6, Sept. 23, 1986, and Oct. 5, 1987, Ronald Reagan to Suzanne Massie, Feb. 15, 1984, Reagan Papers, Author's interview with Suzanne Massie, 2003, Suzanne Massie for CNN, *Cold War*, 1998, *Atlantic*, Feb. 1993, *Boston Globe*, Nov. 12, 1990, *New York Times*, Sept. 28, 1984, and Sept. 26, 1985, *Moscow Times*, June 11, 2004.

"No truck with the government types": Ronald Reagan Diary, Jan. 17, 1984, "I don't want to honor": Matlock, p. 87. "A fatal confrontation" appears in George Bush to Ronald Reagan, Feb. 15, 1984, Reagan Papers. "I have a gut feeling": Ronald Reagan Diary, Feb. 22, 1984. "Any tougher than Y. Frank Freeman": Ronald Reagan Diary, Jan. 13, 1983. "They're utterly stonewalling": Ronald Reagan Diary, May 11, 1984. Mitterrand on Chernenko: Ronald Reagan Diary, June 26, 1984. "A worldwide sensation": Anatoly Chernyaev Diary, Feb. 26, 1985, National Security Archive. "Star Wars scheme": *New York Times*, Sept. 19, 1984. Wirthlin on Star Wars commercials: Wirthlin, pp. 117–19. "The press is after me because": Ronald Reagan Diary, Oct. 21–24, 1984. "Desperate" and "keeps dropping in the polls": Ronald Reagan Diary, Sept. 14 and Oct. 21–24, 1984. "The big day": Ronald Reagan Diary, Sept. 28, 1984.

Gromyko–Reagan meeting: Shultz, pp. 483–84, Gromyko, pp. 306–8, Dobrynin, pp. 555–57, *Washington Post* and *New York Times*, Sept. 29 and 30, 1984. "Didn't pay any attention" and Gromyko exchange with Nancy: Author's interview with George Shultz, 2003, Nancy Reagan interview for PBS, *The American Experience*, 1998. "I have to say I lost": Ronald Reagan Diary, Oct. 6 and 7, 1984. "For political purposes": Ronald Reagan, p. 329. "You'll see that I was smiling": Mondale interview with Jim Lehrer for PBS, *Debating Our Destiny*, 1990. "Beautiful day" and "trying to prove": Ronald Reagan Diary, Nov. 6 and 7, 1984. "What a meeting": Ronald Reagan Diary, Mar. 22, 1985. "To lean on the Soviets": Reagan Diary, Mar. 20, 1985. "It's so out of hand" and "I made it a point to be": Ronald Reagan Diary, Nov. 13, Dec. 1 and 2, 1984.

Chapter Thirty-five: DON'T WORRY THAT I'VE
LOST MY BEARINGS

Chernenko's death and Gorbachev's succession: Shultz, p. 527, Matlock, pp. 105–8. "Crown prince": Chernyaev, p. 10. "Much more effectively": George Bush to Ronald Reagan, Mar. 13, 1985, Reagan Papers. "Psycho job": Ronald Reagan Diary, Mar. 16, 1985. "Too cynical to believe": Ronald Reagan Diary, June 24, 1985. "If they insist": Ronald Reagan Diary, May 22, 1985. "Soviet Union 101": Matlock, pp. 132–35. "No, they would think we're drinking!": Barney Oldfield to Ronald Reagan, Oct. 21, 1985, Reagan Papers. "Thanks for the tip": Ronald Reagan to Barney Oldfield, Oct. 28, 1985, Reagan Papers. "I wonder if they'll print": Ronald Reagan Diary, Oct. 31, 1985. "Learn from stories" and "screwed up my courage": Author's interview with Suzanne Massie, 2003.

Reagan on plans for poolhouse walk: Ronald Reagan Diary, Nov. 16 and 17, 1985. "Protocol is spelled": Kuhn, p. 145. "Lord, I hope": Ronald Reagan Diary, Nov. 18, 1985. Reagan's rehearsals: Matlock, pp. 134–35. "Nancy surprised" and "an irresistible force": Ronald Reagan Diary, Nov. 5 and 18, 1985. "This was the big day": Ronald Reagan Diary, Nov. 19, 1985. Reagan meets Gorbachev and Gorbachev on coats: *New York Times*, Nov. 20, 1985, and Sergei Tarasenko interview for PBS, *The American Experience*, 1998, Kuhn, p. 168. Reagan–Gorbachev first morning meeting, Nov. 19, 1985: Ronald Reagan Diary, Nov. 19, 1985, Memorandum of conversation, 10:20 to 11:30 A.M., Reagan Papers, Author's interviews with George Shultz, Martin Anderson, and Kenneth Adelman, 2003, Mikhail Gorbachev and Sergei Tarasenko interviews for PBS, *The American Experience, Larry King Live*, CNN, Jan. 10, 1991, Matlock, pp. 155–65, Gorbachev, p. 406, Edmund Morris, *Dutch*, pp. 554–60.

Reagan–Gorbachev morning meeting with aides present, Nov. 19, 1985: Memorandum of conversation, 11:27 A.M. to 12:15 P.M., Reagan Papers, Matlock, pp. 156–58. Reagan–Gorbachev walk: Memorandum of conversation, Nov. 19, 1985, Ronald Reagan to Barney Oldfield, Dec. 19, 1985, Reagan Papers, Ronald Reagan, p. 12, Edmund Morris, *Dutch*, pp. 566–67. "The best president": James Kuhn oral history, 2003, Miller Center. "I'd forgotten how really good": Ronald Reagan Diary, Oct. 17, 1986. Reagan on 1980 films: Ronald Reagan Diary, Feb. 14 and Oct. 30, 1981, Aug. 14, 1982. Poolhouse conversation: Memorandum of conversation, 3:40 to 4:45 P.M., Nov. 19, 1985, Reagan Papers, Ronald Reagan Diary, Nov. 19, 1985, Gorbachev, pp. 406–7, Matlock, pp. 158–60. "You could almost get to like": Edmund Morris, *Dutch*, p. 569. "That Raisa" and "Who does that dame": Regan, p. 314, James Kuhn oral history, 2003, Miller Center, Kuhn, p. 171.

"And what a dinner": Ronald Reagan Diary, Nov. 19, 1985. Dinner and toasts, Nov. 19, 1985: Memorandum of conversation, 8 P.M. to 10:30 P.M., Nov. 19, 1985, Reagan Papers. "Here come the little green": Wohlforth, p. 97, and Cannon, p. 42. "I'm *sure* this man": Edmund Morris, *Dutch*, p. 823, Ronald Reagan to Suzanne Massie, Feb. 10, 1986, Reagan Papers. Nov. 20, 1985, morning meeting: Memorandum of conversation, 11:30 A.M. to 12:40 P.M., Reagan Papers, Ronald Reagan

Diary, Nov. 20, 1985, Author's interview with George Shultz, 2003, Shultz, pp. 599–601. "The stuff really hit": Ronald Reagan Diary, Nov. 20, 1985. "Really crushing": Edmund Morris, *Dutch*, p. 823. "I haven't got such a reception" and "the air of success": Ronald Reagan Diary, Nov. 21, 1985.

"Subject was our hostages": Ronald Reagan Diary, Nov. 22, 1985. "Held captive and mistreated": Shultz, p. 735. "Was shown the photos recently": Ronald Reagan Diary, Mar. 21, 1985. "Let myself get euphoric": Ronald Reagan to Suzanne Massie, Feb. 10, 1986, Reagan Papers. "Foolish to believe the leopard": Ronald Reagan to George Murphy, Dec. 19, 1985, Reagan Papers. "The Soviets are becoming increasingly": George Shultz to Ronald Reagan, May 19, 1986, Ronald Reagan to Mikhail Gorbachev, May 23, 1986, Reagan Papers, Shultz, p. 714. Suzanne Massie on Chernobyl and Reagan's reaction: Author's interview with Suzanne Massie, 2003, Frank Carlucci oral history, 2001, Miller Center, Shultz, p. 724, Powell, p. 361, Cannon, p. 757. Daniloff arrest and negotiations for release: Shultz, pp. 728–50, Matlock, pp. 197–202, Reeves, *Reagan*, pp. 334–35.

"Personal assurance": Ronald Reagan to Mikhail Gorbachev, Sept. 4, 1986, Reagan Papers. "Gorbachev's response to my letter": Ronald Reagan Diary, Sept. 7, 1986. "Number one duty": Ronald Reagan to Rudolph Hines, Sept. 26, 1986, Reagan Papers. "A quick one-on-one": Mikhail Gorbachev to Ronald Reagan, Sept. 15, 1986, Reagan Papers. "I opt for Iceland": Ronald Reagan Diary, Sept. 19, 1986. "An isolated city": Shultz, p. 743. "Laying into me": Ronald Reagan Diary, Oct. 1, 1986. "That's a lot of crap": Ronald Reagan Diary, Sept. 19, 1986. "It was dark and raining": Ronald Reagan Diary, Oct. 9, 1986. "Maybe she's ill": Nancy Reagan, p. 344, and Associated Press, Oct. 11, 1986. "Sweep Reagan off his feet": Reeves, *Reagan*, p. 341. Gorbachev's Oct. 11, 1986, proposals, and Reagan's reaction: Ronald Reagan Diary, Oct. 11, 1986, Memorandum of conversation, 10:40 A.M. to 12:30 P.M., Reagan Papers, Author's interview with George Shultz, 2003, Matlock, pp. 218–22, Shultz, pp. 751–80.

Gorbachev covers ears: Ronald Reagan on *Larry King Live*, CNN, Jan. 11, 1990. Officials' skepticism about sharing SDI: Wohlforth, p. 43, Matlock, p. 168. Reykjavik Sunday morning talks: Ronald Reagan Diary, Oct. 12, 1986, Memorandum of conversation, 10 A.M. to 1:35 P.M., Reagan Papers, Matlock, pp. 222–28, Reeves, *Reagan*, pp. 347–49. Reykjavik Sunday afternoon talks: Memorandum of conversations, 3:25 to 4:30 P.M. and 5:30 to 6:50 P.M., Reagan Papers, Shultz, pp. 768–74, Ronald Reagan, pp. 677–79, Matlock, pp. 228–36, Reeves, *Reagan*, pp. 349–53. Discussion in bubble: Author's interviews with George Shultz and Kenneth Adelman, 2003, Reeves, *Reagan*, p. 344. "I was mad" and walk to limousine: Ronald Reagan Diary, Oct. 12, 1986, James Kuhn oral history, 2003, Miller Center, Gorbachev, p. 419.

"We came *this close*!": Donald Regan interview for CNN, *Cold War*, 1998, James Kuhn oral history, 2003, Miller Center. Reagan–Wick exchange: Charles Wick oral history, 2003, Miller Center, Reeves, *Reagan*, p. 353. "I know I made the right decision": James Kuhn oral history, 2003, Miller Center.

Chapter Thirty-six: A MIRACLE HAS TAKEN PLACE

Origins of Iran-Contra scandal: Cannon, pp. 628–29, Reeves, *Reagan*, pp. 313–14, Shultz, pp. 809–13. Reagan pox against bargaining for hostages: Ronald Reagan, p. 494. "Irresponsible press bilge" and "The media looks": Ronald Reagan Diary, Nov. 12, 1986. "Ike for the Sherman Adams": Ronald Reagan to George Murphy, July 21, 1987, Reagan Papers. "Don't think I'm telling": Ronald Reagan Diary, Dec. 1, 1986. "A bitter bile": *Time*, Dec. 8, 1986. "I wore my arms out": Ronald Reagan Diary, Mar. 13, 1981. "What a morale booster": Ronald Reagan Diary, March 28, 1985. "In a daze": Frank Carlucci oral history, 2001, Miller Center. Reagan reads stage directions: Abshire, pp. 120–21, Reeves, *Reagan*, p. 379. Nixon's backstage influence: Ronald Reagan Diary, Feb. 25–26, Apr. 26, Sept. 23, 1984, Nov. 3, 1985, and Sept. 12, 1986, Aitken, pp. 554–62, McFarlane, p. 316.

Reagan's wish to have Nixon dinner: Richard Allen oral history, 2002, Miller Center. Nixon on Nancy Reagan: Anson, p. 144. "Somewhat fuzzy" and Nixon meeting: Nixon memorandum, Apr. 29, 1987, in Aitken, p. 562. "Gotten the noose": Ronald Reagan to George Murphy, July 21, 1987, Reagan Papers. "Ronald Reagan has had the landing lights": Frank Carlucci oral history, 2001, Miller Center. Reagan meeting with Gordievsky: Ronald Reagan Diary, July 21, 1987. "I'm the President": Peter Robinson, pp. 71–99, Wirthlin, 195–96, Reeves, *Reagan*, p. 401. Reagan Berlin Wall address and anger: June 12, 1987, Frederick Ryan oral history, 2004, Miller Center. "Tear down these walls!": ABC News Special Report, June 5, 2004, 6 P.M. EDT. Yakovlev advice: Alexander Yakovlev to Mikhail Gorbachev, c. Dec. 1986, National Security Archive.

"It's lonely at the top": Ronald Reagan to Frank Carlucci, undated, 1987, Reagan Papers. "Why do I hate photo sessions": Ronald Reagan Diary, Jan. 14, 1982. "Might be killed": Ronald Reagan Diary, Feb. 25, 1987. "Those are the workers' houses!": Reeves, *Reagan*, pp. 391–92, *Washington Post*, Oct. 10, 1985. Eisenhower helicopter flight with Khrushchev: Beschloss, *Mayday*, p. 185. "That war is inevitable": Transcript, Ronald Reagan interview with television network anchors, Dec. 3, 1987, Reagan Papers. "Apologist" and "A very weak man": Associated Press, Dec. 4, 1987. Other conservative opposition to INF treaty: William F. Buckley, Jr., to Ronald Reagan, May 5, 1987, Reagan Papers. "Nackey, I'm still": Ronald Reagan to Nackey Loeb, Dec. 18, 1987, Reagan Papers. Washington summit: *New York Times* and *Washington Post*, Dec. 9–12, 1987, Cannon, pp. 773–90, Matlock, pp. 275–82, Reeves, *Reagan*, pp. 432–37.

"Knock 'em dead": *Newsweek*, Dec. 21, 1987. Nancy miffed at Raisa: Nancy Reagan, p. 346. "Good rousing": Ronald Reagan Diary, Dec. 8, 1987. "Mine is Ron" and cufflinks: *Washington Post*, Dec. 9, 1987, Powell, p. 360. Gorbachev discomfort with first names: Edmund Morris, *Dutch*, p. 633. Treaty signing: Dec. 8, 1987, transcript. "Sudden changes" and "a fixed, pleasant expression": Powell, p. 362. Reagan in

Dec. 8, 1987, afternoon meeting: Memorandum of conversation, 2:30 to 3:15 P.M., Reagan Papers, Shultz, pp. 1010–11, Powell, pp. 362–64, Ronald Reagan Diary, Dec. 8, 1987.

"Mr. President, that was a disaster!": Powell, p. 363. State dinner: *Los Angeles Times*, Dec. 9, 1987. DiMaggio baseball and "a witness to history": National Public Radio, May 13, 2006. Dec. 9, 1987, morning meetings: Memorandum of conversations, 10:35 to 10:45 A.M. and 10:55 to 12:35 P.M. Reagan Papers. "Things got a little heated": Ronald Reagan Diary, Dec. 9, 1987. Soviets working "twice as hard as us": Ronald Reagan Diary, Aug. 8, 1984. Reagan anger at Gorbachev lateness: Kuhn, p. 237, and James Kuhn oral history, 2003, Miller Center. Dec. 10, 1987, luncheon: Memorandum of conversation, 12:40 to 2:10 P.M., Reagan Papers, Ronald Reagan Diary, Dec. 10, 1987. "The best summit we've ever had": Ronald Reagan Diary, Dec. 10, 1987. "A big plus": Ronald Reagan Diary, Dec. 12, 1987.

Reagan meeting with Congressional leaders: Ronald Reagan Diary, Dec. 11, 1987, *Washington Post*, Dec. 12, 1987. Reagan on New Year's Eve: Ronald Reagan Diary, Dec. 31, 1987. Moscow summit, general: Shultz, pp. 1101–08, Cannon, pp. 781–90, Matlock, pp. 282–303, Reeves, *Reagan*, pp. 465–75, *Newsweek* and *Time*, June 13, 1988. "We couldn't believe": Ronald Reagan to Armand Deutsch, June 7, 1988, Reagan Papers. Reagan in Red Square: Gorbachev interview for CNN, *Cold War*, 1998, Gorbachev, pp. 457–58, Oberdorfer, pp. 297–99. Reagan–Gorbachev May 29, 1988, talk in Kremlin: Memorandum of conversation, 3:26 to 4:37 P.M., Reagan Papers. Reagan retirement office: Author's interview with Frederick Ryan, 2006, Frederick Ryan oral history, 2004, Miller Center.

"A miracle has taken place": Ronald Reagan to Barney Oldfield, Mar. 14, 1988, Reagan Papers. "No, this couldn't" and "victory lap": Author's interview with Frederick Ryan, 2006, and Frederick Ryan oral history, 2004, Miller Center. "I'll take my ten years as emperor": David Remnick, *Washington Post*, Dec. 26, 1991. Reagan trip to Berlin and Moscow: Author's interview with Frederick Ryan, 2006, *Washington Post* and *Chicago Tribune*, Sept. 13, 1990, *Newsday*, Sept. 19, 1990, *Los Angeles Times*, Sept. 17 and 18, 1990. "The triumph of good": Author's interview with Frederick Ryan, 2006, and Frederick Ryan oral history, 2004, Miller Center. Gorbachev May 1992 visit to ranch: Joanne Drake and Frederick Ryan oral histories, 2003 and 2004, Miller Center, Author's interview with Frederick Ryan, 2006, Barletta, pp. 146–48, 168, Associated Press, May 4, 1992, *New York Times, Los Angeles Times,* and *USA Today*, May 5, 1992.

Governors Island meeting: Memorandum of conversation, Dec. 7, 1988, 1:05 to 1:30 P.M., Reagan Papers, *New York Times* and *Washington Post*, Dec. 8, 1988. Reagan to Gorbachev on Islamic revolution: Nov. 20, 1985, Memorandum of conversation, "Dinner Hosted by President and Mrs. Reagan," 8:00 to 10:30 P.M., Reagan Papers. On Fort Jay and name changes: John Hammond, pp. 37–46, *Columbia College Today*, Sept. 2004.

Epilogue: PRESIDENTIAL COURAGE

Briefings of new Presidents: Central Intelligence Agency, "CIA Briefings," 1996. White House warehouse: Author's conversations with William Allman, White House Curator, 2005 and 2007. "The tremendous power of mass communications": John F. Kennedy, *Profiles,* p. 17. Enhancing White House with artifacts: William Manchester concluded *The Death of a President, The Glory and the Dream,* Little, Brown, 1973, and *American Caesar,* Little, Brown, 1978, by showing how material culture can evoke an epoch. See also Ian Quimby, *Material Culture and the Study of American Life,* Norton, 1978. Washington's death scene: Flexner, *Washington,* pp. 456–62.

SOURCES

MANUSCRIPTS AND RECORDINGS

John and Abigail Adams Papers, Massachusetts Historical Society.
John Quincy Adams Papers, Massachusetts Historical Society.
Eben Ayers Diary, Harry S. Truman Library.
Thomas Hart Benton Papers, Library of Congress.
Nicholas Biddle Papers, Library of Congress.
John Boettiger Papers, Franklin D. Roosevelt Library.
British Foreign Office Archives, Public Record Office, Kew Gardens, Surrey, U.K.
Anatoly Chernyaev Diary, National Security Archive, Washington, D.C.
Henry Clay Papers, Library of Congress.
John Coffee Papers, Library of Congress.
Andrew Donelson Papers, Library of Congress.
Stephen Early Papers, Franklin D. Roosevelt Library.
Gerald Ford Papers, Gerald R. Ford Library.
Elbridge Gerry Papers, Massachusetts Historical Society.
Ulysses Grant Papers, Library of Congress.
Anna Roosevelt Halsted Papers, Franklin D. Roosevelt Library.
Alexander Hamilton Papers, Columbia University.
Hanna-McCormick Papers, Library of Congress.
John Hay Papers, Library of Congress.
Loy Henderson Papers, Library of Congress.
Harold Ickes Papers, Library of Congress.
Andrew Jackson Papers, Library of Congress.
Robert Jackson Papers, Library of Congress.
Eddie Jacobson Papers, Harry S. Truman Library.
John Jay Papers, Columbia University.
Thomas Jefferson Papers, Library of Congress.
Amos Kendall Papers, Library of Congress.
John F. Kennedy Library Oral History Collection.
John F. Kennedy Papers and Recordings, John F. Kennedy Library.
Joseph Kennedy Papers, John F. Kennedy Library.
Robert Kennedy Papers, John F. Kennedy Library.
Rose Kennedy Papers, John F. Kennedy Library.

Tyler Kent Files, Federal Bureau of Investigation.
Arthur Krock Papers, Princeton University.
Abraham Lincoln Papers, Library of Congress.
Robert Lindsey Papers, courtesy of Mr. Lindsey.
James Madison Papers, Library of Congress.
Burke Marshall Papers, John F. Kennedy Library.
John Marshall Papers, College of William and Mary.
George McClellan Papers, Library of Congress.
James McHenry Papers, College of William and Mary.
William McKinley Papers, Library of Congress.
Miller Center for Public Affairs Oral History Collection, University of Virginia.
James Monroe Papers, Library of Congress.
Henry Morgenthau, Jr., Diary and Papers, Franklin D. Roosevelt Library.
William Vans Murray Papers, Library of Congress.
National Security Archive, Washington, D.C.
John Nicolay Papers, Library of Congress.
Richard Nixon Papers and Recordings, National Archives.
Timothy Pickering Papers, Massachusetts Historical Society.
John Randolph Papers, Library of Congress.
Ronald Reagan Papers, Ronald Reagan Library.
Eleanor Roosevelt Papers, Franklin D. Roosevelt Library.
Franklin Roosevelt Papers, Franklin D. Roosevelt Library.
Theodore Roosevelt Papers, Library of Congress and Harvard University.
Theodore Roosevelt, Jr., Papers, Library of Congress.
Sargent Shriver Papers, John F. Kennedy Library.
Theodore Sorensen Papers, John F. Kennedy Library.
Margaret Suckley Papers, Wilderstein Preservation, Rhinebeck, N.Y.
Roger Taney Papers, Library of Congress.
John Toland Papers, Franklin D. Roosevelt Library.
Harry S. Truman Library Oral History Collection.
Harry S. Truman Papers, Harry S. Truman Library.
Martin Van Buren Papers, Library of Congress.
Henry Wallace Papers, University of Iowa.
George Washington Papers, Library of Congress.
Chaim Weizmann Papers, Weizmann Archives, Rehovot, Israel.
Theodore White Papers, John F. Kennedy Library and Harvard University.
Harris Wofford Papers, John F. Kennedy Library.

ORAL HISTORIES AND INTERVIEWS

Kenneth Adelman, interview by author, 2003.
Frank Adler, interview by Daniel Fellman, Harry S. Truman Library, 2004.
Richard Allen oral history, Miller Center for Public Affairs, 2002.
Martin Anderson, interview by author, 2003.
Martin Anderson oral history, Miller Center for Public Affairs, 2001.

James Baker III, interviews by author, 1990–1991.

Cornelius Bliss statement, Hanna-McCormick Papers, 1905.

George H. W. Bush, interview by author, 1997.

Frank Carlucci oral history, Miller Center for Public Affairs, 2001.

Jimmy Carter oral history, Miller Center for Public Affairs, 1982.

Jimmy Carter, interview by author, 2003.

Dick Cheney, interviews by author, 1989–1991.

Clark Clifford, interview by Jonathan Daniels, Harry S. Truman Library, 1950.

Clark Clifford oral history, Harry S. Truman Library, 1971–1973.

Clark Clifford, interviews by Richard Holbrooke, Harry S. Truman Library, 1988.

Clark Clifford, interviews by author, 1992–1993.

Bill Clinton, interview by author, 2003.

Benjamin Cohen, interview by author, 1977.

Matthew Connelly oral history, Harry S. Truman Library, 1967–1968.

Thomas Corcoran, interview by author, 1977.

George Cortelyou statement, Hanna-McCormick Papers, 1905.

Michael Deaver, interview by author, 2003.

James Dempsey statement, Hanna-McCormick Papers, 1905.

Elmer Dover statement, Hanna-McCormick Papers, 1905.

Joanne Drake oral history, Miller Center for Public Affairs, 2003.

George Elsey oral history, Harry S. Truman Library, 1964–1970.

George Elsey, interview by author, 2003.

Abe Feinberg oral history, Harry S. Truman Library, 1973.

Gerald Ford, interviews by author, 1990, 1995.

Max Friedersdorf oral history, Miller Center for Public Affairs, 2002.

Mikhail Gorbachev, interview for CNN, *Cold War*, 1998.

Mikhail Gorbachev, interview for PBS, *The American Experience*, 1998.

Mikhail Gorbachev, interview by author, 1991.

Oleg Gordievsky, interview for CNN, *Cold War*, 1998.

A. J. Granoff oral history, Harry S. Truman Library, 1969.

Loeb Granoff, interview by Daniel Fellman, Harry S. Truman Library, 2004.

Charlotte Rhodes Hanna statement, Hanna-McCormick Papers, 1905.

Loy Henderson oral history, Harry S. Truman Library, 1973.

Theodore Hesburgh oral history, John F. Kennedy Library, 1966.

James J. Hill statement, Hanna-McCormick Papers, 1905.

Elinor Jacobson, interview by Daniel Fellman, Harry S. Truman Library, 2004.

Gloria Jacobson, interview by Daniel Fellman, Harry S. Truman Library, 2004.

Herb Jacobson, interview by Daniel Fellman, Harry S. Truman Library, 2004.

Robert Kennedy oral history, John F. Kennedy Library, 1964–1965.

Tyler Kent, interview by John Toland, Franklin D. Roosevelt Library, 1978.

Martin Luther King oral history, John F. Kennedy Library, 1964.

James Kuhn oral history, Miller Center for Public Affairs, 2003.

Max Lowenthal oral history, Harry S. Truman Library, 1967.

Clare Boothe Luce, interview by author, 1978.

Suzanne Massie, interview by author, 2003.

Walter Mondale, interview by Jim Lehrer for PBS, *Debating Our Destiny*, 1990.
Richard Nixon, interview by author, 1992.
Lyn Nofziger oral history, Miller Center for Public Affairs, 2003.
Nancy Reagan, interview for PBS, *The American Experience*, 1998.
Ron Reagan, interview for PBS, *The American Experience*, 1998.
Donald Regan, interview for CNN, *Cold War*, 1998.
Franklin Roosevelt, Jr., interview by author, 1977.
James Roosevelt, interview by author, 1978.
Dean Rusk, interview by Richard Holbrooke, Harry S. Truman Library, 1988.
Frederick Ryan, interview by author, 2006.
Frederick Ryan oral history, Miller Center for Public Affairs, 2004.
Dorothy Schiff, interview by author, 1978.
Norbert Schlei oral history, John F. Kennedy Library, 1968.
Brent Scowcroft, interviews by author, 1990–1992.
John Seigenthaler oral history, John F. Kennedy Library, 1964, 1970.
George Shultz, interviews by author, 1993, 2003.
George Shultz oral history, Miller Center for Public Affairs, 2002.
Stuart Spencer oral history, Miller Center for Public Affairs, 2001.
Sergei Tarasenko, interview for PBS, *The American Experience*, 1998.
George Taylor oral history, John F. Kennedy Library, 1964, 1967.
Walter Trohan oral history, Harry S. Truman Library, 1970.
Grace Tully, interview by author, 1978.
Sarah Viner oral history, Jewish Community Center, Kansas City, Mo., 1973.
Caspar Weinberger oral history, Miller Center for Public Affairs, 2002.
Charles Wick oral history, Miller Center for Public Affairs, 2003.
Roy Wilkins oral history, John F. Kennedy Library, 1964, 1969.
Harris Wofford oral history, John F. Kennedy Library, 1965, 1968.

BOOKS

Abrams, Herbert. *The President Has Been Shot.* New York: Norton, 1992.
Abshire, David. *Saving the Reagan Presidency: Trust Is the Coin of the Realm.* College Station: Texas A&M University, 2005.
Acheson, Dean. *Present at the Creation: My Years at the State Department.* New York: Norton, 1969.
Adams, John. *Works of John Adams.* Boston: Little, Brown, 1850–1856.
Adelman, Kenneth. *The Great Universal Embrace.* New York: Simon & Schuster, 1989.
Adler, Frank. *Roots in a Moving Stream: The Centennial History of Congregation B'nai Jehudah of Kansas City.* Kansas City, Mo.: Congregation B'nai Jehudah, 1972.
Aitken, Jonathan. *Nixon: A Life.* Washington, D.C.: Regnery, 1993.
Allen, William. *History of the United States Capitol.* Washington, D.C.: U.S. Government Printing Office, 2001.
Anderson, Martin. *Revolution.* New York: Harcourt, 1988.

Andrew, Christopher. *For the President's Eyes Only: Secret Intelligence and the American Presidency from Washington to Bush.* New York: HarperCollins, 1995.

Anson, Robert Sam. *Exile: The Unquiet Oblivion of Richard M. Nixon.* New York: Simon & Schuster, 1984.

Appleby, Joyce. *Thomas Jefferson.* New York: Times Books, 2003.

Arsenault, Raymond. *Freedom Riders: 1961 and the Struggle for Racial Justice.* New York: Oxford, 2006.

Asbell, Bernard. *Mother and Daughter: The Letters of Eleanor and Anna Roosevelt.* New York: Coward, McCann, 1982.

Ayers, Eben. *Truman in the White House: The Diary of Eben Ayers.* Columbia: University of Missouri, 1991. Edited by Robert Ferrell.

Baker, Jean. *Mary Todd Lincoln: A Biography.* New York: Norton, 1987.

Bar-Zohar, Michael. *Ben-Gurion: A Biography.* New York: Delacorte, 1978.

Barletta, John. *Riding with Reagan: From the White House to the Ranch.* New York: Citadel, 2005.

Basler, Roy P., ed. *The Collected Works of Abraham Lincoln.* New Brunswick, N.J.: Rutgers University, 1953.

Bass, S. Jonathan. *Blessed Are the Peacemakers: Martin Luther King, Jr., Eight White Leaders and the "Letter from a Birmingham Jail."* Baton Rouge: Louisiana State University, 2001.

Bass, Warren. *Support Any Friend: Kennedy's Middle East and the Making of the U.S.-Israel Alliance.* New York: Oxford, 2003.

Bassett, John Spencer, ed. *The Correspondence of Andrew Jackson.* Washington, D.C.: Carnegie Institution, 1926–1935.

Bearse, Raymond, and Anthony Read. *Conspirator: The Untold Story of Tyler Kent.* New York: Doubleday, 1991.

Beer, Thomas. *Hanna.* New York: Knopf, 1929.

Bellamy, Francis. *Private Life of George Washington.* New York: Cowell, 1951.

Bemis, Samuel Flagg. *Jay's Treaty: A Study in Commerce and Diplomacy.* New York: Macmillan, 1924.

———. *Pinckney's Treaty: America's Advantage from Europe's Distress, 1783–1800.* New Haven: Yale, 1960.

Benson, Michael. *Harry S. Truman and the Founding of Israel.* Westport, Ct.: Praeger, 1997.

Bent, Silas. *Justice Oliver Wendell Holmes.* Garden City, N.Y.: Garden City, 1932.

Benton, Thomas Hart. *Thirty Years' View.* New York: Appleton, 1854.

Bernhard, Winfred. *Fisher Ames: Federalist and Statesman, 1758–1808.* Chapel Hill: University of North Carolina, 1965.

Beschloss, Michael. *The Conquerors: Roosevelt, Truman and the Destruction of Hitler's Germany, 1941–1945.* New York: Simon & Schuster, 2002.

———. *The Crisis Years: Kennedy and Khrushchev, 1960–1963.* New York: HarperCollins, 1991.

———. *Kennedy and Roosevelt: The Uneasy Alliance.* New York: Norton, 1980.

———. *Mayday: Eisenhower, Khrushchev and the U-2 Affair.* New York: Harper, 1986.

————. *Taking Charge: The Johnson White House Tapes, 1963–1964.* New York: Simon & Schuster, 1997.

Beschloss, Michael, and Strobe Talbott. *At the Highest Levels: The Inside Story of the End of the Cold War.* Boston: Little, Brown, 1993.

Biddle, Charles. *Autobiography of Charles Biddle.* Philadelphia: E. Claxton, 1883.

Biddle, Francis. *In Brief Authority.* Garden City, N.Y.: Doubleday, 1962.

Billias, George. *Elbridge Gerry: Founding Father and Republican Statesman.* New York: McGraw-Hill, 1976.

Bisgyer, Maurice. *Challenge and Encounter: Behind the Scenes in the Struggle for Jewish Survival.* New York: Crown, 1967.

Bishop, Jim. *A Bishop's Confession.* Boston: Little, Brown, 1981.

————. *A Day in the Life of President Kennedy.* New York: Random House, 1964.

Bishop, Joseph Bucklin. *Theodore Roosevelt and His Times.* New York: Scribner's, 1920.

Black, Conrad. *Franklin Delano Roosevelt: Champion of Freedom.* New York: Public-Affairs, 2003.

Blair, Clay, and Joan Blair. *The Search for J.F.K.* New York: Putnam, 1976.

Blight, David. *Frederick Douglass: Keeping Faith in Jubilee.* Baton Rouge: Louisiana State University, 1989.

Blum, John Morton. *From the Morgenthau Diaries.* Boston: Houghton Mifflin, 1959–1967.

Blum, John Morton, ed. *The Price of Vision: The Diary of Henry A. Wallace, 1942–1946.* Boston: Houghton Mifflin, 1973.

Boritt, Gabor. *Lincoln, the War President: The Gettysburg Lectures.* New York: Oxford, 2002.

Bowers, Claude. *The Party Battles of the Jackson Period.* Boston: Houghton Mifflin, 1928.

Bradlee, Benjamin. *Conversations with Kennedy.* New York: Norton, 1975.

Branch, Taylor. *Parting the Waters: America in the King Years, 1954–1963.* New York: Simon & Schuster, 1988.

Brands, H. W. *Andrew Jackson: His Life and Times.* New York: Doubleday, 2005.

————. *Inside the Cold War: Loy Henderson and the Rise of the American Empire, 1918–1961.* New York: Oxford, 1991.

————. *T.R.: The Last Romantic.* New York: HarperCollins, 1997.

Brinkley, Alan. *Voices of Protest: Huey Long, Father Coughlin and the Great Depression.* New York: Knopf, 1982.

Brookhiser, Richard. *Alexander Hamilton: American.* New York: Free Press, 1999.

————. *Founding Father: Rediscovering George Washington.* New York: Free Press, 1996.

Brooks, Noah. *Lincoln Observed: The Civil War Dispatches of Noah Brooks*, edited by Michael Burlingame. Baltimore: Johns Hopkins University, 1998.

Brown, Ralph Adams. *The Presidency of John Adams.* Lawrence: University Press of Kansas, 1975.

Brownstein, Elizabeth. *Lincoln's Other White House: The Untold Story of the Man and His Presidency.* New York: John Wiley, 2005.

Bruce, Preston. *From the Door of the White House.* New York: Lothrop, Lee, 1984.

Bryan, Helen. *Martha Washington: First Lady of Liberty.* New York: John Wiley, 2002.

Bryant, Nick. *The Bystander: John F. Kennedy and the Struggle for Black Equality.* New York: Basic, 2006.

Buell, Augustus. *History of Andrew Jackson.* New York: Scribner, 1904.

Burlingame, Michael. *At Lincoln's Side: John Hay's Civil War Correspondence and Selected Writings.* Baltimore: Johns Hopkins University, 2000.

———. *The Inner World of Abraham Lincoln.* Urbana: University of Illinois Press, 1994.

———. *With Lincoln in the White House: Letters, Memoranda and Other Writings of John G. Nicolay, 1860–1865.* Carbondale: Southern Illinois University, 2006.

Burlingame, Michael, and John Ettlinger, eds. *Inside Lincoln's White House: The Complete Civil War Diary of John Hay.* Carbondale: Southern Illinois University, 1997.

Burns, James MacGregor. *Roosevelt: The Lion and the Fox.* New York: Harcourt, 1956.

———. *Roosevelt: The Soldier of Freedom.* New York: Harcourt, 1970.

Burns, James MacGregor, and Susan Dunn. *George Washington.* New York: Times Books, 2004.

———. *The Three Roosevelts.* New York: Atlantic Monthly, 2001.

Burstein, Andrew. *The Passions of Andrew Jackson.* New York: Knopf, 2003.

Bush, George. *All the Best: My Life in Letters and Other Writings.* New York: Scribner, 1999.

Butler, Benjamin. *Private and Official Correspondence of General Benjamin F. Butler During the Period of the Civil War.* Norwood, Mass.: Plimpton, 1917.

Butterfield, L. H., ed. *Diary of John Adams.* Cambridge, Mass.: Belknap, 1961.

Cabot, James Elliot. *A Memoir of Ralph Waldo Emerson.* Cambridge, Mass.: Riverside, 1895.

Caldicott, Helen. *A Desperate Passion: An Autobiography.* New York: Norton, 1996.

Calhoun, Charles. *Longfellow: A Rediscovered Life.* Boston: Beacon, 2004.

Califano, Joseph A. *Inside: A Public and Private Life.* New York: PublicAffairs, 2004.

Cannon, Lou. *President Reagan: The Role of a Lifetime.* New York: Simon & Schuster, 1991.

Caro, Robert. *The Years of Lyndon Johnson: Master of the Senate.* New York: Knopf, 2002.

Caroli, Betty Boyd. *First Ladies.* New York: Oxford, 1995.

Carpenter, F. B. *Six Months at the White House with Abraham Lincoln.* Lincoln: University of Nebraska, 1995.

Carter, Dan. *The Politics of Rage: George Wallace, the Origins of the New Conservatism, and the Transformation of American Politics.* New York: Simon & Schuster, 1995.

Carter, Samuel III. *The Siege of Atlanta, 1864.* New York: St. Martin's, 1973.

Carwardine, Richard. *Lincoln: A Life of Purpose and Power.* New York: Knopf, 2006.

Catterall, Ralph. *The Second Bank of the United States.* Chicago: University of Chicago, 1960.

Catton, Bruce. *This Hallowed Ground: The Story of the Union Side of the Civil War.* Garden City, N.Y.: Doubleday, 1956.

Chernow, Ron. *Alexander Hamilton.* New York: Penguin, 2004.

———. *The House of Morgan: An American Banking Dynasty and the Rise of Modern Finance.* New York: Atlantic Monthly, 1990.

———. *Titan: The Life of John D. Rockefeller.* New York: Random House, 1997.

Chernyaev, Anatoly. *My Six Years with Gorbachev.* University Park: Pennsylvania State University, 2000.

Chittenden, L. E. *Recollections of President Lincoln and His Administration.* New York: Harper, 1891.

Churchill, Winston. *The Second World War.* Boston: Houghton Mifflin, 1948–1953.

Clifford, Clark, with Richard Holbrooke. *Counsel to the President: A Memoir.* New York: Random House, 1991.

Cockburn, Alexander, and Leslie Cockburn. *Dangerous Liaison: The Inside Story of the U.S.-Israeli Covert Relationship.* New York: HarperCollins, 1991.

Cohen, Michael. *Truman and Israel.* Berkeley: University of California, 1990.

Cole, Donald. *A Jackson Man: Amos Kendall and the Rise of American Democracy.* Baton Rouge: Louisiana State University, 2004.

———. *Martin Van Buren and the American Political System.* Princeton: Princeton University, 1984.

Cole, Wayne. *Roosevelt and the Isolationists, 1932–45.* Lincoln: University of Nebraska, 1983.

Collier, Peter, and David Horowitz. *The Roosevelts: An American Saga.* New York: Simon & Schuster, 1994.

Combs, Jerald. *The Jay Treaty: Political Battleground of the Founding Fathers.* Berkeley: University of California, 1970.

Congress Hall. Washington, D.C.: U.S. Government Printing Office, 1990.

Cook, Blanche Wiesen. *Eleanor Roosevelt.* New York: Viking, 1992, 1999.

Cooling, Benjamin. *Jubal Early's Raid on Washington, 1864.* Baltimore: Nautical & Aviation, 1989.

Correspondence of John Adams and William Cunningham. Boston: True & Greene, 1823.

Croly, Herbert David. *Marcus Alonzo Hanna: His Life and His Work.* Hamden, Ct.: Archon, 1965.

Cullen, Charles, ed. *The Papers of John Marshall,* vol. 4. Chapel Hill: University of North Carolina, 1984.

Cuomo, Mario, and Harold Holzer. *Lincoln on Democracy.* New York: HarperCollins, 1990.

Dallek, Robert. *An Unfinished Life: John F. Kennedy, 1917–1963.* New York: Little, Brown, 2003.

Dalton, Kathleen. *Theodore Roosevelt: A Strenuous Life.* New York: Knopf, 2002.

Dalzell, Robert, and Lee Dalzell. *George Washington's Mount Vernon: At Home in Revolutionary America.* New York: Oxford, 1998.

Daniels, Jonathan. *The Man of Independence.* Philadelphia: Lippincott, 1950.

———. *Washington Quadrille: The Dance Beside the Documents.* Garden City, N.Y.: Doubleday, 1968.

———. *White House Witness: 1942–1945.* New York: Doubleday, 1978.

Davis, Kenneth. *F.D.R.: Into the Storm, 1937–1940*. New York: Random House, 1993.

Davis, Patti. *The Way I See It: An Autobiography*. New York: Putnam, 1992.

Davis, Sammy, Jr., and Jane and Burt Boyar. *Sammy: An Autobiography*. New York: Farrar, Straus, 2000.

Deaver, Michael. *Behind the Scenes*. New York: Morrow, 1988.

———. *A Different Drummer: My Thirty Years with Ronald Reagan*. New York: Harper-Collins, 2001.

DeConde, Alexander. *Entangling Alliance: Politics and Diplomacy Under George Washington*. Durham, N.C.: Duke University, 1958.

———. *The Quasi-War: The Politics and Diplomacy of the Undeclared War with France, 1797–1881*. New York: Scribners, 1966.

Dennett, Tyler. *John Hay: From Poetry to Politics*. New York: Dodd, Mead, 1933.

Dennett, Tyler, ed. *Lincoln and the Civil War in the Diaries and Letters of John Hay*. New York: Dodd, Mead, 1939.

Depew, Chauncey. *My Memories of Eighty Years*. New York: Scribners, 1924.

Detzer, Karl. *Carl Sandburg: A Study in Personality and Background*. New York: Harcourt, 1941.

Dictionary of American Biography. New York: Scribner, 1946–1958.

Diggins, John Patrick. *John Adams*. New York: Times Books, 2003.

———. *The Portable John Adams*. New York: Penguin, 2004.

Divine, Robert. *Foreign Policy and U.S. Presidential Elections, 1940–1948*. New York: New Viewpoints, 1974.

Dobrynin, Anatoly. *In Confidence: Moscow's Ambassador to Six Cold War Presidents*. New York: Times Books, 1995.

Dodge, Daniel Kilham. *Abraham Lincoln: The Evolution of His Literary Style*. Urbana: University of Illinois, 2000.

Donald, David Herbert. *Lincoln*. New York: Simon & Schuster, 1995.

———. *We Are Lincoln Men*. New York: Simon & Schuster, 2003.

Donovan, Robert. *The Presidency of Harry S. Truman*. New York: Norton, 1977, 1981.

Doyle, William. *An American Insurrection: The Battle of Oxford, Mississippi, 1962*. New York: Doubleday, 2001.

———. *Inside the White House: The White House Tapes from FDR to Clinton*. New York: Kodansha, 2002.

Duane, William. *Narrative and Correspondence Concerning the Removal of the Deposits*. Philadelphia, 1838.

Dubovsky, Melvyn, and Warren Van Tine. *John L. Lewis: A Biography*. New York: Quadrangle, 1977.

Dunn, Susan. *Jefferson's Second Revolution: The Election Crisis of 1800 and the Triumph of Republicanism*. Boston: Houghton Mifflin, 2004.

Eban, Abba. *An Autobiography*. New York: Random House, 1977.

Eisenhower, Dwight. *Mandate for Change*. Garden City, N.Y.: Doubleday, 1963.

Elath, Eliahu. *Zionism at the U.N.: A Diary of the First Days*. Philadelphia: Jewish Publication Society, 1976.

Elkins, Stanley, and Eric McKitrick. *The Age of Federalism: The Early American Republic, 1788–1800*. New York: Oxford, 1993.

Ellis, Joseph. *Founding Brothers: The Revolutionary Generation.* New York: Knopf, 2000.

———. *His Excellency: George Washington.* New York: Knopf, 2004.

———. *Passionate Sage: The Character and Legacy of John Adams.* New York: Norton, 1993.

Elsey, George. *An Unplanned Life: A Memoir.* Columbia: University of Missouri, 2005.

Ewald, William Bragg. *Eisenhower the President.* Englewood Cliffs, N.J.: Prentice Hall, 1981.

Farrell, John. *Tip O'Neill and the Democratic Century.* Boston: Little, Brown, 2001.

Fehrenbacher, Don, and Virginia Fehrenbacher, eds. *Recollected Words of Abraham Lincoln.* Stanford, Cal.: Stanford University, 1996.

Felsenthal, Carol. *Princess Alice: The Life and Times of Alice Roosevelt Longworth.* New York: St. Martin's, 1989.

Ferling, John. *Adams vs. Jefferson: The Tumultuous Election of 1800.* New York: Oxford, 2004.

———. *The First of Men: A Life of George Washington.* Knoxville: University of Tennessee, 1988.

———. *John Adams: A Life.* Knoxville: University of Tennessee, 1992.

Ferrell, Robert. *Harry S. Truman: A Life.* Columbia: University of Missouri, 1994.

Ferrell, Robert, ed. *Dear Bess: The Letters from Harry to Bess Truman, 1910–1959.* New York: Norton, 1983.

———. *Off the Record: The Private Papers of Harry S. Truman.* New York: Harper, 1980.

Fields, Joseph. *Worthy Partner: The Papers of Martha Washington.* Westport, Ct.: Greenwood, 1994.

FitzGerald, Frances. *Way Out There in the Blue.* New York: Simon & Schuster, 2001.

Fitzpatrick, John. *George Washington Himself: A Common-Sense Biography Written from His Manuscripts.* Indianapolis: Bobbs-Merrill, 1933.

Fitzpatrick, John, ed. *The Writings of George Washington,* vols. 34–36. Washington, D.C.: U.S. Government Printing Office, 1940–1941.

Flexner, James Thomas. *George Washington: Anguish and Farewell, 1793–1799.* Boston: Little, Brown, 1972.

———. *The Young Hamilton: A Biography.* Boston: Little, Brown, 1978.

Foner, Eric. *Reconstruction: America's Unfinished Revolution, 1863–1877.* New York: Harper, 1988.

Frantz, Douglas, and David McKean. *Friends in High Places: The Rise and Fall of Clark Clifford.* Boston: Little, Brown, 1995.

Freeman, Douglas Southall. *Washington.* Abridged edition. New York: Scribners, 1975.

Gaddis, John Lewis. *The Cold War: A New History.* New York: Penguin, 2005.

Gallup, George. *The Gallup Poll: Public Opinion, 1935–1971.* New York: Random House, 1972.

Gammon, Samuel. *The Presidential Campaign of 1832.* Baltimore: Johns Hopkins University, 1922.

Garraty, John. *Henry Cabot Lodge: A Biography.* New York: Knopf, 1953.

Garrow, David. *Bearing the Cross: Martin Luther King, Jr., and the Southern Christian Leadership Conference.* New York: Morrow, 1986.

Garthoff, Raymond. *The Great Transition: American-Soviet Relations and the End of the Cold War.* Washington, D.C.: Brookings, 1994.

Gentry, Curt. *J. Edgar Hoover: The Man and the Secrets.* New York: Norton, 1991.

Gibbs, George. *Memoirs of the Administrations of Washington and John Adams: Edited from the Papers of Oliver Wolcott.* New York, 1846.

Gilbert, Martin. *Israel: A History.* New York: Morrow, 1998.

Gilmore, James. *Personal Recollections of Abraham Lincoln and the Civil War.* Boston: Page, 1898.

Golden, Harry. *Carl Sandburg.* Urbana: University of Illinois, 1988.

Goodhart, Philip. *Fifty Ships That Saved the World: The Foundation of the Anglo-American Alliance.* Garden City, N.Y.: Doubleday, 1965.

Goodwin, Doris Kearns. *No Ordinary Time: Franklin and Eleanor Roosevelt: The Home Front in World War II.* New York: Simon & Schuster, 1994.

———. *Team of Rivals: The Political Genius of Abraham Lincoln.* New York: Simon & Schuster, 2005.

Gorbachev, Mikhail. *Memoirs.* New York: Doubleday, 1995.

Gould, Lewis. *The Presidency of Theodore Roosevelt.* Lawrence: University Press of Kansas, 1991.

Govan, Thomas. *Nicholas Biddle: Nationalist and Public Banker, 1786–1844.* Chicago: University of Chicago, 1959.

Great Men and Famous Women. New York: Selmer Hess, 1894.

Gregory, Dick. *Callus on My Soul: A Memoir.* Atlanta: Longstreet, 2000.

Grimsley, Mark, and Brooks D. Simpson, eds. *The Collapse of the Confederacy.* Lincoln: University of Nebraska, 2001.

Gromyko, Andrei. *Memoirs.* New York: Doubleday, 1989.

Grose, Peter. *Israel in the Mind of America.* New York: Schocken, 1983.

Gruber, Ruth. *Exodus 1947: The Ship That Launched a Nation.* New York: Crown, 1999.

Guelzo, Allen. *Abraham Lincoln: Redeemer President.* Grand Rapids, Mich.: Eerdmans, 2003.

———. *Lincoln's Emancipation Proclamation: The End of Slavery in America.* New York: Simon & Schuster, 2004.

Guthman, Edwin. *We Band of Brothers: A Memoir of Robert F. Kennedy.* New York: Harper, 1971.

Hahn, Peter. *Caught in the Middle East: U.S. Policies Toward the Arab-Israeli Conflict.* Chapel Hill: University of North Carolina, 2004.

Haig, Alexander. *Caveat: Realism, Reagan and Foreign Policy.* New York: Scribners, 1984.

Hale, William. *Horace Greeley: Voice of the People.* New York: Harper, 1950.

Hamby, Alonzo. *Man of the People: A Life of Harry S. Truman.* New York: Oxford, 1995.

Hamilton, James A. *Reminiscences on Men and Events.* New York: Scribner, 1869.

Hammond, Bray. *Banks and Politics in America: From the Revolution to the Civil War.* Princeton: Princeton University, 1957.

Hammond, John. *Quaint and Historic Forts of North America.* Philadelphia: Lippincott, 1918.

Harbaugh, William. *The Life and Times of Theodore Roosevelt.* New York: Oxford, 1975.

Hay, John. *Lincoln and the Civil War.* Tyler Dennett, ed. New York: Dodd, Mead, 1939.

Helm, Katherine. *The True Story of Mary, Wife of Lincoln.* New York: Harper, 1928.

Henriques, Peter. *Realistic Visionary: A Portrait of George Washington.* Charlottesville: University of Virginia, 2006.

Hersh, Seymour. *The Samson Option: Israel's Nuclear Arsenal and American Foreign Policy.* New York: Random House, 1991.

Hibben, Paxton. *The Peerless Leader: William Jennings Bryan.* New York: Farrar & Rinehart, 1929.

Higham, Charles. *American Swastika.* Garden City, N.Y.: Doubleday, 1985.

Hill, Peter. *William Vans Murray, Federalist Diplomat: The Shaping of Peace with France, 1797–1801.* Syracuse, N.Y.: Syracuse University, 1971.

Hilty, James. *Robert Kennedy: Brother Protector.* Philadelphia: Temple University, 1997.

Hone, Philip. *The Diary of Philip Hone.* New York: Dodd, Mead, 1936.

Humes, James. *Confessions of a White House Ghostwriter: Five Presidents and Other Political Adventures.* Washington, D.C.: Regnery, 1997.

Huntzicker, William. *The Popular Press: 1833–1865.* Troy, Mo.: Greenwood, 1999.

Irwin, Will, ed. *Letters to Kermit from Theodore Roosevelt: 1902–1908.* New York: Scribners, 1946.

Isaacson, Walter, and Evan Thomas. *The Wise Men: Six Friends and the World They Made.* New York: Simon & Schuster, 1986.

Israel, Fred, ed. *The War Diary of Breckinridge Long.* Lincoln: University of Nebraska, 1967.

Jackson, Donald, and Dorothy Twohig. *The Diaries of George Washington,* vol. 6. Charlottesville: University Press of Virginia, 1979.

Jackson, Robert. *That Man: An Insider's Portrait of Franklin D. Roosevelt.* Edited by John Q. Barrett. New York: Oxford, 2003.

James, Marquis. *The Life of Andrew Jackson.* Indianapolis: Bobbs-Merrill, 1938.

Janeway, Michael. *The Fall of the House of Roosevelt: Brokers of Ideas and Power from FDR to LBJ.* New York: Columbia University, 2004.

Jordan, Hamilton. *Crisis: The Last Year of the Carter Presidency.* New York: Putnam, 1982.

Kazin, Michael. *A Godly Hero: The Life of William Jennings Bryan.* New York: Knopf, 2006.

Keckley, Elizabeth. *Behind the Scenes: Thirty Years a Slave and Four Years in the White House.* Chicago: Lakeside, 1988.

Kendall, Amos. *Autobiography of Amos Kendall.* Boston: Lee & Shepard, 1872.

Kengor, Paul. *The Crusader: Ronald Reagan and the Fall of Communism.* New York: Regan, 2006.

————. *God and Ronald Reagan: A Spiritual Life.* New York: Regan, 2004.

Kennedy, David. *Freedom from Fear: The American People in Depression and War, 1929–1945.* New York: Oxford, 2001.

Kennedy, John F. *Profiles in Courage.* New York: HarperCollins, 2003.

Kennedy, Rose Fitzgerald. *Times to Remember.* Garden City, N.Y.: Doubleday, 1974.

Ketchum, Ralph. *James Madison.* New York: Macmillan, 1971.

Kimball, Warren. *Forged in War: Churchill, Roosevelt and the Second World War.* New York: HarperCollins, 1997.

Kimmel, Stanley. *The Mad Booths of Maryland.* Indianapolis: Bobbs-Merrill, 1940.

King, Coretta Scott. *My Life with Martin Luther King.* New York: Holt, 1993.

King, Martin Luther, Jr. *A Testament of Hope: The Essential Writings of Martin Luther King, Jr.* New York: HarperCollins, 1986.

————. *The Autobiography of Martin Luther King, Jr.* Edited by Clayborne Carson. New York: Warner, 2001.

Kirkland, Edward. *The Peacemakers of 1864.* New York: Macmillan, 1927.

Klein, Maury. *The Life and Legend of E. H. Harriman.* Chapel Hill: University of North Carolina, 2000.

Koskoff, David. *Joseph P. Kennedy: A Life and Times.* Englewood Cliffs, N.J.: Prentice Hall, 1974.

Krock, Arthur. *Memoirs: Sixty Years on the Firing Line.* New York: Funk & Wagnalls, 1968.

Kuhn, Jim. *Ronald Reagan in Private: A Memoir of My Years in the White House.* New York: Sentinel, 2004.

Kurzman, Dan. *Genesis 1948: The First Arab-Israeli War.* New York: Da Capo, 1992.

Laas, Virginia, ed. *Wartime Washington: The Civil War Letters of Elizabeth Blair Lee.* Urbana: University of Illinois, 1991.

Lamon, Ward Hill. *Recollections of Abraham Lincoln: 1847–1865.* Lincoln: University of Nebraska, 1994.

Lash, Joseph. *Eleanor and Franklin: The Story of Their Relationship Based on Eleanor Roosevelt's Private Papers.* New York: Norton, 1971.

————. *Love, Eleanor: Eleanor Roosevelt and Her Friends.* New York: Doubleday, 1982.

————. *A World of Love: Eleanor Roosevelt and Her Friends, 1943–1962.* Garden City, N.Y.: Doubleday, 1984.

Latner, Richard. *The Presidency of Andrew Jackson.* Athens: University of Georgia, 1979.

Leech, Margaret. *In the Days of McKinley.* New York: Harper, 1959.

Lettow, Paul. *Ronald Reagan and His Quest to Abolish Nuclear Weapons.* New York: Random House, 2005.

Levenson, J. C., Ernest Samuels, Charles Vandersee, and Viola Winner, eds. *The Letters of Henry Adams.* Vols. 4–6. Cambridge, Mass.: Belknap, 1989.

Lewis, David Levering. *King: A Critical Biography.* Chicago: University of Illinois, 1970.

Lewis, Lloyd. *Sherman, Fighting Prophet.* New York: Harcourt, 1932.

Lodge, Henry Cabot, ed. *Works of Alexander Hamilton.* New York: Putnam, 1904.

Long, Breckinridge. *The War Diary of Breckinridge Long.* Edited by Fred Israel. Lincoln: University of Nebraska, 1966.

Long, David E. *The Jewel of Liberty: Abraham Lincoln's Re-Election and the End of Slavery.* Harrisburg, Penn.: Stackpole, 1994.

Long, E. B. *The Civil War Day by Day: An Almanac, 1861–1865.* Garden City, N.Y.: Doubleday, 1971.

Lorant, Stefan. *The Life and Times of Theodore Roosevelt.* Garden City, N.Y.: Doubleday, 1959.

MacKaye, Percy. *Epoch: The Life of Steele Mackaye.* New York: Boni & Liveright, 1927.

Manchester, William. *The Death of a President: November 20–25, 1963.* New York: Harper, 1967.

Martin, Albro. *James J. Hill and the Opening of the Northwest.* New York: Oxford, 1976.

Martin, John Bartlow. *Adlai Stevenson and the World.* New York: Doubleday, 1976.

Matlock, Jack. *Reagan and Gorbachev: How the Cold War Ended.* New York: Random House, 2004.

McClellan, George B. *McClellan's Own Story.* New York: Charles Webster, 1887.

McCullough, David. *John Adams.* New York: Simon & Schuster, 2001.

———. *Mornings on Horseback.* New York: Simon & Schuster, 1981.

———. *Truman.* New York: Simon & Schuster, 1992.

McDonald, Forrest. *The Presidency of George Washington.* Lawrence: University Press of Kansas, 1974.

McDonald, James. *My Mission in Israel, 1948–1951.* New York: Simon & Schuster, 1951.

McFarlane, Robert, with Zofia Smardz. *Special Trust.* New York: Cadell & Davies, 1994.

McFaul, John. *The Politics of Jacksonian Finance.* Ithaca, N.Y.: Cornell University, 1972.

McGerr, Michael. *The Fierce Discontent: The Rise and Fall of the Progressive Movement in America.* New York: Free Press, 2003.

McGrane, Reginald, ed. *The Correspondence of Nicholas Biddle.* Boston: Houghton Mifflin, 1919.

McMillan, Priscilla Johnson. *Marina and Lee.* New York: Harper, 1977.

McPherson, James. *Battle Cry of Freedom: The Era of the Civil War.* New York: Oxford, 1988.

McWhorter, Diane. *Carry Me Home: Birmingham, Alabama: The Climactic Battle of the Civil Rights Revolution.* New York: Simon & Schuster, 2001.

Meacham, Jon. *Franklin and Winston: An Intimate Portrait of an Epic Friendship.* New York: Random House, 2003.

Merkley, Paul. *The Politics of Christian Zionism.* London: Frank Cass, 1998.

Mieczkowski, Yanek. *The Routledge Historical Atlas of Presidential Elections.* New York: Routledge, 2001.

Miller, Merle. *Plain Speaking: An Oral Biography of Harry S. Truman.* New York: Putnam, 1973.

Miller, Nathan. *Theodore Roosevelt: A Life.* New York: Morrow, 1992.

Miller, Richard. *Harry S. Truman: The Rise to Power.* New York: McGraw-Hill, 1986.

Mitchell, Stuart, ed. *New Letters of Abigail Adams.* Boston: Houghton Mifflin, 1947.

Mitgang, Herbert. *The Letters of Carl Sandburg.* New York: Harcourt, 1965.

Monaghan, Jay. *Diplomat in Carpet Slippers: Abraham Lincoln Deals with Foreign Affairs.* Indianapolis: Bobbs-Merrill, 1945.

Morgan, H. Wayne. *William McKinley and His America.* Kent, Ohio: Kent State University, 2003.

Morgan. Ted. *FDR: A Biography.* New York: Simon & Schuster, 1986.

Morgenthau, Henry III. *Mostly Morgenthaus.* Boston: Ticknor & Fields, 1988.

Morison, Elting, ed. *The Letters of Theodore Roosevelt,* vols. 2–7. Cambridge, Mass.: Harvard University, 1951–1954.

Morison, Samuel Eliot, Henry Steele Commager, and William Leuchtenburg. *The Growth of the American Republic.* New York: Oxford, 1980.

Morris, Edmund. *Dutch: A Memoir of Ronald Reagan.* New York: Random House, 1999.

———. *The Rise of Theodore Roosevelt.* New York: Coward, McCann, 1979.

———. *Theodore Rex.* New York: Random House, 2001.

Morris, Sylvia Jukes. *Edith Kermit Roosevelt: Portrait of a First Lady.* New York: Coward, McCann, 1980.

———. *Rage for Fame: The Ascent of Clare Boothe Luce.* New York: Random House, 1997.

Moser, Harold, and J. Clint Clifft. *The Papers of Andrew Jackson.* Knoxville: University of Tennessee, 2002.

Moss, Norman. *19 Weeks: America, Britain and the Fateful Summer of 1940.* Boston: Houghton Mifflin, 2003.

Munroe, John. *Louis McLane: Federalist and Jacksonian.* New Brunswick, N.J.: Rutgers University, 1973.

Murray, William Vans. *Letters of William Vans Murray to John Quincy Adams, 1797–1803.* Washington, D.C., 1914.

Nagel, Paul. *John Quincy Adams: A Public Life, a Private Life.* New York: Knopf, 1997.

Navasky, Victor. *Kennedy Justice.* New York: Atheneum, 1972.

Neal, Steve. *Dark Horse: A Biography of Wendell Willkie.* New York: Doubleday, 1984.

Neely, Mark. *The Last Best Hope of Earth: Abraham Lincoln and the Promise of America.* Cambridge, Mass.: Harvard University, 1993.

Newton, Joseph. *Lincoln and Herndon.* Cedar Rapids, Ia.: Torch, 1910.

Nicolay, Helen. *Lincoln's Secretary: A Biography of John G. Nicolay.* New York: Longmans, 1949.

Nicolay, John C., and John Hay. *Abraham Lincoln: A History.* New York: Century, 1890.

Nicolay, John C., and John Hay, eds. *Complete Works of Abraham Lincoln.* New York: F. D. Tandy, 1905.

Niven, John. *Martin Van Buren: The Romantic Age of American Politics.* New York: Oxford, 1983.

Niven, Penelope. *Carl Sandburg: A Biography.* New York: Scribner, 1991.

Nixon, Richard. *The Real War.* New York: Warner, 1980.

Noonan, Peggy. *What I Saw at the Revolution: A Political Life in the Reagan Era.* New York: Random House, 1990.

———. *When Character Was King: A Story of Ronald Reagan.* New York: Viking, 2001.

Nossiter, Adam. *Of Long Memory: Mississippi and the Murder of Medgar Evers.* New York: Perseus, 1994.

Oberdorfer, Don. *The Turn: From the Cold War to a New Era.* New York: Poseidon, 1991.

Oberg, Barbara, ed. *The Papers of Thomas Jefferson.* Princeton: Princeton University, 1950–2006.

O'Brien, Michael. *John F. Kennedy: A Biography.* New York: Thomas Dunne, 2005.

O'Toole, Patricia. *The Five of Hearts: An Intimate Portrait of Henry Adams and His Friends, 1880–1918.* New York: Clarkson Potter, 1990.

Parmet, Herbert. *Jack: The Struggles of John F. Kennedy.* New York: Dial, 1980.

———. *JFK: The Presidency of John F. Kennedy.* New York: Dial, 1983.

Parsons, Jacob Cox, ed. *The Diary of Jacob Hiltzheimer.* Philadelphia: William F. Fell, 1893.

Parton, James. *The Life and Times of Aaron Burr.* New York: Mason Brothers, 1858.

———. *Life of Andrew Jackson.* 3 vols. New York: Mason Brothers, 1860–1861. Cited as Parton I, II, and III.

Patterson, James. *Grand Expectations: The United States, 1945–1974.* New York: Oxford, 1996.

Pedersen, William, and Frank Williams, eds. *Franklin D. Roosevelt and Abraham Lincoln: Competing Perspectives on Two Great Presidencies.* Armonk, N.Y.: M. E. Sharpe, 2002.

Persico, Joseph. *Roosevelt's Secret War: FDR and World War II Espionage.* New York: Random House, 2001.

Pessen, Edward. *Jacksonian America: Society, Personality and Politics.* Homewood, Ill.: Dorsey, 1969.

Peters, Charles. *Five Days in Philadelphia: The Amazing "We Want Willkie" Convention of 1940 and How It Freed FDR to Save the Western World.* New York: PublicAffairs, 2005.

Peterson, Merrill. *The Great Triumvirate: Webster, Clay and Calhoun.* New York: Oxford, 1987.

———. *Lincoln in American Memory.* New York: Oxford, 1994.

Pickering, Octavius, and C. W. Upham. *The Life of Timothy Pickering.* Boston: Little Brown, 1867–1873.

Pickering, Timothy. *A Review of the Correspondence Between John Adams and William Cunningham.* Salem, Mass.: Cushing & Appleton, 1824.

Pinsker, Matthew. *Lincoln's Sanctuary: Abraham Lincoln and the Soldiers' Home.* New York: Oxford, 2003.

Pogue, Forrest. *George C. Marshall.* New York: Viking, 1963, 1968, 1989.

Poore, Ben Perley. *Reminiscences of Sixty Years in the National Metropolis.* Philadelphia, 1886.

Potter, Jeffrey. *Men, Money and Magic: The Story of Dorothy Schiff.* New York: Putnam, 1976.

Pottker, Jan. *Sara and Eleanor.* New York: St. Martin's, 2004.

Powaski, Ronald. *Return to Armageddon: The United States and the Nuclear Arms Race, 1981–1999.* New York: Oxford, 2000.

Powell, Colin, with Joseph Persico. *My American Journey.* New York: Random House, 1995.

Pringle, Henry. *Theodore Roosevelt: A Biography.* New York: Harcourt, Brace, 1931.

Quarles, Benjamin. *Negro Soldier in the Civil War.* Boston: Little, Brown, 1953.

Rakove, Jack. *James Madison and the Creation of the American Republic.* New York: Longman, 2002.

Rampersad, Arnold. *Jackie Robinson: A Biography.* New York: Knopf, 1997.

Randall, J. G., and Richard Current. *Lincoln the President: Midstream to the Last Full Measure.* New York: Da Capo, 1997.

Randall, Ruth Painter. *Mary Lincoln: Biography of a Marriage.* Boston: Little, Brown, 1953.

Randolph, Edmund. *A Vindication of Mr. Randolph's Resignation.* Philadelphia: Samuel H. Smith, 1795.

Reagan, Nancy. *My Turn: The Memoirs of Nancy Reagan.* New York: Random House, 1989.

Reagan, Ronald. *An American Life.* New York: Simon & Schuster, 1990.

Reardon, John. *Edmund Randolph: A Biography.* New York: Macmillan, 1974.

Reeves, Richard. *President Kennedy: Profile of Power.* New York: Simon & Schuster, 1993.

———. *President Reagan: The Triumph of Imagination.* New York: Simon & Schuster, 2005.

Regan, Donald. *For the Record: From Wall Street to Washington.* San Diego: Harcourt, 1988.

Reilly, Michael. *Reilly of the White House.* New York: Simon & Schuster, 1947.

Reisner, Christian. *Roosevelt's Religion.* New York: Abingdon, 1922.

Remini, Robert. *Andrew Jackson and the Bank War: A Study in the Growth of Presidential Power.* New York: Norton, 1967.

———. *Andrew Jackson and the Course of American Democracy, 1833–1845.* New York: Harper, 1984. Cited as Remini III.

———. *Andrew Jackson and the Course of American Empire, 1767–1821.* New York: Harper, 1977. Cited as Remini I.

———. *Andrew Jackson and the Course of American Freedom, 1822–1832.* New York: Harper, 1981. Cited as Remini II.

———. *Daniel Webster: The Man and His Time.* New York: Norton, 1997.

———. *The Election of Andrew Jackson.* Philadelphia: Lippincott, 1963.

———. *Henry Clay: Statesman for the Union.* New York: Norton, 1991.

———. *The Life of Andrew Jackson.* HarperPerennial, 2001. Cited as Remini (Abridged).

Renehan, Edward. *The Lion's Pride: Theodore Roosevelt and His Family in Peace and War.* New York: Oxford, 1998.

Reston, James, Jr. *The Lone Star: The Life of John Connally.* New York: Harper, 1989.

Robinson, Corinne Roosevelt. *My Brother Theodore Roosevelt*. New York: Scribners, 1923.

Robinson, Peter. *How Ronald Reagan Changed My Life*. New York: Regan, 2003.

Rogow, Arnold. *A Fatal Friendship: Alexander Hamilton and Aaron Burr*. New York: Hill & Wang, 1998.

Roosevelt, James, and Sidney Shalett. *Affectionately, F.D.R.: A Son's Story of a Lonely Man*. New York: Harcourt, 1959.

Roosevelt, Theodore. *An Autobiography*. New York: Scribner's, 1920.

———. *Life of Thomas Hart Benton*. Boston: Houghton Mifflin, 1887.

———. *The Winning of the West*, vol. 4. Lincoln: University of Nebraska, 1995.

Rosenberg, Jonathan, and Zachary Karabell. *Kennedy, Johnson and the Quest for Justice: The Civil Rights Tapes*. New York: Norton, 2003.

Rosenman, Samuel. *Working with Roosevelt*. New York: Harper, 1962.

Rusk, Dean. *As I Saw It*. New York: Norton, 1990.

Rusling, James. *Men and Things I Saw in Civil War Days*. New York: Eaton & Mans, 1899.

Russell, Francis. *The President Makers: From Mark Hanna to Joseph P. Kennedy*. Boston: Little, Brown, 1976.

Safire, William. *Safire's New Political Dictionary: The Definitive Guide to the New Language of Politics*. New York: Random House, 1993.

Samuels, Peggy and Harold. *Remembering the Maine*. Washington, D.C.: Smithsonian, 1995.

Sandburg, Carl, and Paul Angle. *Mary Lincoln: Wife and Widow*. New York: Harcourt, 1932.

Schlesinger, Arthur, Jr. *The Age of Jackson*. Boston: Little, Brown, 1945.

———. *The Coming of the New Deal*. Boston: Houghton Mifflin, 1959.

———. *Crisis of the Old Order: 1919–1933*. Boston: Houghton Mifflin, 1957.

———. *History of U.S. Political Parties*. New York: Chelsea House, 1981.

———. *Robert Kennedy and His Times*. Boston: Houghton Mifflin, 1978.

———. *A Thousand Days: John F. Kennedy in the White House*. Boston: Houghton Mifflin, 1965.

Schlesinger, Arthur, Jr., and Fred Israel. *History of American Presidential Elections*. New York: Chelsea House, 1985.

Schultz, John, and Douglass Adair, eds. *Spur of Fame: Dialogues of John Adams and Benjamin Rush*. San Marino, Calif.: Huntington Library, 1966.

Schurz, Carl. *Reminiscences*. New York: McClure, 1907.

Schwartz, Philip, ed. *Slavery at the Home of George Washington*. Mount Vernon, Va.: Mount Vernon Ladies' Association, 2001.

Schweizer, Peter. *Reagan's War: The Epic Story of His Forty-Year Struggle and Final Victory over Communism*. New York: Doubleday, 2002.

Seager, Robert II, ed. *The Papers of Henry Clay*, vol. 8. Lexington: University Press of Kentucky, 1984.

Seale, William. *The President's House: A History*. Washington, D.C.: White House Historical Association, 1986.

Sears, Stephen. *George B. McClellan: The Young Napoleon*. Boston: Ticknor & Fields, 1988.

Sears, Stephen, ed. *The Civil War Papers of George B. McClellan*. New York: Ticknor & Fields, 1989.

Shahak, Israel. *Jewish History, Jewish Religion*. London: Pluto, 1994.

Shaw, Peter. *The Character of John Adams*. Chapel Hill: University of North Carolina, 1976.

Shenk, Joshua Wolf. *Lincoln's Melancholy: How Depression Challenged a President and Fueled His Greatness*. Boston: Houghton Mifflin, 1985.

Sherman, William T. *Personal Memoirs*. New York: Appleton, 1886.

Sherwood, Robert. *Roosevelt and Hopkins: An Intimate History*. New York: Harper, 1948.

Shevardnadze, Eduard. *The Future Belongs to Freedom*. New York: Free Press, 1991.

Shogan, Robert. *Hard Bargain*. Boulder, Colo.: Westview, 1999.

Shultz, George. *Turmoil and Triumph: My Years as Secretary of State*. New York: Scribners, 1993.

Simon, John Y., ed. *The Papers of Ulysses Grant*. Carbondale: Southern Illinois University, 1967–2003.

Skinner, Kiron, Annelise Anderson and Martin Anderson. *Reagan: A Life in Letters*. New York: Free Press, 2003.

Smith, Elbert. *Francis Preston Blair*. New York: Free Press, 1980.

Smith, Jean Edward. *John Marshall: Definer of a Nation*. New York: Holt, 1996.

Smith, John David, ed. *Black Soldiers in Blue: African American Troops in the Civil War Era*. Chapel Hill: University of North Carolina, 2002.

Smith, Page. *John Adams*. Garden City, N.Y.: Doubleday, 1962.

Smith, Richard Norton. *Patriarch: George Washington and the New American Nation*. Boston: Houghton Mifflin, 1993.

———. *Thomas E. Dewey and His Times*. New York: Simon & Schuster, 1982.

Smith, Sally Bedell. *Grace and Power: The Private World of the Kennedy White House*. New York: Simon & Schuster, 2004.

Smith, William. *The Francis Preston Blair Family in Politics*. New York: Macmillan, 1933.

Snetsinger, John. *Truman, the Jewish Vote, and the Creation of Israel*. Stanford, Calif.: Hoover Institution, 1974.

Sorensen, Theodore. *Kennedy*. New York: Harper, 1965.

Speakes, Larry. *Speaking Out: Inside the Reagan White House*. New York: Scribners, 1988.

Stahr, Walter. *John Jay: Founding Father*. New York: Hambledon & London, 2005.

Steinberg, Alfred. *The Man from Missouri: The Life and Times of Harry S. Truman*. New York: Putnam, 1962.

Stewart, Donald. *Opposition Press of the Federalist Period*. Albany: State University Press of New York, 1969.

Stimson, Henry, and McGeorge Bundy. *On Active Service in Peace and War*. New York: Harper, 1947.

Stoddard, Henry. *Horace Greeley: Printer, Editor, Crusader.* New York: Putnam, 1946.

Stossel, Scott. *Sarge: The Life and Times of Sargent Shriver.* Washington: Smithsonian, 2004.

Strober, Gerald, and Deborah Strober. *Reagan: The Man and His Presidency.* Boston: Houghton Mifflin, 1998.

Strouse, Jean. *Morgan: American Financier.* New York: Random House, 1999.

Sullivan, Mark. *Our Times: The United States, 1900–1925.* New York: Scribners, 1930.

Syrett, Harold, ed. *Papers of Alexander Hamilton.* New York: Columbia University, 1961–1987.

Tarbell, Ida. *The Life of Abraham Lincoln.* New York: Lincoln Historical Society, 1908.

Teague, Michael. *Mrs. L.* New York: Doubleday, 1981.

Thayer, William Roscoe. *The Life of John Hay.* Boston: Houghton Mifflin, 1915.

———. *Theodore Roosevelt: An Intimate Biography.* Boston: Houghton Mifflin, 1919.

Thomas, Benjamin. *Abraham Lincoln: A Biography.* New York: Knopf, 1952.

Thomas, Benjamin P., and Harold Hyman. *Stanton: The Life and Times of Lincoln's Secretary of War.* New York: Knopf, 1962.

Thomas, Evan. *Robert Kennedy: His Life.* New York: Simon & Schuster, 2000.

Trefousse, Hans. *Andrew Johnson: A Biography.* New York: Norton, 1989.

———. *Thaddeus Stevens.* Chapel Hill: University of North Carolina, 1997.

Trohan, Walter. *Political Animals.* New York: Doubleday, 1975.

Truman, Harry S. *Memoirs.* Garden City, N.Y.: Doubleday, 1955, 1956.

Truman, Margaret. *Bess W. Truman.* New York: Macmillan, 1986.

———. *Harry S. Truman.* New York: Morrow, 1972.

———. *Where the Buck Stops: The Personal and Private Writings of Harry S. Truman.* New York: Warner, 1989.

Tully, Grace. *F.D.R., My Boss.* New York: Scribners, 1949.

Turner, Justin, and Linda Levitt, eds. *Mary Todd Lincoln: Her Life and Letters.* New York: Knopf, 1972.

Twohig, Dorothy, ed. *The Papers of George Washington: Retirement Series,* vols. 1–3. Charlottesville: University of Virginia, 1998–1999.

Van Buren, Martin. *The Autobiography of Martin Van Buren.* Washington, D.C.: U.S. Government Printing Office, 1920.

Van Deusen, Glyndon. *The Jacksonian Era.* New York: Harper, 1959.

Vidal, Gore. *Palimpsest: A Memoir.* New York: Random House, 1995.

Wallace, Paul. *The Muhlenbergs of Pennsylvania.* Philadelphia: University of Pennsylvania, 1950.

Ward, Geoffrey. *Before the Trumpet: Young Franklin Roosevelt, 1882.* New York: Harper, 1985.

———. *A First-Class Temperament: The Emergence of Franklin Roosevelt.* New York: Harper, 1992.

Ward, Geoffrey, ed. *Closest Companion: The Unknown Story of the Intimate Relationship Between Franklin Roosevelt and Margaret Suckley.* Boston: Houghton Mifflin, 1995.

Warren, Louis. *Lincoln's Youth.* Indianapolis: Indiana Historical Society, 1959.

Watts, Sarah. *Rough Rider in the White House: Theodore Roosevelt and the Politics of Desire.* Chicago: University of Chicago, 2003.

Waugh, John. *Reelecting Lincoln: The Battle for the 1864 Presidency.* New York: Crown, 1997.

Weber, Ralph, ed. *Talking with Harry: Candid Conversations with President Harry S. Truman.* Wilmington, Del.: SR Books, 2001.

Weed, Thurlow. *Autobiography of Thurlow Weed.* Boston: Houghton Mifflin, 1883.

Weems, Mason Locke. *The Life of Washington.* Edited by Peter Onuf. Armonk, N.Y.: M. E. Sharpe, 1996.

Weigley, Russell Frank. *A Great Civil War: A Military and Political History.* Bloomington: Indiana University, 2000.

Weik, Jesse. *The Real Lincoln: A Portrait.* Boston: Houghton Mifflin, 1923.

Weisberger, Bernard. *America Afire: Jefferson, Adams and the Revolutionary Election of 1800.* New York: Morrow, 2000.

Weizmann, Vera. *The Impossible Takes Longer.* New York: Harper, 1967.

Welles, Gideon. *The Diary of Gideon Welles.* Boston: Houghton Mifflin, 1911.

West, J. B., with Mary Lynn Kotz. *Upstairs at the White House: My Life with the First Ladies.* New York: Coward, McCann, 1973.

Whalen, Richard. *The Founding Father: The Story of Joseph P. Kennedy.* New York: New American Library, 1964.

Whitcomb, John, and Claire Whitcomb. *Real Life in the White House.* New York: Routledge, 2000.

White, Theodore. *The Making of the President 1964.* New York: Atheneum, 1965.

Wiencek, Henry. *An Imperfect God: George Washington, His Slaves, and the Creation of America.* New York: Farrar, Straus, 2003.

Wilentz, Sean. *Andrew Jackson.* New York: Times Books, 2005.

———. *The Rise of American Democracy: Jefferson to Lincoln.* New York: Norton, 2005.

Wilkins, Roy. *Standing Fast: The Autobiography of Roy Wilkins.* New York: Viking, 1982.

Williams, Frank. *Judging Lincoln.* Carbondale: Southern Illinois University, 2002.

Wills, Garry. *James Madison.* New York: Times Books, 2002.

Wilson, Douglas. *Honor's Voice: The Transformation of Abraham Lincoln.* New York: Knopf, 1998.

———. *Lincoln's Sword: The Presidency and the Power of Words.* New York: Knopf, 2006.

Wilson, Douglas, and Rodney Davis, eds. *Herndon's Informants.* Urbana: University of Illinois, 1998.

Wiltse, Charles, ed. *The Papers of Daniel Webster.* Hanover, N.H.: Dartmouth College, 1977–1986.

Winik, Jay. *On the Brink: The Dramatic Behind the Scenes Saga of the Reagan Era and the Men and Women Who Won the Cold War.* New York: Simon & Schuster, 1996.

Wirthlin, Dick. *The Greatest Communicator: What Ronald Reagan Taught Me About Politics, Leadership and Life.* New York: John Wiley, 2004.

Wister, Owen. *Roosevelt: The Story of a Friendship, 1880–1919.* New York: Macmillan, 1930.

Withey, Lynne. *Dearest Friend: A Life of Abigail Adams.* New York: Simon & Schuster, 1981.

Wofford, Harris. *Of Kennedys and Kings: Making Sense of the Sixties.* New York: Farrar, Straus, 1980.

Wohlforth, William C., ed. *Witnesses to the End of the Cold War.* Baltimore: Johns Hopkins University, 1996.

Wolf, William. *The Almost Chosen People: A Study of the Religion of Abraham Lincoln.* Garden City, N.Y.: Doubleday, 1959.

Wood, Gordon. *Revolutionary Characters: What Made the Founders Different.* New York: Penguin, 2006.

Zornow, William. *Lincoln and the Party Divided.* Norman: University of Oklahoma, 1954.

ACKNOWLEDGMENTS

This book ends in 1989 not only to complete the story two centuries after George Washington took office, but also because I believe it is impossible to write any President's history—with any hope of making lasting judgments—if you do not wait at least two or three decades for the information and hindsight that comes only with time.

During the past four years, I have had a wonderful time researching and writing this book—not least because of the people who have been a part of the experience.

For critiques of the finished manuscript, I am grateful to Professors John Ferling of the University of West Georgia, Robert Remini of the University of Illinois at Chicago, Douglas Wilson of Knox College, Gabor Boritt and Allen Guelzo of Gettysburg College, H. W. Brands of the University of Texas, Alonzo Hamby of Ohio University and John Lewis Gaddis of Yale University.

For additional readings of the manuscript in various stages, as well as all manner of advice, I thank my great friends Mary Graham, Jim Lehrer, Jon Meacham, and Brian Williams. Gordon Wood, Harold Holzer, Frank Williams and Thomas Schwartz also provided counsel.

I have written this book as much as possible from primary sources. For consistency when using quotations, I have occasionally corrected spelling or punctuation, but only when it would not alter meaning.

During my research, Frank Grizzard offered advice on the historiography of George Washington. Celeste Walker advised the author on John Adams and several collections in the Kennedy Library.

I also thank Cynthia Koch and Robert Clark of the Franklin D. Roosevelt Library, Michael Devine, Randy Sowell, Ray Geselbracht and Elizabeth Safly of the Harry S. Truman Library, Deborah Leff, Alan Goodrich, Megan Desnoyers and Stephen Plotkin of the John F. Kennedy Library, Duke Blackwood, Michael Dugan and Ray Wilson of the Ronald Reagan Library, and John Sellers and Jeffery Flannery of the Library of Congress.

For granting access to private papers, I am grateful to Senator Edward Kennedy (portions of the Joseph Kennedy Papers), as well as Frederick Ryan and Joanne Drake of the Ronald Reagan Foundation (for several documents from the Ronald Reagan Papers). Robert Lindsey generously shared with me some of the notes he took while collaborating with former President Reagan on his autobiography.

The White House Curator, William Allman, kindly showed me through almost every room of the Executive Mansion and helped me to understand how it looked in earlier times.

This volume has benefited from thirty-two years of conversations on Presidential leadership with James MacGregor Burns, who began by treating a callow Williams College sophomore as a grown-up and should not be held responsible for the result.

With customary fastidiousness and good humor, Michael Hill helped me to assemble primary materials and printed works. As on my previous book, *The Conquerors*, Michael and Jack Bales checked my final draft against the sources I have cited in the backnotes.

At Simon & Schuster, I am grateful to Jack Romanos, Carolyn Reidy, David Rosenthal, Gypsy da Silva, Sarah Hochman, Jackie Seow, John Wahler, Victoria Meyer, Tracey Guest and especially the legendary Michael Korda, who brought to bear both his fine knowledge of American history and his experience of almost half a century in book publishing. Fred Chase did his usual excellent job as copy editor.

Esther Newberg has been my incomparable agent and guide through the publication of five books. Her friendship has been one of the pleasures of being in this line of work. I am also grateful for the help of her colleagues Chris Earle, Kari Stuart and Liz Farrell. My lawyer and friend Michael Rudell shared his wisdom throughout the process, as did his colleague Neil Rosini.

Above all, I enjoy the immense good fortune of what Theodore Roosevelt called "a happy home life": my two sons, Alexander and Cyrus, now twelve and ten, who, no doubt in deference to their father's sensibility, insist that after their long, illustrious careers in Major League Baseball, they will remember to dash off a few books on baseball history—and their extraordinary mother, to whom this book is dedicated with much love.

Michael Beschloss
March 2007
Washington, D.C.

INDEX

Page numbers in *italics* refer to illustrations.

Martin Luther King in, 261–62,
264–66
Black Muslims, 236, 261, 267
Blair, Francis Preston, 73, 75, 80, 81,
83–84, 88–89, 93, 101, 115
Silver Spring farm of, 104
Blair, Montgomery, 101, 104, 115
Blair House, 73, 101, 227
Bliss, Cornelius, 147, 151
B'nai B'rith, 205, 206, 207, 217
Bonaparte, Joseph, 59–60
Booth, John Wilkes, 106
Boston Post, 88
Bradford, William, 18
Bradlee, Ben, 260
Brandeis, Louis, 223
Breckinridge, John C., 104
Brezhnev, Leonid, 286, 287–88, 291
Britt, Mai, 260
Brotherhood of Sleeping Car Porters,
275*n*
Brown v. Board of Education, 238
Bryan, William Jennings, 129, 150
Bryant, William Cullen, 94
Buchanan, James, 70, 104, 139
"Building of a Ship, The"
(Longfellow), 124, 194–95
Bull Moose party, 173*n*
Bull Run, Battle of, 113
Bureau of Corporations, 145, 146,
147
Burkley, George, 279
Burr, Aaron, 6, 61, 71*n*
Bush, Barbara, 278
Bush, George H. W., 278, 284, 291,
299, 302, 321*n*, 324–25, *325*
Bush, George W., 165*n*, 173*n*, 278
Butler, Benjamin, 140
Byrd, Harry, Sr., 277*n*
Byrnes, James, 183

Cadwalader, Thomas, 76, 78
Caldicott, Helen, 289–90
Califano, Joe, 257
Camp Doniphan, Okla., 205

Cannon, Joe, 137
Carlucci, Frank, 309*n*, 314, 316
Carter, Jimmy, 188*n*, 280, 281, 283,
310
Casey, William, 296, 301
Castro, Fidel, 264*n*
Catholic Interracial Council, 244
Central Intelligence Agency (CIA),
257, 296, 301*n*, 302, 313
Chapman, Oscar, 229
Chase Manhattan Bank, 265
Cheney, Dick, 282
Chernenko, Konstantin, 299, 300, 302
Chernobyl nuclear disaster, 307
China, People's Republic of, 282
Churchill, Randolph, 184
Churchill, Winston, 157, 182, 192,
273, 285
on Anglo-American partnership,
194–95
FDR's Destroyer Deal with, 161,
162, 176–79, 184, 190
Joseph Kennedy and, 160–62, 181,
193
secret correspondence between
FDR and, 159, 161, 162, 163,
179
civil liberties, 66
civil rights legislation, 238, 268, 269,
278, 279
civil rights movement:
Birmingham marches and, 262,
263, 273, 275
Freedom Riders and, 245–46, 247,
248, 273
integration of Ole Miss and,
250–57, 270, 273, 328
integration of University of
Alabama and, 236, 369–70
JFK and, 235–36, 237, 242–48,
262–64, 268–71, 272–77
RFK and, 236, 245, 247, 265–66,
267–68, 273
Civil War, U.S., 96, 101, 102, 122–23,
128, 140, 186, 194

Index

Truman, Bess Wallace, 205–6, 209–10,
223, 229, 234
Truman, Harry, 73*n*, 140*n*, 193,
196–234, *209,* 327
on Abraham Lincoln, 212
Andrew Jackson admired by, 212,
217
anti-Semitic remarks of, 200, 203,
205, 215, 234
background of, 202–3
Bible-reading of, 221–22, 234
diary of, 204–5, 213, 228
Eddie Jacobson and, 205–6, 207,
210, 214, 215, 217, 222, 226–27,
228, 233, 234
in election of 1940, 203
in election of 1948, 228–30
FDR and, 203, 213
on George Washington, 212
as Jackson County judge, 212
Jewish refugees and, 200
letters to Bess Truman of, 205–6,
223, 234
low approval ratings of, 197
and partition of Palestine, 207,
214–15, 218–19, 221, 222, 230
relationships between Jews and,
198–200, 201–2, 203, 204–6, 217,
227–28
religious faith of, 221–22
on Theodore Roosevelt, 213
and U.S. recognition of Israel,
197–98, 222, 224–26, 234, 328
in World War II, 205–6
Zionist lobbying and, 202, 203, 208,
209, 215, 217–18
Truman, Margaret, 210, 213, 218*n*
Truman, Vivian, 221
"trust, but verify" (Reagan), 309, 318,
323
trusts, *see* monopolies and trusts

Ultra-Federalists (or High Federalists),
42, 47, 52, 53, 57, 61
Union Army:

African-Americans in, 109
1864 draft for, 112, 125, 186
failures of, 103, 113
United Jewish Appeal, 204
United Mine Workers, 139
United Nations, 324
and partition of Palestine, 197, 207,
214–15, 217, 219
Taiwan expelled by, 282
United Negro College Fund, 249
United States, USS, 55
United States Telegraph, 73

Van Buren, Martin, 65–66, 71, 77, 85,
88, 93, 94
Vance, Cyrus, 256, 257
Vandiver, Ernest, 242
Van Doren, Irita, 171, 175, 194
veto, Andrew Jackson's use of, 74, 76,
77, 79, 80–83
Victoria, Queen of England, 183
Vidal, Gore, 171*n,* 229
Vietnam War, 168*n*
Viguerie, Richard, 317
Vindication (Randolph), 21
Viner, Abe, 198
Viner, Sarah, 198–99
Virginia, 2
voting rights, 263

Wade, Benjamin, 109, 111
Wade-Davis Bill, 111
Walesa, Lech, 287–88
Walker, Edwin, 256, 257–58, 278
Walker, Jimmy, 175–76
Wallace, George, 236, 266, 269–70
Wallace, Henry, 176, 228, 230
Wallace, Madge, 209–10
Wall Street, Theodore Roosevelt and,
132, 134, 146, 150
War Democrats, 115, 116, 124, 125
War Department, U.S., 185, 186
war hawks, 41, 47, 52, 53, 54
Warm Springs, Ga., 167
Warner, John, 280*n*

[428]

ILLUSTRATION CREDITS

Numbers in roman type refer to inserts; numbers in *italics* refer to text pages.

Victor John Adams, *The Signing of the Treaty of Mortefontaine:* 9
AP Images: 24, 25, 28, 30, 33, 38, 44, *263*
Corbis: 31, 32, 35, 36, 39, *241, 292*
Homer Davenport, *New York Journal,* Sept. 12, 1896: *130*
Dirck Halstead: *325*
John Fanning, *Annals of Philadelphia* (1830): *5*
Frank Leslie's Illustrated Newspaper, Aug. 13, 1864: *105*
Getty Images: 23, 26, 27, 29, 34, *187, 224*
Harper's Pictorial History of the Great Rebellion (1866): 17
Harry Truman Library: *209*
The Hermitage, Home of President Andrew Jackson, Nashville,
    Tennessee: 10, 11
Historical Society of Pennsylvania Collections, Atwater Kent Museum
    of Philadelphia: 12, 13
Houghton Library, Harvard College: 18, 21, 22
Independence National Park: 2 (Charles Willson Peale), 8
John F. Kennedy Library: 35, 36, 37
Indiana Historical Society: 14
Library of Congress: *12,* 16, 19, 20, *20, 90*
Lincoln Museum, Fort Wayne, Indiana: *121*
National Gallery of Art: 3, 6, 7
New-York Historical Society: 1 (Charles Willson Peale),
    4 (John Trumbull)
Ohio Historical Society: 5
Ronald Reagan Library: 40, 41, 42, 43, *298, 320*
White House Historical Association: 15